THE LIMITS OF
GENDER DOMINATION

THE LIMITS OF GENDER DOMINATION

WOMEN, THE LAW, AND POLITICAL CRISIS IN QUITO, 1765–1830

CHAD THOMAS BLACK

UNIVERSITY OF NEW MEXICO PRESS | ALBUQUERQUE

Library of Congress Cataloging-in-Publication Data

Black, Chad T. (Chad Thomas)

The limits of gender domination : women, the law,

and political crisis in Quito, 1765–1830 / Chad Thomas Black.

p. cm.

Includes bibliographical references and index.

ISBN 978-0-8263-4923-1 (pbk. : alk. paper)

1. Women—Ecuador—Quito—Social conditions—18th century.

2. Women—Ecuador—Quito—Social conditions—19th century.

3. Women—Legal status, laws, etc.—Ecuador—Quito—History—18th century.

4. Women—Legal status, laws, etc.—Ecuador—Quito—History—19th century.

5. Women's rights—Ecuador—Quito—History—18th century.

6. Women's rights—Ecuador—Quito—History—19th century.

7. Quito (Ecuador)—Politics and government—18th century.

8. Quito (Ecuador)—Politics and government—19th century.

I. Title.

HQ1560.Q58B53 2010

305.409866′13—dc22

2010028969

Design and composition: Melissa Tandysh

Text composed in Sabon LT Std 10.5/14

For Jenny and Dash

[Women] make their own history, but they do not make it just as they please; they do not make it under circumstances chosen by themselves, but under circumstances directly found, given and transmitted from the past.

—Karl Marx,
The Eighteenth Brumaire of Louis Bonaparte

CONTENTS

ILLUSTRATIONS

TABLES

ACKNOWLEDGMENTS

I am indebted to many people for both direct and indirect help with this book. I would like to acknowledge the following in what is surely a partial list. Financial support for my research was generously provided through a Fulbright-Hays Doctoral Dissertation Research Abroad Fellowship, a PhD fellowship from the Latin American and Iberian Institute at the University of New Mexico, a field research grant from the same institution, and a Howard Rabinowitz Research Award from the History Graduate Student Association of the department of history at the University of New Mexico. I am also indebted to Clark Whitehorn and the editorial staff at the University of New Mexico Press.

I would like to thank Kimberly Gauderman, Elizabeth Hutchison, Linda Hall, Judy Bieber, and the Latin American History contingent at the University of New Mexico (UNM). Also from my time at UNM, I thank Jeffrey Drope, Judy Fetherston, François Gelineau, Doug Hecock, Bob Himmerich, Matt Ingram, Adam Kane, Larry Larrichio, Eric Loomis, Yolanda Martinez and the office staff of the Department of History, Scott Meredith, Margarita Ochoa, Sarah Payne, Pat Risso, Lynn Schibeci, Amy Scott, Joanie Swanson, Ferenc Szasz, Victoria Teerlink, Sam Truett, who even gave me his office for a semester, Gary Van Valen, and Blair Woodard. At the University of Tennessee, thanks go especially to Ernie Freeberg, Jeri McIntosh, Dan Magilow, Bob Morrissey, Lynn Sacco, Robert Stolz, David Worth, and Meghan Worth, but also to Tom Burman, Miguel Gomez, Michael Handelsman, Jay Rubenstein, and the students of the Dissertation

Writing Group. Others who have read, commented on, or sat through panels covering parts of the project include Kathryn Burns, Karen Caplan, Meri Clark, Leo Garofalo, Karen Graubert, Peter Guardino, Jacqueline Holler, Karen Powers, Frank Safford, Pete Sigal, Zeb Tortorrici, and Reuben Zahler. Thanks also to Frank Salomon for help with some Quechua terms.

In Quito, I owe a debt to the staff of the Archivo Nacional del Ecuador, who were ever professional and courteous, and who always provided warm cups of tea on cold, rainy afternoons. I also thank Susana Cabeza de Baca and the staff of the Fulbright office in Quito. Others who deserve special thanks from my time there include Juan Miguel Espinoza and Lori Swanson and their two children, Natalia and Nicolas. Marc Becker, Ernie Capello, John Clark, Joe Eisenberg, Greg Jones, Kris Lane, Liz Roberts, Kate Swanson, and Lisa Swanson formed various parts of my American community in Quito. Thanks to Hugo Andrade and the cycling community of the Concentración Deportiva de Pichincha. Special thanks to Nick Biddle.

Finally, thanks also to family and friends: David Cox, Larry Crowder, Edmundo Echeverria, Kris Knight, Janette and Mark Krier, Andrew Lynch, Mike Pease, Sherrita Roberts, Shaun Slattery, and Stephen Williamson. My parents, Frank and Sue Black, and siblings Paige and Bryant, and Bryant's family have been a super source of support. Most of all I want to thank Jenny Black and our son Dashiell. The two of them are present in every word of this book, except the mistaken ones. Those are all mine.

INTRODUCTION

Governance, Legal Culture, Gender

———•———

This book is about women, the law, political crisis, and institutional authority in the city of Quito, Ecuador, from 1765 to 1830. It is about legal subjectivity and the conflict between popular, customary norms and the changing expectations of absolutists and liberal republicans alike. It is about the political upheavals of the Bourbon and early republican eras, and the impact of those crises on the legal standing of women. The late-colonial and early-republican periods were tumultuous times in this Andean corner of the Spanish Empire. Legal reformers, moral crusaders, bureaucratic infighters, popular tax resisters, and women of all stations, together with a whole cast of local characters, struggled over the nature of authority, justice, and fidelity as the Bourbon kings claimed increasingly centralized power, only to be overthrown in the midst of a trans-Atlantic liberal revolution. Through an examination of judicial documents, legal literatures, and institutional discourses, this book analyzes women's legal, economic, and social status during this period of transitioning governance in order to gauge the relationship between governmentality and the local operation of social authority. It finds that customary legal practice performed a fundamental role limiting gendered domination, preventing the full realization of patriarchal tendencies within Spanish law as well as the consolidation of paternal and conjugal authority modeled on the claims of Bourbon kingship. Furthermore, this vital levee against male domination was dismantled in the early decades of the republican era, as liberals constructed a new form of governance tied to new forms of property and citizenship.

Legal culture and judicial practice were key elements of the social mediation of authority in the Spanish monarchy, which ruled the Americas by means of a judicial bureaucracy. The bureaucratic model developed for the Spanish world in the sixteenth and seventeenth centuries depended on the dispersal of political and judicial power across many competing jurisdictions, placing judicial practice at the center of the empire's effort to govern its numerous kingdoms in the Americas. As a result of this bureaucratic strategy, the voluminous judicial records left in the archives of eighteenth-century Quito provide a revealing look into the interface between the region's institutional authorities and the subjects who sought justice before them. A gendered reading of judicial proceedings in Quito demonstrates that Bourbon attempts to restrict women's access to legal resources were resisted by the expectations and practices of a local legal culture built on traditions of consultation, negotiation, judicial discretion, and contingency. Bourbon colonialists struggled to overcome the persistence of local custom, which long held a structural role in organizing the empire's decentralized rule. For women, the Bourbon struggle against local customary judicial practice had the potential to cut off the legal resources that limited male domination in the region and prevented the consolidation of a full legal, economic, or social patriarchy. While the Bourbons ultimately failed in their assault on women's judicial resources, the transition to republican rule and its associated new legal culture and political organization essentially and effectively began the process that dismantled customary legal protections and ultimately enabled the city's fathers, brothers, husbands, and sons to eradicate women's autonomous legal, economic, and social identities. As such, this book offers a contribution to the genealogy of legal patriarchy in Spanish America, and, as its title indicates, documents the progressive removal of limits to patriarchal power in the waning years of the Spanish Empire.[1]

The processes described in this book wore a very real human face. The many indigenous women, widows, wives, shop owners, daughters, land owners, creditors, adulteresses, and otherwise daily participants in the life of the city who appear in these pages actively laid claim to customary legal rights in the midst of trying and sometimes tragic circumstances. Their self-representations before the court were embodied most often in the participatory identity of the *vecina*, a term that signified not only a woman's residential status, but also her claim to citizenship, to participation in the public life of Quito's barrios.[2] To begin, then, I turn to the story of one such vecina: Ana Arguelles.

ANA FACES HER "PATRIARCHS"

On June 3, 1768, Ana Arguelles appeared before Corregidor Señor General Don Nuño Apolinar dela Cueba Ponce de Leon, a regional judge administrator for the city of Quito and its surrounding five-league jurisdiction.[3] Her complaint brought her directly into conflict with the three closest males of her life: her husband, her brother, and her father. Two and a half years earlier, Ana's husband, Juan Cleto, had borrowed 50 pesos from her brother, Eusebio Arguelles, placing as collateral several pieces of his wife's jewelry. In addition to the original loan, Juan Cleto agreed to pay an impressive 2 pesos per month in interest on the original 50 pesos principal. At the time of the filing, Juan Cleto had fallen behind on the arrangement, bringing Ana and Eusebio into direct conflict. In the absence of interest payments, Eusebio confiscated property belonging to his sister in addition to the jewelry he was already holding as collateral. Ana responded by appealing to the courts in an effort to secure her personal property.

In her initial petition, Ana Arguelles presented herself to the court as a legitimately married woman, a vecina of Quito whose husband was absent, residing in Ibarra. She approached the corregidor under the standard rubric of a right to appear, neglecting any mention of license conferred by her husband. Ana claimed that the confiscation of her property amounted to an illegal act, because her husband's debts had no relation to her personal property. Moreover, she stated that at the time of the original agreement she found her brother's terms to be usurious and therefore contrary to the dictates of canon and civil law, so she renegotiated the terms of the original loan on behalf of her husband to a rate of 5 pesos interest per year. Ana claimed that this second contract was being honored, which, combined with the prohibited terms of Eusebio's initial loan, eliminated any fiscal reason for her brother's actions.

The financial case formed only one element of Ana's legal argument. More significantly, Ana appealed to a combination of legal and cultural logics to deny her brother control of her property. She continued by claiming that the law protected her personal property, reasoning that no son could be held responsible for his father's debt, and likewise neither could a woman be held to the debts of her husband. Because the loan was arranged between Eusebio Arguelles and Juan Cleto, she argued, satisfying the loan and paying the interest was a financial matter involving only her husband's estate. To further enhance her position, Ana then claimed a cultural need for protection of the court, portraying herself as too poor and saddled with too many children to afford repayments even if her brother held some legitimate right to her property. Finally, Ana asserted that in returning her property and relieving her of a debt that was her husband's she would be able to use that property for the beautification of her local church in Tumbaco, a town in the valley east of Quito. Ana's petition concluded with a request that the court order her brother to appear with her property, explain himself, and relieve her of further obligation beyond aiding her husband in paying the principal to recover her jewelry. Corregidor dela Cueba agreed with the petition, and ordered that the local *teniente alguacil mayor* (lieutenant bailiff) notify Eusebio to appear within three days. There is no record of the teniente fulfilling dela Cueba's decree, which, while procedurally unusual, was emblematic of decentralized strategies of resistance to authority.

Two years later, in July 1770, Ana Arguelles again appeared before Quito's corregidor, complaining that she was still without her property. Eusebio had evaded the 1768 order by leaving town with Ana's jewelry. There is question as to whether he was warned of the corregidor's judgment, and Ana complained to dela Cueba that part of the problem resided in "the incompetence of whichever official [was assigned] to the resolution of her petition." Eusebio's evasion was not the last of his attempts to skirt accountability. He claimed that the property he was holding actually belonged to their father, and that it had been returned to him as the rightful owner. Ana rejected this assertion outright, stating, "I find myself out from under [paternal authority] *Patria Potestad*, through emancipation, and . . . the jewelry is mine, not my Father's, much less my Husband's, as the aforementioned Eusebio Areguelles falsely supposes in his maliciousness."4

Ana again concluded the petition with a plea to the corregidor to order her brother to appear within two days with both the jewelry of the original loan and the property he had held for the past two years.

This time, she added a request that a royal official go to Eusebio's house and deliver in person the order to appear to her brother, or his wife, or a servant, or anyone who happened to be there, and to add the possibility of jail time should Eusebio not appear. Cueba issued just such an order on July 6, 1770, compelling Eusebio Arguelles to appear before him within three days of his notification, and to bring any documents relating to the loan and all of the property under dispute. Fourteen days later, on July 20, a notary working for dela Cueba certified that he had notified Eusebio in person, and thus ended the folio.

Ana Arguelles played to the ambiguities inherent in the Spanish legal system to protect her material interests. If the original loan was based on her property, was she not in some way responsible for the loan's security? That her husband effected the transaction and received the 50 pesos apparently opened the door to judicial discretion. Juan Cleto was absent, we learn from the petition, but he was residing to the north of Quito in the town of Ibarra, and therefore not out of reach of a legal system that supposedly required a husband's license for a wife's legal activity. Two years on he remained absent, suggesting a permanent residential separation for the couple. According to Spanish law, Ana should have filed a petition with a magistrate first requesting license to appear in her husband's absence. There was no mention of such a license in the case, yet she held standing before the judge. Ana displayed economic savvy in renegotiating the terms of the interest payments and was able to recognize economic exploitation, apparently better than her husband could. She felt it was legitimate to seek legal remedy, to claim the right to appear before a judge, and to employ a variety of legal and cultural arguments to protect her resources. The combination of legal and cultural argument, referencing simultaneously a woman's right to be insulated from her husband's debts, as well as the much-vaunted image of the poor, miserable woman saddled by children and in need of the charity and protection of the institutions from Spanish justice, formed a matrix of legitimacy from Ana's perspective. She was living in long-term separation from her husband, out from under any purview he may have claimed, in a female-headed household. She may have been a woman of relatively modest property, but she indeed did claim a right to control that property. Ana Arguelles demonstrated considerable pluck in her use of the judicial system. But does her story simply signify the actions of one determined, exceptional woman?

Eusebio Arguelles, whose voice was heard only through Ana, attempted to operate from a position of gender right. He evidently treated his sister's property as collateral for her husband's financial dealings. When pressed in reference to his own lack of claim, Eusebio appealed to a right of their father, in the absence of Ana's husband, to control her property. It was an argument that the corregidor of Quito twice rejected, even if with a certain amount of ambivalence. What would motivate an official whose bureaucratic and judicial responsibilities relied, to a large extent, on the consent of his subjects to rule twice against the interests of the layered patriarchs of Ana's life? Was not the legitimate institutional authority of the Spanish monarchy built on patriarchal right, reaching ultimately to the position of the King himself? If officials of the *corregimiento* of Quito (encompassing the city and its hinterland) felt compelled to undermine the authority of local petty patriarchs, was this not threatening to the concept of authority across society?

Indeed, if Ana Arguelles's actions were exceptional, the answer to such questions would be that the corregidor's willingness to hear her plea and to rule in her favor was of little social consequence. But her actions were far from exceptional. Much as scholars have discovered and documented for more than a quarter of a century in the case of indigenous communities and individuals, women in Spanish America were adroit and ardent litigators who willingly engaged the ambiguities of the Spanish legal inheritance to protect their material and corporal interests.[5] This legal inheritance formed one element of a broader set of cultural logics that eschewed the concentration of power, favoring instead a contingent, negotiated, flexible authority. It was the cultural understanding of legitimate authority in Spanish American society that framed the corregidor's hearing of Ana's plea and ruling in her favor against her "patriarchs," just as other judges did on countless occasions.

Spanish American society was litigious throughout the life of the empire. The courts provided such a stable arena for dispute resolution that in times of serious social flux and even revolt individuals still sought judicial remedy for personal, financial, ethnic, criminal, and marital quarrels.[6] Judicial records therefore provide a wellspring of information for the social history of Spanish American society particularly because judicial forums held such cultural currency. Likewise, the judicial form was integral to the operation of the empire, as bureaucratic appointments, disputes and decisions, economic transactions, personal declarations, testaments, contracts, municipal regulations, dowries, and more shared a language and form of legality that was remarkably similar across the spectrum of legal acts.[7] Because the language and form of justice and legality were utilized in such a wide variety of situations, both quotidian and extraordinary, and, more importantly, because the adherence to legality resulted in a tremendous volume of written records, judicial proceedings provide extensive access to both the cultural and institutional organization of authority in the Spanish kingdoms of America. The picture that emerges from close readings of these records is startling.

As the case of Ana Arguelles hints, the legal operation of social authority was organized neither on the basis of gender equality nor through a strict linear hierarchy of patriarchal domination. A long-established literature on bureaucratic and legal authority in Spain and Spanish America has demonstrated the extent to which, at least during the Habsburg period, the system of rule operated under an ethos of decentralism, contingency, and negotiation through a matrix of competing jurisdictions, contradictory laws, and special privileges.[8] In part because of the threat posed by the first generation of conquerors, in part due to the distance involved in managing a seventeenth-century empire, and in part due to the historical process of reconquest of the Iberian peninsula, the crown of Castile instituted a system of rule that provided legal accommodations to conquered territories, decentralized power through pitched jurisdictional battles, and that prevented the consolidation of power as a challenge to royal authority, paradoxically by empowering local populations to negotiate royal policy. Additionally, the legitimacy of the king's authority continually rested on the perception that the crown ensured the maintenance of justice in the commonwealth by providing a responsive judicial forum for dispute resolution.[9] The net effect was to maintain the king's legitimacy through accommodation rather than fiat, a process of decentralized rule that encouraged communal harmony within the context of endemic inequalities, mediated by the judicial bureaucracy.

This mode of bureaucratic and legal organization provided the context within which cultural authority was performed. The Spanish American historiography has associated a political absolutism with absolutist forms of social relations.[10] According to the view, absolutism as a form of governance, based on the authority of the king, had its equivalence in the authority of the patriarchal household with its paternal power, as well as in the relationship between master and slave. And yet absolutist claims to institutional authority were effectively an advent of the eighteenth century, with the rise of the Bourbons to the throne of Castile. The "absolutism" of the Habsburg period was absolutism in name only. As Owens has observed, during the Habsburg era "The meaning of 'absolute royal authority' did not inhere in the words themselves."[11] Absent were the forms of coercive force and a hierarchical state apparatus generally associated with the eighteenth-century rise of absolutism. Habsburg governance inherited from its Trastamaran antecedents an intense localism that structurally recognized the authority of customary practice and the reality of negotiation, even as kings extolled their absolute royal will. The institutional discourses of the Bourbon period, particularly from the 1760s onward, laid claim to functionally more centralized and absolute forms of authority in both formal and domestic arenas than discourses in the preceding centuries. Legal scholars of the period sought to reformulate the Hispanic legal inheritance to enhance the centralization of authority, as well as those patriarchal tendencies that existed in the labyrinth of Spanish law. Specially empowered royal officials sought to curtail the ability of local bureaucrats to delay or dispel the implementation of royal dictates, particularly those dictates aimed at rationalizing and advancing the military, fiscal, and jurisdictional operation of the empire. Magistrates sought to scrutinize and control more closely the moral behavior and paternal prerogatives of the crown's subjects. And yet Bourbon claims to authority must been seen as assertions, interventions—inventions in the history of Spanish American governance, rather than normalized expressions from which to evaluate the whole of the colonial period.[12]

Bourbon discourses provide an opportunity to evaluate the organization, operation, and relationship between both institutional and social forms of authority, by evaluating the impact of transitioning forms of governance on social relations. As a test case of this relationship, this book investigates the impact of changing sovereignty claims on the operation of gendered social authority in the corregimiento of Quito. One trajectory of recent scholarship on gender in both Spanish America and on the peninsula has questioned whether the patriarchal model best explains how female subjugation operated under Habsburg rule.[13] In the following chapters, I extend this skepticism to the closing decades of the eighteenth century and on to the eve of independent Ecuador in an attempt to trace the legal genealogy of male domination that was increasingly less constrained and more centralized. In order to follow the shifting relationship between the organization of state authority and the operation of social authority, I analyze institutional discourses, bureaucratic struggles, legal literatures, judicial practices, and their gendered effects. My intention in questioning the patriarchal model is not to posit an argument of gender equality for the colonial period or to lessen the reality of male domination. Male domination was a hallmark of Spanish American society. But this book argues for a closer understanding of how this domination was operationalized through the law and courts in early Spanish American society in the specificity of its historical and changing context. As such, it starts from the premise that gender is historically, socially, and culturally constructed and performed.[14]

Because the lived differences of Spain's particular culture of authority diverged so dramatically from its northern European and North American counterparts, it makes sense to carefully define and deploy categories of analysis that reflect that specificity. This is particularly true in the case of the subjugation of women. The Spanish system under assault by the Bourbons and later the new nation states of the nineteenth century formally and customarily recognized autonomous economic, social, and legal positions for women in a manner wholly different from the positions of women in the North Atlantic. Male domination quite simply was made real in a very different and culturally specific manner. The tendency has been to use patriarchy as a metacategorical designation for male domination across time and space, which obscures and subsumes the variety and specificity of historically concrete systems of dominance. I use the category here as a specific rather than as a general or universal category, implicating the legal formation of conjugal and paternal authority. For the purposes of this study, I borrow the definition of patriarchy put forth by Lisa Mary Sousa and delineated as a system:

In which (1) authority is invested in the eldest male; (2) a woman has no individual legal status and, therefore, cannot order testaments, witness legal documents, or legally represent herself in court; (3) a woman has no individual economic status and, therefore, cannot own property or carry out economic transactions without approval of her legal guardian (usually either her father or her husband); and, (4) a woman's identity is derived from her association with the family patriarch (either her husband or her father).[15]

This definition is particularly useful because it moves the discussion from the realm of elite prescriptions and legal abstractions into socially constructed practices that emerge in the documentary base available for the period. Sousa's definition directs analysis of patriarchal systems to the functional role of conjugal or paternal authority in defining a woman's access to and participation in the economic, legal, and social life of the community.

Defining patriarchy is itself a bit of a cottage industry in feminist and gender history. The question of the salience of the term has taken on renewed vigor with the recent publication of Judith Bennett's *History Matters*, which calls for a restoration of the category of patriarchy in western historiography after a generation of reticence.[16] Bennett argues that the term should be used not necessarily for its analytical strength as much as for its rhetorical power and unique ability to characterize male domination over centuries.[17] The danger of this project is that it tends to reinforce ahistorical conceptions of gender relations in which the condition of subjugation becomes a reductive and generalized ontology. Bennett is not alone in viewing patriarchy as a category capable of subsuming the large variety of historically, socially, and culturally specific forms of male domination. The literature on colonial Spanish America has deployed the term to varying degrees of specificity. Gauderman has criticized the most egregious traditions in the literature of presenting patriarchy as "a universal form of social organization," defined by the continuity of gender domination reaching back to the roots of Western Christendom, for their tendency to naturalize male prerogative.[18] She also has criticized work of Latin American scholars who rely on literatures descriptive of northern European family and gender practices, or work focused on the nineteenth century as reinforcing a universalist interpretation of patriarchy.[19] Not all uses of the category are quite as ham-fisted as those critiqued by Gauderman, but the analytical use of patriarchy to describe the operation of gender across the three centuries of Spanish rule in the Americas is becoming increasingly ponderous. Thus, while the definition of patriarchy begins from the initial assumption of male domination, it increasingly came to be defined as women's exclusion from access to formal political power. From there, the category has quickly grown to subsume all manner of women's agency, contradictory cultural structures or practices, and real lived differences as still part of patriarchy. Furthermore, this view of patriarchy as simultaneously flexible and immutable leads scholars to generalize its conditions across the colonial period.[20]

The fallout has been that some historians of the period have tended to see patriarchal logic at work in places it was not. Thus, Stern portrays women in Mexico who sought to exploit overlapping, competing jurisdictions as employing a gender strategy to "pluralize patriarchs," as opposed to engaging in the same type of judicial strategies utilized by elite Spaniards, indigenous communities, and even African and Afro-Mexican slaves and their free counterparts.[21] The women were simply acting like everyone else. Conversely, Sousa, critiquing the patriarchal model for indigenous communities, saw the perpetuation of Mixtec gender parallelism in native women's comparable use of the courts.[22] Part of the argument of this book, however, is that women in the corregimiento of Quito acting as judicial agents along with the women documented by Stern and Sousa were incarnating cultural structures born out of the Spanish system of customary and *fuero*[23] law and governed by unspoken rules that were *shared across* gender, ethnicity, jurisdiction, and caste. It is only in recognizing those cultural structures that the actions of not only female litigants but also judges, royal bureaucrats, municipal officials, and church authorities, along with the interventions of Bourbon rule and the real radicalism of Spanish America's participation in the liberal revolution of the Atlantic world, begin to make sense. Returning patriarchy to a categorical specificity makes clearer the operation of male domination within broader cultural structures of authority and enhances our ability to track shifting forms of subjugation across time, and by this restores history to the legal systems of gender domination in the colonial period.

GOVERNANCE, LEGAL CULTURE, GENDER

The trajectory of women's subjugation in late colonial and early republican Quito follows an inverse relationship to the implementation of emancipatory projects of enlightenment and liberal political and property regimes. In her classic book *The Sexual Contract*, Carole Pateman documents the extent to which the dismantling of medieval and early modern forms of status-based citizenship for liberalism's political, economic, and social contracts was predicated on male domination, and particularly on conjugal right.[24] In Quito, the shift from status to contract entailed the construction of a private sphere of property ownership based on an increasingly restrictive citizenship, even as sovereignty and the law were rearticulated as functions of individual freedom. Terry Eagleton has noted, "Modern European criticism was born of a struggle against the absolutist state. Within that repressive regime, in the seventeenth and eighteenth centuries, the European bourgeoisie [began] to carve out for itself a distinct discursive space, one of rational judgment and enlightened critique rather than of the brutal ukases of an authoritarian politics."[25] In Spanish America, the struggle against absolutism, delayed until at least the 1760s, was not itself a struggle to construct discursive spaces for resistance to the brutal ukases of an authoritarian politics. (Indeed, in a fashion, that did become a struggle in the region some two centuries later.) There already existed a framework for the articulation of resistance to and avoidance of government decisions that claimed too much authority, without necessitating an anticolonial moment pointing toward independence and the particularities of liberal, republican, nation-state modernity. This framework was codified in the governing logic of Habsburg decentralism, in the importance of customary practice to legal reasoning, and in the cultural logic that limited domination through mitigations and negotiations. The connection between these three logics provides a theoretical model for the analysis of late-eighteenth-century Spanish America that allows the various agents of society to speak from a cultural context defined by often-contradictory claims to legal privileges and positions. Thus, for example, an indigenous merchant in Quito could throw rocks while chanting, "Long live the king and death to bad government," without the need to interpret his or her act, or its absence, as either anticolonial or collaborationist. Or a woman could represent herself before one of the city's magistrates while arguing that the terms of a contract she had independently made and fallen awry of were invalid because her husband had failed to grant her permission to make legal acts. Though these two examples are hypothetical, they ring true to the many thousands of small and large legal acts that brought people of all types into the judicial bureaucracy, and they share an underlying logic that, while rarely explicitly articulated, stretched across the spectrum of official and unofficial forms of authority.

In response to these theoretical issues, this book posits a model of inquiry designed to avoid the decontextualization of legal acts and legal actors that were bound by larger cultural structures by investigating three interrelated themes: governance, legal culture, and social authority. The late eighteenth and early nineteenth centuries were a period of transitioning logics of governance (i.e., claims to the constitution of legitimate political authority and its relationship to civil society). The period witnessed three distinct, if overlapping, logics of governance associated with conflicting visions of political and social organization: (1) Habsburg bureaucratic decentralism (to the 1760s), (2) Bourbon colonial centralism (1750s–1820s), and (3) liberal republicanism (1800s on). These overlapping periods witnessed changing state forms, claims to authority, organization of political power, prescriptive legal cultures, and ideological justifications for rule.²⁶ Governance establishes—through the state, ideology, and the exercise of conventional political power—the foundation of formal authority in society. The question remains how this form of power relates to the exercise of social authority, or the informal authority expressed in relations of class, gender, and ethnicity. This book tests the relationship using the legal construction of gender relations as a lens to identify changes in social authority during periods of transitioning governance. Popular perceptions of legitimate social authority are often found in the variety of legal acts of the notary, the civil case, and the criminal trial because these acts occur as contrasting moments of the normal and the abnormal. This is particularly true for the greater Spanish monarchy due to the judicial nature of the state and its exercise of power. Given that the judicial function of the bureaucracy played such a key role in the maintenance of rule, legal culture forms a convenient conceptual hinge in the relationship between governance and social authority, demonstrating the role of law in society while also conversely (and more importantly, from my perspective) expressing how individuals understood legitimate governance.²⁷ As such, legal culture and the documentary trail through which one substantiates it open a window into the relationship between gendered social authority and the ideals of governance. In other words, the political cultures of Habsburg, Bourbon, and republican governance; their associated legal cultures;

and the widespread legitimacy afforded the judicial functions of the state allow an interrelated analysis of social mediation in the culture of authority in the late colonial Hispanic world.

Were, then, the historical experiences of patriarchy in modern Ecuador the result of a colonial legacy, holdovers of a social and economic system of colonial domination? Or did the specific forms of gender inequality that marred Ecuador, and in fact all of Spanish America, in the late nineteenth and twentieth centuries emerge from a later period? The various positions occupied by individuals and groups in Quito were socially and culturally constructed, and an individual had an array of often-contradictory statuses to call on given specific, concrete circumstances. The array of positions, or identifying categories, in the early period were not binaries (e.g., Spaniard/Indian, slave/free, male/female, married/single, and so on), but rather continuums, along which individuals sought to place themselves to maximize their interests, even as institutional authorities sought to do the same. To go further, the array of statuses to which any given person could appeal were not expressions of individual rights in the modern political sense of the term, but rather corporate positions that mapped on the individual the dynamics of fuero law, overlapping jurisdictions, and decentralized, negotiated sovereignty. Just as these dynamics staunched the centralization of power in the empire, the matrix of corporate positions worked to decentralize the body politic. The complex situation through which statuses were daily made formed part of the larger cultural and institutional matrix of power and authority that constituted the gender system of the eighteenth century. Thus, in order to construct a genealogy of gender domination and its legal limits, it is necessary to analyze a broad array of social and cultural moments in a given place to evaluate the trajectory of gendered power in its textual and contextual manifestations. The place that provides the laboratory of my analysis is the city of Quito and its hinterland, known in the eighteenth century as Quito and the Five Leagues.

QUITO AND THE FIVE LEAGUES

Perched high in an intermountain valley of the northern Andes, Quito was the seat of multiple, overlapping bureaucratic and legal jurisdictions from 1563 onward, with the establishment of the Real Audiencia, or royal judicial court.[28] The Audiencia served as both an administrative body and a court for the region extending north to Buenaventura (in present-day Colombia), south to Tumbéz (in present-day Peru), east to the amorphous border with Amazonian Brazil, and west to the Pacific Ocean. Originally the northernmost Audiencia of the Viceroyalty of Peru, in 1739 the jurisdiction was moved to the control of the new Viceroyalty of New Granada, established at Santa Fé de Bogotá. In addition to the Audiencia, the city was home to a municipal council (*cabildo*) and was the center of a corregimiento. The corregidor, the administrative and judicial head of the corregimiento, likewise served as chair of the municipal council, uniting politically the interests of the city and its rural support structure. Together, the city and its cor-regimiento commonly were referred to as Quito and the Five Leagues, or simply as the Five Leagues. Towns included in the Five Leagues stretched from Nanegal in the northwest to Machachi and Aloasí in the south, and from Mindo in the west across the Tumbaco Valley to El Quinche and Yaruquí in the east (see Map 0.1).

Map 0.1. Quito and the Five Leagues.
MAP DRAWN BY LARRY LARRICHIO

The city's elevation (2,850 meters or 9,350 feet) combined with its proximity to the equator (22 kilometers or 13.5 miles north of the city) to provide the region with the mild climate of a perpetual spring. The cool, damp nights, however, proved a source of constant complaint by royal officials whose health was delicate. The city itself was divided into seven parishes, or barrios: El Sagrario (center), San Roque (west), San Sebastian (south), San Marcos (east), San Blas (northeast), Santa Bárbara (north), and Santa Prisca (far north) (see Map 0.2). El Sagrario constituted the center of royal power and was home to the convent of Santa Clara, the monastery of San Francisco, the churches of the Cathedral, La Merced, Concepción, Carmen Alto, San Agustín, and the Jesuit Compañía de Jesus, as well as offices of the bishopric, the cabildo, the Audiencia, and the city's three jails. The other parishes bordered El Sagrario, separated physically as well as conceptually along the fault lines of a number of major ravines, cut through the parishes by runoff from the looming volcano Pichincha

Map 0.2. The Barrios of Quito.
MAP DRAWN BY LARRY LARRICHIO

on the city's western edge. Two exceptions to this rule were Santa Bárbara, which directly bordered the city center, and Santa Prisca, a rural parish wedged between Santa Bárbara and commons land in the north valley.

Santa Bárbara's proximity to both the city center and the rural parish of Santa Prisca reflected more than simple geography. The parish was home both to the city's slaughterhouse and to its customs house, numerous churches, several leading officials and residents, merchants, tradespersons, Spaniards, mestizos, Indians, and more. The amalgam of social groups, oriented toward both the countryside and the city center, position the parish as a good surrogate for understanding the economic, ethnic, and bureaucratic complexities of the corregimiento. Likewise, Santa Bárbara was the focal point of unrest in 1764 and 1765 as Bourbon fiscal reforms arrived in the city. A 1768 census performed by don Manuel dela Lastra, the parish magistrate (*alcalde de barrio*), found approximately 2,740 residents grouped in 182 households arranged along the barrio's forty-seven streets.[29] The ethnicity of each individual resident is not noted in the census; however, ethnicity is provided for household heads and the proprietors of the many shops attached to individual homes when those individuals were indigenous, black, mestizo, or mulatto. Of the 182 households listed for the parish, 73 were listed as female-headed, accounting for a total of 1,132 (41.3 percent) of total barrio residents.[30] Of those households, three were owned by Indian women, one by a mulatta, and the rest by women of undesignated ethnic status. Furthermore, the marital status of these women varied greatly, including married (n=14), married but separated from their husbands (n=6), widowed (n=24), single-unmarried (n=15), and no status listed (n=14). As further markers of status, of the seventy-three female-headed households, forty-nine of those women used the honorifics doña or señora; the remaining used no title or honorific. Female-headed households, just like the male-headed households in the parish, were composed of large extended families and numerous renters of every description, ranging from five to forty-five individuals, including servants. All households averaged 15.5 persons, with female-headed households a very similar 15.3.

Male ownership of the remaining 109 households obscures the variety of family forms found in the barrio's tenants. Take, for example, the following three entries from the census:

(1) House of Alférez Real Don Juan Joseph Chiriboga:
Lived in by Captain Dn [Don] Nicolás Carrión,
    head of the Royal Liquor Monopoly, married   3
Servants   11
Dr. Dn [Don] Pedro de Velasco, foreigner, single   1
Shop: Francisco Paredes, married, grocer and hat
    maker. Family   3
Shop: Xavier Casas, mestizo, married, street vendor   2
Chichería (bar for consuming corn beer/chicha):
    Liberata Plaza, married, Indian   2
Total: 22

(2) House of Dr. Dn. [Don] Pedro Jijón. Family   12
María Nieto, single. Family   3
Manuel Valeriano Escobar, married, with one son,
    laborer   3
María José Villavicencio, widow. Family   3
Martina de Andújar, single   1
Miguel Sánchez, Indian, married, tailor. Family   3
José Tituaña, Indian, carpenter, married. Family   4
José Pillajo, Indian, weaver, married. Family   4
Nicolás Pazmiño, married, tailor. Family   3
Francisca Gualanlima, Indian, single. Family   3
Catalina Carrera, widow   1
José Issa, Indian, cobbler, married. Family   3
María Manosalvas, widow. Family   2
Total: 45

(3) House of Doña Francisca Jarra, married, separated
from her husband   2
Polonia Acosta, single   1
Tomás Trejo, married, chair-maker   2
Alejandro Fernández, married, processional
    cross bearer. Family   3
Vicenta Baca, single   1
Magdalena dela Cruz, widow, with her son   2
Dionisio Pillajo, Indian, cobbler. Family   3
María Josefa Ribas, widow. Family   4
Juana Figueroa, widow, with a son   2

Joaquina Jara, single	1
Ventura Meneses, with her son, separated from her husband	2
María Mejía, widow. Family	5
Total:	28[31]

Note that within these three elite Spanish extended households, a variety of smaller, ethnic, plebeian households existed as tenants. The household census reveals that urban space was not an exclusively Spanish or mestizo space that was only occasionally visited by rural indigenous subjects bound for markets or on official legal or tax business.[32]

Just as home ownership and headship were more diverse than might be expected, so too was proprietorship of the city's many shops. Of the 109 shops listed in the barrio, women operated 48 percent (n=52). Women's shops predominantly sold foodstuffs; their shops operated either as fresh meat and produce stores (*chagras, carnecerías,* and *pulperías*), or as shops that sold prepared food in the eighteenth-century equivalent of restaurants and bars (*estancos* where cane liquor was sold, *chicherías* where *chicha* [corn beer] was sold along with simple fare, and *olleras* where prepared meals could be bought). Thirty-two of the female-operated stores had no indication of their business, while the remaining twenty were food service. The proprietors were of varied marital and ethnic status as well, comprising no-ethnic-status (n=32), Indian (n=17), black or mulatta (n=3); and no-marriage-status (n=9), married (n=13), married-but-separated (n=5), widowed (n=13), and single-not-married (n=12). Meanwhile, the fifty-seven male-run stores listed in the barrio were heavily dominated by married men (n=51), with married-but-separated (n=1), single-not-married (n=3), and widowed (n=2) rounding out the balance. The male-owned shops also covered a wide array of trades, including bricklayer, musician, chichería, cigar maker, barber, grocer, tailor, weaver, cobbler, estanco, rope maker, sexton, butcher, linen maker, and more. Twenty of the shops were run by Indian men, two by mestizos, and the rest by those without ethnic designation. Beyond the individual shops, the census includes trade designations for 230 men and women, totaling fifty-seven different occupations. (See Appendix I.) The largest category by far was servant, accounting for sixty-seven people. Certain trades were clearly dominated by indigenous workers, including bricklayers, barbers, carpenters, cobblers, weavers, and those who sold produce. Indians also had a presence as tailors, owners of chicha establishments, butchers, embroiderers, and day laborers. Positions of power, such as the royal standard-bearer, two court lawyers, two city magistrates, and two notaries lived coterminous lives with a number of rural workers, indigenous tradespersons, and hawkers of fruits, produce, and meats. Agricultural goods were grown in gardens within the parish limits, as well as on the farms surrounding the city. The many small shops at which such goods were bought and sold were meeting points, along with the streets themselves, where men and women of various social and ethnic statuses mingled. The provisioning of the city by merchants and hawkers from all social and ethnic statuses forged close ties between the city and the rural hinterland of the corregimiento.

Residents of the corregimiento brought to town their legal needs and judicial disputes along with the fruits of their labors. Both residents of the barrios and of the corregimiento performed baptisms; notarized contracts; and filed criminal complaints, tax disputes, and creditor actions in the various parishes of the city and before the various magistrates of the Audiencia, cabildo, and corregimiento. The jurisdictional authority of a wide variety of city, Audiencia, and provincial officials overlapped, providing a network of judicial avenues along which individuals could pursue justice. The short list of magistrates available to hear disputes in the city and its hinterland included two town magistrates elected by the cabildo (*alcaldes ordinarios*), the rural police magistrate of the Holy Brotherhood (*alcalde de la Santa Hermandad*), the corregidor, the judges of the Audiencia who heard both appellate and, in certain circumstances, first-instance litigation (*oidores de la Real Audiencia*), commercial magistrates, the bishopric, the Holy Office of the Inquisition, and especially empowered officials of various tax levies. Add to this list both Spanish and indigenous local officials from the rural villages and the cadre of individuals with some claim to jurisdiction over the legal needs of the corregimiento's subjects, and the legal system quickly seems unwieldy. And yet the often ponderous, petty wrangling between various authorities over jurisdictional claims was itself integral to the operation of Quito's own decentralized legal culture.

According to Minchom, the 1781 census counted the population of the city at approximately 25,000, with the corregimiento as a whole totaling 65,935. Indigenous subjects constituted some 66 percent of the total population, at 43,535.[33] Eight years later, the viceroy's (vice king's) Secretary Francisco Silvestre reported for the whole Audiencia a population of 585,460 with 34 percent white, 50 percent Indian, and the remaining 16 percent divided between "free of various colors" and slaves. Interestingly, the category of mestizo was not utilized, and presumably persons of mixed race were lumped together with whites. The secretary further reported the Audiencia was 56 percent male and 44 percent female, with a total of 114,204 recognized marriages.[34] For the corregimiento of Quito itself, including the city and the thirty villages of the Five Leagues, the secretary detailed 59,382 subjects, with 39,791 Indians, 19,083 whites, and 508 slaves.[35] Both of these calculations are significantly less than the figure 130,000 provided by Audiencia judge Juan Romualdo Navarro in 1764, but likely represent a more realistic estimation.[36] Regardless, the corregimiento of Quito placed in close contact a dense indigenous population with a significant center of Spanish bureaucratic and judicial power. While the Audiencia lacked the mining wealth of its neighboring viceregal jurisdictions, the region did maintain a demographic complexity that was in many ways representative of the core areas of Spanish control in the Americas. Taken together, the demographic, jurisdictional, and occupational realities of the corregimiento of Quito provide an excellent setting to evaluate the impact of changing governance and institutional discourses on social relations, and particularly gendered social relations, across the varied ethnic and economic terrain. Moreover, these realities are readily accessible through the judicial documents left in the archives of Quito.

SOURCES AND ORGANIZATION

In order to document as closely as possible both the persistent and the changing in the local legal culture of the corregimiento of Quito, this study centers on, but is not restricted to, an analysis of the cases collected under the auspices of the office of the First Notary of Quito (1NJ). Generally speaking, judicial cases in the National Archive of Ecuador are divided either thematically (criminal, marital, land, indigenous, civil, and so on) or by the office of the presiding notary. There were six enumerated notaries in the eighteenth century. I chose the First Notary because it is the most extensive and complete of the offices for the period under consideration. The disputes transcribed in 1NJ are most important to the study because they tend to be first-instance litigation filed before the city's alcaldes ordinarios and alcaldes de barrio, and before the corregidor and alcaldes de la Santa Hermandad. To a lesser extent, the judges of the Audiencia heard appeals and occasionally first-instance litigation recorded by the First Notary. As such, the vast majority of the cases analyzed herein originated from Quito and the Five Leagues. By contrast, the cases collected thematically primarily were cases being heard before the Audiencia, and therefore originated throughout the Court's geographic jurisdiction. For the purposes of this study, however, I have largely restricted the cases under consideration to those within Quito and the Five Leagues.

The case set for the 1NJ runs the gamut of types of disputes. There are, in no certain order, financial disputes over petty loans, criminal prosecutions for rape, murder, theft, receiving stolen goods, assaults, and injurious words, testamentary disputes, marital conflicts over adultery, domestic violence, and property, as well as tax disputes, land conflicts, and more. As a result, the 1NJ cases cover virtually all types of civil and criminal litigation in Quito and the Five Leagues, providing ample evidence for evaluating the operation of local legal culture, and particularly gendered legal culture. Because of the extreme volume of litigation, the case set for this study is constituted of alternating decades: 1765–1774, 1785–1794, 1805–1814, and 1825–1834, for a total of 1,600 cases.[37] Documents from the 1NJ section were further supplemented by cases from the topical series for the same periods from Criminales, Civiles, and Matrimoniales. Chapter 2 relies principally on cases from the Criminales section of the archive.

Utilizing this vast body of evidence, the book is divided into two sections that pair a late-colonial political crisis with two chapters on its effects on legal practices involving women. Section I follows Bourbon efforts to reform the fiscal and administrative practices of the Audiencia of Quito and the resulting political crisis of the Rebellion of the Barrios. Chapter 1 turns to this crisis of governance sparked by the fiscal reforms pursued by New Granada's Viceroy Pedro Messia dela Zerda. The chapter begins with the troubled attempts to reform the administration of the state liquor monopoly, first at the local level and then by a special emissary appointed by the viceroy for the express purpose of reform. In May and June of 1765, the city of Quito erupted into open riots and rebellion in response to the heavy-handed attempts to reform the collections, as the culmination of a period of failed negotiation. Local elites had sought to staunch the speed and extent of reform by playing bureaucratic games through an articulated right to consultation in all governing decisions that would have a direct impact locally. The process of failed negotiation, followed by the events of the summer of 1765, represented something greater than just a political crisis, however: the root of the conflict between Bogotá and Quito signified a broader clash over governance, legal process, and the legitimate authority. Finally, the chapter charts the postrebellion reconstitution of royal authority, the machinery of fiscal exaction reformed, and resistance to the institutional exercise of authority returned to the judicial venue.

The next two chapters turn to the legal-system-in-practice in the wake of the rebellion, and follow the effects of the disjuncture between customary conceptions of criminality, and women's legal status, issues of licensure through the revealing ancillary details of the cases. Chapter 2 looks to the gendering of crime beginning with the restoration of authority following the Rebellion of the Barrios, from 1765 to 1795. In a bid to reestablish royal authority in the barrios, the Quito cabildo constructed an infrastructure of surveillance through the appointment of a new coterie of neighborhood magistrates who worked in conjunction with the city's ordinary magistrates to monitor barrio behavior. Through an analysis of arrest statistics, the chapter demonstrates a significant increase not only in raw confinements, but also especially in morality arrests. This policing of morality targeted both men and women, but, interestingly, the increase in arrests did not initially result in an increase in prosecutions. However, twenty years out from the uprising the city continued its scrutiny of moral behavior with a redoubled commitment to prosecution as well. The surveillance of the barrios proved to place women's bodies under direct public scrutiny, belying a split between private female spaces and public male spaces. The prosecution of sexual crimes demonstrated a continuity of cultural logics by way of the mode in which men and women marshaled legal resources. Though the imperative to control people's moral bodies and behaviors took on new form in the closing decades of the colonial period, local expectations for justice and harmony continued to drive individual reactions to the invasive state. Again, Bourbon policy ends were hampered by an inherited legal culture.

Women did not find themselves embroiled in the legal system solely as victims or perpetrators of criminal acts. Chapter 3 uses the civil litigation collected by the city's First Notary to excavate the broader question of women's autonomous legal identity. Beginning with the legal procedures of licensure, the chapter demonstrates the extent to which *quiteña* women of all marital statuses were able to access the courts independent of their brothers, husbands, and fathers. From there, the chapter looks specifically at the economic roles inhabited by women as found in the documents: women as debtors, creditors, business operators, and defenders of economic self-interest under the divergent pressures of bad marriages, testamentary hopes, and aggressive bureaucrats. Likewise, the conflicting languages utilized by female defendants and plaintiffs in property disputes is analyzed in order to understand the tactical reasons that the language of inferiority was employed, or the reasons that men represented women in legal proceedings.

Section II brings the narrative back to political crisis, and looks at the impact of shifts in governance and legal culture during the revolutionary period of 1809 to 1830. It also documents the downstream effects of these political upheavals on the legal construction of gendered domination in Ecuador's transformation from Audiencia to Republic. These culminating chapters of the book make plain one of my core arguments: that the dissolution of the Habsburg form of governance and legality was the first step in undermining the avenues of mitigation available to women in Spanish American society.

Chapter 4 analyzes the crisis of the opening phases of independence that began with the Napoleonic invasion of Castile in 1809. In the initial stages, the crisis of political legitimacy sparked by the abdication of Fernando VII once again pitted Quito against the viceroy in Bogotá. As in the 1760s, this antagonism was articulated through fidelity to an absent king (though in this instance, absent quite literally). Fernando's resumption of the throne and subsequent backlash toward liberal political innovation sparked the second phase of agitation, culminating in Quito's liberation from Spanish rule as an integrated state in Simón Bolívar's newly constituted Gran Colombia. The Gran Colombian period was significant in the reformulation of legitimate political authority, reliant on liberal constitutional concepts. Further consolidated in fully independent Ecuador, this new vision of governance aided the transformation of legal culture in Quito through a new understanding of policing, legal precedent, and judicial hierarchy that ultimately would undermine women's position in society as both economic and legal actors. At its essence, citizenship in the new state was gendered male, and women were constitutionally written out of existence.

Chapters 5 and 6 document how quickly the levees of protection from the patriarchal flood deteriorated under the liberal regimes of late colonial and early postcolonial rule. Through analysis of arrest records, verbal case hearings, and civil litigation, the chapters demonstrate the immediate attack on women's economic resources from the beginning of the liberal revolution. Women were denied their customary position as heads of household in community decision making. Their legal disputes initially were pushed through a new system of mediation that added a layer of male intervention and extrajudiciality to the cases. Gendered violence escalated. The protections from debtor's prison enforced under Spanish rule were dismantled in the postcolonial period, the first of a number of policies aimed at diminishing the legal measures women had routinely used to protect their material interests. Furthermore, Chapter 6 documents the privatization of the disciplinary functions of the state in the domestic arena. Whereas Bourbon institutional authorities had sought to regulate the moral behaviors of men and women in the city and its hinterland, republican police regulations forbade magistrates from interfering in domestic conflict or entering citizens' homes. Republican policing created a private sphere where before one had not existed, in large part because the shift from status to contract, to borrow Sir Henry Maine's famous phrase, required a private sphere of property for the emergence of a public sphere of politics.[38] The net effect of these trends, as in the well-documented case of indigenous communities, was the removal of structural means to protect women's social, economic, and legal interests.

SECTION I

1765–1809

In Viscaya they observe various special privileges, in Aragon, their fueros, in the Indies their municipal laws, in Peru, their ordinances, as with every Province and place in the District. For, as the proverb says, he who goes to Rome must live according to Roman custom.

—Joseph Lazo dela Vega, 1764

The dramatic upheavals of the late colonial Andes played out in a raucous, and often-violent collision between local political expectations and the expansionist claims to absolute authority by the Bourbon crown. Quito provided an opening salvo of the great age of Andean insurrection with its very own Rebellion of the Barrios, sparked by an attempt to reform the Audiencia's liquor monopoly and sales tax collections. The events leading up to the rebellion pitted customary practice against governing intention, mirroring the conflict over women's legal position in the decades following the restoration of royal authority. Thus, the political crisis represented by the Rebellion of the Barrios provides the essential context for understanding women's experience in the judiciary at the close of the century. Chapters 1 and 2 document that experience in both criminal and civil arenas as women found themselves before or sought audience from a wide variety of the corregimiento's officials. As with many of the other Bourbon reforms, the institutional desire to put women in their place, so to speak, clashed with a formidable customary practice perpetuated through legal fictions that ignored or hid women's marital status.

CHAPTER ONE

QUITO *1765*

Justice, Rebellion, Reform

———•———

INTRODUCTION

Bourbon restructuring of the fiscal organization of Spain's American kingdoms had wide-ranging effects on the relationship between local subjects and the imperial system of rule.[1] The assorted reform initiatives pursued by the crown and its representatives during the eighteenth century met with varying degrees of success in the Andes. Following the War of Spanish Succession, the consecutive governments of Felipe V, Fernando VI, Carlos III, and Carlos IV pursued to varying degrees the fiscal, administrative, and military reorganization of the many holdings of the king of Spain. Until the reign of Carlos III, the majority of efforts centered on the crown's European possessions. An early step toward the reorganization of the American kingdoms came in 1739 with the first of two attempts to restructure the administration of the jurisdictions of South America. The Audiencia of Quito, along with the jurisdictions of Santa Fé de Bogotá, Venezuela, and Panama, were removed from the control of the Viceroyalty of Peru and placed under the direction of the newly formed Viceroyalty of New Granada. The formation of the new viceroyalty had a relatively small effect on the administration of its constituent jurisdictions for about another twenty-five years. The second major restructuring of South America came in 1776 with the establishment of the Viceroyalty of Río de la Plata in Buenos Aires, a move that further divested Lima of control over the area now comprising Argentina, Bolivia, Paraguay, and Uruguay.[2]

In the wake of the Seven Years War, Bourbon officials undertook with renewed interest their efforts to rethink the colonial relationship between the peninsula and the Americas, particularly the fiscal and military administration of the latter. The war left the government of Carlos III with numerous debts, and revealed the military vulnerabilities of the empire's port cities. In response to the situation, Madrid sent especially empowered officials (*visitadores*) to investigate the military and fiscal administrations of two of its most important American holdings: Cuba and New Spain. The investigations of Alejandro O'Reilly (Cuba) and José de Gálvez (New Spain) resulted in a number of reform proposals, including the liberalization and rationalization of commercial trade and tariff policy, the formation of permanent militias, and the fortification of coastal entrepôts. In the case of New Granada, no visitador was ever appointed to investigate the administration of the still newly formed viceroyalty's military or fiscal affairs.[3] Additionally, New Granada was the only one of the viceroyalties in the Americas not to carry out any appreciable military reform. This is somewhat surprising, given the importance of Cartagena as a military post. Kuethe attributes the negligence to New Granada's secondary importance to the revenue streams of the empire. In fact, leading into the 1760s, the viceroyalties of Peru and New Spain were remitting five and ten times, respectively, the amount remitted by New Granada. The paltry contribution of this viceroyalty, even at the time, was credited to the vigor of illicit trade in the region, and the inability of royal government to "harness, manipulate, and tax the commerce of New Granada, which flowed in and out with little interference and seldom paid any duties."[4]

Viceroy Pedro Messia dela Zerda (1761–1772) endeavored to change this situation, and took it upon himself to reorganize the fiscal administration of New Granada, beginning with the Audiencia of Santa Fé de Bogotá. His effort to extend the reform out to the other jurisdictions under his command precipitated a crisis of governance. The desire to increase exaction required a thorough reconceptualization of authority under a much stricter hierarchy in order to sidestep the traditional processes of negotiation that had been the norm throughout the preceding centuries of Habsburg bureaucratic decentralism. In the case of Bourbon Quito, Messia dela Zerda's effort to reorganize the administration of the Audiencia's cane liquor monopoly (*estanco de aguardiente*) and sales tax (*alcabala*) collection spawned conflict precisely over the organization and operation of authority under the new procedures of Bourbon rule. In October 1764, a special representative of the viceroy, Juan Dias de Herrera, was sent to Quito to take over direct administration of the cane liquor monopoly and sales tax collection, sparking indignant opposition from the city's various social sectors. The crisis culminated in open rebellion in the streets of Quito for much of 1765, a revolt that was the direct result of the failure of the customary function and organization of authority.[5] In the wake of the Rebellion of the Barrios, royal government was faced with the difficult task of reestablishing its legitimacy, while being under constant pressure from the viceroy to restart fiscal reorganization. In the end, resistance to the centralization of tax collection was ineffective, and during the ensuing decades residents of the Audiencia would become subject to one of the most efficient and far-reaching tax systems in the world.[6] More significantly, the failure of negotiation to avert the crisis of 1765 marked a watershed in the governance of colonial Quito. Surprised by the ferocity of the city's barrios, local elites threw their support behind the reestablishment of a much stricter and more interventionist governing power. While the logic of Bourbon governance was temporarily rebuffed by the violent success of the barrios, the lapse was only temporary. In the 1780s, with the arrival of Audiencia President Ramón García de León y Pizarro, reform of the Audiencia's finances took on a new urgency.

Even as fiscal reform was delayed for some twenty years, the Rebellion of the Barrios marked a new claim to surveillance over the bodies of the city's inhabitants. The city's magistrates began to take a keen interest not only in debt, theft, and violence, but also in broadly defined morality crimes. The policing of the city represented a new imperative of control over the subjects of Quito, whose relationships to imperial rule were brought under the scrutiny of an increasingly interventionist judicial apparatus. Both the resistance to fiscal reform and the increased scrutiny of behavior in the barrios after the rebellion shared a language of justification that emphasized loyalty to the public good, though to divergent ends. The concept of the public good, along with justice, royal interest, and good government, were abiding linguistic tropes traditionally utilized to advocate for local benefit in the negotiation of royal policy.

This chapter will document the failure of negotiation, the resultant crisis of governance, and the aftermath of the rebellion for the shifting logic of royal governance. The expectations engendered by earlier understanding of the primacy of local custom and the contingency of royal authority patterned the quiteño response to viceregal attempts at reform. These expectations were based on something deeper and more fundamental than the belief in political rights, and appealed to implicit cultural understandings of legitimate authority. The failure of the Quito elite to successfully mitigate the central authority of the viceroy, therefore, sparked not only a political crisis, but also a more generalized crisis of the relationship between government and authority. The contours of this calamity patterned the behaviors of Quito's insurrectionary barrios during the uprising and in its aftermath.

THE FAILURE OF NEGOTIATION: TOWARD 1765

When Viceroy Pedro Messia dela Zerda trained his sights on Quito's sales tax collection (alcabala) and cane liquor monopoly (estanco de aguardiente) in 1764, he found an Audiencia languishing in economic trouble and moribund leadership. At the death in 1761 of the previous president, the Marqués de Selva Alegre, only one judge of the court and the crown attorney (fiscal) were active in the city. The other members were either absent or, in the case of Don José de Quintana, too old to serve effectively in office.[7] The presidency matriculated to the longest-serving member of the court, Don Manuel Rubio de Arévalo, who was from Seville but who had been in residence in Quito's Audiencia since 1720. His career had been lengthy, but undistinguished.[8] Long-serving ministers on the court formed strong local ties, resulting in continual, petty infighting over local resources. To a large extent, though, the weak leadership of the Audiencia was of secondary importance to the desperation of quiteño society by midcentury. A combination of economic and natural disasters left the region in a marginal position relative to the centers of wealth and power in Buenos Aires, Lima, and Bogotá.

The most significant problem facing the quiteño elite in the eighteenth century was the contraction of the region's textile economy. During the peak years of Quito's textile (obraje) sector, the province was producing annually some 100,000 meters of cloth, dominating the supply to both New Granada and Peru. Annual sales of cloth accounted for some 1 to 2 million pesos, largely tied to provisioning the mining sectors in the neighboring kingdoms.[9] But a confluence of events brought the halcyon days of Quito's textile economy to an end by the 1740s. Beginning with the importation of French textiles in the wake of the War of Spanish Succession (1700–1716), and then with the expansion of trade liberalization in the 1740s, European textiles quickly came to dominate the markets once controlled by the Quito textile elite. Competition from cheaper imports caused a collapse in the price of quiteño cloth that amplified the crisis throughout the economy because, Andrien has noted, "when cloth exports declined, so too did imports, commerce and government tax receipts."[10] Andrien has also noted that in elite circles the economic crisis in the obraje sector led to intense factionalism among the region's elites as they fought over cloth tariffs and "control of local agricultural markets."[11] As prospects for profit in the textile market continued to diminish, elites turned increasing attention to the most lucrative sector of the agricultural economy: sugar cane and cane liquor. Thus, when the viceroy took aim at the aguardiente economy, he was threatening the livelihood of an already battered elite as well as their creditors in the city's monasteries and religious corporations.

The economic instability of the mid-eighteenth century was complicated further by a series of natural disasters. On June 15, 1742, Cotopaxi, a volcano near Quito, awoke from its slumber and began a four-year continual eruption of steam and ash. Though the direct effects of the eruptions were restricted largely to the province of Latacunga, Cotopaxi's awakening signified a period of intense seismic activity. In 1755, a series of quakes, the largest on April 28, severely damaged Quito. Two years later, another strong quake struck Latacunga during carnival celebrations, causing the Iglesia del Noviciado de la Compañía to collapse on some two hundred celebrants, killing forty Jesuits, two priests, one junior, and one novice. The economic impact of these disasters was far reaching, as the Audiencia suffered from the contraction of the obraje sector, its attendant effects, and a real shortage of specie to pay for repairs.[12] Finally, in 1764 and 1765, the corregimiento of Quito was simultaneously suffering through a drought and epidemic disease.[13]

Decisions on policy and action to deal with the many challenges facing Quito were made within a number of overlapping jurisdictions. The Audiencia, cabildo, and corregidor all laid claim to various aspects of the city's administration.[14] Throughout 1764, prior to the arrival of the viceroy's emissary, all three jurisdictions were consumed with managing the economic, natural, and bureaucratic struggles facing the province. The municipal council spent much of the year trying to find someone willing to assume control of provisioning the city with pigs and cattle for slaughter, preparing for the arrival of a new bishop and festivals for which the occasion called, hearing petty tax disputes, licensing doctors to deal with the epidemic assailing the barrios, deciding which of the city's many cults of the Virgin Mary should be paraded to combat the epidemic, and managing encroachments into the city's communal lands in Añaquito and Turubamba.[15] The cabildo was also deeply involved in a dispute being heard by the Audiencia over a new proposal for the administration of the aguardiente monopoly. The monopoly was founded in 1746 as a special tax intended to fund the construction costs of a new Royal Palace.[16] For the next two decades, tax farmers, who paid rent for the right to administer the monopoly, bought bottled aguardiente directly from producers at fixed prices, and then resold the liquor to distributors.[17] The system was rife with evasion, and as a revenue underachiever, it was a target for reorganization.

At the end of 1763, the viceroyalty put forth an order to standardize the production, administration, and collection of the aguardiente monopoly.[18] The main goal of reorganization, along with all the other fiscal initiatives pursued in the 1760s, was to increase tax collections in order to increase remissions to the viceroyalty to be used for the defense of Cartagena. In January 1764, the aguardiente monopoly for the corregimiento of Quito was opened to bidding, a process that resulted in a maelstrom of political struggles. Two competing bids emerged as the leading contenders for control of the estanco. Don Pedro Guerrero offered to assume control for the customary price of 8,000 pesos, and to maintain the status quo arrangement for production and distribution of the liquor. The furor, though, was caused by the rival bid of Audiencia lawyer Don Melchor Ribadeneyra, who offered a higher rent of 10,000 pesos, accompanied by a number of conditions. Foremost among these were that the administrator would reserve the right to set the prices and quantities at which bottled liquor would be purchased from provincial distillers. Additionally, Ribadeneyra requested permission to open an official estanco distillery, cutting out the intermediaries and establishing the monopoly as a primary consumer of the sugar and honey used in distillation.[19]

In effect, the reorganization would shift the profitability and balance of power of aguardiente production away from the myriad small and medium producers (hacienda owners, religious corporations, and merchants) and toward a centralized structure under royal control. Ribadeneyra claimed that the current method of running the estanco violated the very concept of royal monopoly, in that the administrator was at the mercy of the various hacienda owners and distillers who colluded to determine the price at which the estanco would be provided the finished product. It was contrary to royal interests to be beholden to such local control. The only means by which to put the estanco "in order, and method" would be to break with local custom and enable the agent to "freely make and buy aguardiente."[20] This was precisely the idea Viceroy Messia dela Zerda had for the estanco. The proposal was a metaphor for the tension between a local political culture of decentralism and a centralized governance emergent in the Bourbon period. It was also ill received.

Within days of the filing of Ribadeneyra's proposal, interested parties submitted protestations to all of the interested jurisdictional bodies: the viceroyalty, Audiencia, and cabildo. Ribadeneyra had the support of the outgoing administrator, Alguacil Mayor Don Sebastian Solano de la Sala, the Audiencia's attorney, Doctor Don Joseph Cistue, and the viceroy. Solano submitted a supporting petition that specifically connected Ribadeneyra's proposal as important to the effort to "defend Cartagena from the dangers threatening it." Another petition claimed the proposed changes for the estanco would bring Quito in line with the practices of the more profitable estanco in Santa Fé.[21] Ribadeneyra and his supporters had crafted petitions in language designed to appeal directly to the interests in Bogotá, emphasizing that the proposal would provide thousands more pesos to the crown than Guerrero would have provided. Also, the language of royal interest and empowerment over local custom appealed to the viceroy's concern for tightening fiscal control over his dominions.

The vested interests of the Quito aguardiente market saw the proposal for what it was: an attempt to crack down on tax evasion, illicit aguardiente sales, and local control. The petitions filed by Ribadeneyra's opposition followed a customary path by appealing to multiple jurisdictions in the name of minimizing local harm. At its January 25, 1764, meeting, the municipal council heard a number of protests and proposals portraying Ribadeneyra's plan as rife with "injurious conditions against the good of the Public Cause." The cabildo was lobbied to appoint Don Joseph Gomez Lazo dela Vega, a member of the council, to represent the interests of the city's vecinos and distillers before the Audiencia. The cabildo so ordered, allying themselves with the faction trying to maintain local, customary practices.[22] Further petitions were filed directly with the Audiencia. A group of thirteen distillers and prelates complained that, while Ribadeneyra's proposal claimed to serve the royal interest as well as the well-being of the city's religious communities and leading townspeople, in reality it would "advance the royal interests to the detriment, and complete ruin of [Quito's] loyal subjects."[23] Signatories to the petition included Provincial Vicar Fray Francisco Esculero of the Augustinian order, Alferez Real Don Juan Joseph de Chiriboga y Luna, and Doña Juana Jasinta Aveladeve, acting as a public and interested party to the reform. Further allegations were made against Ribadeneyra, questioning the ability of a mere lawyer to come up with the level of capital he was proposing to invest in the estanco. Conspiracy theorists posited that Ribadeneyra was acting on behalf of Fiscal Cistue and former administrator Solano, or as a proxy for sugar interests from Ibarra, to the north of Quito. To quell this angle, Cistue ordered that Ribadeneyra appear before a notary to swear out a declaration affirming that he was operating free of coercion, which he did.[24]

Ultimately the pressures applied by local hacienda owners, distillers, religious leaders, and the cabildo (as an institutional representative of the interested parties) prevailed, and the Audiencia refused to grant the estanco to Ribadeneyra. Most significantly, the dispute set the stage for further struggle between the centralizing drive of the viceroy in Bogotá and the decentralized ethos of local customary practice. The dispute also patterned a modus operandi of how to fight objectionable policy within acceptable boundaries of fealty. Opponents to the Ribadeneyra reform engaged in legal action across overlapping and competing jurisdictions, arguing for the primacy of local impact over the abiding royal interest to maximize revenues. They utilized the judicial form, submitting notarized petitions on paper carrying the royal seal, to provide functional legitimacy to carefully chosen language laying claim to advancing the public good. The case showed bureaucratic decentralism in operation, and placed the city of Quito on a collision path with the new legal and bureaucratic culture of Bourbon-era reform.

The viceroy was not pleased with the outcome of the bidding process. In March 1764, he ordered that the administration of the estanco be removed from the tax-farm system and placed under direct control of the royal treasury (*real caja*), an announcement met with near universal derision.[25] Messia dela Zerda decided to appoint Félix de Llano, a member of the Quito Audiencia, as judge administrator (*juez conservador*) of the estanco. Llano immediately complained that if he attempted to reform the estanco in line with the viceroy's wishes it would cause havoc and "would not only be damaging to the hacendados of the area, it would also threaten public order by provoking disorder among the students, friars, and plebeians of the city, already notorious for their turbulent dispositions."[26] In order to ensure the reform go forward, Messia dela Zerda then decided to appoint a special envoy to take direct control of the estanco as well as administration of the alcabala.

Juan Dias de Herrera was chosen by Messia dela Zerda to reorganize the aguardiente and alcabala departments as a result of the success with which he had administered receipts in Bogotá.[27] The failure of local quiteño officials to increase revenues, as represented by the dispute between Rivadeneyra and Guerrero, helped persuade the viceroy to sidestep the infighting of local elites in favor of a specially empowered official. Dias de Herrera's appointment was one step farther in the centralization of tax collection, following the March 1764 announcement that the aguardiente monopoly was to be moved directly under control of the royal treasury. The severity of the response to both the Rivadeneyra proposal and the viceregal order intervening in various branches (ramos) of royal revenue should have served as a warning of the firestorm Dias de Herrera was about to enter. The viceroy's determination to appoint a special representative deviated from the traditional method of negotiating important changes in royal policy. The traditional process, exemplified by the "I obey but do not execute" formula, relied on the ability of local groups to delay or prevent the implementation of new policy. Phelan describes the formula:

> The "I obey" clause signifies the recognition by subordinates of the legitimacy of the sovereign power who, if properly informed of all circumstances, would will no wrong. The "I do not execute" clause is the subordinate's assumption of the

responsibility of postponing the execution of an order until the sovereign is informed of those conditions of which he may be ignorant and without a knowledge of which an injustice may be committed.[28]

The formula provided a legal avenue by which to evade royal orders, and was exemplary of the governance of the pre-Bourbon period. It was anathema to the absolutist designs of Bourbon governance, and it was exactly this form of evasion and delay that Messia dela Zerda desired to obviate.

Dias de Herrera arrived in Quito on October 2, 1764, to a number of unwelcoming pasquinades posted throughout the barrios.[29] Rumors had spread prior to his arrival that Dias de Herrera was coming not only to reorganize the estanco and the alcabala, but also to establish new taxes on a variety of effects: tobacco, viticulture, salt, potatoes, women's jewelry, and even babies in the womb.[30] One contemporary complained that Dias de Herrera did nothing to quell these rumors once he was in the city, and instead went about his work with no consultation.[31] The rumors thus continued to spread, adding to the tension in the city. The municipal council reacted by immediately challenging Dias de Herrera's qualifications to administer the estanco and the alcabala. On October 10, the city sent council member Joseph Lazo dela Vega as a representative to the Audiencia, requesting to see a viceregal dispatch validating the office. Meanwhile, Dias de Herrera was already about his work. His design for the estanco went farther than the proposal of Don Melchor Ribadeneyra, in that he planned to construct a single royal distillery for the corregimiento. This distillery, which he set up in the barrio of Santa Bárbara, would purchase sugar directly from producers, then distill, mix, and distribute all aguardiente for the region. It was to be a true monopoly. The aguardiente interests represented by the cabildo immediately sought a means by which to prevent the construction. The council received Dias de Herrera's plan to construct the official distillery on October 19.[32] The plan called for the construction of a permanent connection to the aqueduct providing water to the neighboring barrios of Santa Prisca and San Blas. Dias de Herrera explained that the water was necessary for the process of distillation, mixing, and curing the aguardiente, and therefore the distillery would need continual access to water. He explained, "for this reason it is indispensable for me to consult with you, with all due respect and veneration, that in order to proceed in this Commission for which I find myself responsible, that you would permit me to divert more water."[33] The administrator insisted the project would cause no harm to the public good (*causa pública*), and in fact would result in great benefit to the townspeople along the route of the new aqueduct, as they would now have access to a reliable water source. The cabildo, for its part, saw the water issue as a means to subvert Dias de Herrera's work. At their October 23 meeting, Joseph Lazo dela Vega reported that the Audiencia still had not provided the requested documents empowering Dias de Herrera. The council then voted to appoint both Lazo dela Vega and the interim standard bearer, Francisco de Borja, to go directly to Dias de Herrera to request to see the documents, in order that they might protect the public good.[34] Finally, on November 7, the cabildo received a copy of the order naming Juan Dias de Herrera as administrator of the estanco and the alcabala, empowered to reform their management under the same organization as was being used in Santa Fé de Bogotá.[35] This first delaying tactic failed to deter Dias de Herrera.

Faced with Dias de Herrera's resolve to go forward with the reform, Francisco de Borja began working to organize a broader resistance. The municipal council, largely through the activities of Borja and Lazo dela Vega, became the focal point of opposition to the reform, much as it had in the struggle over Melchor Ribadeneyra's proposal. The other elements of the earlier coalition (ecclesiastics, hacienda owners, merchants) joined the municipal council to discuss their opposition with the convening of a *cabildo abierto*. A cabildo abierto, literally "open council," was a special meeting of town notables, the bishop, and representatives of the religious orders, called in order for locals to deliberate with the municipal council on issues of vital importance. A cabildo abierto might be called, for example, in time of war. Convening a cabildo abierto was an uncommon though not unprecedented occurrence. It had been used, for example, as part of local resistance to the original implementation of the alcabala in the closing decade of the sixteenth century.[36] A formal request by the city's prelates to convene a cabildo abierto was submitted to the council on November 14. The "Reverend Fathers of the Religious orders presented petition, in which they express the harm that will befall them in regards to the alcabala and aguardiente estanco, and request permission for a cabildo abierto, in which all will be able to explain the damages, and dangers to both private and public interests."[37] The council's representative wrote to the Audiencia, arguing that a cabildo abierto was necessary due to the severity of the situation caused by the

> notorious indifference to the damage to property that could result from the administration of the Royal Departments of the Alcabala, and the Aguardiente monopoly, as it has come to be practiced by Don Juan Dias de Herrera, [imposing] some new taxes, which, given the miserable condition of the people, are insupportable and harmful to the public good.[38]

On the advice of the tribunal's attorney, President Rubio de Arévalo agreed to the gathering on November 23, issuing an order that granted the municipal council's representative permission to call an assembly "in order to celebrate cabildos abiertos, as is fitting for the common good and public cause . . . in order to prevent protests and disorders set against those ends."[39]

Two weeks later, on December 7, 1764, the cabildo abierto was called to order in the presence of the members of the Audiencia, cabildo, the bishop, representatives of the city's many religious corporations, and other important vecinos and vecinas. Petitions were filed and short orations given by representatives of the city's various corporate groups, including Indians, monasteries, secular clergy, the cabildo, the leading citizens of the city, hacienda owners, and merchants. The majority of representatives arose to voice their concurrence with a document that Francisco de Borja had prepared. The contents of this petition and a supplement by the municipal council's lawyer (*procurador general*) Joseph Lazo dela Vega reveal the cultural logic that impelled the opposition to the reform. Borja's presentation questioned not only the reorganization of the estanco, but also the legitimacy of its existence all together. In an appeal reminiscent of the "I obey but do not execute" formula, Borja opened his petition claiming it was his responsibility to inform the viceroy of the harm that would befall the community if the reform went forward. Borja reminded the viceroy, "the Royal will must always incline to the relief of its subjects," and as the viceroy is only the representative of the monarchy, it would be inappropriate for him to diverge from this principle. Borja continued, "Therefore, his Excellency, with very wise and serious reflection will end the present project, and its establishment, based on the condition that *it will exact a noteworthy burden on the community.*[40] The evidence for community harm was threefold, and contradictory. First, Borja argued that the estanco would cause economic harm to the region's agricultural economy because Dias de Herrera's plan would no longer allow for private distillation and bottling of aguardiente, and also would result in reduced prices for sugar cane and, Borja claimed, a net loss of 3 pesos per bottle of finished product. Removing the profitability from sugar production would cause contractions across the agricultural sector.

Borja's second point centered on the moral ambiguity of the government profiting from the vices associated with liquor consumption. He claimed that the moral depravity of many of the city's inhabitants was the direct result of the original formation of the estanco. Royal sales of liquor, even under the old method, had led to widespread drunkenness, which in turn had produced a corrupted community, "lacking even the least shame, without fear of God, or for Justice, conducting themselves with great insolence, and daring, with every lewd act and abomination that follows on such unspeakable vice. . . . What monopoly is there in this city, except that which is the public office of every offense against God, where with impunity people commit the gravest sins, lewdness, slander, robbery, thievery, dishonor, and a thousand more scandalous acts that contribute to the ruin of everyone."[41] The greatest victims of this injustice, he argued, were the Indians, who lacked the ability to resist the potency of the liquor, and who referred, he claimed, to the royal estanco as the royal destruction (*real estrago*). Much worse than their simple moral degradation, in the case of indigenous subjects aguardiente led to a reduction in tribute receipts and therefore harm to the royal exchequer. For this reason alone, he argued, the estanco should be abolished.

Finally, Borja appealed to the general financial ruin in which the quiteños found themselves in the wake of the collapse of the textile economy. The unfortunate, miserably poor subjects of Quito "had nothing to mine, except for the production of cloth, and other products of the land," and were already subject to the most "immense exaction with mortgages, tribute, sales taxes, tithes, harvest taxes."[42] Borja explained that, regardless of the method and success of tax policies in Cartagena or Bogotá, the specific circumstances of Quito negated their applicability because of the harm they would cause to the public good. Borja crafted his petition in such a way as to appeal to the cultural logic of decentralism. In it, he delineated the responsibilities of royal agents to act justly, and to not cause harm to the financial, moral, and social conditions of the jurisdictions under their purview. The arguments were, to a certain extent, contradictory. On the one hand, he decried the monopoly's impact on the financial prospects of the region's sugar growers, aguardiente distillers, and sales merchants. On the other, he disparaged the social effects of liquor consumption, as if desiring the abolition of drink altogether.

The addendum of Joseph Lazo dela Vega provided a legal justification for opposition to the reform by appealing to the concept of fuero rights. Though no formal set of special legal privileges was ever granted the municipalities of the Americas, Lazo dela Vega claimed specifically that the "practices and customs" of Quito carried the same weight as the many fuero rights respected by the crown. The practices and customs were determined by the climate, temperament, and land of a given area, not by the residence or will of royal officials. The many, diverse kingdoms of the Spanish monarchy, then, each had its own privileges:

> In Viscaya they observe various special privileges, in Aragon, their fueros, in the Indies their municipal laws, in Peru, their ordinances, as with every Province and place in the District. For, as the proverb says, he who goes to Rome must live according to Roman custom.[43]

This observation is key to understanding the structural nature of his argument, as Lazo dela Vega placed local, customary practice at the same level of legal currency as any formal fuero, ordinance, or legal charter to emanate from the crown. Finally, in accordance with the traditions of decentralized governance, Lazo dela Vega requested the viceroy grant permission for and pay the costs of sending a representative of the municipal council directly to Madrid to plead their case, essentially bypassing the authority of the viceroy. He offered three names of individuals, including Francisco de Borja, as candidates for the position of representative. Taken together with the Borja petition, the addendum presented a comprehensive scheme to avert the implementation of undesirable legislation under the logic of Habsburg governance. This logic reached beyond the jurisdictional organization of a bureaucratic decentralism to widely held cultural values that saw the concentration of power as inimical to the legitimate operation of authority in society.

Following John Leddy Phelan's interpretation of the 1781 Comunero revolt in New Granada, McFarlane argues the petitions of the cabildo abierto represent the articulation of a constitutional, political right to consultative governance.[44] Phelan and McFarlane rightly note that this tradition of consultative governance had its roots in "an ideological tradition fed by the concepts and conventions of Hispanic political theory in the Golden Age, rather than by the new ideological currents emanating from the European Enlightenment."[45] This tradition held that local subjects had a right (a constitutional right, in Phelan's parlance) to provide consult to the king and his council in the formation of policies that directly affected the local context. While neither Phelan nor McFarlane argue that the assertion of a constitutional right to political consultation in the Hispanic world was rooted in the struggle for constitutional monarchy in France or Britain (including its colonial agitators), there is in this line of interpretation an equivalence drawn between the tax resistance and the demand for representation in tax policy that drove much of the political crisis in the North Atlantic world from 1765 onward. Andrien has characterized the petitions of the cabildo abierto as too narrowly drawn to be "a relatively sophisticated constitutional argument," amounting instead to a simple airing of grievances, noting, "[the arguments] did outline very directly the economic and political agenda articulated by the quiteño élite since the economic crisis began late in the previous century."[46]

The use of the cabildo abierto and the petitions produced by the various social sectors for the meeting represent something more significant than an asserted right to political consultation or a mere list of grievances. The contradictory nature of the claims put before the viceroy in an effort to deter reorganization of the estanco and the alcabala were expressions of a deeper cultural logic that sprang from an understanding of authority and legitimacy. It seemed perfectly reasonable to the participants in the cabildo abierto to claim, for example, that alcohol was a social evil that caused harm to both Christian and economically productive behaviors, while also claiming that the viceroy's move to wrest control of the liquor market would cause irreparable harm to the economic interests of the region's religious and secular elites who needed the proceeds from sugar production, liquor distillation, and market supply to offset the deterioration of the textile economy. The logic of such argumentation relied on a contingent, localized, and decentralized understanding of authority that could embrace such contradictory ends. The petitions of the cabildo abierto went beyond a simple conflict over political representation, and represented the clash of two very different ways of conceiving authority in society—one decentralizing and on the wane, the other centralizing and on the rise. It was this clash that determined the severity of the crisis in the coming year of 1765.

In the weeks after the cabildo abierto, Dias de Herrera found it increasingly difficult to freely pursue his labors. Hostile pasquinades again appeared in the streets of the city, and he felt threatened enough to request a guard for personal protection.[47] In the interim period between the assembly and the viceroy's response, work on the estanco and the alcabala continued. The cabildo continued to offer legal challenges to the aqueduct that had been proposed the previous November. The council appointed Francisco Borja to represent its interest in the water dispute, and the conflict between the two men continued to escalate. The council claimed that the city's water supply could not support the needs of both the community and the liquor factory. Dias de Herrera claimed otherwise, and personally examined the existing infrastructure, submitting a report to the Audiencia. Borja countered on January 11, 1765, that, had Dias de Herrera been from Quito, he would know that winter was the rainy season, and therefore that no evaluation of the city's water supply could be made until the following summer, in July or August, when the supply was at its lowest. This was an attempt to push the construction of the aqueduct off for months, effectively delaying the transfer of liquor distillation to the estanco factory. Borja then requested that the Audiencia appoint council member Sebastian de Salzedo y Oñate to perform a second assessment. Dias de Herrara was incensed, firing a response back to the Audiencia in the beginning of February that the question of supply was ridiculous, and that Francisco de Borja "always prefers private benefit to the utility of a proposition and the growth of the Royal Treasury." The Audiencia struck a compromise solution, ordering the city's main aqueduct (acequia) be cleaned and maintained so as to maximize the flow of water, but refusing to give the distillery guaranteed full access to the water supply year-round. The amount of water that would be diverted would depend on the judgment of the city's water arbitrator. Judge Félix de Llano, who had been charged the prior year as juez conservador of the estanco, issued the ruling on February 7. Six days later, Borja swore his compliance to the order, and, on February 20, the acequias were cleaned and the distillery's connection to the system established.[48] Eleven days later, on March 1, 1765, Juan Dias de Herrera officially opened the new distillery. Tensions rose yet again.

The viceroy did not pen a response to the cabildo abierto until May 7. He was completely dismissive of the arguments put forth in the petitions by Borja, Lazo dela Vega, and the authors of the other included petitions. His ruling stated tersely that the complaints put forth by the cabildo of Quito against the aguardiente monopoly were completely without cause. He then went on to explain that his understanding of the situation lent credence only to the explanation that quiteños were corrupted by the habit of tax evasion, arguing that in a place where "many thousands of pesos are either owed or have disappeared, it is only natural to find the whole province in opposition, conspiring against the important end of [a just Administration and collection of Royal levies]."[49] Messia dela Zerda then proceeded to ridicule the logic of Borja's petition, pointing to the willingness of the ecclesiastical community and vecinos of Quito to maximize their sales of aguardiente and overlook any supposed "pernicious damages of its use." The one consolation Messia dela Zerda granted was permission for the city to send a representative to Madrid to lobby the king's council directly, but with two conditions: (1) The citizens of Quito had to pay all the expenses themselves, and (2) The deputy could be anyone except for Francisco de Borja. Despite having employed their most sophisticated arguments, steeped in the cultural logic of bureaucratic decentralism, the elites of Quito had been soundly rebuffed. The viceroy granted no legitimacy to either the logic or the substance of their arguments, and demanded the city stop resisting his authority. The customary right of local communities to moderate royal orders, based in an understanding of the decentralized and contingent organization of authority in Hispanic society, was rejected. The significance of this failure would soon become clear, as the city erupted into open rebellion and the calculus of legitimate authority was permanently changed.

MAY 22—BARRIOS UNITE!

In early May, Felix de Llano was removed as juez conservador of the estanco and replaced by Juan Romualdo Navarro.[50] On May 15, Dias de Herrera established a new customs house for the administration of the sales tax. The office was installed in a house on the Santa Bárbara central square (*plazuela*) that had formerly been an oidor's residence, adjoining the customs house to the estanco distillery and parish church in the neighborhood of the carnecería. This concentration of physical manifestations of the reform policy provided a convenient space for the coming protest. On May 20, Dias de Herrera published a list of punishments for individuals caught trying to evade any of the new alcabala and then proceeded to have his agents register properties in the barrio of San Roque. On May 21, he sent his assistants under the direction of Don Bartolomé Puyol to census plots in the barrio of San Sebastian. The registration of plots was for a planned tax of 4 pesos per holding.[51] Jesuit Father Bernardo Recio reported that the opening of the customs house and registration of plots by Dias de Herrera's agents sparked a new wave of rumors throughout the barrios, as word spread that Dias de Herrera was planning to implement new taxes on eggs, charcoal, and firewood, and "all the fruits of the land."[52] Recio also reported the rumors affected the city's indigenous population most, and indeed the products he lists as subjected to rumored tax expansion were controlled by the city's indigenous hawkers. To tax Indian products under the alcabala would have signified a breach of the tributary contract, under which indigenous subjects were exempted from virtually all other forms of taxation as long as they maintained their tributary status. Recio characterized the city's Indians as simpletons, easily duped to believe in threats to their well-being by unscrupulous merchants.[53] McFarlane states these were more than rumors, and that indigenous marketers were forced to pay taxes "on small quantities of salt, vegetables, peppers, eggs, and other provisions, and their goods were confiscated if they did not pay." Additionally, he notes clerics were being forced to pay tax on goods they accepts as alms. Actions such as these spurred further rumors that plans were in the works for "high land taxes, tribute on children in the womb, and taxes on the river stones used by washerwomen, and to create government monopolies on salt, tobacco, potatoes, sugar, and maize."[54]

As tales of new and oppressive taxes spread throughout the barrios of the city, so too did word of an impending uprising. On the morning of May 22, posters appeared throughout the barrios proclaiming, according to Gonzalo Súarez, "in very large and legible letters . . . an imminent uprising in the barrios of Quito against the customs [house] and aguardiente monopoly."[55] Additionally, Recio reported that, early in the day, masked men appeared before the priest of the Santa Bárbara parish church, warning him to remove the host from the church lest it be caught in the impending conflagration. Recio believed these men to be discontented members of the city's merchant class, and likely the authors of the protest.[56] At 8 p.m. on the evening of May 22, fireworks and church bells signaled the masses to pour forth from their homes, particularly in the barrios of San Roque, San Sebastian, and San Blas, and converge on the plazuela of Santa Bárbara, where they proceeded to burn the customs house, ransack the distillery, empty the casks of aguardiente, and dismantle stone by stone the customs building itself.[57] Young men, old men, women, and children together yelled in the streets against the perceived tyranny of Dias de Herrera and Viceroy Messia dela Zerda. Estimates of the participants vary from 3,000 to the obviously inflated number of 18,000 to 20,000 claimed by the anonymous author of the *Relación sumaría*.[58] Juan de Velasco reported some twenty-five years after the events that the crowd was led in part by a few masked men along with sixty butchers from the nearby carnecería, echoing the assertions of Recio of the presence of masked agitators presumably rousing the plebe. Likely, the crowd numbered in the region of 8,000, but regardless of the actual number of participants, the crowd succeeded in the destroying the physical symbols of viceregal authority.

Apparently, the parish priest of Santa Bárbara had kept to himself the warnings of impending arson, as the actions of the throng caught the Audiencia and other royal officials in a panic. It is hard to imagine that the coordination involved in the uprising, combined with the (literally) public signs of its coming, could have left the authorities so ill prepared. It may well be that Dias de Herrera's provocative actions and unwillingness to observe the customary rules of consultative governance had left the city's authorities ambivalent, when not outright hostile, toward his interests. The twenty or so guards attached to the Audiencia manned what arms were at the government's disposal to protect the reported 80,000 pesos held in the royal treasury, but had few resources with which to quell the disturbance.[59] As a result, the crowd's actions went unabated. At 11 p.m. the parish priest of Santa Bárbara brought the Eucharist out of the church, hoping its public presence would calm the crowd. It did not, and he soon retreated with the host to the Iglesia de Carmen Bajo a few blocks to the east of the plazuela. The Audiencia publicly called for support amongst the city's vecinos, asking them, according to McFarlane, "to take up arms and to illuminate the streets by lighting their doorways, windows, and balconies."[60] A core of royal officials, including the members of the Audiencia, Fiscal Cistue, Alguacil Mayor de Corte Antonio Solano de la Sala, his lieutenant Mariano Alvarez Monteserín (also an *alcalde ordinario* of the cabildo), Corregidor Manuel Sanchez Osorio y Pareja, and a few responsive vecinos such as merchant Angel Izquierdo attempted to organize patrols (*rondas*) to regain control of the streets. They were met with a shower of stones, the weapon most readily available to the mob. Juan Dias de la Herrera quickly sought refuge in the palace, where he pleaded for action from the Audiencia. The court decided to deposit him in the San Francisco monastery for safekeeping.[61]

By the morning of May 23, the crowd had finished its work in dismantling the customs house, undeterred by any attempted interventions by royal authorities and loyalists. The Audiencia was in a weakened position, and the desire to restore order to the city prompted a number of attempts to negotiate with the throng. The process of reconciling the protestors began overnight, as four respected Jesuit priests were dispatched by quiteño Oidor Romualdo Navarro as emissaries of the government. The protestors had two significant demands: (1) A full pardon for all involved in the night's activities, and (2) Suspension of any further attempts to reform the estanco and alcabala. The priests made promises to this effect, and together with the bishop attempted to "reassure the populace that neither the king nor the viceroy wished to harm common interests."[62] Promises from both the priests and Navarro that the demands of the crowd would be respected were deemed insufficient, as was an official general pardon order (*auto de perdón*) issued by the Audiencia but vague in its wording. It was not until Navarro, accompanied by the bishop and a notary, came to the plazuela under armed guard to issue a signed and sworn pardon that the barrios were satisfied.[63] The exploits of the rebellious crowd and the reconciliation offered by the government both gained legitimacy, or authority, through the performance of a legal act, and in particular through the judicial form. This adherence to legality in the midst of widespread and violent insubordination expressed the cultural standards of contingent authority, in which the participants viewed their extreme measures as carrying their own legitimacy as a response to the irreparable harm assured in the actions of the viceroy and his representatives. Why demand a notary? Why not accept the earlier writ of pardon from the Audiencia in hiding? The public act of producing a notarized petition of general pardon conferred to the resolution the authoritative voice of the judicial form, which carried with it an explicit cultural authority. The judicial form, even in the midst of patently defiant behavior, conveyed legitimacy.

The results of the May 22 uprising were amplified by the caution of the Audiencia in dealing with the rebellion. In addition to the grant of pardon, temporary end of the estanco, and suspension of the alcabala, the ronda was stopped and Dias de Herrera was forced to remain in hiding along with his closest advocates and employees.[64] Furthermore, the battle lines of the coming June explosion were clearly drawn. The rioters reflected the demographic realities of the city, led by the artisan class and composed of a mix of mestizos, poor whites, and Indians. The officials and vecinos who stood against the actions of the barrios (and their tradesperson leaders) would become the initial targets of the more serious June violence. A tenuous and unsustainable peace settled on the city. Over the course of the next month, small commotions continually threatened to escalate into larger actions. On May 29, word spread that Oidor Hurtado de Mendoza was convening an investigation into the previous week's events; barrio residents took to the streets proclaiming their intent to burn his house along with those of the city's other royal officials. The situation was defused by the intervention again of ecclesiastics.[65] As May turned into June, agitations continued to grow. On June 2, a patrol led by the corregidor rounded up thirty-six young men who were publicly drunk and dancing. The corregidor decided to put them on display in the *plaza mayor* as an example to the rest of the city.[66] Sanchez Osorio y Pareja's actions had the opposite of their desired effect. On June 8, more pasquinades appeared on the city's thoroughfares, this time calling for the expulsion of European Spaniards from Quito. A week later, they appeared again, renewing the call.

On June 14, six indigenous men raided the city jail and liberated a compatriot who had been incarcerated. On June 18, residents of San Blas arrived at the bishop's residence to demand they be able to choose their own parish priest. The next day, members of the same barrio had to be repelled by an armed guard under the direction of

Romualdo Navarro when they tried to free a barrio resident detained in the city jail.[67] Mariano Monteserín arrested the detainee for having assaulted and stabbed two young men. In an attempt to exploit the distrust of the barrio, the detainee's brother, Mateo Ballinas, agitated for an assault on the jail; during the day on June 20, his brother was freed by a group of San Blaseros. The following day, realizing they had been duped, representatives from all the city's barrios together turned the Ballinas brothers over to Monteserín. The action signified that the Quito plebe was not interested in subverting authority per se, but rather in resisting government actions they deemed illegitimate and harmful to the public good.[68]

The Audiencia used the weeks following the May riot to organize its defenses. In part because royal authority continued to be perceived as weak, formerly reticent vecinos, particularly European Spaniards, responded to the need to protect the palace and royal treasury from the hostile mob. A group of approximately three hundred men was formed into a security detail; these men constructed defensive positions for the protection of royal property and were provided private weaponry to the city's aging stockpile. Barracks were constructed on the plaza mayor and parapets in front of the royal palace. The various positions were then armed with the few mortars and cannon possessed by the palace guard.[69] Each night during June, shifts of the city's vecinos operated the parapets in an attempt at a well-armed display of strength and protection of the royal interests.[70]

Surprisingly, the cabildo met just once in May (on May 11, close to two weeks before the riot), and once in June. The riot was never officially discussed. The June 20 meeting dealt with two petitions, both concerning issues in the Tumbaco River valley, part of the corregimiento of Quito to the east of the city. The first related to the meat supply in the pueblos of Tumbaco, Puembo, Pifo, and Yaruqui; the second related to the construction of a bridge over the Tumbaco River.[71] The eerie silence of the cabildo on the momentous events of May and June concealed a rift within the body. The presiding officer of the council, Corregidor Manuel Sánchez Osorio y Pareja emerged as the most severe critic of the government's conciliatory approach toward the rabble. Meanwhile, Francisco de Borja continued to be seen by the barrios as the city's leading advocate in what was still considered a standoff with external interests. That Osorio y Pareja was a European Spaniard confirmed in the minds of barrio residents the perception of equivalence between oppressive policy and metropolitan provenance. Ultimately, the equivalence was just a matter of perception, since only thirty of the seventy-six resident European Spaniards would come to the aid of the Audiencia in the coming late June troubles.[72]

JUNE 24—DEATH TO THE CHAPETONES!

It was Corregidor Sanchez Osorio y Pareja's insistence on the hard line that provided the pretext for insurrection the night of June 24. The date was significant, marking the celebration of the saint's day festival of San Juan. San Juan remains one of the most significant festival days of the Andean calendar, coinciding with the summer solstice. During the colonial period, the festival also marked the biannual payment of tribute from the indigenous communities of the Audiencia. The coincidence of the date, with the preparations for Catholic, indigenous, and fiscal celebrations, eased the process of communication for the city's popular sectors as the city swelled with arriving representatives of the region's indigenous communities and weekend marketers of agricultural goods, all of whom mingled with the resident populace. Over the weekend of June 22 and 23, the corregidor insisted, against the objections of the more conciliatory factions of the Audiencia and cabildo, on performing street patrols of the barrios. On June 23, patrols of San Roque and San Sebastian yielded forty-four arrests, including the detention of thirteen women. The corregidor ordered the detainees be publicly whipped in order to communicate to the plebe that the government would not tolerate another May 22 riot. The detentions and whippings had the opposite effect.[73]

The next day, pasquinades again appeared in the streets of the city, this time calling on all of the barrios to unite in resistance to the unjust actions of Corregidor Sanchez Osorio y Pareja. On the evening of June 24, crowds began to gather in the plaza of Santo Domingo, many of them armed with crude weapons, stones, farming implements, and the occasional lance. Recognizing the seriousness of the situation, oidores Luis de Santa Cruz y Senteno and Juan Romualdo Navarro, Fiscal Joseph Cistue, and Protector Fiscal Joseph de Herrera gathered at the palace along with other supporters of royal government from 7 to 9 p.m. to prepare for an anticipated attack. President Manuel Rubio de Arevalo was absent due to health and age issues, so Santa Cruz assumed leadership on the scene. This indeterminacy led to confusion, exploited by the corregidor, over who had actual authority to decide on a response to the expected street fighting. Sanchez Osorio y Pareja insisted on performing another patrol of the barrios with a well-armed coterie of his closest (and almost exclusively European Spaniard) supporters. Santa Cruz and Navarro, joined by Oidor Hurtado de Mendoza, explicitly and vehemently objected to the proposal, seeing the action for the provocation it would be. The corregidor, however, had sent two European Spaniards to convince Rubio de Arevalo to support his call for street patrols. The president, isolated from the reality on the streets, listened to the corregidor's plea for strength in the name of royal interest, and ordered the patrols as requested. The conflicting chain of authority took control of the situation out of the hands of those oidores actively operating the artillery pieces on the plaza mayor.[74]

Claiming support from the president, Sanchez Osorio y Pareja set out around 10 p.m. with a group of approximately twenty men, armed with muskets (*fusiles*), to patrol the barrios. Officials gathered at the plaza mayor let off a cannon shot, a prearranged signal to the city's vecinos that the time had come to immediately rally to defensive positions around the royal palace. It seems Santa Cruz and Navarro recognized the response with which the patrol would be faced. The ronda set out for San Sebastian, and on the way came across a crowd amassing on the plaza of the Santo Domingo church. The corregidor attempted to arrest a number of the revelers as an example to the crowd. It was a poor decision. Those gathered assailed the patrol with stones and lances, threats that were returned with a fusillade reportedly causing the death of two or three rebels, with another two severely injured. It was the first clash of what would prove to be a violent, insurrectionary evening.[75] The patrol retreated northwest toward the Audiencia, greatly outnumbered by the ever-growing throng of barrio mutineers. Over the course of the next twelve hours, royalists and quiteño rebels clashed in the streets as the multitude decided (through consultation, according to one observer) to attack specific points it associated with the tyrannical authority of the city's European Spaniards.

At least three officials' houses were set ablaze and destroyed, including those of Corregidor Nuño Apolinar dela Cueba Ponce de Leon, alguacil mayor of the Audiencia court jail Antonio Solano dela

Sala, and merchant and captain Angel Izquierdo. All three of these officials were European Spaniards who had participated in resistance to the May 22 riot, while both the corregidor and Izquierdo were on the patrol that sparked the violence the night of June 24. Reportedly, Izquierdo was chosen as a target because he was the most readily identifiable member of the ronda on account of a distinguishing white suit he was wearing. His house was just two blocks off the plaza, where a crowd of some eight hundred men and women showed up around 12:30 a.m., intent on burning it down. Izquierdo's wife and children were present at the time, terrified by the pounding on the doors and windows as the assailants attempted to enter and ransack the house. Izquierdo's family escaped, seeking refuge in the nearby home of the Marquesa de Maensa. Meanwhile, the merchant heard of the assault on his property and rushed to the scene, accompanied by a handful of soldiers and one of the guard's six artillery pieces. They fired on the crowd, but were soon put into retreat, overwhelmed by the numbers and intentions of the mob. In the process, Izquierdo lost the cannon as well as his house, which was roundly ransacked and then burned to the ground.[76]

The mob then turned its attention on the plaza mayor. Through the night and into the next morning, the crowd, armed with stones, lances, and an increasing number of fusils and artillery pieces (eventually numbering three), gained in the chaos, skirmished with royal forces holding artillery positions on the parapet of the palace as well as a position manned by Juan Romualdo Navarro on the corner of the plaza mayor in front of the city's Jesuit church. The increasingly desperate palace defenders repelled wave after wave of attack, running dangerously low on gunpowder supplies. Cries of "*¡Viva el Rey! ¡Mueran los chapetones! ¡Abajo el mal Gobierno!*" (Long Live the King! Death to the Europeans! Down with bad Government!) rang forth from the mob. They were met with the retort, "*¡Viva el Rey, pícaros! ¡Mata a estos traidores! ¡Avanza, mata!*" (Long live the King, you knaves. Kill these traitors! Let's go, kill them!).[77] By morning, the rising sun illuminated the casualties of the night's fighting, totaling just two dead of the 150 defenders of the Palace, including a soldier of the guard and the Escribano de Provincia Antonio Dueñas. The insurgents were not so lucky. Eyewitnesses put the death toll at between two hundred and five hundred. Fighting continued until 11:30 a.m., when residents of San Roque were the last to withdraw from the plaza.

The barrios were not finished, though. Despite a number of moves intended to calm and disperse the crowds, as dusk approached the throng made its way back to the plaza mayor. During the day, a number of Jesuit emissaries had sought to bargain with the leaders of the barrios, but their overtures had been rebuffed. In another religious appeal, a group of ecclesiastics paraded the city's barrios carrying crosses, the Eucharist, and images of the Virgin. The scene left a serious impression on participating priest Bernardo Recio, who reported, "here was a dead mestizo, and there lying an Indian; and they said that in a nearby ravine there were bodies galore," all the aftermath of the night's fighting.[78] As he and the rest of the religious delegation continued their procession through the city, they discovered the extent to which the rebellion was a full community project. Recio continued, "I saw, then, what is a civil war. Women were coming and going loaded with stones, as well as their children."[79] For the plebe, the fight was a family affair. The procession of the Eucharist, escorted by the priests' singing, was intermittently interrupted by the sound of artillery fire. Upon entering San Roque, the convoy found the most ardent resistance. Armed barrio guards stood at the entrance to the barrio, arranged in ranks. The party's approach was met with a shower of stones. Recio reported that they then prostrated themselves on the ground, making the sign of the cross and asking for the barrio captain to allow their entrance. On his order, the crowd let the procession continue to the barrio church where the ecclesiastics read to those gathered the offer of peace proposed by the bishop, at the behest of the Audiencia. As they continued through San Sebastian, the group encountered more hostility, punctuated by the occasional cry of "Long live the king! Let's have peace!"[80] They continued on through the rest of the city's barrios, from San Sebastian north to San Marcos, San Blas, and Santa Bárbara, spreading word of the offer of peace.[81]

By nightfall, however, the crowds had returned to El Sagrario intent on renewing their battles with the remaining loyal guard and European Spaniard contingent. Realizing the precarious position in which they found themselves, members of the Audiencia, the corregidor, and the remaining guard took refuge first in the Monasterio de la Concepción, and then finally in the Convento de San Francisco.[82] From this haven, over the next few days the Audiencia bargained a peace with the barrios, effectively ceding control of the city. The atmosphere was electric, as the triumphant insurgents celebrated their victory in the streets, accompanied (with a touch of irony?) by much drinking and revelry. On the morning of June 26, Recio reported that patrols of mestizos set forth throughout the city, visiting the homes of known European Spaniards, and rejoicing when those homes were found empty. For a known European unlucky enough to be discovered on the streets, "they threw themselves upon him like rabid dogs, as happened to a Catalan who had only recently arrived in Quito."[83] The religious communities of the city, for their part, continued their processions, marching the icons of Nuestra Señora del Rosario and San Francisco's Madre Dolorosa. The processions still fell short of their intended effect, and Recio and his companions were met with taunts from women on street-side balconies who yelled down, "Blessed Father, go back to Rome."[84]

During the day on June 26, the Audiencia and the bishop met with Francisco Borja and two Jesuits who acted on behalf of the barrios to negotiate an end to the violence. The barrio demands were stiff, much more so than the preceding May, and included the mass departure of all Europeans from the city, a second general pardon for participants in the insurrection, the release of all prisoners from the city's jails, an exchange of prisoners held by the barrios for those awaiting execution, dismantling of the city's gallows, and the expulsion of the fifty or so men who made up the royal guard. In return for these demands, the barrios would concede the weapons they had won, depositing the artillery pieces, lances, and fusils in the Convento de Santo Domingo. Despite the agreement, the crowd only returned the lances and fusils, holding back the cannon, which they set up in defensive positions in the barrios. The government was ultimately powerless to enforce the agreement, and at last a peace descended on a city that was well and truly in the hands of the plebe.[85]

The following day, June 27, representatives chosen by the barrios continued to press the issue of the presence of European Spaniards in the city, guaranteeing that if the Audiencia did not order and enforce their expulsion, the crowd would return in strength in eight days time to enforce the order themselves. The number of resident and nonresident Europeans totaled eighty-six, including three judges of the Audiencia, the corregidor, the captain of the royal guard, the Audiencia's official notary, the alguacil mayor of the court's jail, the royal treasurer, a German watchmaker, and one Italian and one French doctor, among others. The Audiencia yielded, issuing a combined general pardon and proclamation of expulsion in a public ceremony, ordering, "everyone of the European nation to leave under the bogus slander that [they] had abandoned the defense [of the city]" by taking refuge in the monasteries and convents.[86] Angel Izquierdo remarked bitterly the following year that this decision was, "the most shameful action, to see the royal image and standard raised in the presence of the Tribunal, a Pardon given to the vile, rebellious plebe, [the Tribunal] having been unable to preserve our King (may God protect Him) from the indignity of such a ceremony and to them, in his image and edict, [the Audiencia] acted to provide in this most vile ceremony to this most depraved people, Pardon."[87] It was not only the order that compelled the Europeans to want to leave Quito, but also fear for their safety. Long-term resident and alguacil mayor de corte Antonio Solano dela Sala petitioned the Audiencia on July 4 to relieve him of his office so that he could vacate Quito as a result of the destruction of his house and general hostility of the population to his presence. The Audiencia granted the petition and within days had named Mariano Alvarez Monteserrin as interim. Interestingly, the adherence to formal legal procedure for such bureaucratic decisions continued despite the virtual powerlessness of the Audiencia to affect policy in the corregimiento.[88]

Within the eight-day evacuation period, Izquierdo, Solano dela Sala, Sanchez Osorio y Pareja, and the other European residents of the city had departed, leaving the city in de facto control of the barrios. On July 4, the barrios again converged on the plaza mayor to formally end the actual rebellion where, "amidst protestations of fidelity and repentance, they handed over the captured arms. The oidores were forced to restate the pardon they had granted, and the arms were then solemnly returned, amid much public clamor. Finally, as a symbol of the city's loyalty, the royal standard was raised on the balcony of the Audiencia palace, to be kept illuminated for three days and nights."[89] Under continued negotiation, new barrio representatives were chosen with the Conde de Selva Florida picked for San Roque, Nicolas Calixto de Alarcon for San Sebastián, Marian Perez de Ubillas for San Blas, Joseph Lazo dela Vega for Santa Bárbara, and Manuel Gonzalez and Francisco de Borja for San Marcos. These barrio representatives then took over most of the municipal posts of the city, and ruled in an uneasy peace with the barrio populace.[90] In a symbolic gesture of obedience lacking all capacity for compliance, the cabildo met on July 9 and finally swore compliance to the viceroy's May response to the petitions of the cabildo abierto. The meeting was supervised by Joseph Herrera, an oidor of the Audiencia, and ratified by the remaining members of the cabildo.[91] They would not meet again until September, at which time they again would consider petitions concerning the provisioning of meat to the city, as well as a debt claim by the Convento de La Merced for 50 pesos owed by the cabildo for the celebration of the Natividad de Nuestra Señora from the preceding year. The September meeting conferred an ersatz appearance of normalcy, but the violence and disruption of the summer of 1765 resulted in a relative vacuum of royal authority until the arrival on September 1, 1766, of troops under the direction of Juan Antonio Zelaya, the former governor of Guayaquil.

Though many of the Europeans who had been run out of Quito in July had returned by October, they were unable to reestablish any semblance of the political and bureaucratic control and security they had had prior to the uprisings. For example, on October 14, 1765, the officials of the royal treasury complained to the Audiencia that the nine men charged with providing security for the strongbox of the royal treasury were stretched very thin by the continued danger in the city. The officials requested the Audiencia budget a salary for an extra guard to be assigned from the city's commercial police (*guardia mayor de comercio*), currently charged with patrolling the streets and shops of Quito to ensure compliance with good commercial practices, to the royal guard. Present in the salon of the tribunal were judges Rubio de Arévalo, Santa Cruz, Romualdo Navarro, and Hurtado Mendoza y Zapata; Joseph de Herrera served as fiscal in the place of Joseph de Cistue. Herrera responded on October 20 with a recommendation to grant the petition, which was formalized by the members of the Audiencia on November 11 with an order to Salvador Sanchez Pareja (treasurer, and brother of controversial Corregidor Manuel Sanchez Pareja y Osorio). The order for payment and provisioning of an extra guard was not rescinded until the following October 1766, when the royal troops under the direction of Zelaya had been in Quito for more than a month.

RESTORING ROYAL ORDER

In the aftermath of the rebellion, Viceroy Messia dela Zerda's primary concerns were to reestablish royal authority, quell further unrest in the barrios, and return to fiscal reform. The first steps toward restoring royal authority occurred with the appointment of Juan Antonio Zelaya to lead a force from Guayaquil to Quito to pacify the region. Messia dela Zerda received word of the June uprising a little more than a month after its occurrence. On July 28, he issued a decree from Bogotá to Zelaya, then serving as governor of Guayaquil, to mobilize a militia in the port and await the arrival of troops under the command of Brigadier General Francisco Javier Moreno y Mendoza, with whom he would then mount an expedition into the highlands. Zelaya would then take control as general commandant of a force comprising Guayaquileño, Panamanian, and Limeño troops. The necessary funds for the expedition were to come from the Guayaquil treasury. Zelaya's instructions were to assemble the troops, then lead them to Guaranda, the seat of government for the province of Chimbo, and the gateway to the Andes southwest of Quito. From Guaranda, it was Zelaya's responsibility to judge the fidelity of the surrounding cantons and determine the extent to which the provinces were sympathetic to the Quito uprising. Once Zelaya was assured of the loyalty of the provinces, he would move to Quito itself.[92]

Three days later, the viceroy sent a second communiqué claiming he had received word from the Audiencia in Quito claiming the authors of the insurgency were ready to sign a capitulation. Messia dela Zerda requested that Zelaya determine the extent to which this news was true, "to verify the agreement and repentance proposed by the authors and accomplices of this seditious, continued uprising."[93] In fact, no such capitulation had actually occurred. The confusion over the trajectory of the situation in Quito was directly the result of the distance involved. So, too, was the delay in Zelaya's mobilization. On September 24, the viceroy sent a further set of instructions to Zelaya on the military expedition, reiterating the messages on July 28 and August 1, and adding news that a battalion of two hundred men had been dispatched from Panama.[94] A little more than a week later, Messia dela Zerda added in a subsequent message that the troops from Panama were also bringing 24,185 pesos provided by the Panamanian treasury to cover expenses, as well as munitions and gunpowder provisions. The message also included a series of general orders for Zelaya's use in compelling the cooperation of the provinces surrounding Quito; these orders were meant particularly for Joseph Phelipe de Arechua, corregidor of Chimbo.[95] Despite this initial energy from the viceregal office, it was months before Zelaya assembled the troops and eventually set forth to scale the heights into the Andean interior.

Meanwhile, life in Quito continued in an uneasy peace. Zelaya, it would turn out, had little to fear from the provinces. Royal government in the surrounding corregimientos never tipped toward support for the rebellion, and in fact determined to prevent its spread in part by denying Quito access to combatant materials. In August 1765, Quito's fireworks masters were forced to petition the Audiencia for a writ ordering the corregidor of Latacunga and assistant administrator of the royal gunpowder factory, located to the south, to sell small quantities of gunpowder for use in saint's day celebrations and other festivities. The gunpowder monopoly was resistant to selling to the fireworks technicians, in particular because of their role in rallying the barrios on May 22. Furthermore, from June 29 onward, the monopoly was operating under an embargo on sales to any jurisdiction within the Five Leagues of Quito for fear that the material would be used in the insurrection. Interim fiscal Joseph de Herrera's take on the petition was conciliatory, noting that within the boundaries of reason and precaution, the director of the monopoly should resume sales to responsible officials, including those members of the fireworks guild. To make sure that only the appropriate individuals should receive gunpowder, the fiscal suggested the administration develop a list of everyone who purchased the product, when, and how much. It was so ordered on September 13 by Romualdo Navarro, Rubio de Arevalo, and Hurtado de Mendoze y Zapata.[96] Such attempts to accommodate the city's interests (in this example the availability of fireworks for annual festivities celebrated by the city's religious communities) marked the activities of officialdom through the end of 1765 and into 1766. In December, Manuel Rubio de Arevalo officially stepped down as president of the Audiencia, and was replaced on an interim basis by Oidor Santa Cruz, who carried out no reprisals on the rebels and rather sought to bring the elected barrio leadership back into the fold of royal authority.[97]

Word finally reached Quito in March 1766 that a military expedition was on its way. There was talk that the troops would immediately reestablish the tax infrastructure and seek to punish at the gallows the many participants in the year's insurgency. The fears were not allayed until the troop actually arrived some six months later on September 1,

1766. The troops entered the city with relative ease. Recio described the significance of their arrival:

> The period came to an end with the arrival of many soldiers, some from Lima, others from Panama, all by way of Guayaquil. Upon seeing such a large company, the barrio agitators began to flee, this time without the least bravery. Quito took up the yoke of the law, subordinated itself to it. And to assure that she would not raise her head again, there were above all many soldiers.[98]

With the arrival of the soldiers, Zelaya posted instructions to the wayward barrios that defined just what taking up the yoke of law would mean. The instructions were an interesting mix of language, articulating the return of formal royal authority within the matrix of common good, peace, and sovereignty that played to the cultural values that had impelled the barrios to resist Juan Dias de la Herrera's impertinence in the first place. The orders began,

> May it be known to all residents and inhabitants of this City, of whatever station, class, or condition that whereas his excellency the Viceroy of these kingdoms, Señor Doctor Pedro Messia dela Zerda, has placed in my care the Command of Arms and pacification of this Province in order to return to it the tranquility and peace necessary to conserve the Sovereignty of His Majesty, respect for Justice, the well-being of the community, and the profit and benefice of each and every individual of this City and Province. And having experienced, not withstanding the recent revolutions, all the towns of the region and residents of this City that yielding and submitting is to the great benefit to all who work to achieve peacefulness . . . in the protection of His Excellency the Viceroy, whose orders are the most gracious and kind.[99]

Zelaya's claim to legitimate authority, preceding the actual instructions for the populace, sought to rearticulate the formulas of the past in order to reestablish royal government. Zelaya appealed to renew the image of the viceroy as a collaborator and guarantor of justice, whose ultimate aim (standing in the stead of the king) was to ensure the well-being of his loyal subjects. Zelaya then followed the appeal with three very specific instructions, from the stick to the rhetorical carrot:

1. In the space of three days, all weapons (fusils, pistols, arquebuses, muskets, carbines, lances, daggers, pikes, swords, and so on) be turned in to the palace guard along with the names of the owners. The penalty for evasion was three years exile for nobles and two hundred lashes plus five years exile in one of the presidios to the south for plebeians.
2. No one was to speak in public or secret or to have any conversation concerning the uprising, its causes, or its motives, nor to congregate after 6:30 p.m. publicly in groups of more than two. Furthermore, Zelaya instituted a citywide curfew at 9:30 p.m.
3. It was finally prohibited to use or display publicly for any reason, without express permission of the government, fireworks, explosives, or any type of fire, under the penalties already laid out in the law.[100]

These three strictures were designed to alleviate the remnant social pressures that might prolong the threat to royal authority. The entire experience of barrio insurrection was to be removed from the vocabulary of local reality, along with the implements of insurrection.

From this start, on September 3, 1766, Zelaya set forth to rebuild royal governance within the corregimiento. The presence of the royal troops, no doubt, enhanced his position. Corregidor Manuel Sanchez Osorio y Pareja, who sparked much of the unrest in June 1765, was replaced by Don Nuño Apolinar de la Cueva Ponce de Leon (the same corregidor who heard the case of Ana Arguelles that is discussed in the Introduction). Francisco Borja, who had been a key agitator on the side of the barrios, returned the office of alferez real to Juan Chiriboga. In July 1767, Zelaya relinquished his interim appointment and handed the Audiencia over to a new president, the Spaniard Don José Diguja. Diguja's first acts in office were to suspend all investigations the Audiencia was pursuing on the issue of the uprisings, and to dismantle the gallows erected in the plazas of the city.[101]

The new leadership sought to restore a balance of power between the Audiencia, corregimiento, and cabildo. Elites who were daunted by the ferocity of the popular sector involvement in the second stage of the rebellion were eager to cooperate with the various jurisdictions to maintain order. There was, however, continued pressure to reform the fiscal apparatus of the province. As early as October 27, 1766, Messia dela Zerda was writing to Zelaya insisting he begin again the reorganization of the aguardiente estanco as well as the alcabala collection. He wrote again in January 1767 to complain that he had not yet heard from Zelaya of any progress. Zelaya responded two months later that he had appointed two local officials to investigate on how best to organize and operate the estanco and the alcabala, and that consultations were ongoing, in essence putting off Messia dela Zerda.[102] In order to push forward fiscal organization, the viceroy appointed Don Seraphin Veyan y Mola, a member of the Quito Audiencia only since April 30, 1765, as juez conservador in charge of administering the royal treasure. On March 3, 1768, Veyan y Mola opened an investigation of the books of the royal accounts in an attempt to determine the exact state of affairs in the Quito treasury.[103] Despite such steps, Messia dela Zerda would complain at the end of his tenure in 1772 that Quito continued to resist, reporting to his successor,

> Despite having pacified the province of Quito, and attempted to reestablish royal revenues, I draw your attention to their remarkable decadence. With every year, receipts from aguardiente fall, which with more than enough reason I attribute to the negligence and carelessness of the administrator, and the lack of activity or conscientiousness of his immediate supervisors.[104]

Resistance to taxation targeted not only alcabala and aguardiente receipts, but also the core collection of indigenous tribute. In September 1768, President Diguja was already writing the viceroy to complain that, according to his protector of the Indians, the indigenous communities of the corregimiento of Quito would in no way be able to meet tributary obligations.[105] Messia dela Zerda's successor, Manuel de Guirior, continued the push to reorganize aguardiente and alcabala collections to the standards of operation in Bogotá. The Audiencia successfully resisted the move.[106] Guirior was effective in establishing an expanded royal monopoly of tobacco during the period. This purpose was enhanced by the availability of convict labor for the two main tobacco factories in Quito and Guayaquil.[107] It would not be until the 1780s, under the appointment of José García Leon y Pizarro as president of the Audiencia, that significant improvement of tax remissions would occur.[108]

The political calculus had changed by the 1780s. García Leon successfully revamped the fiscal structures of the Audiencia, ultimately constructing a tax apparatus unrivaled in the Hispanic world, and possibly in the entire world.[109] Revenues skyrocketed during the decade. Tables 1.1 and 1.2 follow the growth of tax receipts in the Audiencia across the period 1753 to 1800 in the revenue categories of the alcabala, aguardiente, tribute, and total collections. From relatively flat collection rates in the 1750s and 1760s, to modest growth in the 1770s, to skyrocketing revenues in the 1780s, the political culture attached to taxation went through a dramatic shift during the postrebellion period. The massive increase in revenues coincided directly with the tenure of Garcia Leon as Regent of the Audiencia. Aguardiente, alcabala, and tribute receipts all grew roughly threefold from the early high in 1762 to the historic peak of 1786. Overall tax receipts, however, expanded more than sevenfold across that same period, growing from 1762 receipts of a mere 236,018 pesos to the 1786 climax of 1,772,019 pesos! Aguardiente receipts actually decreased in significance, from an average of 7 percent of revenue in the decade 1755–1764 to just 2.6 percent of revenue in the decade 1780 to 1789, during the reign of Garcia Leon (1778–1784) and his successor Juan José de Villalengua y Marfil (1784–1790). A similar decrease is detectable in the alcabala, constituting 5.1 percent of receipts from 1755 to 1764, diminishing to 1.5 percent of overall revenues for the decade 1780–1789. In fact, much of the expansion in revenues during the 1780s was driven by a doubling of revenue categories, as well as an expansion of remissions from Guayaquil and Cuenca directly into the coffers of the Audiencia.[110]

Garcia Leon removed oversight of revenue collection from the officials of the royal treasury and created a centralized tax directorate (dirección general de rentas) charged with consolidating and improving collections across the Audiencia. In large part, this bureaucratic restructuring removed tax collection from the same easily corrupted tax farm system that had been a target of Juan Dias de Herrera in the 1760s reform. Garcia Leon's success was driven in part by his authority as regent, president, and visitor general (visitador general) of the

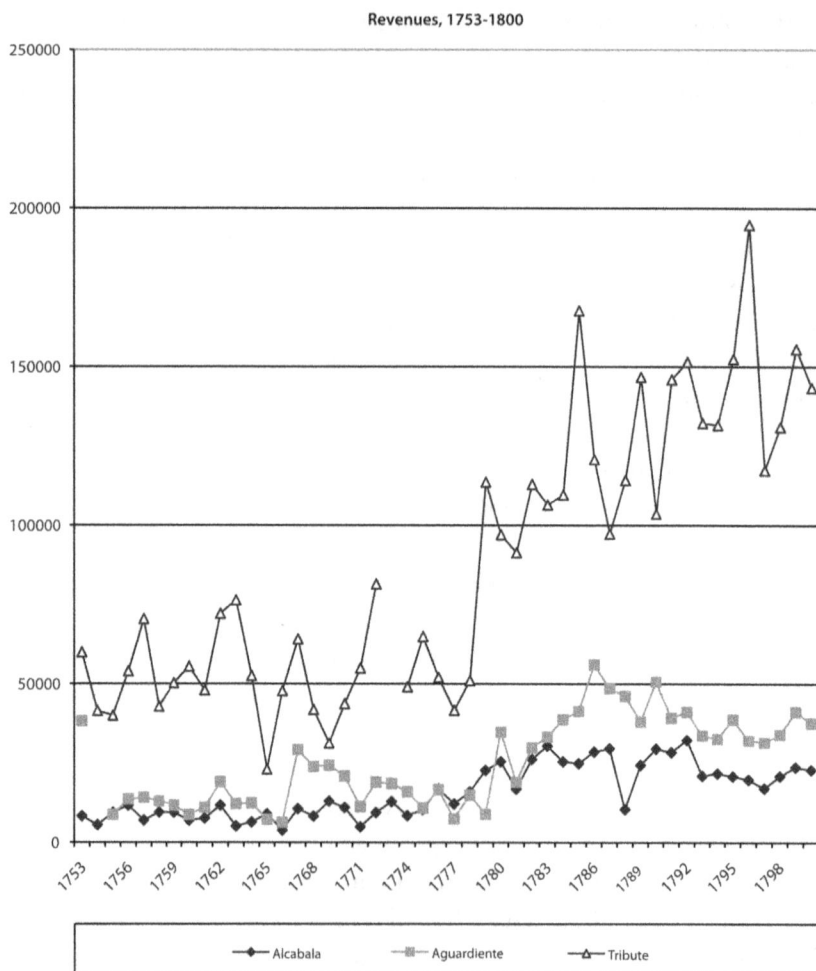

Table 1.1 Alcabala, Aguardiente, and Tribute Revenues, 1753–1800
SOURCE: JARA AND TEPASKE (*1990*): *123–64*.

jurisdiction. The position of regent was newly created with his administration, and carried more authority than serving simply as president
and member of the Audiencia council. Moreover, as visitador Garcia
Leon was specially empowered to investigate and institute reforms,
much as Messia dela Zerda had attempted to do twenty years earlier.
An Audiencia transformed in the wake of the 1760s further aided
Garcia Leon and Villalengua in their reform efforts. Whereas the

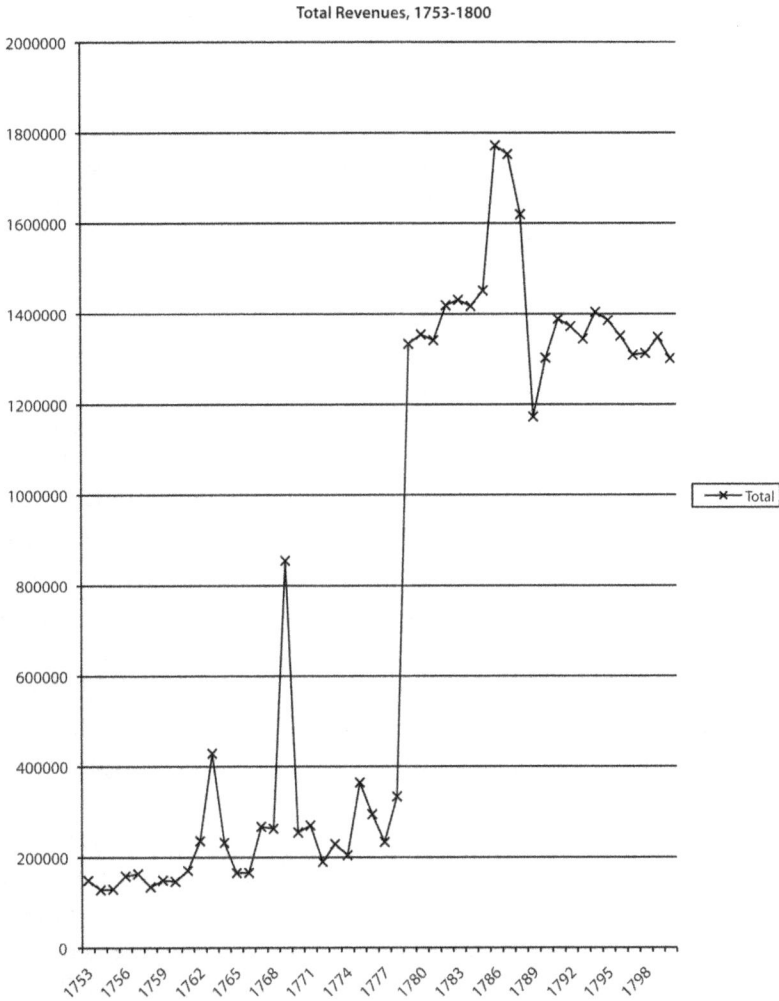

Table 1.2 Total Revenues, 1753–1800
SOURCE: JARA AND TEPASKE (1990): 123–64.

moribund council of the 1760s had been dominated by judges with very long tenures in the Audiencia, whether "peninsulars" or "creoles," the judges and fiscals of the court in the 1770s and 1780s brought to the court a more professional, detached service. Of the oidores who served on the court from 1775 to 1795, only Gregorio Ignacio Hurtado de Mendoza y Zapata had ties to prerebellion Quito.[111] This more professional bureaucracy lent its support to constructing the new taxation apparatus, rather than resisting its implementation. From a fiscal perspective, then, the 1780s would seem to have been a complete repudiation of the successes of 1765.[112]

The groundwork for the expansion of royal power in the 1780s was laid in the preceding decades. Much of this was the result of the emergent machinery of surveillance that became a core element in disciplining the barrios into compliance with royal dictates.[113] It was also the result of the crown's ability to gain information. Beginning in the years immediately following the uprising, and continuing through independence, a number of localized censuses were taken with the aim of increasing the reach and efficiency of taxation. President Diguja ordered a survey of the city in 1768, carried out by barrio magistrates.[114] Two years later, Diguja received an order from Bogotá requesting a full accounting of the Audiencia, detailing the towns, cities, and villages that constituted his jurisdiction, and how many inhabitants there were in each, as well as their professions. Initial attempts to comply with the order caused a few ripples in the provinces. The indigenous residents of San Felipe and Saquisili, in the corregimiento of Latacunga to the south of Quito, rebelled against the local corregidor when he attempted to survey the population in March 1771, fearing that the census was designed to increase tribute exactions.[115] Five years later, an order came from Spain that priests should submit yearly diocesan censuses, particularly of indigenous parishes for the purposes of augmenting the colonial economy and tribute receipts. The attempt to complete the first full-scale census of the jurisdiction from 1776 to 1779 was directed by Audiencia Fiscal Juan José de Villalengua y Marfil, who later would succeed Garcia Leon as regent and president. This order in turn caused disturbances in 1777 in the indigenous communities of the cantons of Otavalo and Cayambe, north of Quito, as well as in the corregimiento of Riobamba in 1778.[116] Not every jurisdiction rebelled against the numeration, and Villalengua was successful in his count in the corregimientos of Quito, Latacunga, Ambato, Ibarra, and Chimbo. Violent resistance to census taking was not without reason, as the aims of Bourbon-era information collection were invariably intended to expand taxation. But unlike the heady days of 1765, the violence remained contained to sporadic outbursts of a few local communities. The widespread challenge to royal authority did not occur again in the Audiencia until 1809.[117]

This is not to suggest that resistance to policy changes ceased. Rather, resistance to policy changes shifted back to traditional venues of the quotidian and the judicial. As a case in point, the fiscal changes of the regencies of Garcia Leon and Villalengua led to a dramatic increase in tribute remissions, as well as a dramatic increase in detentions for tribute evasion and litigation seeking protection from zealous tribute collection. The word "zealous" seems appropriate when considering the arrest records from Quito. In 1789, 186 unnamed Indian tributaries (*indios*) were listed in the rolls as being apprehended for owing tribute. The number is astonishing in comparison with earlier counts of the city's jails, when, for example, from January 1767 through July 1770 only two individuals were detained for derelict tribute payments![118] In the decades of the 1780s and 1790s, precisely when royal revenues dramatically increased, so too did aggressive state detentions, individual enforcement of fiscal categories, and judicial reactions against those actions. In the case of tribute, this process manifested through a dramatic increase in litigation for formal declarations of mestizo status.[119] The Villalengua census was officially compiled in 1780, and presumably informed the tax collection process from that year forward. Table 1.3 demonstrates the expansion of suits requesting official designation as mestizo coinciding with the implementation of the Villalengua's census. The judicial acts sought to verify mestizo identity for the sole purpose of obtaining exemption from tribute.

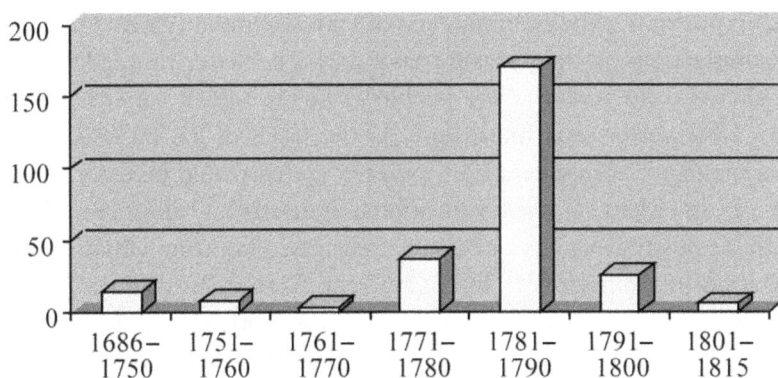

Table 1.3 Declaration of Mestizo Suits Filed by Decade
SOURCE: "GUÍA DEL FONDO MESTIZOS DEL ARCHIVO NACIONAL" Quitumbre 9 (1995): 123–40.

Within the organized resistance to census taking and tribute collection, ordinary men also took refuge in the judicial form. Only men filed for declarations of mestizo because, from the institutional perspective, an Indian was defined as a tribute-payer, who was by definition conceived of as being male. The rules for determining mestizo identity in the 1780s were largely derivative of the ethnic status of fathers for legitimate sons, and mothers for natural children. For example, the legitimate son of a mestizo father and indigenous mother would follow his father's exempt status, whereas the natural child of an indigenous mother would be required to pay the Indian tax. The legitimate son of an Indian father would likewise follow his tributary status. Mestizo identity was distilled, ultimately, to a derivative tax status.[120] New regulations on mestizo applications included extensive explanations of legitimate and illegitimate birth and communal location, but no commentary on language, food, dress, or even occupation. They also emphasized paternal descent when paternity was known as part of the broader Bourbon agenda to enhance paternal authority.

The standards had an immediate impact on the legal appeals for exemption from tribute obligations. For example, in his appeal for mestizo status in 1785, Enrique Ordoñes, a resident of the indigenous pueblo of Lican in the jurisdiction of Riobamba to the south of Quito, pled within the framework of legitimate birth and fiscal practice.[121] Ordoñes, who called himself as well as his father highland mestizos (*montañeses*), presented the court with baptismal documents establishing his position as the legitimate son of a mestizo father, Pedro Ordoñes, and indigenous mother, Visenta Ynquibay. The plaintiff noted that his mother was the native of the pueblo of Lican, rather than his father. This observation was important, as the town of his father's origin was the place from whence his own tax status would be determined. Finally, in order to prove his position as a mestizo, Ordoñes presented with his position a stack of alcabala receipts, a tax from which tribute payers were exempted.[122] The same year, Marcos Rodriguez filed to be declared mestizo on the strength of his mother's reputed ethnicity. Rodriguez's baptismal certificate noted he was the natural child of "Thomasa Olano *Mestiza*, and an unknown father."[123] The word mestiza was underlined in the original, emphasizing that as a natural child, Rodriguez's tributary status should follow the ethnicity of his mother. Rodriguez filed out of desperation, as he had been confined by the administration of tributes in the San Roque textile factory. The cache of testimony provided to the court by the Audiencia-appointed lawyer charged with assisting the poor on Rodriguez's behalf included statements from three different witnesses, all of who testified to the public recognition of Rodriguez's status as a mestizo, as well as that of his mother. On March 10, 1785, Mariano Oyeda testified he knew Marcos Rodriguez, and more importantly his parents, his mother a "mestiza *limpia*," the father an "*español*": (his mother was a "clean" mestiza, and his father pure Spanish). It turned out that the identity of Rodriguez's father remained secret because his father was married, while the mother remained single. Interestingly, the next witness was one Dr. Don Ygnacio Rodriguez, the tithe (*diezmo*) collector for the pueblos of Oña and Nabon in the jurisdiction of Cuenca, who testified that while he did not know the father of Marcos Rodriguez, he was certainly willing to testify that Marcos had always been known as a mestizo. Was this Doctor Rodriguez the unidentified Spaniard who fathered the namesake Marcos Rodriguez? By the rules of mestizo qualifications, it was not that important of a question.

The petitions of both Marcos Rodriguez and Enrique Ordoñes were fashioned to meet the expectations of a new legal standard, but used according to the customary means of the judicial form. These two men, along with many others caught up by the overzealous expansion of the machinery of fiscal enforcement in the 1780s, submitted their requests for justice (*pido justicia*) before the customary forum in which subjects of the kingdoms of the Americas had long sought personal justice: the various magistrates of the Audiencia. This process pitted the conflicting desires of varying elements of the bureaucracy against one another, in this case the desire for a peaceful, just community against the pressures of increased revenue collection. The system of adjudication was far from perfect. Marcos Rodriguez, for example, spent a total of two months confined in the obraje of San Roque before the administration of tribute collection accepted the Audiencia's writ officially recognizing his mestizo status. But the courts remained a recommendable venue of recourse, even for those (like Marcos Rodriguez) who were too poor to afford to contract their own legal counsel. Both Rodriguez and Ordoñes found themselves vulnerable to the persecution of fervent tribute officials because they were originally from outside the jurisdiction of the corregimiento of Quito, leaving them without the local resources of support needed for protection against policy implementation. Even so, judicial action still provided an avenue to mitigate the severity of their situations. In the case of declarations of mestizo, this meant that an impressive 73 percent of applicants were granted the exemptions.[124]

CONCLUSION

The transformation of taxation and tributary practice in the closing decades of the eighteenth century placed indigenous and mestizo subjects under much closer state surveillance. The process by which individuals were subjected to closer policing for the enhancement of revenue generation was patterned initially in the policing of the barrios of Quito in the years after the rebellion. This greater claim to control over people's bodies emerged as an imperative after the collapse of governance by negotiation. The violent actions of the summer of 1765 had their roots in the Habsburg ethos of decentralized governance, in which the sovereignty of the crown and its representatives was limited by the customs and practices of intense localism. By dismissing the rules of acceptable authority, Viceroy Pedro Messia dela Zerda and his emissaries provoked the explosive reactions of May 1765. And yet the actions of the barrios went too far the following June, destroying the ability of Spanish authority to maintain control over the varying social and economic sectors of quiteño society. The attack on the city's European inhabitants grew out of disgust with certain Spaniards' unwillingness to recognize the grievances of the barrios in the wake of the May riot. The determination of individuals such as Corregidor Sanchez Osorio y Pareja and Fiscal Joseph Cistue to resist any conciliatory posture, and to parade an attitude of strength and militarism through continued, provocative street patrols, led to an association of their position in local society with the tyrannically perceived policies handed down from Bogotá, sparking the anti-European sentiment that overflowed in June. Yet this sentiment never took the final step of divorcing quiteño identity from its position within the broader Spanish world of the late eighteenth century. Rejection of individual Spaniards, much like the rejection of unwanted policies, was ultimately rooted in the inherited ethos of decentralism.

When Antonio Zelaya arrived carrying the stick of military force, he decided foremost to engage the barrios with the language of public good and justice that were traditionally associated with kingly sovereignty. The rhetorical move eased the return of royal authority into the corpus of rebellious neighborhoods. Conciliatory moves on the behalf of royal officials in the succeeding years, though, masked a significant shift in the perception and constitution of governance, a shift that led to the construction of the hemisphere's most effective apparatus of tax collection. While this process was marked by a decline in collective, violent reaction to an increasingly invasive institutional authority, individuals sought recourse through customary legal appeals to the public good and balanced justice. Habsburg legal culture would prove to be one of the most difficult obstacles to the Bourbon's reconceived coloniality.

CHAPTER TWO

PRACTICE I

Sexed Crimes

———•———

ASSAULT!

On Wednesday, March 16, 1785, Mariano Thena stopped by a shop in the barrio of Santa Bárbara operated by Thomasa Cusallos to retrieve a jackknife that he had hocked a few days earlier.[1] He entered the shop, took off his hat and cloak, and demanded Cusallos return his property without his having to pay the one *real* needed to redeem the pawn. When she refused, Thena picked up the jackknife and cut her across the face, putting her at risk of losing an eye. A surprised and wounded Cusallos screamed, and the noise of the commotion drew the attention of Maria Rosa Correa, Maria Flores, Maria Ponze, and Casimera Tigre, four women who lived in the neighboring houses. As everyone spilled out onto the street, the witnesses found Cusallos with her face "bathed in blood" that emanated from her mouth, nose, and eye. In the midst of the turmoil, Cusallos closed the door to her shop and set out, holding her bloodied eye, to find one of the city's magistrates to immediately file a complaint against Thena. Thena's cloak was still in the store, while he found himself on the street besieged by the neighborhood. In the confusion, his wife, Rosa Muños, arrived on the scene, picked a stone up from the street (a cobblestone maybe?) and entered the store where she found Cusallos's unsuspecting daughter, Bernarda Vera. Muños slammed the stone into Vera's head, and was pulling back for a second blow when Maria Rosa Correa grabbed her arm, preventing what could have been a devastating blow. Muños whirled around to Maria Rosa and called her, "Old whore! Pimp! Low life!"[2] She then furiously and recklessly searched the shop and living quarters for her husband's cloak, departing with a new round of insults, this time directed at Bernarda Vera: "Whore! Adulterer! Home wrecker!"[3]

Four days later, the barrio magistrate of San Blas and Santa Bárbara (*alcalde del barrio de San Blas y Santa Bárbara*) Don Visente Enrriquez de Guzman forwarded to the judge in charge of criminal cases for the Audiencia the witness testimony, a statement by a surgeon verifying the extent of the injuries suffered by Thomasa Cusallos and her daughter, along with his own corroboration of the charges against Mariano Thena and Rosa Muños. Based on the information gathered during the barrio magistrate's investigation, Oidor Lucas Muños y Cubero found the couple guilty of criminal offense and issued an order that Thena be promptly confined in the city jail for the flagitious assault on Thomasa Cusallos. His wife was to be arrested and held in the women's jail (*recogimiento de Santa Marta*) for both the physical assault and the injurious words against Bernarda Vera. Justice, in this instance, was quick. The persuasive force of the surgeon's physical examination of the injured bodies, eyewitness testimonies to the ferocity of the couple's bodily and verbal battering, and the availability of a neighborhood magistrate to perform a prompt and thorough investigation of people with whom he likely was familiar combined to make the judicial system responsive to the victims' needs.

The office of alcalde del barrio was less than two decades old in the city of Quito, and had been formed in the wake of the 1765 tumult. While the role of barrio alcalde injected into the case a minor procedural peculiarity from the perspective of normative imperial judicial practice, the insults and assaults themselves were all too familiar. The procedural development of the case followed an established chain of events: criminal act, complaint, acceptance of the complaint, medical examination (in cases of bodily injury), collection of eyewitness testimony, and detention. While the documentary record of this case ends with the detention of the offenders, procedural standards usually followed on with the confession of the defendants and definitive sentencing.

Other observations of this particular case stand out. First and foremost, the public arena of Santa Bárbara's streets and shops was a remarkably female space. Of the eight principal actors in the case, seven were women, including the two victims, one of the assailants, and all of the witnesses. Thomasa Cusallos was brought into the conflict as an economic actor, the proprietor of a small shop that acted in part as a source of petty credit.[4] Indeed, prior to this incident, Mariano Thena had sought out credit from her. Cusallos filed the complaint on behalf of herself and her daughter, against male and female assailants responsible for physical and honorific assaults. The four witnesses who provided testimony to Alcalde Enrriquez were women aged twenty-four to forty, and their statements were taken without misgiving. In other words, these women of majority age were deemed to hold a legal status that conferred reliability to their sworn testimony. Finally, the second assault acted out by Thena's wife combined physical attack with gendered insult. Specifically, Rosa Muños's words struck at the sexual reputations of Bernarda Vera and Maria Rosa Correa. "Whore! Adulterer! Pimp! Home wrecker!" Such epithets bring to the fore the potency not only of women's public reputations, but also the place of communal surveillance of sexualized bodies.[5] In the years following the Rebellion of the Barrios, social control of moral behavior became an institutional imperative, so that the intimacy of neighborhood observations took on serious punitive implications. Sexualized public observations moved from the realm of insult to prosecutable criminal accusation.

This chapter will follow the cues provided by Thomasa Cusallos's unfortunate moment of public, corporal crisis to investigate the gendering of criminality in Quito during the period 1765 to 1795. In an attempt to reestablish royal authority over the intractable barrios of the city, the Audiencia and the cabildo worked together to construct a system of social surveillance that primarily targeted moral behaviors.[6] A key element of the government's plan was to form a new assemblage of neighborhood magistrates, the alcaldes del barrio. These new magistrates were charged to work in conjunction with the city's ordinary magistrates and Audiencia judges to supervise the barrios. Using arrest statistics and criminal complaints, this chapter documents the process by which moral policing came to preoccupy the city, its differential effects on men and women, and how defendants utilized their inherited legal culture to deal with a greatly expanded claim by institutional authorities to control their bodies and behaviors. Section 1 describes the procedures and officials involved in the prosecution of criminal offenses. Section 2 analyzes the arrest statistics of the city's three jails (the city jail, the court jail, and the women's jail) for the years 1767–1770 and 1789 in order to demonstrate trends in apprehension. Who was arresting whom, and why? The section documents the rise of moral policing, the relationship between the city's varying types of magistrates, and their personal tendencies in law enforcement. Finally, Section 3 turns to actual prosecutions of sexual crimes to analyze the means by which men and women, brought under the purview of the disciplinary state, mobilized legal resources for prosecution and defense. The new interest in sexualized bodies opened opportunities to settle old scores. Often, publicly scandalous behaviors that had endured for years became of very sudden interest to the city's magistracy. While the period immediately following the rebellion saw a dramatic increase in detentions of men and women for sexual offenses, these detentions led to relatively few prosecutions. This situation had changed by the 1780s, as both detention rates and prosecutions of sexual crimes continued to rise. Through stories of adultery, cohabitation, rape, and homosexuality, this chapter will probe the gendered significances of body, morality, and criminality.

1. PROCEDURES AND OFFICIALS

There were a dizzying array of officials in the corregimiento of Quito with arrest and prosecutorial powers, each of whom also shared at some level in the bureaucratic administration of the province. Despite attempts by Bourbon-era legal commentators to draw jurisdictional lines clearly between the various officials charged with policing the cities of the empire, the sometimes-conflicting roles of the many magistrates enlisted in the province provided a certain degree of flexibility for both plaintiffs and defendants who found themselves embroiled in the system. No fewer than ten different entities held jurisdiction over criminal disputes in the corregimiento. The offices included the Audiencia's alcalde de corte, the corregidor, the cabildo's two alcaldes ordinarios, the various alcaldes de barrio (from 1768 forward), the alcalde de la Santa Hermandad, provincial magistrates (alcaldes de provincia) the alférez real, the bishop, and the inquisition. Ecclesiastical courts were generally only involved in criminal cases that involved religious defendants. The purview of the inquisition was not specifically over criminal actions; however, the Holy Office did prosecute cases of bigamy and polygamy, which were considered criminal acts. The office of the royal treasury also ordered detentions, though strictly over tax and debt issues.[7]

In a second tier below the officials who ordered arrests was a body of city and provincial officials largely charged with enforcing magistrate rulings, mainly arrest warrants, investigations, and punishments. These officials included the alguacil mayor and his lieutenants, the village judge bailiff (*juez pedaneo*), soldiers and deputies (*ministros de justicia*) who accompanied the alcaldes on their nightly rounds, and the public notaries. The latter were involved intimately in each step of a criminal prosecution, recording eyewitness testimony, preparing petitions, documenting confessions, registering judicial orders, and notifying the varying parties attached to a piece of litigation of the judgments as a case moved its way through the judicial process. Within recognized indigenous communities, a parallel structure existed with judicial powers vested in the offices of governor, indigenous chief (*cacique*), and alcalde de indios.

Finally, many litigants sought representation in judicial proceedings from the region's *abogados* (lawyers) and *procuradores* (attorneys).[8] Generally speaking, individuals were represented before the court by procuradores, who required less legal education and met a lower standard of licensure than did the abogados registered with the Audiencia. Procuradores usually presented to the court a formal power of attorney, and were available for free for minors (*procurador de menores*) or those officially declared too poor to afford representation (*procurador de pobres*).[9] Just as the Audiencia-appointed procuradores offered legal council to their respective groups, indigenous subjects had access to free legal representation through the office of the protector of the Indians (*protecturía de naturales*). The Audiencia had its own legal counsel in the office of the fiscal (prosecutor), which was divided from 1776 forward in two, one for criminal cases and the other for civil litigation. Judges of the Audiencia consulted the fiscal for legal interpretation of issues that arose during the course of litigation, particularly concerning sentencing criteria. Because of the labyrinthine nature of the Spanish legal tradition, a capable fiscal was key to the Audiencia's ability to respond to the contradictory legal arguments utilized by litigants' attorneys, lawyers, and notaries.

Together, this coterie of officials formed the human face of the institutional machinery of justice in the corregimiento of Quito. Despite the presence of the Audiencia and its criminal court (*sala de crimen*), the lion's share of first-instance criminal arrests, investigations, and prosecutions were managed by the two alcaldes ordinarios of the municipal cabildo. Complaints from anywhere within the Five Leagues could be filed with one of the two magistrates, elected each January by the cabildo from its ranks to serve one-year terms. The first round of voting produced the alcalde ordinario of the first vote (*de primer voto*), with the second round providing the alcalde ordinario of the second vote (*de segundo voto*). Many officials were elected or appointed at the first January meeting in this manner, including the alcalde de la Santa Hermandad, the city acalde de aguas (charged with arbitrating water disputes in the corregimiento), the alguacil mayor, the procurador general of the cabildo, the lieutenants of various positions, and from 1768 forward, the alcaldes del barrio of the city's parishes.[10]

Criminal complaints followed a fairly standard procedural path from the filing of charges through definitive sentencing. Cases could be started through one of three means: denunciation, accusation, or government initiative (*de oficio*). Third parties made denunciations, while victims made accusations. In both cases, a properly formed petition would be submitted to one of the judicial authorities of the corregimiento explaining the crime committed and requesting judicial intervention. The presiding magistrate would then accept or reject the cause, in the case of the former opening an official investigation. The investigatory phase (*prueba*) of the case proceeded on the presumption of the guilt of the accused. An official notary who interviewed and transcribed witness testimony according to the information provided by the complainant managed the prueba. Of note, the denouncing or accusing party, who certainly would choose individuals sympathetic to his or her cause, usually provided the names of witnesses for the prueba. A witness provided her name, occupation, marital status, age, and place of residence, and then swore to tell the truth, before making the sign of the cross. The witness was then either read a copy of the allegations or asked a series of questions provided by the plaintiff. In this way, testimony was front-loaded in favor of denunciation. In the Andes, translators were provided to witnesses who spoke "the language of the Inga [Inca]," and could not understand Spanish. If this were the case, the notary made note of it in the document. Finally, if the witness was literate, he or she would sign the notary's narrative of the testimony. If not literate, this too would be noted. In the case of physical violence, an examination of injuries by a surgeon supplemented witness testimony. At the end of the prueba, all relevant written material was submitted to the judge for his consideration.

Based on the accumulated evidence, the magistrate would either dismiss the case (highly unlikely) or issue an arrest warrant if the defendant was not yet imprisoned. From jail, defendants had the opportunity to respond in writing to the charges brought against them. Based on the response and the weight of the prueba information, the next step was for the judge to order a confession to be taken. The term "confession" was a bit of a misnomer. Because the Hispanic legal system assumed guilt, the official questioning proceeded with an interrogatory that placed the inmate in a defensive position, forced to deny allegations that were framed as positive indictments. So while the confession might contain no actual admissions of guilt, the burden of proof was in the strength of the denial. Confessions could include the use of torture, but this method seems to have been exceedingly rare in the Audiencia. The use of torture in eliciting a confession likewise had its own set of procedural rules. Following the confession, the defendant also had the opportunity to respond in writing to the specific allegations leveled against her, as well as to level charges against her accuser. She could offer a counter-interrogatory as well as a list of witnesses in her defense, which would be followed by a second-round prueba.

This back and forth between accuser and accused could continue for several rounds. At any point during the progression of the case, if legal arguments were presented that required interpretation, the judge would forward the petitions to the royal fiscal (a state's attorney of sorts), who would parse the complicated legal arguments for an official government position. When the judge felt the arguments had been exhausted, he would make a final ruling called the "definitive sentence" that would detail the specific punishment to be meted out on the apparently guilty party. A definitive sentence did not signify, however, a definitive end. There were numerous means to appeal the sentence, either for its revocation or for mitigation or clemency. Because the entire process was dependent on the submission of written petitions, the expertise of a party's chosen notary or attorney could have great effect on the success of their requests. Face-to-face encounters were usually limited to arrest and questioning, moments already skewed against the rights of the defendant.[11]

De oficio cases followed an almost identical procedural path. The main difference, of course, was that a judge or magistrate brought initial charges in his institutional capacity. Murders were almost exclusively de oficio cases. During the 1780s, de oficio prosecutions of morality crimes became a somewhat common occurrence, the result of vigilant enforcement of public morality by magistrates and judicial officials on the ronda. De oficio procedures also deviated from the norm in that interrogatories and witness identification fell on the shoulders of the presiding judge instead of a complainant. This, however, did not shift the burden of proving innocence in any way off the shoulders of the accused. In fact, because the judge who opened the investigation and brought charges against the defendant also decided the case, it is every bit as likely that the burden on the accused to prove his innocence was actually greater than in denunciation or accusation cases. Following the prueba, de oficio cases followed the standard procedural development of written response and legal wrangling.

The benefit for the historian of the procedural reliance on written submissions based on templates is that criminal cases from the period quickly reveal not only information germane to the crime, but also procedural and linguistic sleights of hand in which deviations from or additions to the template, often as silences, speak volumes of local legal and social norms. For example, when a certain phrase repeatedly appears in cases on similar charges, the meaning of the phrase takes on a rhetorical character, as part of a checklist of accusation. The language ceases to transparently describe a specific criminal act or historical moment and is transformed into a normalized appeal. This problem is further complicated by the tendency of savvy litigants to craft their petitions to specifically appeal to the jurisdiction or even the individual magistrate being approached.

This is particularly the case for sexual crime prosecutions. Traditionally, the enforcement of sexual norms in early Spanish America has been placed within the realm of the Catholic Church. In large part due to the ecclesiastical role in establishing and enforcing standards and practices of marriage, it was assumed that the proper venue for the adjudication of sexual behaviors outside the marital norm fell to the ecclesiastical authorities.[12] In fact, there were limits to the interests and involvement of the ecclesiastical courts in adjudicating sex crimes, which most often found their proper venue of trial in the secular halls of justice.[13] While the religious authorities continued to moderate divorce, annulment, and separation cases (many of which included allegations of sexual impropriety), the secular authorities held jurisdiction over the prosecution of criminal acts, including those of a sexual nature. Sex crimes prosecuted by the civil authorities included adultery, illicit sexual behavior by singles, prostitution, solicitation, violent rape, statutory rape, incest, bestiality, and sodomy. At times, the difficulty of establishing guilt outside catching individuals in the act led to interesting standards of investigation and proof. Public rumor was considered valuable, if not absolute, evidence; in addition, physical examinations were called on to substantiate penetration of males and females alike.[14] Sexual crime, unlike property or violent offenses, carried with it a claim to police both behavior and body, uniting the moral and the corporal. As such, sexual propriety was a perfect proxy for the Bourbon bureaucrats to enforce their new governance, based as it was on a hierarchical, patriarchal imperative.

2. POPULATING THE CITY'S JAILS

In the years after the 1765 uprisings, the most immediate manifestation of a renewed royal authority came in the form of the policing of the barrios.[15] During the period 1767 to mid-1770, the city experienced a startling increase in detentions in the city's three jails: the public jail of the cabildo, the court jail of the Audiencia, and the women's jail at the recogimiento of Santa Marta.[16] From an average of sixty detentions per year in the period prior to the rebellion, arrests rose to 372 in 1767, 453 in 1768, 514 in 1769, and 262 in the first seven months of 1770.[17] Extrapolated out for the full year, that final number suggests the city was on course for 450 detentions. Not only was the growth in apprehensions dramatic, but also it was sustained. Arrest statistics from the period reveal an important shift in the objectives and effects of the policing. The primary goal of the city's magistrates was to reaffirm order in the barrios, which in effect resulted in a closer surveillance and control over the bodies of barrio members. Second, it became increasingly clear that this surveillance and control would concentrate on moral crimes. The addition of a new, lower level of alcaldes at the parochial level enhanced a sense of community policing. These magistrates likewise centered their activities almost exclusively on moral regulation. Finally, the statistics make clear that the shift in social control affected both men and women in the barrios, though in different ways.

The responsibility for detaining individuals fell on the many judicial officials of the city. The arrest statistics bear out the expectation that the majority of arrests were ordered by the two ordinary magistrates of the municipal council. From 1768 forward, the newly formed office of barrio magistrate augmented their work. Royal officials had experimented with barrio magistrates for a brief period in the early 1730s. Then, also at the behest of the Audiencia, the office was established to amplify the nightly ronda. Based on an order from the Council of the Indies, Herzog reports the task of the office was to give its "attention to public crimes and sins." Herzog explains that in order to effectively make their rounds, barrio alcaldes, "could walk around armed and carrying the insignias of justice; they had the ability to prevent crimes, seize delinquents, and break up games and dances. They utilized spies, gave payments to their collaborators, and required, when they judged it necessary, that not only members of the commercial patrol, but also vecinos accompany them."[18] The office lasted only from 1729 to 1732, when a combined resistance from within the municipal council and in the neighborhoods effectively undermined it. While this first experiment with neighborhood policing was short-lived, it was extremely prescient in both its objectives and methods: the neighborhood magistrates would come to form the front lines of royal surveillance and social control in the closing decades of the eighteenth century. Though the Audiencia had first- and second-instance jurisdiction over many forms of criminal and civil litigation that could result in detention, they were responsible for a relatively small percentage of inmates. Audiencia-ordered detainees were held in the court's own jail (carcel de corte), while others generally were placed in the municipal council's public jail (carcel pública). The corregidor or a magistrate of the Santa Hermandad usually investigated criminal behavior within the Five Leagues of the city's hinterland. Other individuals who ordered detentions include the bishop, the inquisition, the royal treasury and its provincial judge, and the alferez real.

In 1767, a total of twelve different officials ordered detentions, with the majority of the burden evenly split between Alferez Real Juan Chiriboga, Corregidor Apolinar de la Cueba Ponce de Leon, and the city's two ordinary magistrates, together responsible for 83 percent of arrests. In the coming two years, however, the offices of alferez and corregidor drew back from such extensive enforcement. In 1768, a total of eighteen different officials ordered arrests, with ordinary magistrates responsible for 63 percent, the new barrio magistrates for 15 percent, and the Audiencia for a mere 5 percent of detentions. In 1769, a total of thirteen officials ordered arrests, with the two ordinary magistrates accounting for 87 percent, the barrio magistrates for only 7 percent, and the Audiencia for a meager 3 percent of confinements. It should be noted that one of the ordinary magistrates, Manuel Lastra, who had served the year before as the barrio magistrate for Santa Bárbara, was personally responsible for 64 percent (n=329) of the year's arrests. Interestingly, these statistics indicate that the real work of reestablishing authority in the barrios fell on the members of the same body, the municipal council, which was the key fount of agitation before the rebellion. Lastra himself was a European Spaniard who had participated in the defense of royal interests against the plebe. Finally, during the first seven months of 1770, only eight individuals issued the arrest orders for 262 detainees. Lastra again led the way, responsible for 57 percent of arrests (n=150), with alcalde ordinario de segundo voto Guerrero y Ontañon a distant second with 21 percent of arrests (n=55). The Audiencia ordered but one arrest in 1770, while together the barrio alcaldes combined for thirty-five. Interestingly, the barrio alcaldes only detained people for morality crimes, and at a very skewed rate of four men to thirty-one women.

The composition of the arrest rolls, from both gendered and categorical perspectives, provide more compelling evidence for a shift in surveillance and social policing than the growing numbers of arrests and the individual magistrates involved in the detentions. The reasons for detention can be divided into six broad categories: debt, moral crime, property crime, slavery issues, violent crime, and undetermined reasons. Detentions for debt were fairly straightforward, and averaged 155 pesos per detainee across the period. Moral crime includes such offenses as illegal gambling, prostitution, illicit cohabitation, adultery, rape, statutory rape, bigamy, detention at the request of a parent or spouse, disrespecting royal officials, drunkenness, and providing false testimony. Also included in this category are arrests that occurred during nightly rounds of the city. The vast majority of ronda arrests were for suspicion of illegal activity, often sexual dalliance. That said, a very few ronda arrests were for suspicion of robbery. Property crime included petty theft, jewelry heists, accusations of robbery, cattle or mule rustling, and receiving or selling stolen property. Slavery-related detentions invariably involved one of two justifications: the request of a master or the search for a master. Violent crime included any number of assaults and batteries, as well as murder. Finally, a total of twenty-nine detentions across the period were of undetermined cause. Tables 2.1 and 2.2 summarize the gendered division of the detentions. Table 2.3 analyzes moral crimes specifically. It is immediately evident that female defendants were apprehended for moral crimes at a rate inordinate to male defendants. Close to 30 percent of total arrests were women accused of moral crimes, particularly illicit cohabitation and apprehension by the ronda. Both men and women were detained at the request of spouses or parents. What is not expressed in the rolls, though, are the reasons for the requests. Detentions of women

Table 2.1. Arrests by Gender and Category, 1767–1770

GENDER	CATEGORY	1767	1768	1769	1770	TOTALS
MALE	Debt	54	64	30	34	182
	Undetermined	8	7	2	2	19
	Moral Crime	62	60	112	45	279
	Property Crime	73	98	94	56	321
	Slavery Issues	25	28	5	3	61
	Violent Crime	9	7	39	11	66
	TOTAL MALE	231	264	282	151	928
FEMALE	Debt	8	4	3	0	15
	Undetermined	4	4	0	2	10
	Moral Crime	73	130	174	86	471
	Property Crime	42	27	42	22	133
	Slavery Issues	8	7	0	0	15
	Violent Crime	6	17	13	1	37
	TOTAL FEMALE	141	189	232	111	681
TOTAL DETAINEES		372	453	514	262	1609

SOURCE: AN/Q, 1NJ 45, 1767.

Table 2.2. Arrests by Gender and Category as Percentages, 1767–1770

GENDER	CATEGORY	1767	1768	1769	1770	TOTALS
MALE	Debt	14.5%	13.9%	5.8%	13.0%	11.8%
	Undetermined	2.2	1.5	0.4	0.8	1.2
	Moral Crime	16.7	13.0	21.8	17.2	17.2
	Property Crime	19.6	21.3	18.3	21.4	19.7
	Slavery Issues	6.7	6.1	1.0	20.2	4.3
	Violent Crime	2.4	1.5	7.6	4.2	3.9
FEMALE	Debt	2.2	0.9	0.6	0.0	0.9
	Undetermined	1.1	0.9	0.0	0.7	0.7
	Moral Crime	19.6	29.9	33.9	32.8	29.1
	Property Crime	11.3	5.9	8.2	8.4	8.5
	Slavery Issues	2.2	1.5	0.0	0.0	0.9
	Violent Crime	1.6	3.7	2.5	0.4	2.1

SOURCE: AN/Q, 1NJ 45, 1767.

for sexual offenses more than tripled in the course of the three years, from twenty-one in 1767 to eighty in 1769.

Male arrests for sexual offenses grew at a similar rate, from fourteen in 1767 to fifty in 1769. But the very disparity between concubinage arrests for men and women demonstrate the higher likelihood that women would be taken into custody for suspicion of improper sexual behavior. Just as in the case of sexual offenses, women were apprehended in much higher numbers than men were by the ronda. Over the course of three years, a total of seventy men were taken on nightly rounds, with a peak of forty-five in 1769. Over the same period, 144 women were detained, peaking in 1769 with sixty-eight arrests. Given the reduced rates of violent and property crimes committed by women, it can be assumed that this greater interest in women at night related to the dangers of illicit moral activities. For women, sexual crime constituted 40 percent of moral crime detentions, while the ronda accounted for another 39 percent across the whole period 1767 to mid-1770. In contrast, sexual crime accounted for 38 percent of men arrested, with the ronda providing for only 28 percent of

Table 2.3. Moral Crime Arrests by Gender, 1767–1770

TYPE	1767 M	1767 F	1768 M	1768 F	1769 M	1769 F	1770 M	1770 F
Concubinage	9	15	14	37	32	69	21	33
Illicit Alcohol	2	0	1	2	0	0	0	0
Bigamy	2	0	2	0	2	1	0	0
Disrespect/Honor	0	0	3	0	6	2	1	1
Illicit Sex	4	6	5	13	4	11	2	4
Gambling	17	0	11	0	11	0	6	0
Other	6	7	11	5	4	5	1	2
Sexual Assaults	1	0	2	0	7	0	5	0
Holy Inquisition	1	2	3	4	0	0	0	0
Request of Parents	0	1	0	0	0	0	0	0
Request of Father	1	0	2	0	0	1	0	0
Request of Mother	0	5	0	3	0	3	0	2
Request of Spouse	0	8	0	14	1	14	2	6
Request of Master	0	2	0	1	0	0	0	0
Ronda	19	25	6	51	45	68	7	38
Undetermined	0	2	0	0	0	0	0	0
TOTAL	62	73	60	130	112	174	45	86

SOURCE: AN/Q, 1NJ 45, 1767.

moral crimes from 1767 to mid-1770. What men did engage in that women did not was gambling. Arrests for gambling were responsible for 16 percent (n=45) of detentions of men for moral offenses.

What do these statistics suggest concerning the policing of the city in the years after the rebellion? First, the sheer increase in arrests indicates a heightened attention to the need for social control in the wake of the disruptions. The numbers of detainees were unprecedented in the history of the city. To a certain extent, the data suggest that one factor in this growth was the zeal with which certain magistrates approached their work, but it is hard to determine simply from the rolls the extent to which the individual magistrate's volition was causal. Regardless of who ordered the arrest, moral crimes constituted the single largest category across the board. Taken together, male and female moral crimes were 46 percent of arrests in the three-and-a-half years under consideration. At their peak in 1769, moral crimes were responsible for 56 percent of total arrests! Within the moral category, both male and female detentions for sexual crime rose across the period, but without question women were much more likely to fall under the eye and hand of the city's magistrates. Finally, the statistics do indicate a sea change in the extent to which the state claimed the right and authority to control the behavior of its citizen subjects. The honorifics don and doña were almost completely absent from the arrest rolls, as were ethnic terms such as blanco or español. The vast majority of detainees were of no ethnic designation, indicating they likely came from the city's large mass of mestizos and from the middling sectors that had been so active in the summer of 1765. As Table 2.4 demonstrates, the city jails were populated largely by the undesignated masses.

In part, the lack of extensive ethnic categorizations could suggest that racialized categories were as yet not central to the penal strategies of the city. In other words, it could be that, from the institutional perspective, racialized categories had not yet hardened, and the attribution of the three main categories above (none, Indian, and slave) were indicative of an institutional status distinct from a determinative ethnic identity. For example, the terms "pardo," "mulatto," "black" (*negro*), and "slave" (*esclavo*) were used interchangeably in the rolls, with slave being the most common designation.[19] Likewise, it is conceivable that the designation of Indian was dependent on the broader, noncultural, institutional status indicating an individual tied directly to an indigenous community through tribute and land usage.

Table 2.4. Arrests by Ethnicity, 1767–1770

	WHITE	NONE	INDIAN	BLACK, MULATTO, SLAVE
1767	1	271	71	29
1768	0	353	89	19
1769	0	436	71	8
1770	0	239	18	5

SOURCE: AN/Q, 1NJ 45, 1767.

It was the city plebe that the institutional authorities sought to control, with the full cooperation of the jurisdictional bodies that had fought so hard to restrict a centralized operation of authority as envisioned by the viceroy from 1764 to 1766. The crisis of governance sparked by the fiscal and administrative reforms of the Audiencia of Quito reflected a broader crisis over authority and legitimacy. Coming out of that moment, local institutions of rule emerged with an enhanced need to watch and control the dangerous plebe. That burden, as the statistics make evident, was largely carried by individual magistrates, whose personal preferences greatly affected the operation of community policing. The dependence of the system on denunciation and accusation played to a judge's discretionary power to admit or reject a complaint. Likewise, the zealousness with which the ronda invaded private spaces, as will become clear, depended on the initiative of the presiding magistrate. In the second half of the 1760s, the magistrate responsible for the vast majority of arrests was Manuel dela Lastra. From his start as a barrio alcalde for Santa Bárbara, through two terms as alcalde ordinario, Lastra was the most active individual in the Quito judiciary. As barrio alcalde, Lastra was relatively limited in his contact with the city, having jurisdiction only over the residents of the parishes of San Blas and Santa Bárbara. Even so, he was responsible for 35 percent of total ronda arrests, 10 percent of concubinage arrests, and 10 percent of requested detentions (requested by a spouse or parent). The following two years, as alcalde ordinario with jurisdiction over not only the city, but also the corregimiento, Lastra greatly expanded his operation. In 1769, he was the ordering officer in 46 percent of ronda arrests, an astonishing 82 percent of concubinage detentions, and 79 percent of requested confinements. Finally, during the first seven months of 1770 Lastra slipped to 16 percent of ronda arrests, 54 percent of concubinage detentions, and 70 percent of requested confinements. Such statistics indicate that indeed judicial discretion could serve the purposes of tightening control by royal authorities. It is likely, for example, that wives, husbands, mothers, and fathers sought out Lastra with requests for confinement of their sons, daughters, and spouses, knowing that he would be sympathetic to their desires. The same could be said of accusations and denunciations of adulterous relationships. As becomes clear in the litigation, the increased attention on surveillance and prosecution of sexual behavior opened the door to accusations rooted in any number of motivations, from the settling of scores to genuine harm. Whatever the motivation of the complainant, savvy litigants, collaborators, and vengeful souls looked to the friendliest jurisdiction, hoping to find their personal flavor of justice. In the 1780s, this brought the president regent of the Audiencia directly into the policing of the city.

Twenty years hence, the arrest rolls continued to attest to an aggressive, involved judiciary seeking to monitor and control the behavior and bodies of city residents. Memories of 1765 coincided with fears of indigenous rebellion spurred by the confluence of locally aggressive fiscal reorganization and news to the south of the conflagration consuming the Andean heartland in the form of the Tupac Amaru and Tupac Katari rebellions, and to the north of Indian revolt in Pasto.[20] Borchart de Moreno has found that for the early 1780s, President Regent Garcia de Leon y Pizarro began to take a personal interest in the policing of moral behavior in Quito. She attributes this personal interest to the large numbers of men and women incarcerated in the 1782 jail census, which documents 329 men and 127 women for a total of 456 detainees.[21] As we have seen above, however, this level of policing and apprehension emerged in the years immediately following the Rebellion of the Barrios.

In the 1789 jail census, a total of 555 individuals were listed on the rolls, with 211 men and 14 women held for debts, and 162 men and 182 women detained for criminal acts.[22] The debtor numbers are skewed by large roundups of indigenous men at the end of the year for being derelict in tribute payments. If we correct for this incongruity, the census yields 369 total detainees, reducing the number of men held for debts to twenty-five. Interestingly, this elevates the percentage of total detainees who were women to an astonishing 49.3 percent (Table 2.5). On par with the earlier data, a total of fourteen officials ordered the detentions, including five different members of the Audiencia, the alcalde ordinario de primer voto, the alcalde ordinario de segundo voto, the dirección de rentas (the office charged with administering the royal monopolies on aguardiente, gunpowder, and tobacco), the director of royal tribute collection, as well as barrio alcaldes for San Roque, San Sebastian, San Marcos, and the combined San Blas and Santa Bárbara. Noticeably absent from this list are the corregidor, the bishop, the inquisition, the Santa Hermandad, and any provincial judges or magistrates. The city's two alcaldes ordinarios were responsible for 248 of the 369 nontributary arrests, amounting to 67 percent of detentions; barrio alcaldes combined for ninety-five, or 26 percent of arrests. Members of the Audiencia directly ordered seventeen detentions, with President Regent Villalengua leading with eleven. These numbers obscure the involvement of the Audiencia in policing the city, however, as many of the warrants attributed to barrio alcaldes were actually ordered by a presiding Audiencia judge called the *oidor juez superior de barrios*. The only exceptions were detentions made by barrio alcaldes on the ronda. Yet even in these cases, barrio alcaldes reported to the juez superior, at which point incarcerations were either terminated or extended by the oidor. These trends hint toward a significant shift in the policing of the city, a shift documented in the litigation of the 1780s. During the decade, members of the Audiencia and the president regent himself were intimately involved in the policing

Table 2.5. Arrests by Gender and Category, 1789

GENDER	CATEGORY	RAW	ADJUSTED FOR TRIBUTE
MALE	Debt	211 (56.6%)[1]	25 (13.4%)
	Undetermined	2 (0.5)	2 (1.1)
	Moral Crime	50 (13.4)	50 (26.7)
	Property Crime	86 (23.1)	86 (46.0)
	Slavery Issues	3 (0.8)	3 (1.6)
	Violent Crime	21 (5.6)	21 (11.2)
	TOTAL MALE	373	187
FEMALE	Debt	14 (7.7%)	14
	Undetermined	0	0
	Moral Crime	99 (54.4)	99
	Property Crime	52 (28.6)	52
	Slavery Issues	1 (0.5)	1
	Violent Crime	16 (8.8)	16
	TOTAL FEMALE	182	182
TOTAL DETAINEES		555	369

SOURCE: AN/Q, INJ 107, 16*1*1789.

1. The percentages represent the percent of arrests within each gender (i.e., 211 debt arrests represent 56.6 percent of male detainees in the raw numbers).

Table 2.6. Moral Crime Arrests by Gender, 1789

| | NUMBERS | | PERCENTAGES | |
TYPE	M	F	M	F
Abandoned Marriage	0	1	0.0%	1.0%
Concubinage	16	30	32.0	30.6
Bigamy	1	0	2.0	0.0
Disrespect/Honor	1	11	2.0	11.2
Drunkenness and Illicit Alcohol	1	1	2.0	1.0
Illicit Sexual Activity	3	3	6.0	3.1
Gambling	0	0	0.0	0.0
Other	1	2	2.0	2.0
Sexual Assaults	3	0	6.0	0.0
Holy Inquisition	0	0	0.0	0.0
Quarrelling	0	3	0.0	3.1
Removal	6	1	12.0	1.0
Request of Parents	0	0	0.0	0.0
Request of Father	0	0	0.0	0.0
Request of Mother	0	1	0.0	1.0
Request of Spouse	0	1	0.0	1.0
Request of Aunt	0	1	0.0	1.0
Request of Master	0	2	0.0	2.0
Ronda	17	41	34.0	41.8
Vagrancy	1	0	2.0	0.0
Undetermined	0	0	0.0	0.0
TOTAL	50	98		

SOURCE: AN/Q, INJ 107, 16-1-1789.

of the city, and particularly in the surveillance, prosecution, and punishment of immoral behavior in the plebe. The council's involvement operated through a close relationship to the barrio magistrates, who during the late 1760s and 1770s had largely worked in concert with the municipal council's ordinary magistrates. From both jurisdictional and procedural perspectives, this relationship was innovative and signaled an ever-growing interest by Bourbon-appointed and -influenced officials in controlling the bodies and behaviors of American subjects by circumventing traditional judicial venues. In a somewhat ironic twist, it was the jurisdictional imprecision of the Habsburg model that enabled the Audiencia to lay claim to first-instance litigation, and by extension to impose its vision of normative morality on the barrios.

In comparison with the earlier data, the morality arrests show some interesting trends (Table 2.6). The rate at which both men and women were arrested at the request of a parent or spouse dropped dramatically. Furthermore, as a percentage of moral arrests, for both men and women the ronda followed by concubinage were the two leading causes for detention. The obvious disarticulation between the two gendered categories came with removal, sexual assault, and honor and respect crimes. Men were arrested at a much higher rate for removing girls from the purview of their guardians without permission and for sexual assaults (largely statutory rapes), while women led detentions for quarrels and effrontery to honor. One final note of comparison, whereas gambling was a consistent moral crime filed against men in the late 1760s, no one was arrested for it in 1789.

The tributary roundups of October, November, and December again skew the statistics on ethnicity. Corrected for those detentions, the vast majority of male and female inmates had no ethnic status noted in the 1760s. Non-designated ethnicity accounted for 86.8 percent of women and 77.9 percent of men in the corrected rolls. Indian men and women accounted for 18.8 and 12.6 percent of the total population, respectively. Counting the anomalous tributaries, nonstatus males were just 38.4 percent, with Indian men jumping to

Table 2.7. Arrests by Ethnicity, 1789

	MALE WITH TRIBUTARIES	MALE W/O TRIBUTARIES	FEMALE
No ethnicity given	143	143	158
Esclavo/Slave	3	3	1
Mulatto	3	3	0
Negro/Black	2	2	0
Indian	221	35	23

SOURCE: AN/Q, INJ 107, 16ᵃ1ᵃ1789.

59.4 percent. In the 1789 census, free blacks and mulattos do show up in addition to slaves (who carry no exact "ethnic" designation), as opposed to the 1760s when all derivations of Africans and mixed-Africans showed up on the rolls as slaves (Table 2.7).

What accounts for these shifts, particularly for the diminution of individuals incarcerated at a family member's request? In part, as will become clear in the following discussion of specific cases, requested arrests likely diminished with a concomitant rise in spousal denunciations for specific crimes of interest to institutional authorities. It should also be noted that the raw numbers of individuals arrested for broadly defined morality crimes were significantly less than in the years immediately following the rebellion, particularly for women. The decrease, however, mirrors the overall decrease in detentions when we correct for tributaries. This does not signify an actual decrease in overall arrests for the corregimiento. Details within the cases themselves indicate that rather than rely on the three city jails, officials began to utilize a number of subsidiary locations for incarceration including the presidio of the royal guard, the royal tobacco factory, and the city poorhouse (ospicio de pobres).[23] The expansion of locations of incarceration likewise hints at a transformation of punishment objectives toward a more modern understanding that combined the punitive with the reformatory through productive labor and surveillance.[24]

One final statistical observation: It is difficult to account for the increase in arrests during the late 1760s through actual litigation. For the period 1765 to 1774, there are only six instances of sexual crime prosecutions combined in the 1NJ and Criminales sections of the archive. By comparison, those two divisions of the archive house sixty-nine prosecutions for the decade 1785 to 1794. What explains this more than tenfold increase in prosecutions for two decades with comparable arrest statistics? It could be, of course, indicative of litigation lost throughout the intervening two hundred years. And yet the trend holds for all types of criminal litigation between the two decades. The 1780s and 1790s witnessed an explosion of all types of litigation. Were adultery cases remanded to ecclesiastical authorities? It seems unlikely that the increased state interest in the policing of morality would have resulted in secular authorities punting jurisdiction to ecclesiastics. Or was it enough to temporarily jail offenders as an object lesson? The details of the litigation do suggest a real transformation—in policing, prosecution, and punishment of sex crimes in the corregimiento. This transformation was the result of Bourbon bureaucrats who utilized the legal system to enhance the centralization of a paternal royal authority in the city under control of the Audiencia. The arrest rolls do not indicate the extent to which the processes that transformed the state into a stricter, less-contingent repository of authority also transformed the social and legal expectations of quiteño subjects. Only a discursive analysis of the large body of litigation sparked by the social policing of the plebe will indicate the extent to which the larger legal and social culture of the city was transformed by the experience.

3. A NOTORIOUS, SCANDALOUS LIFE

On April 20, 1770, Alexo Merino filed a plaintive petition with alcalde ordinario Manuel dela Lastra protesting that his wife, Francisca Naranja, had abandoned her spousal obligations for more than fifteen years on account of her "notorious adultery and daring haughtiness."[25] The proof of Francisca's infidelities stretched back thirteen years, to the first time she was caught by the ronda cavorting in a public store with her lover, soldier Xavier Sandoya, by then–alcalde ordinario Don Mariano Uvillus. While she was incarcerated, Merino had Jesuit Father Juan Hospital pay her a visit to educate and council her to return to married life. As if to prove her questionable character, Merino noted in his opening line that his wife was also known by the alias la Xarra (literally jug, or pitcher), a name he continually used in the rest of the petition. Certainly only shady figures of dubious morals and intention go by aliases. Apparently, la Xarra's haughty pride and disregard for either her husband or their public reputations was not easily chastised, and she was caught by the ronda in the early 1760s by Francisco Borja, who placed her again in Santa Marta. This time, with the intervention of Juan Hospital, a second Jesuit, Father Josef Peres, and president of the Audiencia Manuel Rubio de Arevalo, the wife's lover Xavier Sandoya apparently was banished to Guayaquil.

In response to his wife's incorrigible behavior, Merino claimed he repeatedly sought judicial recourse before the bishop, fruitlessly requesting a formal separation of the marriage. Furthering his disgust, Merino reported his wife had given her lover 300 pesos to fund his removal to Guayaquil and his eventual return. Nothing, it seemed, could discourage his wife's iniquities. Finally, in April 1770 she found herself again in Santa Marta, placed there by the alcalde of San Blas and Santa Bárbara, whom Merino alleged la Xarra had tried to bribe with an offer of 500 pesos. In his desperation, after these many long years of suffering his wife's embarrassing behavior, Merino avowed it would serve Justice if alcalde ordinario Manuel Lastra would "mandate that [Francisca Naranja] be held in [Santa Marta], or in the monastery of Your determination, and Sandoya in the Yaruqui textile factory for the space of two years, or for the time period Your Honor determines." Within the week, Lastra had collected testimony from three witnesses suggested by Merino, all of whom swore to the long-term adultery of Francisca Naranja and Xavier Sandoya, as well as to the rest of Merino's story. Based on Merino's petition and the witness testimony, on April 27, 1770, Lastra issued an official arrest warrant for Naranja to continue to be held in Santa Marta and for Sandoya to be confined to the city's military barracks. Sandoya was spared the city jail because as a soldier he was entitled to the protections of the military fuero. Officially, the couple's crime was public, scandalous cohabitation.[26]

Merino's petition and the witnesses he provided set the tone for the official investigation and prosecution of his wife's crimes. Because the Hispanic judicial system assumed guilt, defendants in a case stood at a distinct disadvantage to their accusers. Following procedure, Lastra took the confessions of Sandoya and Naranja from their jail cells with an interrogatory patterned on the accusations of Merino. Though the couple each denied specific accusations, Lastra did not find their testimony compelling. In particular, both defendants denied that Sandoya had been exiled to Guayaquil, and claimed instead that he had been sent there in his capacity as a soldier. They also claimed that their relationship had been intermittent over a period of just eight years and that la Xarra had offered the alcalde de barrio just 25 pesos to dispense with their seizure by the ronda. Following established procedure, the content of the confessions was communicated to Alexo Merino, who filed a response calling for Sandoya to be banished from Quito, to a point far enough away that he could not return easily. He also requested his wife be retained in Santa Marta for whatever period of time Lastra would deem required for her "to know her reformation."[27] Merino reasoned that the penalties were more than justified since the couple was "apprehended in the actual act in which they were engaged in total scandal and freedom, nestled together in an underground room in order to enjoy themselves, hidden from the conscientious vigilance of Justice."[28] He further argued that canon and civil law provided the death penalty for adulterers, particularly those caught in the act, and that the husband should be the arbiter of the severity of punishment, up to and including death. It was in the interests of "charity," "justice," and "good conscience" that Merino repudiated such calamitous punishment in favor of the more lenient castigation he requested. Murder of the offending spouse and her lover was acceptable in Hispanic law only if the husband himself discovered them flagrantly in the act, and only if he, consumed by an intoxicating passion, killed both offenders. Merino's rather casual interpretation of the law was disingenuous, but certainly designed to enhance his personal standing before the judge. The reason for this desire soon became clear.

On May 18, the latest petition of Alexo Merino was forwarded to the imprisoned defendants, who produced responses that impugned the character, behavior, and legal reasoning of their accuser. Interestingly, Sandoya's response questioned the a priori presumption of criminal adultery from a variety of angles. First, he claimed that any actual consummated adulterous acts began more than five years earlier, placing the relationship outside the statutory limitations for accusation. Furthermore, he claimed that for adultery to exist, there had to be a functioning marriage. "It is equally certain that legally there is no Adultery if there has been no violation of the Conjugal Bed."[29] As evidence that Sandoya could not have violated his lover's marriage, he explained that from the moment they wed, Merino had lived a "scandalous life," cheating on his wife, beating her to the point of causing a miscarriage (abortar) during an early pregnancy, and voluntarily abandoning her to live a separate life. "It was in these circumstances that I met [her], the marital bed of his wife abandoned for years. One could not call [their relationship] conjugal, as the word insinuates the cohabitation of consorts."[30] Given the situation, Merino denied the possibility of having committed adultery. Their marriage was wrecked by Merino's own behavior, and therefore, Sandoya reasoned, "in view of the fact that Merino cannot hold me responsible for breaking up his marriage, nor could he fault his wife's prostitution, nor can Merino condemn as Adultery a friendship that was not the cause of the disasters that proceeded it; . . . nor can a man be faulted for coming to know a married woman free from Subjection because she was abandoned by her husband."[31] If there was no functional marriage to break up, then there could have been no adultery, particularly if the accusing spouse was himself culpable for the offense. Merino's particular sin, in the eyes of his wife's lover, was in abandoning his marital responsibilities in the first place, leaving her without semblance of a real marriage. The argument deconstructs concepts of marriage, fidelity, adultery, and scandal by placing these concepts along a continuum of acceptability. The greater sin was Merino's, not his wife's. Her transgression was rooted in the search for companionship in a substitute relationship when faced with an abusive, duplicitous husband.

Francisca Naranja's petition echoed the arguments of her lover. Claiming the honorific doña, Naranja requested that Lastra investigate her husband's infidelities before he pass judgment on her unfortunate lot. The picture framed by Naranja and Sandoya was a mirror opposite to that posited by Merino. Moreover, the arguments employed open the question of popular versus institutional understandings of marriage. Naranja reasoned, "it is well known through municipal, canon, and civil law that in order for a male spouse to have the right and ability to accuse his wife of the crime of adultery, it is necessary to have complied exactly with the obligations of an honorable husband; that is, to provide to her with food and clothing . . . as well as to be well ordered in his habits and morals, to be a good example to his wife, that she enjoy the love and good treatment required of both spouses to give one another."[32] With this expression of legitimate matrimony, Naranja then proceeded to catalogue the mistreatments, infidelities, and neglect occasioned her by Merino, detailing in depth his "scandalous incorrigibility." Doña Francisca's appeal to the law was inexact, containing no references to specific entries in the *Siete Partidas*, the *Recopilación*, or any other recognized legal corpus. Rather, she referenced the vague notion of municipal, canon, and civil law as upholding a certain form of honorable marital obligation. The phrase "it is well known" parallels the standard for punishable illicit sexual activity—that an act be public and notorious—and as such inverts the meaning of legitimate and illegitimate marital behaviors.

As the weeks passed, Sandoya and Naranja continued to labor in their confinements while Merino protested their maligning of his character. In July, the two detainees produced their own interrogatories as well as three witnesses each to testify on their behalf. Sandoya produced three men, two merchants and a third resident of Quito;

Naranja produced another three men, one merchant, a presbyter, and a resident of Tumbaco. They also carried their case to the Audiencia, seeking to circumvent Lastra and the municipal authorities. As a result of their cumulative paper production, Naranja and Sandoya were released from prison by order of Audiencia judge Sebastian de Salzedo y Oñate. Salzedo was unwilling to accept the force of the couple's deconstruction of the meaning of marriage and its relation to adultery, but justified their release in the verity of Merino's complicity in the same transgression. The adultery of both parties cancelled each other out. Naranja and Sandoya's freedom came with an admonition to abandon their illicit friendship under pain of future severe punishment lest they be caught again. Finally, all three parties were required to bear the costs of the litigation equally.

Salzedo's ruling was not handed down until September 8, and while the accused couple ultimately regained their freedom as a result of Merino's duplicity, they spent almost five months confined in Santa Marta and the city's barracks. Merino, for his part, escaped scathed only by one-third of the costs of the case. The procedural development of the case demonstrated the advantages of being the first to speak, along with the power of denunciation and of accusation. By all rights, Francisca Naranja could have followed the path of many other women in similar circumstances and denounced her husband, setting the discursive stage for his incarceration. She did not, it seems, because she had long before come to an acceptance that her marriage to Alexo Merino was a farce. In fact, it was only the public act of being caught by the ronda that motivated Merino to make his own accusation. It was the invasive presence of royal authority in the form of a vigilant barrio magistrate that brought the relationship to "public" light and forced a very long-term relationship into the realm of scandal and notoriety. One cannot imagine, however, that a relationship of a decade or more was not public knowledge prior to its entry into the judiciary. Surveillance made the adultery to fit the requirements of prosecution.

By 1770, however, institutional authorities were not able to overcome the limitations and mitigations of the labyrinthine legal system. Both plaintiff and defendants marshaled legal arguments that referenced the codes of Quito, Castile, and the Vatican to bolster their positions. Even for an offense as serious as adultery, judicial discretion and the interests of communal justice enabled Naranja and Sandoya to mitigate the serious punishments to which they were subject. Definitions of marriage, fidelity, and legality were vague enough to provide room to maneuver. This would not be the case fifteen years later.

The case of Alexo Merino, Francisca Naranja, and Xavier Sandoya represents the convergence of vigilance and discretionary justice that marked the increased surveillance and moral policing of the barrios in the years immediately following the rebellion. While the barrio magistrates worked closely with the municipal council's ordinary magistrates to supervise the barrios, the judicial will evidently was not yet present to overcome judicial discretion in the interests of disciplinary punishment. It is significant that the moderating role in the case came in the form of an Audiencia intervention. From 1780 onward, that would not be the case. Likewise, the array of punishments requested and considered in the case look back to the traditional means of settling adultery suits—banishment for the man, confinement to a monastery or recogimiento for the woman, and even mention of murder of the offenders by the husband. Just fifteen years later, the likelihood was that all three parties would have been punished with internment in the royal tobacco factory, combined with the confiscation of half of everyone's property.

In the six cases of sexual prosecution from the corregimiento de Quito extant in the Criminales and First Notary sections of the archive, the offended spouse filed all but two. Three wives and two husbands, including Alexo Merino, filed denunciations of their partners for adulterous relationships, including a case of mutual denunciation.[33] Generally, the adultery was prosecuted in reaction to its exposure by the ronda, and sentences tended to display the same level of discretionary mitigation discussed above. In 1765, Maria Alexandra de Silba filed a complaint against her husband's recidivist adultery, in this instance with a servant girl. The alcalde ordinario ordered Gaspar Arboleda to stop the affair under threat of future imprisonment to force his reformation.[34] In 1773, Josefa Escobar complained to alcalde ordinario Pedro dela Barrera that her husband, Bacilio Thorres, had maintained an illicit relationship with Petrona Ortuño for three of the eight years of their marriage. Based on her petition, the two lovers were confined for the duration of the investigation, but were ultimately released under the admonition to abandon their errant ways and return to honorable lives. Ortuño was threatened with two years in a Riobamba convent should any new legal action be brought against her, while Thorres was promised that any future transgression would be met with appropriate punishment.[35] As in the case of Alexo Merino's complaint, punishments were far below that which was provisioned by the law.

The one piece of non-adultery-related litigation during the period points to a customary means of adjudicating sexual improprieties, in this case illicit but consensual sexual activity. In June 1766, Ana Sanches filed a provocative complaint against Doña María Josepha Morales to force her to pay for the support of a child conceived of an illicit relationship with the defendant's son, Don Mariano Guijalva.[36] In the wake of Ana and Mariano's relationship, Ana presented Doña María Josepha with a legal instrument designed to guarantee that she would participate in raising the child as if he were a legitimate grandson. Doña María signed the contract, but eight months into the life of her new grandson had yet to give Ana any money. Ana sued for restitution of two reales a day, a rate that Doña María protested as exorbitant. Ultimately, the judge ruled that Doña María had to pay Ana at a rate of half a real a day, plus an additional 5 pesos for forcing Ana to use the courts. It is interesting to note that Doña María Josepha Morales was representing the interests of her son, while there is no mention of her own marital status. Likewise, the lack of marital status did not prejudice her use of the honorific doña. The instrument presented by Ana carried with it the force of law, despite having been drawn up by two women in resolution of illicit and illegal sexual activity. Ana's lack of honorific title and María Josepha's use of doña indicate unequal social standing between the two parties, but apparently do not indicate the court's willingness to find in Ana's favor. Finally, the court was actually protecting the interests of a child born out of an illicit relationship, respecting the request of a mother who could not technically have guardianship of her son. Neither did the court seek to force Ana and Mariano to marry, and thus legitimate the status of the child, though no apparent impediment to marriage surfaced during the suit.

A negotiation obligating the assailant's family to provide child support was a customary, extrajudicial means of dispute settlement, though it should be noted that Ana Sanches did take pains to legally document the terms of their agreement, terms supported by the judiciary. There is evidence that in the 1780s institutional authorities heightened their involvement in community moral affairs while simultaneously disregarding popular perceptions of appropriate punishments and the flexibility of concepts such as marriage, fidelity, scandal, and adultery. But, in cases of statutory rape (*estrupo*), particularly when eased by promises of marriage, informal arrangements continued.

TO CORRECT PUBLIC SINS

On January 28, 1785, widow Maria Ximines filed a complaint with president and regent Villalengua accusing Josef de Leon of the statutory rape of her daughter, Francisca Moscoso.[37] Francisca, just fifteen years old, had disappeared from the family home for an alarming three-day period, when her family finally discovered her with Leon on the street near the college of San Buenaventura. The two were taken into custody by the barrio alcalde of San Roque. Upon the occasion of her apprehension, Francisca Moscoso made an official declaration claiming that Leon had promised to marry her, that the two were planning on moving to Ambato for the wedding, and that she had spent the past three days staying with Leon's grandmother while he prepared for their relocation. She had indeed lost her virginity to Leon, but only because they were to be married. Maria Ximines then provided three witnesses to testify to her daughter's story, as well as her known virginity, jealously guarded for all of her fifteen years. As if to doubly emphasize the point, Don Xavier Sarrao's testimony portrayed Francisca as a "virginal girl," never separated from her mother's side.[38]

Based on this summary information, Villalengua ordered Josef de Leon's confession be taken from his cell in the court jail. The confession was taken on February 18, and the case was moving on its procedural way to sentencing by the Audiencia. Then, suddenly, on March 2, 1786, Maria Ximines wrote to President Villalengua requesting the case be ended, and that Leon be released from jail. Ximines claimed the two parties had come to a mutual consensus, and the prosecution was no longer necessary. Villalengua complied, and ordered Josef de Leon's release with the caveat that if he were brought before the court again or if he "proceeded in his bad behavior," he would be sentenced to two years service in the royal tobacco factory. Leon's five weeks of imprisonment ended with an indication of the type of punishment he was about to receive, but averted through a mutually acceptable resolution with the family of the victim.[39]

The case between Maria Ximenes and Josef de Leon hinted at the continued operation of nonjudicial sexual dispute resolution; it also pointed to shifts in the adjudication of sexual crime in the decade following the Rebellion of the Barrios and the intensive reform administrations of the 1780s. Most significantly, the Audiencia as a body and the president regent as an individual took on direct roles in policing and first-instance prosecution of moral crime in the corregimiento of Quito. Although the jurisdictional flexibility had long existed for individuals to bypass municipal magistrates, the corregidor, or other local judicial officials, and to plea directly with the Audiencia, this was very rarely done in first-instance litigation. In the 1780s, however, the office of the presidency openly encouraged residents of the city to petition directly to the Audiencia for resolution of moral crimes. Furthermore, the presidency and the Audiencia consolidated their enforcement position by coopting the alcaldes del barrio, forcing the neighborhood magistrates to report their judicial activities to either the presidency or the presiding judge of the council's criminal court. This administrative shift effectively placed the ronda and its vigilance over moral behavior under the leadership of the Audiencia. Though the two ordinary alcaldes of the municipal council continued to make street patrols, morality arrests, and prosecutions of all types of property, violent, and moral crimes in the city and in the Five Leagues, they did so in a continuing jurisdictional tension with the de facto expansion of Audiencia authority. Finally, the sentence that Villalengua hinted he would have handed down signals a shift in the punishment objectives from those traditionally meted out to criminals.

This is not to suggest that all statutory rape cases ended in extrajudicial arrangements. In the two other cases from the corregimiento heard by the Audiencia, the files abruptly end after the prueba and issuance of an initial arrest warrant.[40] The lack of definitive sentencing suggests the possibility of informal settlement. But in May 1786, Geronimo Ruiz filed a complaint against Josef Segura for having corrupted his thirteen-year-old daughter with a promise of marriage.[41] Audiencia judge Lucas Muños y Cubero accepted the case and forwarded it to the barrio magistrate of San Blas and Santa Bárbara for investigation. Following the investigation and confession of Josef Segura, he was sentenced to pay the family of Angela Ruiz 150 pesos and to pay court costs and a 10-peso fine to be applied to public works in the city, "to punish the crime and as an example to others."[42] Segura also was promised that should he come before the court again on any similar charge he would be given five years in the royal tobacco factory of Guayaquil. In December 1792, Antonio Pazmiño filed charges against Ventura Hidalgo for the rape of Maria Pazmiño, his daughter, slighting him as a "young bum."[43] In a similar case, Rafaela Gonzales sued Pedro Velastigui for the rape of her daughter Bernarda Bargas.[44] Velastigui was found guilty and sentenced to monetary recompense. He pled poverty, and so the presiding judge ordered that one-third of the sales from a shop operated by Velastigui be garnished to pay Gonzales and to pay for the court costs of the case. He was not sentenced to spend any additional time in jail or one of the royal factories, but rather was ordered to return to live with his wife and refrain from all communication with the victim or her family. The abiding state interest, it seemed, was to mend Velastigui's broken marriage. Sexual propriety belonged in the marriage bed, and could only be reconciled thusly.

In 1785, President Villalengua published and publicly displayed an order calling for the vigilance and correction of "public sins."[45] This secular initiative to monitor and control the city's moral behavior was part of a broader trend that expanded the jurisdictional claims of secular authorities into areas traditionally deemed the purview of religious authorities. The classic example of this expansion was the 1776 issuance of the Royal Pragmatic on unequal marriage, which was extended to the American kingdoms in 1778.[46] Designed to enhance parental ability to prevent unacceptable marriage choices by legitimate children, the Pragmatic sought to move adjudication of such disputes out of the more sympathetic ecclesiastical forum.[47] But its purpose was not explicitly an attack on religious authority per se. As Saether has argued, "the most important object of the law was to strengthen paternal authority and filial obedience, *and* in this manner enhance the power of the King, who, according to the Bourbon absolutist rhetoric, was the father of all fathers. In other words, the law was meant to fortify the paternalist, hierarchical bonds on which the empire was thought to rest."[48] As in the case of moral policing of the city, what was at stake was not so much an expansion of secular authority at the detriment of religious authority as it was the expansion of a specific mode of organizing authority conceived of as patriarchal prerogative. The Pragmatic became a new legal resource, and sometimes led to interesting litigation supported by ecclesiastical authorities. For example, in August 1785, Don Ygnacio Solano dela Sala, son of the former administrator of the aguardiente monopoly Don Antonio Solano dela Sala, had his attorney file a petition with the Audiencia alleging his father was colluding with the bishop to prevent his desired marriage to Doña Antonia Bustos y Piedrahita.[49] The bishop was involved in the case because Ygnacio and Antonia were first cousins, and required special dispensation to marry. Interestingly, the bishop's denial of the license referenced the Pragmatic on unequal marriage, rather than simply denying the request on grounds of the incestual impediment. The bishop went as far as to claim that, based on the Pragmatic, he was required to obtain paternal permission to grant the dispensation. Ygnacio's father was plainly against the union, and had, Ygnacio claimed, secretly instructed the bishop to deny the dispensation by whatever means necessary. And so, without support for his marriage choice in the Ecclesiastical See, the son turned to the secular authorities, claiming that the justification for denying the couple permission to marry was fundamentally errant on two accounts: First, paternal authority played no role in the conference of dispensations to marriage impediments. And second, as first cousins, Ygnacio and Antonia were obviously social equals and therefore exempt from the strictures of the Pragmatic. Finally, Ygnacio admitted that he and Antonia had engaged in sexual relations, and that the overriding concern of all involved must be the protection of her honor through marriage. This ingenious bit of legal reasoning, jurisdictional wrangling, and moral positioning resulted in a much-delayed victory for Ygnacio and Antonia on March 12, 1786. Presiding Judge Doctor Andres Salvador reasoned that the strictures of the Royal Pragmatic were not applicable to the couple's situation who were patently equals by virtue of their familial ties; as such, they must be conferred the requested dispensation to marry.

The strange twist of this case, in which the secular authorities supported marriage choice over a paternal prerogative to which the religious authority was lending its support, demonstrates the intractability of customary legal practice. The Audiencia's ruling lent more importance to the protection of Antonia Bustos y Piedrahita's sexual propriety than to Antonio Solano dela Sala's wishes. Sexual expression was the foremost preoccupation of the vigilant correction of "public sins." Sex had its place only in marriage, even if it was between cousins. Absent a criminal complaint against Ygnacio Solano dela Sala, the abiding state interest was in ameliorating public morals by circumscribing sexualized bodies. Indeed, of the many types of sexual impropriety and unnatural acts open to prosecution, it was improper activity by married men and their lovers that dominated the Audiencia's attention.

In response to Villalengua's call to police public morality, there was a veritable explosion of sex prosecutions in the corregimiento. The Audiencia oversaw forty investigations in the decade 1785 to 1794 alone. By comparison, the city's ordinary magistrates prosecuted twenty-nine instances, as recorded by the First Notary[50] (Table 2.8). The arrests for sexual crimes fit into eight categories, dominated by adultery and cohabitation cases, with rapes (largely statutory) a distant second. Of significant note, the case set includes two prosecutions of sodomy, including a rare instance of two women accused of a sexual relationship (Table 2.9).

Note that denunciations by husbands were strongly clustered with the Audiencia and its barrio magistrate agents. Parental and third-party denunciations were evenly split, while the Audiencia and its barrio police dominated cases of de oficio investigations. This represented a significant shift in the locus of law enforcement and surveillance in the corregimiento. In either case, whether the magistrates radiated from the cabildo or the Audiencia, they were mostly

Table 2.8. Sex Crime Arrests by Section and Type of Complaint, 1785–1794

	INJ	CRIMINALES	TOTAL
DENUNCIATION TOTAL	23	25	48
Husband	2	8	10
Wife	8	6	14
Mother	3	3	6
Father	3	2	5
Other	6	6	12
ACCUSATION	1	1	2
GOVERNMENT (DE OFICIO)	5	14	19
TOTAL	29	40	69

SOURCE: AN/Q, 1NJ 88–144; CR 108–158.

Table 2.9. Sex Crimes by Section and Type of Crime, 1785–1794

	INJ	CRIMINALES	TOTAL
Adultery and Concubinage	19	27	46
Estrupo and Rapto	7	5	12
Alcagueta	0	2	2
Bigamy	1	1	2
Homosexuality	0	2	2
Incest	0	1	1
Mal vivir	0	1	1
Other illicit sexual behavior	2	2	4
TOTAL	29	41	70

SOURCE: AN/Q, INJ 88–144; CR 108–158.

Note: Criminales and the overall total are one higher than in Table 2.8 because one case involved a prosecution of two separate individuals, for estrupo and for alcagueta.

interested in adultery, confirmed by both the arrest data and the actual extant litigation.

Adultery and illicit cohabitation led the total with 65.7 percent of prosecutions. Such actions were invariably the result of spousal denunciations or de oficio government investigations, though occasionally third-party tips prompted a visit by a barrio alcalde on the ronda and the start of litigation. Rape prosecutions were customarily started by parental denunciation, distributed equally in the case set between mothers and fathers. *Alcagueta* referred to the procurement of illicit sexual activity, but could occur without money changing hands, and was a crime investigated by official investigation or denunciation by a third party. *Mal vivir*—bad living—was invariably a part of domestic disputes. The term was a legal trope that, along with public, scandalous, and notorious, formed a predictable part of the etymology of adultery charges. It indicated the abandonment of marital obligations for immoral living, and impugned the defendant for his poor public example. But, along with the other terms listed above, mal vivir was not a fixed, precise accusation. Rather, it stereotyped the offending spouse's behavior and morality in order to strengthen the accusing spouse's own side of the case. As such, the accusation was a regular part of adultery or concubinage denunciations. The one case that solely prosecuted mala vida (and no other crimes) was brought by a husband against his wife.[51] The instances of bigamy and sodomy were pursued as government investigations, and were often the product of invasive ronda activity.

The president's call for public vigilance against immoral behavior sparked the majority of these prosecutions. Individuals were encouraged to inform on long-term relationships, and the city's various magistrates spied and eavesdropped on residents during their nightly patrols.[52] Members of the patrols would enter houses unannounced based on personal suspicions or questionable noises emanating from within, or when tipped off. Relationships, particularly long-term relationships, were carried on with public knowledge, but only became scandalous or notorious (prerequisites for prosecution) through the act of denunciation, accusation, or vigilant surveillance. The combination of the public call for information, knowledge of sympathetic judicial officials, and a willingness of institutional authorities to impose themselves quite literally in people's bedrooms opened the door to malicious and vindictive accusations as well as to legitimate denunciations that served the material and honorable interests of both men and women in the corregimiento.

"ASÍ ES JUSTICIA."

On February 6, 1786, the barrio alcalde of San Roque, Manuel Pacheco, wrote to inform President Regent Villalengua that two nights earlier while out on patrol he entered a Sanroqueño house unannounced, only to find Miguel Lagos passed out on the floor while his wife, Petrona Ayala, slept in bed with Miguel's brother, Fernando Lagos.[53] Pacheco reported that the couple was found lying together in one bed, "naked under the same blanket, their bodies united as if they were married, just a short distance from where [Miguel Lagos] was on the floor."[54] Pacheco asked Miguel how he could let his legitimate wife sleep with his brother, to which Miguel responded that Fernando was a good man who did not "make use of women." With a certain element of disgust, Pacheco took all three into custody, placed them in the royal court jail, and referred the case to the president in the interests of justice. Villalengua ordered a notary of the court to accompany Pacheco on a preliminary investigation of the crime and circumstances of the arrest. The two interviewed the four men who had accompanied Pacheco on the ronda, and, based on their statements, Villalengua decided on February 15 to forward the case to the Audiencia's sala de crimen where it was ordered all three should give their confessions.

In his confession, forty-year-old Miguel Lagos stated that when the patrol entered his room, he was drunk, passed out on the floor. He further admitted that his brother often slept with the married couple because the couple could only afford one bed. He insisted it was a totally innocent practice. Fernando claimed the same and further suggested the whole situation was the product of a verbal fight his sister-in-law had had on February 4 with a number of other women who lived in the house. Petrona Ayala, who was less than twenty-five years old, was assigned a guardian by Pacheco before her confession was taken. The guardian was the substitute alguacil mayor of the jail, and therefore the official charged with her imprisonment. Still, Petrona's testimony echoed that of Miguel and Fernando. She claimed that as they only had one bed in the room, everyone slept together, usually with herself and her daughter on one side, her husband in the center, and her brother-in-law on the opposite side. It was, she also insisted, entirely innocent. This night was different only in that her husband was so drunk that he failed to make it to the bed.

The stakes of the case were high for the accused, because the allegation was not simply that of adultery, but also second-degree incestuous adultery. Villalengua ordered the confessions and earlier summary information be forwarded to the Audiencia's fiscal for clarification of the legal implications of the case. Despite the universal denials of the three parties involved, Fiscal Merchante reasoned that by discovering Petrona and Fernando in bed together, the couple was caught in the act by alcalde Pacheco, "which is the best proof one can have." Therefore, "these offenders should be punished with the penalty indicated by the law." Merchante continued,

> Law 7, Title 17, *Partida* 7 provides that a husband who incurs this crime should be castigated with the punishment for adultery. And based on this, Antonio Gomes comments that Law 8 of [the *Leyes de Toro*], number 73, teaches he should be given the death penalty. [. . .] Law 9, Title 20, Volume 8 of the *Recopilación de Castilla* mandates that a consenting husband like Miguel Lagos should be punished

with the same penalty as pimps and public procurers, which is the first time to be paraded in public shame, carrying a sign of their crime, then sent to ten years service on the galleys; and then the second time to give them 100 lashes and permanent service on a galley. For their part, Law 3 Title 18 *Partida 7* says the incestuous adulterers . . . should be given the penalty of banishment to some island, and that their property be confiscated. Law 7 of Title 20, Volume 8 of the *Recopilación de Castilla* . . . condemns them to lose half of their property. Antonio Gomes, in Law 15 of the cited volume and based on the practices of the Kingdom, teaches that in order to conform to the law of the *Ordenamiento* they should be punished with an expedient sentence and have half of their property confiscated. By reason of the law, and taking note of the nature and condition of the offenders, it appears that Miguel de Lagos should be condemned to the penalty of public shaming with the insignias of his crime and to eight years of service in one of the royal tobacco factories. The two incestuous adulterers, Fernando de Lagos and Petrona Ayala also should be assigned to serve four years each in one of the royal factories with rations, but without salary, and have half of their property confiscated. . . . and such is Justice. [*Así es Justicia.*]

Merchante's commentary demonstrated the complexity of legal interpretation. The law provided traditional punishments of public shaming, banishment, and economic exaction for sexual crime. The punishments appear particularly harsh. Merchante adapted the conflicting advice of the various legal resources at hand to craft a sentence recommendation that served an intermediary penal purpose. While Miguel Lagos would be publicly shamed for allowing the supposed adultery in his presence, his real punishment would come in the form of eight years of impressed service in a royal tobacco factory. Fernando and Petrona were to suffer confiscation of their property, as well as four years impressed service. The alleged perpetrators of the sexual crime received lower recommended sentences than the husband, who had failed in his conjugal responsibilities to ensure the sexual propriety of his wife. Merchante ended his brief with the boilerplate phrase, "such is Justice."

The recipients of such justice must have immediately realized they were in over their heads upon receiving Merchante's report. Under provisions in Castilian law, however, they were provided an attorney, in this case Thomas Garcia y Sierra, to represent them because all three were too poor to hire representation on their own. Miguel Lagos claimed his occupation was day laborer (*labrador*); Fernando listed farmer (*granjero*). Petrona listed no occupation. Certainly if the trio could not afford more than one bed, a hired attorney was out of their reach. Through their crown-appointed attorney, the three requested the opportunity to provide their own witnesses, and proffered an interrogatory for further investigation that was accepted on March 29, more than seven weeks after the arrests. Three witnesses were questioned: Juan de Avila, 55; Reimundo Salazar, 63, printer; and Father Maestro Fray Juan Obando of the Order of Nuestra Señora dela Merced. The witnesses testified to the moral character of the accused, to their good Christian living, as well as to the well-known public affection between Miguel Lagos and Petrona Ayala.

The second prueba served only to mitigate Miguel's punishment. On April 5, 1786, judges Muños y Cubero and Quadrado of the Audiencia handed down the definitive sentence:

> Hear this: following the recommendation of the Señor Fiscal, we condemn Miguel Lagos to public shame, which he will suffer being conducted through the customary streets with the insignias of his crime, and also to serve for a period of five years with rations but without salary in the Royal Tobacco Factory of this capital. Further, for the same period of time Petrona Ayala, wife of the aforementioned Miguel, is condemned to serve in the same manner. Fernando Lagos is condemned to leave in banishment from this city a distance of 50 leagues [250 kilometers] for a period of ten years. We declare as well that half of the property of the aforementioned defendants be confiscated, the notice of this sentence be given to the President Regent, and that [this order] be complied without any restraint.

It was a devastating order. The next day a sentry of soldiers escorted Miguel Lagos, mounted on a horse, through the streets of Quito, stopping at each corner to cry his deeds. Fernando Lagos appealed for at least fifteen days to prepare for his banishment; he was granted three.

Six months later, Juana Muños de Ayala, mother of Petrona Ayala, began petitioning the court for leniency for her daughter. Petrona was suffering greatly in the tobacco factory, repeatedly hurting herself in accidents, and her health had deteriorated to the point that she was bleeding constantly from her mouth. The Audiencia ruled she could serve out her prison term in the city hospital, but that she would not be released unless she could pay a 50-pesos fine to commute her sentence. She filed her own petition the following February, still confined in the factory and unable to pay the fine, and still suffering from deteriorating health. The Audiencia would not extend clemency, but granted a transfer to the poorhouse where she was instructed to work off the rest of her term. She continued to get worse, and again requested clemency eight months later. The fiscal and the Audiencia recognized she was no longer capable of providing physical service to the crown, but refused to release her and ordered she be held in the hospital to convalesce the remaining four years of her term. The punishment was devastating to all involved.

Fernando Lagos's testimony suggested other members of the larger household tipped off the barrio alcalde and his patrol, presumably as retribution for an unrelated argument. Such was the power of denunciation in a city where institutional authorities were consumed with moral enforcement. The other residents of San Roque knew a suggestion to the local barrio alcalde would be enough to exact revenge. The institutional authority for enforcement of sexual norms would be receptive to neighborhood vigilance, regardless of motivation, and the nightly patrol would be the tool of enforcement. Often defendants claimed they were being accused for purposes of revenge.[55] In many instances, the ronda suddenly turned its attention to long-term adulterous relationships because of secret tips or their own spying eyes while on patrol. When right, such suspicions invariably led to spousal denunciations since it was impossible to ignore adultery once it had been made scandalous and public by the ronda.[56] Of course, suspicions were not always correct. In July 1787, the Alcalde of San Sebastian was passing a home across the street from the Convent of the Predicadores when the patrol heard "scandalous noises" emanating from within one of the rooms.[57] The patrol entered the house to investigate, which the alcalde claimed they did with total courtesy. Inside they found Vicente, Felipe, and Lorenzo Basques Alban y Palis, brothers, who chastised the patrol for entering the room of a married woman uninvited. The alcalde replied that it was the sound of male voices in a married woman's room that had prompted him to investigate. A scuffle ensued that left one member of the party, Lieutenant Alguacil Mayor Mairano de Araujo y Ortega, violently beaten on the head, back, and right hand. The Palis brothers continued to berate the soldiers of the patrol as they were escorted to jail. The entire incident resulted from the actions of a zealous royal official looking for sexual impropriety to punish. On the whole, the ronda was very productive in responding to allegations and as a projection of royal surveillance of the barrios.[58]

The objections of the Palis brothers were not entirely outlandish. In August 1788, Antonia Navarrete complained to the Audiencia that the lieutenant barrio alcalde of San Sebastian Francisco Ortiz de Ceballos had attempted to extort her for 10 pesos under threat of incarceration.[59] According to Navarrete, she was locked in her house trying to avoid her abusive husband when Ceballos broke in, threatened her with arrest, and offered her the opportunity to pay a 10-peso bribe to make him go away. Immediately upon making public her petition, the complaints began piling up. Manuela Escobar claimed she and her husband had been arrested by Ceballos while on patrol, accusing the two of adultery. They paid him a 4-peso "fine," as was the custom to make the situation go away. Rafalea Sparza and Eugenio Maldonado Montañez had been arrested for refusing to pay a 6-peso fine as adulterers, even though the two were married. Pedro Fernandez, a cobbler from the neighborhood, was arrested for speaking to two women in his shop while Ceballos passed by. All three were detained, and later visited by Ceballos who offered them the chance to make the charges go away by paying him and the jailer a small fee. Fermina Chaberria complained that Ceballos had entered her home at the foot of the Panecillo Mountain unannounced, searched it, and took a cape, two containers of chicha, and an old hat. He came back the next day and stated that if Chaberria wanted the property back it would cost 4 pesos. Asencia Perez told of an incident one month earlier when she had gone to the grocery store on the corner of her street at 11 p.m. in order to purchase some aguardiente and bread to settle her sick stomach. Another customer, a mulatto traveling to Pasto, entered the store to buy some tobacco and papers on his way through town. Ceballos passed by on patrol and arrested the two, alleging they were lovers despite attestation by witnesses to the contrary. All told, seventeen individuals, mostly women, registered complaints with the investigating judge during the course of the investigation. Ceballos was ordered into custody for confession, and the manuscript ends without final sentencing. Corrupt officials could easily exploit a situation in which the Audiencia leadership zealously pursued sexual improprieties.

Denunciations and street patrols were not the only means by which sexual improprieties were identified and prosecuted. In January 1785, Catalina de los Reyes initiated a suit against Josef de Mena in an attempt to recover a pair of gold and pearl earrings worth 50 pesos that she had "loaned" Mena under the pretext of restoring the image of Santa Tereza. Mena was taken into custody, and a flood of complaints followed of similar tenor.[60] Doña Bernarda de Herrera alleged she had loaned him a pair of emerald earrings worth 50 pesos five months earlier, which he had never returned. This complaint was followed by a third from Doña Maria Rosa de Velasco y Maldonado concerning an emerald worth 6 pesos she had loaned Mena twenty days earlier to use as an adornment for the Christ child. The Audiencia ordered Mena to return the jewelry, which he was unable to do because he had pawned it to pay the costs of wooing his lover. It was an inelegant con, and certainly Mena had to realize it would catch up with him. The investigation into his debts to three separate women in the city led to the revelation of an illicit sexual relationship, which immediately became the focus of Villalengua's prosecution. Rumor had it that the woman on the receiving end of Mena's largess was named Manuela Martines; with the exposure of the relationship, Mena's mother, Doña Leonor Chiriboga, filed suit against her. Chiriboga justified the complaint because Mena was not yet of majority age, and as a legitimate child (*hijo de familia*), remained under her paternal authority (*Patria Potestad*).[61] Villalengua immediately swore a warrant for Manuela Martines's arrest. The Manuela Martines they apprehended was the legitimate wife of Don Joaquin Ribadenerya, guard of the estanco de aguardiente. Following customary procedure, Villalengua probed Martines's behavior and moral standing by interviewing three witnesses, in this case Don Juan Matheo Navarrete, Real Hacienda notary Mariano Navarrete, and Gregorio Villamaior.

All three testified that it was publicly and notoriously known she had maintained an illicit friendship with Don Alenzo Feyjo, but the details of her alleged relationship with Mena were less clear. But Martines was known to have abandoned her husband, and because she had been seen in public with Mena, rumor had it they were involved. It was enough for Villalengua, who, based on this scant testimony, condemned Martines to be banished thirty leagues from Quito. If she refused to leave, or did not go far enough, Villalengua threatened her with four years in the royal tobacco factory in Quito. The sentence was handed down just four days after Chiriboga filed the complaint.

It may have been premature. On February 19, Maria Manuela Martines filed a response to the punishment handed down for her "scandalous life." She began by admitting that it was true that due to, "my fragility and poverty I have fallen into some miseries, but not accompanied by the scandal or depravity which Your Lord has inferred." Martines went on to explain that she had known Josef de Mena a mere four months, during which time she had witnessed him constantly lose money gambling. Gambling debts explained the jewelry con, not a sexual relationship with Martines. She claimed she only wanted to live a good Christian life, which was possible in Quito where she had sisters and relatives who could help her. Finally, she revealed she was pregnant, and that banishment would cause her to miscarry due to the rigors of travel by horse or wagon. Villalengua ignored the balance of the petition, and zeroed in on this last claim. He ordered a midwife visit her in jail to determine if "it will be dangerous for her to mount a beast of burden." Midwife Francisca Xaviera Caeza de Baca, a married white woman age fifty, examined Martines and determined that indeed she was five or six months pregnant, experiencing some bleeding, and would miscarry if forced to ride a mule. With this information, Martines was released into the custody of three women of known virtue and good judgment on February 22, 1785.

Josef de Mena would not be so lucky. The investigation into his moral depravities continued through February. A suit from two years earlier, in which Mena had been arrested by the barrio alcalde of San Sebastian for disrespect, was located by the investigating magistrate Mena had proclaimed at 9:30 a.m. on a street corner in front of witnesses to magistrate Josef Chacon that he had an inflated opinion of himself, and that any mestizo with 200 pesos could be a barrio alcalde. His disrespect to a minister of justice, combined with the current evidence of his gambling, adultery, and general licentiousness, merited serious punishment. Villalengua indicted Mena's character in the strongest language possible, accusing him of living "a scandalous and licentious life, full of the abominable vices of adultery, prohibited gambling, fireworks, and more, adding up to eight different proceedings, and likely hastening more and more with his crimes, with little fear of God." In punishment for his incorrigibility, Mena was sentenced to depart the city immediately with troops headed first for the River Marañon, and farther on to Napo to fight Indians in the Amazon basin. It was a virtual death sentence handed down just one day after Martines was released from jail. Mena knew this, and tried repeatedly over the coming weeks to prevent or delay his sentence. He even claimed he was needed by his mother to take her to Peru. When questioned by the judge, Leonora Chiriboga responded, "[T]here is no trip to Lima. I mean, the whole world knows his father lost my dowry, and left him without a single real of inheritance. If this young man stays in Quito, he will further scandalize with prohibited gambling, fritter away that which I don't have, and disobey Justice." Mena left Quito at the beginning of March. Two years later, Leonora Chiriboga was still involved in legal actions to settle the court costs and child support for her illegitimate grandson. A woman named Martina Campoverde, her son's actual mistress, had brought the action for child support.

By 1790, the court moved beyond its reliance on denunciation, street patrols, and serendipity to directly identify and prosecute offending couples. In response to royal instructions, the juez pedaneo and the governor of Chillogallo put together a dossier on all the couples maintaining illicit relationships in their jurisdiction.[62] The officials identified twenty-four couples, and included data on the marital status of each of the offenders, the current known status of their relationship, and ethnic status *if* the offenders were indigenous (Appendix II). The information was submitted to the Audiencia on May 10, 1790; the following August, the court ordered the alguacil mayor of Quito to go to Chillogallo and determine which of the allegations could be substantiated through the testimony of two or three witnesses with knowledge of "the scandalous life, and disorderly conduct of those contained in the report." The alguacil presented his findings one month later, accounting for eleven of the twenty-four accusations.

Based on the information gathered, the fiscal recommended, and the Audiencia ordered, "in order to remedy the scandal and put right the people of [Chillogallo], compel the married to reunite [with their spouses], and the singles, who find themselves able, to marry. Finally, punish the incorrigibles with the penalties established by law, and give an account of all that is done. Thereby proceed with Justice." It should be noted that, somewhat surprisingly, the investigation centered on the improprieties of Chillogallo's male inhabitants, who were impugned for abandoning their marital and patriarchal responsibilities. Reconciliation of sexual activity within the confines of marriage remained the goal of government enforcement, without the expected wink and nod of double standards.

But what of sexual activity that could not be reconciled through marriage? We have already seen the severity with which institutional authorities dealt with incestuous suspicions. While the burden of proof to substantiate an allegation of incestuous sexual activity was lower than in other cases of adultery, it was even lower in prosecutions of sodomy. The mere suggestion to a judicial authority that sodomy was suspected resulted in some form of punishment for the accused. There were two prosecutions of sodomy in the 1780s pursued by city officials, one involving a group of young men and the other involving two young women.[63] In both cases, the court fell short of demonstrating actual, penetrative sexual activity. There was no moment *en delito flagrante*, and therefore the prosecutions ultimately relied on circumstantial evidence.

In early May 1788, Custodio Legendres, a twenty-year-old copyist employed by the estanco de aguardiente, found himself denounced for sodomy before the Audiencia by Mariano Espinosa. In his petition to the president of the court, Espinosa accused Legendres of "degenerating the nature of man, with infamy for Religion [by] maintaining a nefarious cohabitation with one Justo Santana, with notorious scandal."[64] Prior to making this allegation, Espinosa was already involved in a legal dispute with Legendres who had filed a complaint with Oidor Lucas Muñoz y Cubero against Espinosa for a physical assault. It is likely that the allegation would not have surfaced if Legendres had suffered the violence silently. The allegation of sodomy was clearly a reprisal, though dressed in high-minded language of fealty. Espinosa explained, "I can do nothing less in attention to Justice than unload my conscience and present to Your Highness the primary motive behind [Legendres' suit against me], and the maliciousness with which he presents himself omitting the iniquitous origin of the action."[65]

This simple allegation by a third party opened an investigation into the sexual activities of ten of Quito's young men for associations with Legendres (Table 2.10). Information for the investigation initially was gathered through interviews with seven different young men, all of whom testified that Legendres had carried on a series of affairs in which he treated his male partners as if they were wives or women. Examples of such treatment included giving his partners gifts, holding them in his arms, taking them out for strolls through the streets of Quito, dressing them in fine clothing, enviously guarding their attentions, sharing a room with a single bed, and providing them with food, "as if he were his lady."[66] In one instance, Legendres threw a jealous fit when a lover decided to marry. In his initial testimony, Gregorio Rios admitted that when he was younger he had had a relationship with Legendres, and "that being just a kid, and innocent he had fallen in his turpitude some twenty times in the space of the three months they had been friends."[67] The admission led to his arrest. Once held in custody, Rios backtracked on his story and claimed they had never actually engaged in sodomy. While the investigating magistrate had interpreted the admission as a confession of anal sex, Rios later explained during his confession that, "[Legendres] took [Rios's] shame in his hand," and masturbated him, catching the semen in a hand towel. Rios then returned the favor.[68] The other witnesses testified to one extent or another of their own (platonic) friendships and their familiarity with neighborhood rumors that Legendres was a sodomite. In particular, they all alleged that Legendres was involved with Justo Santana, a guayaquileño with whom he shared his bed. Legendres and Santana were detained and questioned, but, unlike Gregorio Rios, they consistently rejected all allegations of improper sexual activity and brushed aside stereotyped assertions of impropriety.

Because of Rios's retraction, the judge was left without any admissions or witnesses to actual sodomy. The fiscal commented,

> According to the summary and other actions, the accusation
> of sodomy, or the nefarious sin, made by Mariano Espinosa

Table 2.10. Witnesses and Accused Sodomites Attached to Custodio Legendres

NAME	AGE	OCCUPATION AND ROLE IN THE CASE	LITERATE
Custodio Legendres	20	Scribe, Administration of Aguardiente, Accused	Yes
Justo Segura y Santa Ana, el Guayaquileñito	17	Tailor, accused	Yes
Gregorio Rios	21	Musician, Scribe, accused	Yes
Manuel Flores	18	Silversmith, accused	Yes
Miguel Jimines	16	Violinist, witness	Yes
Manuel Fernandes	20	Scribe, Tribute Collection, accused	Yes
Antonio Cortes	19	Bookseller, accused	Yes
Josef Fernandez	18	Organist, accused	No
Leandro Paredes	18	Black Slave, accused	No
Pedro, son of a Tailor named Pablo	?	Unknown, absent in Barbacoas, accused	?

SOURCE: AN/Q CR 126 10∞V∞1788, "AUTOS SEGUIDOS SOBRE EL FEO, Y ABOMINABLE DELITO."

against Custodio Legendres has not been justified according to the method and form prescribed by the law for ordinary punishment contained in Law 2, Title 21, Partida 7 and in the pragmatic 85 of the Kingdom. As a result another class of crime is justified, that of incontinence against nature, following that which was specified in the confession and confrontation of Gregorio Rios. . . . [I]t seems to the Fiscal that it would be useful for Your Highness to condemn Custodio Legendres, Justo Segura y Santa Ana, and Gregorio Rios to four years service in the royal tobacco factory of this city . . . in order to serve as a warning to others, and satisfaction of public vindication. And for the levity and ease with which Mariano Espinosa proceeded with his denunciation, slandering Custodio Legendres, attributing to him the nefarious crime, which has not been verified in all of its strictures, as was said before, it seems to the Fiscal that it would be useful for Your Highness to condemn him as well to four years service in one of the tobacco factories.

Merchante's advice was not fully taken. The Audiencia handed down sentences of four years of service on a ship of the royal navy for Custodio Legendres and two years each for Gregorio Rios and Justo Santana y Segura. Until an appropriate ship could be identified, Legendres and Rios were to serve as bookkeepers in the tobacco factory in Guayaquil, where Santana would labor. Finally, all three were to bear the court costs equally. Mariano Espinosa, it seems, escaped punishment. Interestingly, absent any immediate evidence of actual penetration, the case rested on Legendres's public behavior toward his lovers. The accusation that he acted toward them as a man legitimately should act toward a woman opens a window to understanding normative gendered courting and marital behaviors. That the Audiencia would punish still so harshly the decoupling of this gendered behavior from acceptable avenues absent legal proof of sodomy suggests that the sexual act itself was not the sole concern of their moral regulation.

Such a conclusion is further supported by the experience of Josefa Lara and Manuela Palis.[69] On July 29, 1787, San Marcos Barrio Alcalde Antonio Freyre de Andrade reported to the Audiencia that, based on numerous denunciations, he had taken into custody the two women for an illicit relationship that included "the abominable act of sodomy."[70] During the nightly ronda, Freyre had caught the two sleeping in the same bed, but provided no further lurid details.[71] Oidor Fernando Quadrado ordered Freyre to perform a full investigation of the allegations and take the confessions of the accused accompanied by Doctor Don Manuel Josef de Borja, a lawyer attached to the court. The evidence against the two boiled down to circumstantial testimony provided by their sisters, Flora Lara and Juana Palis. Both placed the responsibility for the relationship on the shoulders of Manuela Palis, who for the past year had engaged Josefa Lara in a torrid affair. Another witness, Ygnacia Cordero, asserted that, prior to this relationship, Manuela had carried on with another neighbor named Paula Martines, who was a friend of Flora's. Flora often visited Paula and Manuela in the room they shared together, and on occasion brought her sister Josefa along. When the two separated, Manuela apparently propositioned Josefa and their love affair began. Though again there was no physical evidence to substantiate a sexual relationship between the two, all five witnesses in the investigation testified to the behavior between the two associated with normative heterosexuality. Manuela reportedly took Josefa on strolls around the streets of Quito, took her out to eat and drink liquor in bars (*estanquillos*), often slept with Josefa in the same bed, took her dancing at parties (*fandangos*), and beat her in a public brawl over Josefa's possible engagement to a man. In the investigative phase of the case, this behavior was characterized by witnesses and the inter-rogating magistrate as, "how men [treat] their concubines or lov-ers."[72] In their confessions, both Manuela and Josefa admitted to the facts arrayed against them, but with a different interpretation. Yes, they walked about and drank publicly together, but did so with other young women as well. Yes, they occasionally slept together in the same bed, but only in the manner that platonic girlfriends do when it was too late or one of them was too drunk to be wandering the streets home at night. They engaged in these acts innocently, as "comrades," friends, including the night the alcalde busted into the room while out on patrol. In no instance, both insisted, did their friendship take a wicked, immoral, depraved turn to illicit sex. The violent episode was dismissed as patently bogus.

Unfortunately for the two young women, their denials carried little weight with the barrio alcalde, Audiencia lawyer, and judges on the court. On August 11, 1787, the court sentenced Josefa Lara two years in the royal tobacco factory of Quito in order to "correct [her] excesses," and Manuela Palis to two years in the poorhouse. As an addendum to the sentence, Regent Villalengua ordered that under no circumstances was Josefa Lara ever to be transferred from the factory to the poorhouse.

Manuela Palis's reputation for preferring women to men had led the neighborhood to interpret her public actions within a matrix of customary sexual comportment. Just as was the case with Custodio Legendres, the damning evidence used to convict the pair was Manuela's public treatment of Josefa. In this case, she acted as a man toward a woman while Custodio treated another man publicly as one would his wife. Youthful indiscretions of drunkenness, dancing, dining, and cavorting at night took on a different meaning when one party paid for the other's entertainment. Furthermore, Manuela pub-licly assaulted Josefa, apparently to chastise her for considering a com-peting offer of affection. In an atmosphere of surveillance and moral enforcement that sought to instill a patriarchal ethic of circumscribed sexuality, such gender bending required severe correction.

CONCLUSION

In the two decades following the Rebellion of the Barrios, the institutional authorities of the corregimiento of Quito conspired to erect a machinery of moral surveillance and enforcement that laid a newly invasive claim on subject bodies. The restoration of royal authority was to be wrought from those bodies by tearing down any protective wall between public and private spaces. Women's bodies bore a disproportionate burden of surveillance, particularly through the effective spying eyes of the nightly ronda. And yet even as the president regent sought to expand his personal authority over moral enforcement in the Five Leagues, he was dependent on the procedural imprecision of the Spanish legal inheritance to surmount the jurisdictional space necessary to flex his moral muscles. The secular authorities firmly took the reins of moral enforcement through the ronda, the jail, the court, and the factory. But these activities depended in part on citizens' willingness to denounce bad husbands, as well as bad wives. In several instances, women who sued their husbands over infidelity did so claiming license from the very targets of the litigation. Most women did not. What did the participation of women on both sides of criminal prosecutions suggest concerning women's broader legal status in the closing decades of the eighteenth century? More specifically, if a woman claimed her husband's permission to punitively bring him before a judge, what did this signify for mediated access to legal resources? The details of the criminal cases suggest that quiteña women occupied a broad spectrum of public, economic, and legal spaces in the closing decades of the century, even as institutional authorities sought to enforce a new understanding of paternal authority and hierarchical obedience. The next chapter will excavate those spaces further.

CHAPTER THREE

PRACTICE II

Women, Property, Civil Dispute

———•———

"Whereas it is in accordance with the Law, I appear before
Your Mercy, and say. . . ."[1]

INTRODUCTION

Women did not find themselves embroiled with the legal system
only as objects of sexual surveillance or victims and perpetrators of
criminal acts. Most litigation in the corregimiento dealt with civil disputes over property. Of the 266 cases collected by the First Notary in
the decade 1765 to 1774, only thirty-four (14 percent) were criminal
prosecutions. By contrast, there were ninety-one civil disagreements
over monetary debts during the same period, accounting for 34 percent of cases. When all types of property litigation are added together,
they account for 189 instances (71 percent) of the cases transcribed
by the office of the First Notary (Table 3.1). Women's participation in
the legal system mirrored this general pattern.

Access to legal resources for recourse of property disputes was a
major bulwark in protecting women's economic interests in the corregimiento. It also was a key way in which legal practices diverged
from the prescriptive literature. The gendering of property rights in the
Hispanic system limited the ability of men to divest women through
both explicitly protective law and custom practice, such as partible
inheritance, the dowry, and the division of marital property into both
communal and personal accounts, shielding spouses from each other's
debts. Likewise, women were prevented from being arrested for debt

Table 3.1. First Notary Cases by Category, 1765–1774

CATEGORY	NO.	%
Pesos/Monetary	91	34.3
Testamentary	43	16.2
Criminal	37	14
Other	23	8.6
Religious Corporation Loans and Chaplaincies	16	6
Lands	15	5.7
Houses	9	3.4
Royal Orders, Laws, and Rulings	8	3
Slaves	4	1.5
Marriage	3	1.1
Bodegas and Groceries	3	1.1
Clothing	3	1.1
Taxation	3	1.1
Legitimation	2	.8
Indigenous	2	.8
Aguardiente Estanco	2	.8
Ecclesiastical	2	.8

SOURCE: AN/Q 1NJ 43*57.

in all cases except those where the debts were incurred through criminal activity.[2] But Bourbon-era legal interpretation emphasized the restrictive rather than the protective features of the Spanish legal tradition, and particularly attempted to deconstruct protective customary practices. Legal commentaries emphasized the process of licensure, in which women could gain access to legal resources only through explicit permission from their father, husband, or a judge acting in their stead. The restriction of licensure sought to mediate gendered legal status primarily as an expression of conjugal authority, and secondarily as an expression of paternal authority. The provision by which a judge could grant permission in the absence of other male authorities reinforced Bourbon governance that favored hierarchical fealty and institutional patriarchalism. As in the case of criminal enforcement, there was a disjuncture, though, between institutional priorities and social values expressed in customary practices and legal wrangling.

This chapter will excavate further customary legal practices in the closing decades of the colonial period in order to evaluate women's operative legal status within quiteño legal culture. In the conflict between customary legal expectations and Bourbon prescriptions, legal practice structurally favored the local over the imperial, a tendency that Bourbon reformers never fully overcame. This tendency was exemplified in the issue of licensure, which this chapter will analyze among female litigants, beginning with a surprising commercial contract dispute. We open with the story of Doña Ygnacia Sanchez, after which we will turn to the prescriptions of legal commentaries and the broader trends of licensure in practice. Analyzing marital status, licensure claims, and forms of male representation for the periods 1765–1769, 1785–1789, and 1805–1809, this section will present a comprehensive picture of women's court presence across the closing decades of the colonial period. Furthermore, I will highlight the language and process of legal representation and litigant self-representation to illustrate the tactical deployment of gendered legal concepts. Finally, the chapter ends with a discussion of the economic implications of women's presence in civil litigation. As women continued to assert autonomous legal identities across the period 1765–1809, they did so in order to protect and expand their already significant economic roles as creditors, debtors, and otherwise as property owners who richly added to the texture of daily economic life in the corregimiento. Now for some of that texture we turn to the story of a shrimp sale gone afoul.

A CASE OF BAD SHRIMPS

During the second week of January 1809, Antonio Ruiz, a local of Ambato, approached Doña Ygnacia Sanchez, the proprietor of a number of shops (*tiendas*) in Quito, with an offer to supply her with a certain quantity of shrimp (*camarones*).[3] He promised that the camarones on offer were large, crystalline, delicious (*riquisimos*), and that she would not be disappointed. They agreed on a price, and Ruiz returned a few days later with the shrimps. In fact, he returned with quite a few more than Doña Ygnacia was expecting, and their dispute began. Doña Ygnacia maintained that the agreement was for a single *quintal* (roughly twenty-five pounds), whereas Ruiz delivered four, and then demanded 12 pesos in payment. Doña Ygnacia refused to pay the price for this rather large mass of camarones, disputing both the amount delivered and the price charged. Her decision prompted Ruiz to bring her before the local commercial judge for a verbal hearing. Based on the testimony of Ruiz, Doña Ygnacia, and an unnamed witness, the magistrate issued a verbal judgment ordering her to accept and pay for the entire delivered product.

It is at this point that the case entered the written record. Given the judgment against Doña Ygnacia, on January 11 her husband, Don José Santiana, filed an appellate petition before the same commercial magistrate. Don José's approach to the appeal and the judge's response are very telling. To begin, Don José feigned surprise at hearing his wife had been brought before a commercial judge, and that the judge had ruled against her. Upon learning of the case, he went directly to his wife to inquire what had happened and why, to which she responded she had been approached by Antonio Ruiz with an offer to sell some great shrimp, and that she had agreed to buy one quintal, "assuming [her husband's] consent." She then reported that Ruiz had shown up with four quintals, forcing her to take and pay for them all after telling her that she could certainly sell the shrimp in the four stores she ran in the city. From this set of "facts," Santiana set forth this argument for the nullification of the contract: because Doña Ygnacia Sanchez was his wife, and because Ruiz had contracted with her instead of him, the contract was of no value. To fortify his argument, Santiana then employed Castilian law:

> Just as a woman, during marriage and without the license of her Husband, cannot make a contract, nor can she break or waive any contract in which she is involved . . . nor can she take part in any court case, not even in defense, without the license of her husband.[4]

Finally, based on this legal argument, Don José claimed that not only were the contract and sale null and void, but the judge's verdict in the verbal suit was illegitimate because his wife should not have had standing on her own before the court.

Antonio Ruiz responded with a direct attack on this argument of gender rights, as well as on Santiana's retelling of the "facts" of the case. In his rejoinder, Ruiz argued the case was a simple dispute over "a contract for the sale of four quintals of shrimp negotiated in public shops [*tiendas públicas*], and celebrated with [Santiana's] wife, Doña Ygnacia Sanchez." Ruiz rejected the notion that he had negotiated in bad faith by dealing directly with Doña Ygnacia, and maintained that the negotiation established a fair price of 3 pesos per quintal, a contract upheld by the verbal hearing. While these were issues related to the facts of the case, Ruiz also engaged Santiana's legal argument for gender right, stating

> The point of law is not applicable, because nothing is more valid than contracts made by married women who work publicly in business away from the presence of their husbands. The assumption of their husbands' knowledge has all the more force when their actions explain better than words his outlook on the matter. Santiana's wife is one such woman, as she has commissioned stores where she buys and sells without the intervention of her husband. This is why only she appeared in the verbal case, which she lost due to the declarations of witnesses put forth in favor of the contract. . . . Certainly [Santiana] knows this very well, and is now just trying to get out of the contract, claiming the incapacity of his wife to make contracts.[5]

Ruiz pointed out that Santiana never disputed the terms of the contract, only the contract's validity. Therefore, he argued, because the contract was valid, the terms must be respected. Furthermore, given the very high rates at which women were involved with public commerce in the city, the gears of daily economic life would grind to a halt if routine business transactions could be routinely challenged in this manner. The commercial judge agreed, and on January 17 issued a second ruling in the case:

> [B]eing public and notorious that Da [Doña] Ygnacia Sanchez makes contracts by herself in a public store, and that her husband Dn [Don] José Santiana admits in his petition that she assumes to already have his permission to negotiate frankly and ratify commercial dealings: in which case the privilege of other married women to cede [their right to make contracts]

in deference to their husbands ceases . . . the claim of nullification set forth against the verbal judgment is declared without cause. What is more, this court finds with certainty Da
[Doña] Ygnacia to be a public merchant, and furthermore
responsible for the four quintales of shrimp with the exception of one arroba . . . and that the price is normal by virtue
of the testimony of witnesses produced by the plaintiff.[6]

Additionally, the judge ordered that Santiana was responsible for all
court costs.

Despite the setback, Santiana was not through. On the same day
the verdict was issued, Santiana filed a power-of-attorney motion
appointing José Paz de Albornoz as the couple's official representative
before the court. Paz immediately appealed the second decision of the
commercial judge to the Audiencia. While the Audiencia was considering the case, the disputed camarones were removed to the care of a
neutral merchant. Paz's petition before the Audiencia was much more
sophisticated in its arguments, but decidedly less gendered in its logic.
Under the new line of argumentation, the validity of Antonio Ruiz's
contract behavior rather than the gendered issue of license for public
conduct took center stage.

In this retelling of the fact set of the case, Antonio Ruiz approached
Doña Ygnacia with an offer to sell her a portion of camarones from a
larger quantity he was delivering to Quito for another merchant, one
Señor Duprat. Doña Ygnacia agreed to take one quintal of shrimp at
a yet-to-be-determined price, dependent on the quality of the product.
The problems began with Ruiz's return. The petition claimed that
Ruiz delivered the camarones to Doña Ygnacia's tienda, which spe-
cialized in "edible trifles," while she was absent. Ruiz then sought out
and found Doña Ygnacia, demanding she pay 12 pesos for the impos-
sibly large quantity of four quintals. Upon returning to her shop, she
found not only this mass of shrimp, but, to her surprise, the shrimp
were not of the highest quality. Thus she refused to pay, either the
price or for the ridiculous quantity. Paz claimed that this situation was
directly the result of Ruiz's malicious behavior and willingness to take
advantage of the "imbecility" of Doña Ygnacia's sex. Paz presented
the question of negotiating in bad faith as the central argument, while
the gendering of dispute moved away from Doña Ygnacia's ability
to have public presence either as a hawker of food or as a defendant

before a commercial judge. Instead, the attorney moved discussion of gender inequality to the much more familiar ground of the need for protection of the interests of supposedly weaker groups in society.

The Audiencia agreed, and issued a compromise ruling negating the verbal and written decisions of the commercial judge. The writ did not absolve the merchant couple of all responsibility, though, and required Doña Ygnacia to take and pay for one quintal of shrimp, as she had originally contracted. Likewise, both parties to the suit were required to pay for expenses incurred to that point. The ruling was issued on January 19, and one can only imagine that all parties lost their shirts on the deal, as the shrimp had been sitting in unrefrigerated storage in Quito, at this point, for nine days!

A number of observations can be drawn from this suit. On the procedural level, the case provides evidence for the use of verbal hearings of middling contract disputes. In this suit, both the first and second instances were heard before the same commercial judge, who in the first instance viewed Doña Ygnacia Sanchez as a legitimate defendant within the judicial structure of the city's merchants. The direct and ancillary details of the case show an active woman, central to the daily economic life and comestible provisioning of the city. There were enough women selling things in the city that it seemed normal for a supplier to deal directly with Doña Ygnacia, and for the courts to recognize her position as a commercial agent. It seems that Doña Ygnacia found herself in this unfortunate situation through the plotting of Ruiz and the illusive Señor Duprat. It turns out that the latter gentleman was the witness who testified against Doña Ygnacia in the initial verbal hearing, only to be revealed by José Paz de Albornoz as the other quiteño merchant for whom the balance of the shrimp had been intended. Likely, Duprat realized how poor the seafood was, refused to purchase it, and suggested they pawn it all off on the unsuspecting Doña Ygnacia Sanchez. With the conspired testimony arrayed against Doña Ygnacia, it is not surprising she lost the initial hearing before the commercial judge. At that point, Doña Ygnacia's husband made a conscious decision to employ gender rights as a legal tactic. The logic of argumentation of the case in its various stages opens the door to a split between the ideal and the actual in judicial practice.

Don José Santiana's consciously chosen tactic of representing his wife's interests before the court was not a gendered obligation because of his wife's inability to stand before the court. Indeed, while Santiana correctly quoted Castilian law concerning a wife's legal standing in contracts and courts, the law did not matter because of the primacy of local customary practice that, as in the verbal dispute, recognized Doña Ygnacia's legitimate legal status. Interestingly, the assumption of license for the public activities of Doña Ygnacia radiated from the fact of her daily participation in public activities. Customary practices and expectations trumped formal legal strictures. While it is true that the case lacks a written record of Doña Ygnacia's voice, and rather includes that of Santiana, Ruiz, Paz de Albornoz, and judges—all men—the case is exceptional in this respect to the many hundreds of cases I have collected from the period which are filled with women's voices that are significantly less filtered. Finally, the fact that the line of argumentation changed when a professional attorney was engaged to argue before the Audiencia suggests that those most intimately involved with litigation recognized the tendency of courts to maintain the tension between local custom and metropolitan law, a tension at the heart of the judicial state. Paz took the gendering of the dispute away from a priori questioning the legitimacy of Doña Ygnacia's economic behavior and legal status, and moved the litigation toward a gendering that emphasized the obligation of the Spanish judiciary to perform the function of ensuring a protective justice. In either case, the tactical deployment of gender prerogative by both Santiana and Paz were belied by the realities of Quito's daily commercial activities, as evidenced by the case's ancillary details. Thus, the interests of communal harmony in a situation where women were regularly involved in commercial dealings required the correction of Ruiz's exploitative actions and the maintenance of Doña Ygnacia's economic identity. These practical realities were more important than the procedural vagaries of the law. The discretionary nature of Spanish justice posed a significant challenge to the centralization of authority so clearly dear to the hearts of Bourbon-era Spain.

LEGAL PRESCRIPTIONS

What, then, were the procedural prescriptions intended to bind women's access to legal resources? Legal actors had an array of practical publications to turn to in the form of judicial manuals. As with economic, administrative, and religious practices in the late eighteenth century, legal prescriptions suffered from the confusing, contending labyrinth of inherited custom, Habsburg practice, and Bourbon aspiration. As Charles Cutter has noted, "[The Spanish Empire] was a government of judges, where nearly every appointed official exercised some sort of judicial authority."[7] The concentration of judicial and political power into the hands of individual magistrates and offices of the bureaucracy has often led to depictions of colonial administration as "ponderous, tyrannical, arbitrary, and corrupt."[8] That depiction misses the adaptability of the system, however, in which the melding of judicial and political power was tempered by the structural conflicts of overlapping jurisdictions, the malleability of Hispanic law, the primacy of local customary legal practice (derecho vulgar), and the power of judicial discretion.[9] On an operational level, jurisdictional authority over bureaucratic and judicial functions tended to be reproduced across administrative entities.[10] Thus, for example, secular authorities could not enact policies concerning marriage without taking into account the ecclesiastical position on the issue. As a corollary, litigants were able to search out the authority most likely to support their position in a dispute.[11] What litigants found when appearing before the judge of their choice could vary greatly across the empire. The famous dictum, "I obey but do not execute," was a formula that gave primacy to local customs and conditions over royal wishes, providing "an institutional device for decentralizing decision making."[12] Jurists' decisions on any one set of facts presented in a case were likely to be most responsive to the same local customs and conditions that enabled them to resist implementing crown dictates. Justice, as a result, existed at the confluence of law, custom, and a desire for local communal harmony.[13]

If a judge desired to base decisions just on written law, though, he was faced still with a labyrinth of contradictions. The history of Hispanic law into the nineteenth century was one of accrual rather than of precedence. A plaintiff, her attorney, and the presiding court had at their disposal a body of law extending back as far as the Roman Empire, and included the Justinian Code (529 to 565, also known as the Codex Justinianus), the Fuero Juzgo (654, also known as the Lex Visigothorum and the Liber Judiciorum), the Siete Partidas (1251) of Alfonso X, the Fuero Real (1250s), the Ordenamiento de Aclalá (1348), the Ordenanzas Reales de Castilla (1485), the Pragmática Real, Los Capítulos de Corregidores y Jueces de Residencia (1500), and the Leyes de Toro (1505), along with such compilations as the

Nueva Recopilación de Leyes de Castilla (1536), the *Recopilación de Indias* (1681, in the Americas), the *Autos Acordados* (1770s), and the *Novísima Recopilación* (1805). Local municipalities, certain kingdoms, and corporate groups (military officers, ecclesiastics, indigenous peoples, merchants, and so on) also possessed their own particular fueros, legal charters or privileges.[14] Add to this already impressive list any number of royal orders (*cédulas*), laws (*leyes*), and special laws (*pragmáticas*) issued by the Castilian monarchy, which retained their stature regardless of when they were handed down.[15] Kagan's observation, "Castilian justice in the sixteenth and seventeenth centuries was a hodgepodge of confused laws and competing jurisdictions that crafty litigants exploited to their advantage," aptly depicts the kingdoms of Spain in the Americas into the eighteenth century.[16]

The position of women within the legal inheritance of Habsburg governance was ambiguous, but reflected a governing ideology that privileged the decentralization of authority through institutionalized conflict. Just as the king's authority was tempered by the evasions and squabbles of both the secular and religious bureaucracies, the position of male authority was tempered by marriage, dowry, inheritance, and legal practices.[17] Likewise, a woman's marital station carried with it related legal obligations and privileges, much as did membership in one of the numerous fueros recognized in Hispanic law.

The Hispanic legal tradition placed individuals according to their position in numerous categories, each of which determined elements of one's legal identity. One's place along a number of continuums (slave/free, Spanish/Indian, male/female, minor/adult, legitimate/illegitimate) delineated a complicated set of legal positions.[18] Gender formed but one element of the matrix, and adroit litigants would emphasize or de-emphasize the various constituencies to which they belonged, depending on the requirements of a legal circumstance. Gauderman has described this process in the seventeenth-century example of indigenous market women (*gateras*), who were able to exploit the complexities of their unique matrix of professional, racial, and gender statuses to dominate street marketing in the city of Quito. As Indians, the gateras were able to sell their wares free of the commercial taxes from which all Indians were exempt. As women, they were freed from the obligations of the tributary rolls, which only recorded male community members. When taken to court by nonindigenous male grocery store owners, the gateras took recourse to the right to free representation by the crown-appointed protector de indios. The intersection of racial and gendered legal statuses enabled Quito's gateras to dominate much of the commercial activity that provisioned the city by providing them with a competitive advantage over their male counterparts, both Spanish and indigenous.[19] Such ambiguities inherent to the Hispanic legal tradition mitigated the patriarchal tendencies that lay beneath Habsburg decentralism, in the cultural values of inequality intrinsic to a caste-based society. The prospect of tightening the legal culture of the Hispanic world, of more clearly delineating an orderly chain of authority that enlivened the rationalist Bourbon mind, was the hope of reformulating the practice of gender inequality across the social spectrum—in law, economy, and social relations.

The desire of Bourbon reformers to bring some clarity and order to the judicial functions of the state is reflected in the judicial manuals published during the eighteenth century, as well as the revival of works written during the legal publishing boom of the late sixteenth century.[20] There was a veritable explosion of works published in the second half of the eighteenth century, at a time when litigation was expanding as well.[21] The period bears significant resemblance to the explosive era of litigation that accompanied the first wave of practical legal publishing documented for Spain by Richard Kagan.[22] Many of the classic works of that period were revived in the interest of clarifying the Spanish legal labyrinth, but they also were joined by many new works. Below I discuss one of the new manuals of the eighteenth century with Juan y Colom's *Instrucción juridical*, as well as the revived manual of Alonso Villadiego, *Instrucción política y práctica judicial*, which was published originally in 1612 at the tail end of the sixteenth-century Castilian legal revolution, and in numerous editions from the 1740s on.[23] These were not the only manuals to be written or to gain renewed enthusiasm during Spain's Bourbon legal revolution, but they are representative of the confluence of legal idealisms from the two periods.[24] In addition to Juan y Colom, the late eighteenth-century witnessed as well the publication in numerous editions of Joseph Berni y Catalá, *Instrucción de alcaldes ordinarios* (1763), José Febrero, *Liberia de escribanos, é instruccion juridical theorico práctica de Principiantes* (1790), Francisco Antonio de Elizondo, *Practica universal forence de los tribunales de España y de Indias* (1792), Count (*Conde*) de la Cañada, *Observaciones practicas sobre los recursos de fuerzo* (1793), and Juan Sala, *Ilustración del derecho real de España*

(1806), among others. In addition to the revival of Villadiego, Gabriel de Monterroso y Alvarado's *Práctica criminal y civil* (1566) and Juan de Hevia Bolaños's *Curia philipica* published originally in Lima in 1602, made the rounds of the empire's magistrature.[25]

In contrast to some legal writings of the preceding centuries, Bourbon commentators sought to produce a didactic literature emphasizing an organized and practical presentation of legal concepts, procedures, and forms, and to emphasize earlier manuals that did the same.[26] Writing in Castilian as opposed to Latin, scholars in both Spain and America shunned esoteric dissertations and the internecine arguments of the doctors of the law in favor of works that were "fundamentally compendiums intended to facilitate the work of judges, lawyers, and scribes."[27] Moreover, the force of these works rests in their push for some measure of predictability in a vast array of legal situations. Predictability, though, would come at a cost to derecho vulgar, jurisdictional squabbling, and judicial discretion.

JUAN Y COLOM

Joseph Juan y Colom's *Instrucción jurídica* consists of three books: Book I. On Justice, Right, Law, Jurisdiction, and Privileges: Their Definition and Use; Book II. On Marriage; and Book III. On Advisors and Companions of Common Judges. Book I is the most theoretical of the three, prone to long discourses defining foundational concepts of law, right, jurisdiction, and justice. The author provides general descriptions of each idea, and then further divides them into rubrics of type, breaking individual concepts into further subcategories with their own definitions and functions. So, for example, *derecho* is defined as, "a good and fair art, whose precepts are to live honestly, cause no harm to others, and give to each that which is his."[28] This general definition is then broken into three types:

1. Natural Right: that which is common to all of the human genus, both the rational and irrational, who are inclined by their natural instinct towards self preservation and survival, through the procreation, care, and nourishment of children. . . .
2. Rights of Men: that which men established by mutual agreement in prudent judgment.

3. Positive Right: that which is imposed at the will of the supreme Monarch, be he Emperor, King, or Prince, and which recognizes no greater temporal authority, and which changes according to the circumstances of the times . . . It is divided between Canon and Civil law.[29]

The process of general definition followed by etymological classification is repeated for justice, law (*ley*), and jurisdiction. Thus, Juan y Colom proceeds for the remainder of the book to follow this instinct toward classification as a means to rationalize the law and its practice. The desire for classification and clarity was confounded, though, by the realities of jurisdictional imprecision and the chaotic mass that was the body of law for the many kingdoms of the Spanish monarchy. For example, following an extensive lineage of Hispanic law, Juan y Colom advises jurists to apply the following hierarchy of legitimacy to the various legal compilations at their disposal:

1. *Nueva Recopilación*, including the *Reales Pragmáticas* and *Autos Acordados*.
2. *Fuero Real*.
3. *Fueros Municipales*.
4. *Siete Partidas*.
5. Local custom.
6. Laws collected in the *Ordenamientos Real*, the *Fuero Juzgo*, and the *Derecho Canónico*, the *Civil Romano*, and "which ever laws are adaptable to natural reason."
7. In the absence of laws speaking directly to the type of case being adjudicated, a judge should turn to the closest law he can find.[30]

Municipal fueros and local custom often existed in direct contravention to the royal will, as well as varies bodies of codified law. Juan y Colom was not, however, able to fully dismiss contradictory codes or practices, because of their traditional recognition. In effect, then, the best he could do was to subordinate competing law codes to the most recent compilation of royal law collected and issued in the *Nueva Recopilación*. As demonstrated in the chapters that follow, this subordination never really occurred until the liberal revolution of the nineteenth century.

The most agonizing attempt to bring order to a chaotic situation notably occurs in the longest chapter of the first book, on determining which judge should hear which type of case. As a guiding principle, Juan y Colom advises that the judge of first instance should always be the corregidor, chief local magistrate (*alcalde mayor*), or alcalde ordinario of the town or territory where the defendant resides unless, of course, it is a real estate dispute, in which case the judge of the place where the disputed land is located has jurisdiction; or in cases of vagrancy in which the appropriate judge is the residing magistrate of the place where the vagrant was found; or in criminal cases where the defendant committed his crime in a region outside of where he is a resident, in which case the local magistrate again has jurisdiction. And what if someone stole something moveable? Or if the act was committed at sea? Likewise, the corregidor, alcalde mayor, or alcalde ordinario may not have primary jurisdiction if the dispute occurred within Five Leagues of an Audiencia, in which case certain disputes become the primary provenance of the Audiencia court.[31] Just as the legal foundation of judicial discretion could not be easily dispensed with, the jurisdictional confusion inherited from the Habsburg period was not easily overcome. In all, Juan y Colom needed seventeen pages to spell out the intricacies of the jurisdictional assignment. To a large extent, the specificity and enumeration of each entry point to thoroughness as an avenue around complexity. By covering as many contingencies as possible, Juan y Colom endeavors to remove the ambiguity that long served the venue-shopping interests of litigants.

The section on jurisdiction is also where Juan y Colom first broaches the subject of women in the courts, stating, "the arbiter of a suit against a woman should be the Judge who would have had jurisdiction over cases involving her husband."[32] Juan y Colom's positioning of a woman's standing before a judge as derivative of her husband's standing was indicative of the eighteenth-century redeployment of male authority and household representation. The line of argumentation is continued in Book II, On Marriage. Comprising thirteen chapters, the book endeavors to delineate the privileges and restrictions within married relationships. Juan y Colom recognized the religious nature of marriage, but his definition hinges on the conjugal right of a husband to control female sexuality:

Marriage is the con-joining or sexual union of a man and a woman, with the intention of living forever together, without separating one from the other, nor he knowing another woman, nor she another man. It is called matrimony and not patrimony because it is composed of the Latin words, *matris* and *munium*, which is in the romance, charge of the mother, because she bears more work with the children than the father. She carries them in the womb, births them with pain, feeds them from her breast, and when they are young, they need her more than their father. [. . .] [Marriage] was instituted in two principles; which are, before Adam sinned, for the propagation of the human species, and after, when it was elevated to being a Sacrament, in order to evade the sin of fornication.[33]

The definition ties marriage as an institution to an imagined primordial history of sexual purity and orderly succession dating back to Adam. The sacramental nature of marriage, he argues, is tied directly to ensuring the sexual purity of the community, but particularly that of the woman whose responsibility it is to bear and raise the children resulting from sexual activity. In his opening phrase, marriage is at its essence the act of sexual union. Juan y Colom continues to specify the importance of this connection in listing the benefits of marriage: lineage, faithfulness, and sacrament. The primary benefit of marriage consisted in "having legitimate children" which must be "the intention of the married couple, even if they do not have children or are not able to have them naturally."[34] The other two benefits exist in the married couple's ability to guard each other's fidelity and ensure the relationship's long-term security. Thus, for Juan y Colom, in the eyes of the law marriage constitutes a dual contract—both natural and sacred—whose complementary design was the protection of lineage and sexual fidelity. In eighteenth-century Quito, this preoccupation with marriage-as-sex became an obsession of secular authorities, who saw in the sexual lives of married people an analogy for the orderliness of royal authority.[35] Writing in 1736, and renewing the sentiments in 1795, the exposition placed the surveillance and control of marriage firmly in the hands of a rationalist state, in line with the movement of the crown against ecclesiastical control of marriage embodied in the

1776 *Pragmática* against unequal marriage.[36] Furthermore, the secular matters of legal behavior (emancipation and legitimation of children, Patria Potestad, penalties for adultery) and contracts (dowries, marital profits, inheritance) dominate the text. On the first account, Juan y Colom's interpretation is unambiguously patriarchal, whereas on issues of property the plot is decidedly more mixed.

In describing the operational relationship between a man and a woman in marriage, Juan y Colom adopts the classic patriarchal metaphor of body and head, stating that in "depicting the married husband and wife as of one flesh and body . . . the husband should be the head of this body, and wherever he wants to dwell, so should the wife as his subject."[37] The extent to which Juan y Colom envisioned male headship as determinative of a wife's status is revealed in his argument that a noble woman who marries a commoner loses her noble privileges as long as they remained married.[38] Within this position of headship, the husband has the right to administer and control his wife's property.[39] Furthermore, in virtually every form of legal and economic activity, Juan y Colom's vision of women is derivative from men's authority:

And the married woman, during her marriage, cannot repudiate an unexpected inheritance without license from her husband. . . .

Nor can a woman sign any contract or waive any action undertaken, [. . .] nor appear as the plaintiff in any suit, nor in her defense without license from her husband. *Ley 2. tit. 3. lib. 5. Recopilación.* But her husband can confer to her a general license to make contracts, and to do all that she is unable to do without a license. Under this form, all acts of the woman are valid. *Ley 4. tit. 3. lib. 5 Recopilación.*

A judge, hearing a legitimate case, based solely on the summary information of witnesses, can compel the husband to grant her license. . . .

Likewise, a judge, in hearing a legitimate case that is necessary or beneficial to the woman, can grant her license to act and appear in the case if her husband is absent.

A husband can also ratify an action of his wife, engaged without his license.[40]

Patriarchal prerogative as articulated by Juan y Colom was the conjugal prerogative of husbands over wives, not that of fathers over
their children. Limits to women's access to the courts were not to
be restricted to cases outside the marriage. Juan y Colom advised
limits to women's ability to sue or bring criminal charges against
their husbands, advocating that judges only admit the most serious
of suits, and not elevate "flippant" disputes, establishing a standard
for women's participation in the law far stricter than that dictated by
either law or custom.[41] He then continues in the following chapters to
enumerate the restrictions and privileges associated with dowry and
inheritance wealth. The discussion includes the legal definitions of the
dowry, varying types of marital property, profits, who must provide a
dowry, the nondowry property brought into a marriage by the woman
(*parafernales*), and processes for the restitution of the dowry.[42] The
integrity of dowry wealth was threatened, according to Juan y Colom,
only by the act of adultery: "The married woman who commits adultery loses her dowry, the groom's wedding gift to the bride [*arras*], and
marital profits, which should be transferred to the husband."[43] But the
discussion of the dowry, and particularly the means to restitution of
the dowry, point to enduring legal protections of women's access to
their personal property within the Hispanic tradition. These protections were intended to maintain clear lines of ownership, particularly
in the event of one or the other spouse's death. Likewise, the eluci-
dation of procedures for inheritance, in which a wife was entitled to
the property she brought into the marriage in addition to 50 percent
of the profits of the marriage, demonstrates that it was difficult for
those who would disfranchise women of their property or legal rights
to overcome long-established practices.

Following his lengthy discussion of the dowry and marriage property, Juan y Colom then turns to defining categories of legitimacy
for potential heirs of marriage unions—legitimate children, natural
children, orphans, adopted children—and their enumerated rights to
inheritance. Within this section, the author also explains the legal
concept of patria potestad, or paternal authority, based the *Siete
Partidas*.[44] Patria potestad references the authority of fathers over
their legitimate children, and from which natural children (children

born out of wedlock whose parents have no impediment to marry), illegitimate children (born out of wedlock with legal impediments to their legitimation, including incest or being the result of adulterous relationships) are categorically excluded. Juan y Colom notes that children who do not fall under Patria Potestad by cause of the absence of a legitimately married father are not by extension under such authority of their mothers. Likewise, the authority over children does not default to the mother or her antecedents in case of a father's absence. In describing the prerogatives of patria potestad, Juan y Colom explains that, at its core, the authority rests on the father's ability to own and control the wealth, profits, inheritances, gifts, and so on accrued while the children were of minority age.[45] Sons and daughters could free themselves of this authority by reaching the age of majority (twenty-one for women and twenty-five for men), by marrying, or through emancipation. Children were emancipated through a variety of means: (1) death of the father; (2) civil death of the father (loss of citizenship rights through abandonment or royal proclamation); (3) remarriage of a father after the child's mother's death in a manner contravening the law (for example, remarriage to a professed nun); (4) by taking a religious profession; or (5) by judicial writ, in which the child and father appear before a magistrate and request emancipation.[46] Additionally, a son or daughter could ask the court to compel emancipation in cases of cruelty, or in cases where the parents forced their children to act criminally as prostitutes or thieves, or in cases of other forms of abuse.[47]

Parents were obligated by law, and, according to Juan y Colom, by natural right, to provide food, shelter, clothing, and the like for their children in consort with their own standard of living. For the first three years, it was the mother's primary responsibility to feed and care for a child. But, as a remnant of marital law that kept separate the estates of husbands and wives, the wealthier parent was obliged to pay for the child's upkeep out of his or her assets.[48] Juan y Colom restricted this obligation to legitimate or natural children, stating that parents had no duty to care for illegitimate offspring with no hope for legitimation. Essentially, the stricture prevented parents from being sued for alimony or from having their estates distributed to illegitimate progeny. This interpretation of the law contradicted the standard analysis established by Gregorio Lopez in his authoritative gloss of the *Siete Partidas* published in 1555, who argued that both parents and grandparents were obligated by natural and canon law to support children, even if they were the product of incestuous or adulterous liaisons.[49] Juan y Colom specifically notes the disagreement, consciously tightening the legal interpretation of normative family and parental obligation.

Juan y Colom's redeployment of Spanish law emphasized the traditions of male control and domination of women over the mitigations of the law. One the one hand, women's legal activity was to be subsumed in the authority of the leading males of their lives. On the other hand, venerable traditions that protected their access to property, even from their husbands' desires or debts, carried the force of law in spite of his authority. This tension between the centralizing, rationalizing authority of Bourbon reform and the messy yet flexible customs of Hispanic law, was emblematic of the tension between Iberian designs and American expectations.

VILLADIEGO

Alonso Villadiego's *Instrucción política*, published originally in 1612 and then again in 1747, took Juan y Colom's penchant for covering all contingencies to a new level. Villadiego wrote at the end of the sixteenth-century Castilian legal revolution, and sought to bring sense to the perceived chaos of jurisdictions and frivolous litigation of the era. Comprising some five hundred pages in eight chapters, Villadiego clarified the procedural application of the law from a suit's inception through its final appeal. Rather than utilizing a topical organization built on foundation concepts, like that employed by Juan y Colom, the *Instrucción política* is divided by case type (civil, criminal, appellate, and investigations of royal officials [*residencia*]) in addition to chapters dealing with good governance in the office of corregidor and proper testaments. Finally, approximately 40 percent of the text comprises formulas for petitions. Much like Juan y Colom, Villadiego structures his work to move from the general to the specific. Each step of a civil—and later a criminal—suit is defined, the rules governing that step are enumerated, and then contingencies discussed. Above all, the *Instrucción política* emphasizes the importance of proper form and procedure in the successful ajudication of disputes. The example of the initial petition (*demanda*) will suffice to demonstrate this form of prescription as used by Villadiego.

Villadiego begins by explaining that civil suits "can be pursued in five ways: against the defendant in his presence, in contempt, in his absence, after his death, or as a case [prosecuted] by the Court."[50] Regardless of how the case is brought, there are six phases through which it must pass: petition, reply, order of investigation, publication of witnesses, definitive sentencing, and appeal. Villadiego's chapter then follows these steps in order. The initial petition as the first step in the process is further elaborated. Villadiego explains that an effective petition required five specific elements: the name of the plaintiff, the name of the defendant, the dispute and its attendant details, the penalty desired, and certification that the information provided is sworn testimony.[51] Villadiego then further defined each of these elements, with examples. Finally, the section ends with Villadiego's clarification of exceptions to the normal procedure. Of key concern was who had the ability to file a petition before a judge. It is here that women first appear in the *Instrucción:*

> And if the plaintiff is an hijo de familia, or a minor with a guardian, or a married woman, she cannot bring a suit without license from her father, guardian, or husband. And furthermore, any member of these categories has to request a license at the beginning of the demanda, or petition for it first.[52]

Grouping together women and children in a discussion of licensure reinforces the perception of a woman's legal minority. But Villadiego further clarifies that licensure for women worked differently from the obstacles to minors' legal agency.[53] In following his pattern of defining, explaining, and excerpting, the passage continues by describing cases in which the license is not necessary, including requests for the restitution of the dowry for women. The rest of Villadiego's work proceeds in this manner, allowing a judge or scribe to turn at any point during a proceeding to the applicable section and read a synopsis of the ideal form of the relevant procedure as well as exceptions to the rules.

Finally, at the end of the work, Villadiego includes some two hundred templates for petitions, covering every conceivable action taken in judicial proceedings.[54] The importance of this section to the author cannot be understated. In fact, Villadiego asserts that it is in proper form and procedure that justice is located: "The successful creation of a petition . . . is of the utmost utility, and essential for the litigant to get justice, because a well-crafted petition carries virtually all of the force of a suit."[55] The numerous petitions designed for women emphasize the particular relationship they are to have with the court. The standard petitions assume male participants, with special templates for women's actions, largely restricted to marital and inheritance disputes. Defining the woman's relationship to a man—be it her husband, father, deceased husband, or the court standing in for one of the above—legitimates these special petitions.[56] Furthermore, while Villadiego's manual does not include a separate section that segregates and subsumes women's legal position in family law, the templates do reinforce this impression by specifying women's participation as gendered forms.

LICENSURE IN PRACTICE

Returning to the case of Doña Ignacia, the central argument of Don José Santiana's initial foray before the commercial judge was to question the legitimacy of both the contract and the judicial ruling by contending that they had been formed without his consent or license. Licensure was intended to place women in a subordinate and mediated position vis-à-vis legal acts. As referenced above, Joseph Juan y Colom's summarization of the *Recopilación de Castilla* on the issue appears rather cut and dried: no contract, no judicial demand, no judicial defense without license of her husband, or through judicial provision. Villadiego further tied the issue of licensure to paternal prerogatives:

> And if the litigant is a legitimate child [hijo de familia], a minor with a guardian, or a married woman, she or he cannot appear in court without license of his or her father, guardian, or husband. Any of the above must request the license from them at the initiation of the complaint, or at the time of their first petition. . . . But, if a married woman is requesting [restitution] of her dowry, or its security from a husband who is going about impoverishing them, spending the dowry, she very well may appear in court without a license from her husband.[57]

While Villadiego's juxtaposition of women, minors, and hijos de familia reinforces the perception that women were considered perpetual legal minors, legal minority is not the appropriate descriptor. Unlike legitimate and illegitimate minors, married women formally possessed legal prerogatives that minors did not, particularly in relation to the maintenance and protection of dowry and personal estates and inheritance practices. Women also brought criminal charges against their husbands for domestic violence without requiring license, and customarily did so for adultery as well.

In both legal commentaries, licensure follows what was perceived as a woman's natural progression from being a minor under the tutelage of parents to being in the marital relationship under the auspices of a husband. The prevalence of nonmarried female-headed households, widows, separated married couples, and long-term absent husbands confounded the supposed succession of patriarchs. In cases of an absent spouse, a woman carrying general permission from her husband was obligated to request from the court license to act, for example, in the collection of debts owed to the couple. Villadiego's template for this circumstance states,

> *Name*, as a woman who belongs to *Name*, my husband, with his consent, say, that some individuals from such and such place owe my husband and me a certain quantity of maravedis, which I need for my sustenance; and, that my husband is absent and I do not expect him to return promptly. I ask and implore Your Honor, based on this information that you order I be given license so I may collect the referenced debts, and to be in court, in agreement with my rights.[58]

Single women of majority age, widows, and divorcees, however, had no special provision established for gaining permission to access legal resources, either in the form of litigation or in the form of making contracts. It is likely this omission was because single women of majority age, divorcees, and widows did not fit the natural progression expressed in the ideal world of the legal commentaries. It is also remarkable, given the commentaries' tendency to cover all contingencies in formularies and legal exegeses. The omission suggests the extent to which the real world of local legal culture and social authority could and did differ from the Bourbon ideal. One final category of women who regularly required license to engage in judicial or contractual actions was members of religious communities. The issuance of license for members of religious communities, whether male or female, was governed by the ecclesiastical fuero, which required that the bishop or other ranking ecclesiastic grant permission for religious individuals or corporations to act in a secular context. This license, which mirrored that given to soldiers protected by the military fuero when engaged by civilian courts, enabled the religious to act outside the protections of their fuero.[59] This was a renunciation of privilege and protection, which may well be the best explanation for the local understanding of the operation of gendered licensure in the corregimiento.

The phrase "with his consent" or "based on his consent" (*premisa la venía* or *premisa su venía*) was one of two generally used tropes to claim license in a legal act, the other being a form of "with license" (*bajo licensia, previa licensia*, or *con su licensia*). That was, of course, when legal actors deemed it necessary to present permission, which was surprisingly not all that often. Despite the far-reaching insistence of Bourbon legal commentaries, licensure and, as a corollary, male representation of women in legal acts was far from normative in quiteño legal culture. It was much more common to find women appearing before the court under the gender-neutral boilerplate of this chapter's epigraph, "whereas it is in accordance with the law, I appear and say," the same language utilized by men. Appendix III contains tabulations for license claims, male representations, and unlicensed activities by marital status for the periods 1765–1769, 1785–1789, 1805–1809, 1810–1814, and 1825–1829 as represented by primary litigants (defendants and plaintiffs) in the cases transcribed by the First Notary. The numbers are quite startling. For the five-year period 1765–1769, only four women claimed license, three married and one married with an absent husband. A further five women were represented by men before the court. Of those five, three hired attorneys, one appointed a third party to represent her interests, and only one was represented by her husband. By contrast, twenty women represented themselves in litigation without reference to license. As one would expect, widows and single women were prominent in the nonlicensed category, together accounting for 35 percent of the actions. Women whose status never was noted in the course of litigation accounted for another 35 percent of the cases. Surprisingly, the remaining 30 percent of nonlicensed actions were taken by four married women and two married women with absent husbands. Taken together, then, nonlicensed legal actions totaled 69 percent of women acting as primary litigants for the period

1765–1769. The remaining 31 percent was evenly distributed between licensed appearances and male representations. It should be noted that attorneys were usually hired by women on their own accord, and therefore served no purpose different from the purpose served by attorneys hired by male litigants.

These ratios remained fairly constant for the ensuing decades. For the period 1785–1789, 63 percent (n=122) of women acted without license, 24 percent (n=47) were represented by men in court, and the remaining 13 percent (n=25) presented license. The licensed individuals included three religious women, twenty-one married women, and one who woman who was married but whose husband was absent. Male representatives included eight husbands, four husbands representing both spouses, six fathers, fourteen attorneys, five lawyers from the office of the protector of the Indians, and ten third-parties. As above, representation by an attorney was not a gendered prerogative, but rather a strategy employed by all types of litigants. Nonlicensed actions included one religious, two divorced, one married with an absent husband, twenty married, five singles, thirty-five widows, and again a predominant fifty-eight with no status indicated. Combining the various categories of married women, thirty-four presented license or were represented by their husbands, as compared to twenty-three who acted alone. This comparison does not include married women who hired attorneys or indigenous married women who were represented by the office of the protector of the Indians.

Finally, for the period 1805–1809, 69 percent (n=204) of women acted without license, followed by 23 percent (n=67) represented by men, and 8 percent (n=24) appearing with license. The relative drop in license presentations was accounted for in an increase in nonlicensed self-representation. Married women presented twenty-one spousal licenses, one license by a woman who was separated but married, and two rare license that had been granted by the presiding judge in a husband's stead. Husbands, who represented either their wives or the marriage's communal interests in twenty-four instances, dominated male representation for the first time. Twenty attorneys, fifteen protectors of Indians, six third parties, and two fathers standing for their daughters followed. Meanwhile, 53 percent (n=108) of litigants without license were of no denoted status. Forty-three widows combined with twelve single women to complete the categories traditionally outside of consent requirement.

Taken together, then, in the fifteen years compiled for the closing decades of Spanish rule in Quito, 518 women were involved as primary litigants in disputes compiled by the First Notary. Of those, 67 percent (n=346) claimed no license to appear before the court. An additional 10 percent (n=53) appeared claiming license, while 23 percent (n=119) were represented in some capacity by men. Of those in the last category, only 7 percent (n=37) of total female litigants were represented by their husbands. What are we to make of sixty-eight married women acting without license, while forty-eight claimed permission? What do these numbers signify? Is it safe to assume that women who presented petitions before the court or who signed contracts without reference to marital status were themselves single? Ancillary details of the cases suggest this assumption cannot be made safely and universally. The answer to all these questions is that the devil is in the details. As predicted from the legal commentaries, single women of majority age and widows never sought or presented permission for legal acts. But the licensure of married women was much more complicated than the simple instructions of Villadiego and Juan y Colom.

There are numerous examples of cases that followed the rules: In April 1769, Josepha Villafaña filed suit to legitimate her parentage in hopes of gaining inheritance. Her husband was absent from the city, but she still presented a formal, notarized writ of license from him. The text of the license restricted the permission to this specific instance of litigation. In gaining legitimation of her questionable heritage, Villafaña stood to gain a significant inheritance. It may be she felt her dubious parentage required a higher attention to procedural formalities to impress the court. In December 1772, Doña Elena de Leon y Otalero, the legitimate wife of General Don Phelip Arechua y Sarmiento, filed suit with his license to regain the proceeds of a commercial venture she contracted with Manuel Barraza.[60] Barraza had carried unspecified goods for sale to Guayaquil. Upon his return, Barraza refused to divulge to Doña Elena what he had sold, for how much, and what her cut of the proceeds should have been. She brought suit, and the court attempted to compel Barraza first to produce a memorial of the activity, and later to pay Doña Elena. Ultimately, she had Barraza placed in jail for noncompliance.

In January 1785, Doña Ysidora Sanchez, the legitimate wife of Josef Carcelen who was absent in Latacunga, claimed permission to appear before the court to request a royal financial grant for her son to attend college.[61] The scholarship was awarded for the following period of matriculation. By that time, the son to whom the award was assigned was too sick to attend classes and Josef Carcelen, who had returned to Quito, resumed the case, petitioning the Audiencia to reassign the grant to another son. In December 1787, Manuela Gomez Astudillo, wife of Josef dela Cruz, claimed permission to file criminal charges against the city's lieutenant tribute collector for a set of pearls she claimed he had unjustly taken from her.[62] The dispute originated from an attempt to impress a mestizo named Mariano Santos into tribute payment. Gomez stood up for Santos, angering the lieutenant, who proceeded to confiscate her pearls for Santos's supposed tribute debt.

Finally, in June 1805 Doña Mariana Paez y Coleti, legitimate wife of Prospero Ocampo, sought and received judicial license (*premisa la benia del juzgado*) to bring suit against her father-in-law, Don Gregorio Ocampo.[63] She alleged that her husband had taken property she had inherited from her parents and given it to Gregorio Ocampo against her wishes, and was suing for its return. In all likelihood, Prospero Ocampo refused to support the legal action, since he was responsible for funneling the property to his father. The court concurred with Doña Mariana, and ruled in her favor.

Each of these cases represented procedurally correct but varied forms of criminal and civil litigation in which married women specifically sought licensed consent to appear before the court, including those with absent or, in the last case, uncooperative husbands. Much of the licensed litigation was not so transparent. For example, in April 1788 Doña Maria Ventura Padilla, a resident of Quito and legitimate wife of merchant Don Pedro Herrera, filed suit against her husband over abandonment and financial support.[64] Doña Maria Ventura phrased her opening petition with the expression, "based on the necessary [permission]," and then proceeded to catalog the disastrous behaviors of her husband.[65] In his response to the petition, Don Pedro Herrera feigned shock that his wife would complain to the court of his treatment of her, particularly that she would assume the right to appear in court. Technically, married women could sue their husbands for alimony, since food, shelter, and clothing were marital obligations, so the reference to consent was unnecessary. The court ignored Herrera's surprise and allowed the case to continue. In January 1789, Doña Ysidora Aguayo filed charges with an alcalde ordinario alleging her husband, Francisco Xavier Garzon was engaged in an adulterous relationship with a mulatta (*parda*) woman named Josefa Larrea that had lasted the entire length of their marriage.[66] As would be expected, Aguayo filed the complaint without permission of her husband, and the alcalde ordinario immediately arrested Garzon. Two weeks later, Aguayo appeared before the magistrate again, this time utilizing the phrase "premisa su benia," to request her husband be released from jail. In the interim, the couple had reconciled and she no longer wanted to sustain the complaint. Interestingly, now that Aguayo was filing a petition on behalf of her husband's interests, she referenced his consent.

In a similar case from December 1805, Tomasa Saures, a resident in the nearby village of Pomasqui, claimed license from her husband to file charges against his lover Juana Molineros for adultery.[67] Included in the complaint was also a list of physical and verbal assaults that Suares had suffered at the hands of Molineros who publicly called her a derogatory term for black (*samba*) and a thief. In response to the complaint, the alcalde ordinario ruled that Suares could not file against Molineros for concubinato, claiming, "The woman cannot bring charges of adultery," and requiring Suares to consult an attorney to conform her complaint to the law.[68] In response to the alcalde's ruling, Suares changed her tactic and refiled a criminal complaint for verbal and physical assault against Molineros. A second plaintiff, Margarita Ortis, whose marital status was never noted, joined her in the new case. With the charges moved from adultery to injurious words and actions, Saures dropped the claim of license and proceeded to file petitions before the court together with Margarita Ortis without reference to consent. There no longer was a perceived tactical advantage to the consent. Interestingly, though the alcalde was a stickler for the procedural details of adultery allegations, contrary to local customary practice, he never questioned Margarita Ortis's unlicensed status, nor the shift for Tomasa Saures. In certain instances, the claim of consent plainly confounds logic. In September 1806, Doña Josefa Ypes filed a suit against her husband, Don Nicolas Araujo, in secular court to complement divorce proceedings under way before an ecclesiastical judge.[69] The secular charges amounted to attempted murder for an assault Araujo perpetrated against her with a knife. Still, in filing the opening petition of the criminal complaint, Ypes utilized the standard phrase, "premisa la venia."

Women often utilized license language in instances where they were representing the interests of the marriage, their husbands, or their legitimate children. If a husband was incapacitated by an assault and unable to petition the court directly, his wife could represent the husband under his consent.[70] The privilege extended beyond assault cases, as well, with wives occasionally representing their husbands before the court out of convenience.[71] In either case, the extension of license appeared to work much the same as power of attorney given to third-party representatives and lawyers. Contrary to expectations, it appears from the litigation that fathers were unlikely to represent their legitimate children except in cases in which daughters were sexually assaulted. Five of the eight cases filed by fathers on behalf of minors were cases of estrupo; the other three involved monetary disputes.[72] Women, conversely, represented the interests of their sons, daughters, and servants on a much wider variety of cases, both with and without license from their husbands. In January 1767, Manuela Aguirre, legitimate and licensed wife of Mathias Carbajal, filed charges against Mariano dela Cadena for assaulting her daughter in a fit of jealous rage after she rebuffed his courtship.[73] Two decades later, but without expressed consent, Agustina Araus filed charges against Ventura, Tomasa, and Luisa dela Zenda for beating up her sixteen-year-old legitimate daughter, Doña Nicolasa Baldes y Arauz.[74] A year later, in June 1788, Beatris Seballos's mother, Doña Roza Navarro, filed a criminal complaint against Agustin Fiallos for sexually violating her daughter with no reference to marital status or consent.[75] Mothers also represented their sons and daughters in inheritance and dowry disputes, against abusive employers, and for protection from abusive royal officials, among other things.[76]

Some of the most telling information on the customary attitudes toward paternal consent in the legal system comes from cases, like that of Doña Ygnacia and her shrimp, in which licensure was made a specific point of legal argument. In June 1772, Don Gaspar Antte had his attorney file a brief with the Audiencia in response to a credit action taken against his mother, Doña Dionicia Donazo.[77] On the face of it, this action would tend to suggest Doña Dionicia's access to the court was linked to her relationship with her son, likely the oldest male left in her life. Doña Dionicia found herself in a precarious position, owing some 5,000 pesos to two creditors, who together held a lien on her hacienda. The attorney's rejoinder was in response to the creditors' request for an appraisal of the hacienda in a move to foreclose on Doña Dionicia's debt. The complication for a gendered reading of this case comes in the form of the lead representative of the creditors: Doña Ysavel dela Flor, the legitimate wife of Don Gaspar Antte. Doña Ysavel dela Flor was joined in the action against Doña Dionicia by the Marqués de Villa Orellana (himself an alcalde ordinario charged with upholding the law in Quito), and yet it was Doña Ysavel dela Flor who initiated and managed the legal action. Don Gaspar's attorney used this fact as a platform to challenge the suit, claiming that neither the original loan nor the current suit were valid because Doña Ysavel operated without license from her husband, arguing,

> It is indisputable, that in order to appear in a suit, a woman must legitimate her person by extending, as an unavoidable requirement, license from the husband. . . . The opposing party having omitted the formality, the petition should be rejected for this reason.

The attorney employed this argument of gender right as one element of the petition, arguing further that any garnish against the profits of Don Gaspar's mother's hacienda would prevent her from meeting other important obligations, most notably the payment of royal tribute for the property's resident Indians. But this economic argument was based on a mode of defense that was different from the first. The gendered argument questioned the legitimacy of the court action a priori, whereas the economic argument was a plea to mercy in the interest of the royal treasury. Unfortunately, the folio ends with an order by the judge to pass on the petition to the creditors, so we do not have the response of Doña Ysavel to the attorney's line of reasoning.

The ancillary details of the dispute speak to normative actions outside the framework of licensure. The case against Doña Dionicia was filed initially by Doña Ysavel; the Audiencia accepted it in due course. It can be inferred from the text that Doña Ysavel did not have license from her husband to bring the suit, but this did not deter the Audiencia from accepting her petition and forwarding it to the defendant. Don Gaspar's response was crafted by an attorney, Mariano Coello, who would have been familiar with the intricacies of Castilian law, and who sought to exploit the gender rights of his client as a tactic for dismissing the case. It should be noted that this argument could only have come in the name of Don Gaspar, as his mother could not have invoked gender right as a legal strategy. Finally, the underlying facts of the quite substantial loan between Doña Ysavel and Doña Dionicia points to an independent and legally documented economic contract between women. Clearly, in this case, the argument of the gendered right to consent employed by Gaspar and his attorney was a tactical option, chosen as a last-ditch effort to protect his mother's property and his future inheritance.

Husbands were not the only ones who attempted to tactically employ gendered legal procedures to get out of sticky situations. In May 1806, Doña Victoria Ponze, legitimate wife of Juan Teran, found herself indebted to various creditors she could not afford to repay.[78] In a rather unusual maneuver, Doña Victoria petitioned the court to abolish her debts, arguing, "the obligations that I have signed are null because I took them without the intervention of my husband, and because they are expressly usurious."[79] The court rejected the argument outright, and Doña Victoria was required to liquidate her personal house in the barrio of San Roque and other belongings to the tune of 555 pesos in order to satisfy her creditors. Doña Victoria's argument was surprising to her creditors. In at least one case, the loan receipts showed Doña Victoria had borrowed money together with her husband and included an instrument that spoke of her requesting and demanding license from Juan Teran, though this was an exception to her many debts.

The one instance when women regularly requested license from their husbands was when married couples mutually borrowed monies with formally notarized instruments. The standard language normally utilized by notaries in this instance explained that the married couple appeared before the notary to make a legal instrument; the woman, before all other acts, "requested and demanded" license from her husband to sign and swear the instrument. Once granted by the husband, the license could not be revoked. This legal act was then followed by a declaration in which the married couple proclaimed they were borrowing money, buying property, or whatever was to occur with one voice, jointly [de mancomún]. In effect, the declaration placed the personal property of both the husband and the wife at peril of debt collection, which required the couple to renounce the legal protections in Spanish law against a husband or wife being responsible for the spouse's debt. In essence, the request and demand for license in this situation acted as a legal renunciation of those privileges, and clarified to all parties involved that dowry property, communal property, or the husband's personal estate were all subject to repayment of the loan or as collateral on the property. Interestingly, in cases where married couples borrowed from women, the creditors' marital status was rarely, if ever, noted, nor any license indicated.[80]

Female lenders controlled all of the cumulative debts of Ponze. Only one of the loans was made with a formal, notarized instrument—the same that carried license. The rest of the debts were made with simple instruments, witnessed and signed, but not notarized. The court still enforced these debts. Ponze's report of her debts included the following:

Doña Manuela Sandoval,	
with a notarized loan instrument	220 pesos
Doña Gregoria Salazar,	
with a simple instrument	110 pesos
The widow of Señor Angulo,	
with a simple instrument	73 pesos
Señora Doña Antonia Donoso,	
without an instrument	20 pesos
Doña Francisca Arias,	
with a simple instrument	50 pesos
Doña Josefa Andrade,	
with a simple instrument	60 pesos
Doña Antonia Velasquez,	
with a simple instrument	30 pesos
Doña Rosa Arisa,	
with a simple instrument	38 pesos
Doña Petrona Camacho,	
without an instrument	30 pesos
Plus, monies she owed her son,	
Don José Ribadeneyra	30 pesos
Total debts:	661 pesos

In the instruments presented in the case, none of the lenders ever referenced either marital status or any form of consent for the loans made. The largest of the loans was the only one certified by an official notarized document (*protocolo*). The extensive use of simple, non-notarized contracts suggests that women's participation in an informal debt economy was extensive, and largely invisible to analyses of the debt economy dependent on protocolos. Likewise, those simple instruments of the informal debt economy were always gender neutral. The court's rejection of the argument questioning those loans made without male intervention provides further evidence for customary autonomous female economic identities.

Issues of gender right were most likely to appear at moments of tactical necessity: this was the case in the arrest of Maria Ortiz and Ygnacia Paredes in April of 1774.[81] Maria and Ygnacia found themselves in the recogimiento of Santa Marta for having publicly insulted an officer of the court and the administration of royal justice, hurling at an alcalde of the cabildo the most "denigrating words." Maria and Ygnacia had come to the cabildo court for a verbal hearing of a petty dispute with an unidentified third party. When the presiding magistrate, Alcalde Ordinario Don Pablo de Unda y Luna, ruled against the women, they began to berate him as unjust, and continued to do so outside the court in the plaza mayor. Don Pablo proceeded to have the two arrested and put in jail, despite their protestations that an alcalde ordinario did not have the ability to arrest married women. The claim is interesting, because the women had initiated a verbal hearing outside the presence of the husbands, and because it was only in the face of possible punishment that they invoked their status as married women (*mugeres casadas*), arguing that Don Pablo's actions contravened the right of the women's husbands to manage their relationship to the legal system. His actions, though, were upheld upon further investigation, and the women remained in jail. Gender rights, including rights in the form of licensure, most often appeared in cases where the litigants perceived a tactical advantage in the prosecution or defense of a claim. Given that 67 percent of cases involving women as primary litigants did not invoke licensure or male representation, either as a proactive proclamation or as a reactive defensive maneuver, it would appear that the relative tactical appeal of gendered prerogatives was weak in the corregimiento. In fact, the majority of women in the corregimiento of Quito who engaged the legal system in the closing decades of Spanish rule did so assuming an independent legal identity that included the right to make and defend both criminal and civil legal actions without the intervention of the men in their lives. What then, do the cases say of the broader concept of women's legal and socioeconomic status and identity?

ECONOMIC INTERESTS, LEGAL ACTIONS

The corregimiento's nonlicensed litigants performed every imaginable legal and economic role, as plaintiffs, defendants, creditors, debtors, guardians, executors of wills, eyewitnesses, and even as contract witnesses. As discussed above, the bulk of civil litigation transcribed by the First Notary dealt with property disputes, largely loan and testament conflicts. These cases were clearly dominated by women of all types of known and unknown marital status acting without consent, as independent legal and economic agents. The loan disputes provide significant evidence for the important role women played as mid- and small-level lenders in the corregimiento. As with religious corporations and secular male lenders, women readily utilized legal resources to force derelict debtors to pay overdue loans. Female lenders regularly requested that male borrowers be jailed in order to force repayments. Female nonpayers also were sued, but, with one exception, were not jailed. This gendered difference was a special privilege afforded in the Spanish legal heritage, which, as mentioned above, prevented women from being arrested for their own debts barring criminal activity or for the debts of others, including for the debts of their husbands.

The debt litigation demonstrates the important role women played as small and medium lenders in the corregimiento. Sixty-three debt prosecutions from the fifteen sample years (1765–1769, 1785–1789, 1805–1809) included nonlicensed female plaintiffs and defendants. Of a total of ninety-one litigants, fifty-nine were plaintiffs suing to ensure repayment of monies owed them by male or female debtors. The remaining thirty-two female litigants were defendants. Both categories were dominated by women who omitted reference to their marital status, with widows a distant second (Table 3.2). Note, however, that widows were proportionately represented much higher as defendants. The amounts under dispute ranged from a paltry 8 pesos up to an astounding debt of 6,000 pesos.[82] The role women played as creditors radiated from their ready access to the limited market of liquid cash through the service economy as well as hard assets, particularly in the form of jewelry and real estate.

Table 3.2. Nonlicensed Debt Litigants by Status

	NO STATUS	MARRIED	WIDOWED	SINGLE	RELIGIOUS	TOTAL
Plaintiffs	37	6	9	4	3	59
Defendants	15	7	8	2	0	32
TOTAL	52	13	17	6	3	91

SOURCE: AN/Q 1NJ 43#47, 87#112, 220#255.

Several clues as to women's position as creditors have already emerged in Chapter 2. Harkening back to the assault of Thomasa Cuellos in Santa Bárbara in 1785, the attack was prompted by a dispute over property Cuellos was holding in pawn at her street-side shop.[83] The prominence of women in the petty commerce sector of the economy placed them in a convenient position to make the type of short-term and low-quantity loans typical of the pawnshop. The tragic case of Josef de Mena, who borrowed jewelry from numerous quiteñas to finance gambling and young women, likewise suggests that specifically female forms of moveable property like jewelry were a potential source of cash.[84] The jewelry Mena borrowed from three different women eventually was located on the shelves of another street-side shop, pawned for cash. Evidence suggests that pawning and loaning out jewelry was practiced by anyone with access to property, large and small. On February 17, 1794, slave Rafaela Matheu performed postmortem inventories of the jewelry and clothing of her recently deceased master, the Marquesa de Maenza, at the request of the estate's executor.[85] The inventory included records of the ingress and outflow of various types of property reaching back into the 1780s, providing an intensive view into credit flows managed, surprisingly enough, by a slave woman. There was a dizzying array of pieces of jewelry and bundles of different types of cloth loaned out on behalf of the Marquesa, as well as pieces she held in pawn for people, including many diamonds, pearls, emeralds, necklaces, earrings, crosses, broaches, candlesticks, jewel-encrusted butterfly figurines, reliquaries, bracelets, silver plates, glasses, jeweled buckles, velvets, brocades, alter cloth, sheets, towels, other types of cloth, gold pens with diamond tips, and more. The Marquesa had pawned one particular pair of bracelets for 500 pesos. The inventories demonstrated a continual flow of jewelry, cloth, and other pieces of movable property changing hands in short-term loans for use or cash. Even wealthy individuals used property in this manner, in part because of the short supply of minted monies in the city. The Marquesa certainly was a wealthy woman, and Rafaela's inventory also included a list of nineteen slaves, including her, that belonged to the estate.

Accepting hocked assets for small loans or outright purchase and resale made shopkeepers vulnerable to accusations, sometimes well founded, of fencing stolen goods. Twice in just five years, merchant Antonia Perez (also known as *La Corbacha*)[86] was accused of selling stolen goods. In September 1785, she first found herself under arrest at the request of Dr. Ramon Yepes, a lawyer of the royal Audiencia, for attempting to sell a set of silver candlesticks that were supposedly his.[87] The attorney provided the court-sworn testimony from three separate silversmiths who stated the candlesticks were the same as a pair originally made by master silversmith Manuel Rodriguez that had gone missing from the home of Doña Rosa Chiriboga, wife of the Alferes Real Don Mariano Donoso. Furthermore, Yepes claimed that Antonia Perez had attempted to influence Rodriguez and a second silversmith, Andres de los Rios, into providing false testimony concerning the provenance of the candlesticks. In her own written response to the charges, Perez admitted the candlesticks came from Chiriboga, but she claimed they were part of a transaction for a gold rosary and several pieces of silver Chiriboga had purchased from Perez's store. At her request, the notary took the actual candlesticks to the home of Rosa Chiriboga for her identification. Chiriboga claimed she did not recognize these particular pieces, and so the court ordered that the case proceed to the confession stage. Perez's confession began with her self-identification as "Antonia Perez, native of this city, 35 years old, widow of Antonio Miño, and merchant business dealer." After the confession, Perez requested that she be cleared of the charges and released to care for the Christian education of her children. Yepes then made a new round of theft charges, identifying a number of silver pieces in her store he claimed had been stolen. The dueling testimony between the accusers of Antonia Perez (La Corbacha) and the defenders of Antonia Perez, merchant, continued through November 1785 when she was ultimately released.

In July 1790, Perez found herself in Santa Marta again, this time accused of fencing jewelry robbed from the home of Don Jose Freyle y Ante.[88] Freyle, appearing on behalf of his wife Doña Maria Ygnacia Osorio, claimed that several pairs of his wife's earrings showed up for sale in Perez's store. Perez responded with sworn statements from Dr. Don Josef Cevallos, a priest, and Doña Alexandra Lara who claimed they witnessed Maria Ygnacia Osorio give the earrings to Perez to sell on her behalf. This time, rather than languish in jail, Perez also requested and was granted representation by Mariano Suares y Castrillon, then serving as the at-no-cost crown-appointed attorney for the poor. Perez was again vindicated, largely, it seems, by the strength of testimony on her behalf. It appears from the case that the charges stemmed from Osorio's decision to sell property unbeknownst to her husband. In both cases, the frequent use of general stores in the city as a means to the cash economy through either pawn or consignment opened the city's small merchants and vendors to allegations of trafficking in stolen property.

Women's participation in the credit-debt system of the city was not limited, however, to running pawns and owning jewelry. As in the case above of Victoria Ponze, female lenders repeatedly appeared on lists of creditors in legal proceedings against bankrupted individuals. For example, in October 1790, Josef Marsilla provided the court a memorial of all the individuals he owed and who owed him.[89] Marsilla, who listed his occupation as embroiderer (*franjero*) found himself at the time in the Audiencia court jail at the requested of his creditors. He itemized his debts and credits as

Señora Marquesa de Selva Alegre	200 pesos
Doña Basilia Ante	100 pesos
Doña Ygnaica Freyre	51 pesos
Maria Balberde	60 pesos
Petrona Carrera	75 pesos
Justa Ximenes	77 pesos

Thus, Marsilla found himself in jail at the request of six women to whom he owed a total of 563 pesos. Note that the lenders carry as a group a combination of honorifics—one Señora Marquesa, two doñas, and three women without any special title. As such, the list indicates the role of creditor was occupied by women across the social spectrum, dependent only on access to property available to loan. Four individuals also owed Marsilla:

Señor Mayorazgo Don Francisco Freyre	76 pesos
Doña Basilia Ante	6 pesos
Ramon Villalva	24 pesos
Mariano Baca	8 pesos

So, together his debtors owed him a paltry 118 pesos, including the 6 pesos from his creditor Doña Basilia Ante. It is likely that the debt totals from each individual represented both debts from single loans as well as those accumulated over time.

Another memorial involved Don Manuel Velasquez Choquicondor, the principal cacique and indigenous governor of the pueblo of Guápulo, which is located on the eastern edge of the city, just off the barrio of San Blas. The pueblo was of note to the religious and social life of Quito as home of the Virgin de Guadalupe, a statue often paraded through the streets of Quito to combat illness, earthquakes, and other natural disasters. Don Manuel had amassed a rather impressive 1,690 pesos of outstanding debt, a slight majority of which was held by women:

Doña Josefa Canisares	500 pesos
Don Andres Saez	200 pesos
Don José Solis	100 pesos
Don Nieves Velasquez	400 pesos
Doña Laura Parra	200 pesos
Doña Juana Andrade	100 pesos
Doña Agustina Moro	60 pesos
Don Manuel Hidalgo	100 pesos
Doña Pasquala Justato	20 pesos
Don Vicente Solis	10 pesos

The cacique was seeking protection from imminent collection and foreclosure on his home. He explained he was unable to pay his creditors "due to unfortunate circumstances and setbacks I have suffered in the form of daily losses and bad breaks I have experienced in the business negotiations I have kept."[90] The cacique was granted, with "the tacit consent of the creditors" a not-unusual five-year extension on repayment of his obligations. Of significance to this current discussion, women held a sizeable 880 pesos, or 52 percent of the indigenous official's debts.

As the information on nonlicensed litigants in debt and property disputes suggests, together with these memorial examples, gender was not a limiting factor of the ability of creditors to legally press their debtors for repayment. Indeed, women may well have been at a certain competitive advantage in the lending game because they had access to capital through jewelry, houses, dowry wealth, the arras, and other property brought into marriage, as well as protections against debtors' prison for themselves. Thus, it was conceivable that women could also borrow sums of money to be redistributed in the revolving debt economy without fear of imprisonment for nonpayment.

The debt disputes hint at the active role women played in greasing the economic wheels of the city in the closing decades of Spanish rule. Creditor was but one of the economic roles occupied by women in the cases of the First Notary. Many other clues point to their centrality in the economic life of the city. An 1805 list of subjects targeted for collection of a special tax to pay for repairs to the main thoroughfare in the barrio of San Sebastian included forty-four neighborhood residents expected to contribute between 4 reales and 8 pesos.[91] City government itself provided 52 pesos and 1 real, in addition to the requested individual contributions. Twenty-two of the forty-five residents required to pay were women, who together accounted for 158 pesos, 3 reales, of the total amount the municipality intended to collect. On the tax roll, assessed at the household level, these women represented themselves as legal heads of household. Of course, none of the residents was thrilled with the prospect of paying a one-time contribution of up to 8 pesos for the construction project, and the list of names is followed in the folio by a long procession of complaints opposing the exaction, filed by both men and women.

It is likely that many of the women on the list were employed provisioning the city with bulk and prepared foods, cloth, and other comestibles from permanent street-side stores and in the public markets. Evidence points to women as direct and indirect proprietors of such stores. In May 1785, for example, Doña Rosalia Pasmiño was arrested in her tienda under suspicion of colluding with a number of other female grocers to sell sugar at less than the price fixed by the cabildo.[92] In her confession, another store owner, Ysabel Freyre, alleged the price collusion was done at the behest of the source of their sugar supply, the administrator of the office that administered expropriated Jesuit properites (*junta de temporalidades*) in Ibarra, which led to accusations that the scheme represented another attempt by Ibarran sugar interests to take control of the Audiencia sugar trade as they had in the lead-up to the 1765 aguardiente crisis. The public face of the intrigue was not sugar magnates, but rather women who owned and operated street-level groceries.

One month later, in June 1787, Manuela Ñassu, a married indigenous resident of Quito, was arrested on accusations of robbery; the accusations were made by Clara Santos.[93] Ñassu worked in the city cleaning a number of stores, including one owned and operated by Santos. No details on Santos's marital status were mentioned in bringing the complaint against Ñassu, only her proprietorship of the store. As an Indian, Ñassu was entitled to and received representation in the case by the general protector of Indians. Santos argued that Ñassu's access to her store, along with the others she cleaned, provided her alone with the opportunity to steal the missing property. In October 1785, widow Mariana Reyes had the manager of a pulpería she owned in Quito arrested for embezzling both the store's profits and stocks.[94] In November 1788, Salvadora Velasquez was sued by Gabriel de Zenisagoya for back rent owed on a Quito store of his.[95] She was ordered to appear in three days and pay the 30-peso debt.

Women from a variety of social statuses, not just the proprietors of various types of stores or those with access to vast amounts of jewelry or other goods, found their way to the courts to seek legal redress as part of economic activities. In September 1786, Ana Tereza de Arias, a resident of Quito, brought suit against the estate of her long-term employer Don Felipe Nicolas Gonzales for back wages.[96] Arias and her daughter had served as domestics for Gonzales reaching back to 1772; they had been employed to wash his clothes, darn his socks and stockings, and press his best clothes twice a week. In return for this service, Arias was promised an annual salary of 24 pesos. For years, on every Thursday and Sunday, Arias washed, ironed, and repaired Gonzales's clothing, as well as that of other members of the household. When Gonzales died, the executor of his estate refused to pay her for that year's labor. The judge, referring to Arias as a *concierto* (a term generally applied to indigenous servants or hacienda workers), accepted her complaint and ordered an investigation into her claims.

Unfortunately, the file ends abruptly without a recording final ruling, but the anecdotal data contained in the litigation as well as the cases discussed above provide solid evidence for a broad economic presence for women in the corregimiento of Quito, active as buyers and sellers, borrowers and lenders, laborers and employers. It may well be that a preference for using simple loan instruments, rather than formally notarized writs, and consignment sales or pawning of moveable goods have concealed the extent to which women acted as creditors by keeping much of their activity out of the notaries' books. It must be noted, however, that simple instruments were still enforced by the courts. The ancillary details of the litigation discussed above, with its prevalence of nonlicensed actors and economic agents, confirms the presence of women as homeowners, household heads, taxpayers, and shopkeepers revealed in census materials such as the Santa Bárbara Padrón. Customary actions and customary presence found women in late-Spanish Quito possessing significant economic autonomy.

CONCLUSION

In June 1809, Ventura Guzman filed suit before one of the municipal council's ordinary judges to compel Julian de Echeverria to resolve a disputed house sale worth 840 pesos.[97] Ventura presented with the petition two receipts for payment to Echeverria, including the original purchase agreement. Under this agreement, Guzman paid 200 pesos up front to Echeverria, with an additional 400 pesos to be paid two months hence when she was to finish selling another house she owned near the Cruz de Piedra. The remaining 200 pesos, plus 5 percent interest, was going to be paid as rent. Guzman was buying a property in the neighborhood of the La Merced Church, in the parish of Santa Bárbara, in an area known as de los Barberos (Neighborhood of the Barbers). In the instrument, she is described as "Doña Ventura Guzman, resident of this City, of celibate status."[98] As a single woman, she carried no consent to engage in this rather large real estate transaction, but rather stood on her own legal identity as Doña and vecina. The moniker of celibate status (*estado celibe*) began to appear to indicate unmarried women in place of the adjective single (*soltera*) in the first decade of the nineteenth century, perhaps as fallout from the *fin de siècle* institutional obsessions with sexual behaviors. Guzman, for her part, complied with the details of the deal, only to discover that the provenance of the house she bought was contested, and Echeverria did not have the right to make the sale. That sparked litigation to recover Guzman's 840 pesos. This time, the calculus of her legal identity changed a fraction. In petitioning the municipal court, Guzman dropped reference to both her title (Doña) and her marital status, and instead filed under the rubric, "Ventura Guzman, Indian resident of the city, in conformance with the law, appear before Your Honor and Say. . . ."[99] The doña purchasing an expensive house in the parish of Santa Bárbara, not far from the center of royal power in El Sagrario, became an indigenous woman in need of the special protections offered by the crown's protector of the Indians. Guzman appealed to this right, and was granted access to the legal resources freely available to the crown's indigenous subjects. With representation of the Audiencia-appointed attorney, she was able to force Echeverria to make restitution on the fraudulent real estate deal, as well as for the costs incurred by the litigation.

Guzman craftily reinvented her legal self to maximize the legal resources available to protect her material interests. Her statuses as a single woman, as a vecina of Quito, as an Indian, as an honorable doña, as a homeowner, as a debtor, and as a plaintiff were nodes along a spectrum of identities to which she could appeal, given the exigencies of concrete, historical circumstances. Guzman's decision to emphasize various points on this spectrum reflected perceived tactical advantages in the broader strategy of asserting whatever special privileges, and downplaying whatever potential restrictions, applied to her legal personhood. This ability to assert contingent identities was the essence of the Spanish legal inheritance, which granted through a formal recognition of customary practice, both legal and economic identity to Ventura Guzman. Despite the restrictive impulses of Bourbon-era imperial discourses and the whims of governing bureaucrats, gender was not the determinative factor in women's ability to maintain either autonomous economic or autonomous legal identities. In large part, this protection was due to the special privileges of the legal inheritance, privileges that cunning litigants were able to manipulate to their advantage. These litigants were not just wealthy Spanish women, but included all social groups of the city, from washerwomen to society matrons, mestizas to pardas, and Indians to Europeans. The unlicensed economic and legal activities of the corregimiento's women constituted significant evidence for independent economic and juridical identities, carved out of male domination through customary practice and assertive legal protections. What, though, would become of the customary ability of women to assert their property and legal rights when those special privileges were removed? What effect would "equality before the law" have on the ability of women and other dominated groups in the new society of Ecuador to mitigate their domination?

SECTION II

1809–1830

Since the French nation has subjected through conquest nearly all Spain, and José Bonaparte has crowned himself king in Madrid, and, therefore, since the Junta Central, which represented our legitimate sovereign, has been extinguished, the people of this capital—faithful to God, the patria, and the king—have created another [junta] equally supreme and interim . . . until His Majesty recovers the Peninsula or comes to America to govern.

—Marqués de Selva Alegre
Quito, August 1809[1]

As with the case of the Rebellion of the Barrios and Bourbon rule, the arrival of Atlantic liberalism to the Audiencia of Quito was marked by a flashpoint political crisis. And, as before, this local political crisis had its genesis in royal actions from the peninsula. Section II follows the story of a transformed legal culture in Quito by first recounting the emergence of local ruling juntas in the city, and by then documenting the effects of Spanish liberalism, and then Gran Colombian xx republicanism on women's access to legal resources. The changes of the early republican period began in the contest between local and imperial liberalisms during the era of Fernando VII's exile from the throne. Many of the legal changes associated with the Gran Colombian period actually date to this moment, under the guidance of Spain's Cádiz Constitution. Ultimately, the age of independence proved the beginning of a quick decline in women's legal standing, including the end of their informal political participation as vecinas. The particularities of the political crisis of 1809–1813 provides invaluable context to understanding that process of decline.

CHAPTER FOUR

QUITO *1809*

In Defense of Religion, King, and Patria

———•———

INTRODUCTION

The era of Bourbon governance was coming to an end even as indigenous Doña Ventura Guzman played to the ambiguities of the Spanish legal system to recover her 840-peso investment in the Santa Bárbara house. Would she have imagined just two months later, in August 1809, the quiteño elite would step into a leading, if temporary role in the political revolutions sweeping the Spanish monarchy? Could she have imagined that in just two short decades those revolutions would end with the dismantling of almost the entirety of the Spanish Empire, and the emergence of a slew of modern nation-states, Spain and Ecuador included? In the course of this political revolution, the legal culture that allowed Doña Ventura to reconstruct her judicial self-representations was transformed by the larger Atlantic liberal revolution. The years of royal abjuration (1808–1814) were revolutionary throughout the Spanish monarchy, and certainly in the corregimiento of Quito, which witnessed the establishment of two local autonomist juntas in 1809 and 1810.[1] The events that brought about the collapse of the Spanish Empire radiated, as had the political crises of the 1760s, from questions of authority and legitimacy. Unlike the 1760s, this crisis ultimately yielded a new state built on a new theory of sovereignty and a newly conceived legal culture. The labyrinthine heritage of Spanish jurisprudence, with its overlapping jurisdictions, special privileges, subject obligations, accumulated laws, and structural recognition of customary practice, was abandoned in favor of the principles of equality before the law, separation of powers, and legal precedence that were essential to the liberal republicanism.

In the early years of the republic, Spanish law persisted as the new government of Gran Colombia reaffirmed the continued authority of the *Siete Partidas*, the *Recopilación de Leyes de Indias*, and the *Nueva Recopilación de Leyes de Castilla*.[2] However, the context within which these laws were enforced dramatically transformed their specific implications for dominated groups in quiteño society. The colonial system of contradiction, legal fiction, and custom, messy as it was, maintained a rough tension between communal harmony and justice and the interests of dominating institutions and elites. Dominated corporate groups such as indigenous communities and women vested the colonial courts with significant legitimacy, and used legal resources quite effectively. The flexibility and contingency inherent in the judicial state's messy labyrinth of legal codes, jurisdictional disputes, magistrate clientelism, and special rights had enabled women to constrain the patriarchal tendencies of the law and, to a significant extent, within quiteño society itself. . . . Special status rights and obligations, rather than simply serving the interests of a moribund nobility, combined with the structural role of customary practice to limit male prerogative systemically. The liberal revolution that birthed the new republic retheorized the legal organization of sovereignty, property, and justice. As counterintuitive as it may seem, this sea change in the relationship among law, justice, and sovereignty would ultimately prove to be a dramatic step backwards for women and indigenous communities alike in the coming decades.[3]

At the heart of this transformation was a realignment of sovereignty, away from the king's privileged position as the arbiter of a judicial state engaged by its subjects through an array of potential juridical statuses. In its place emerged the executive and legislative authority of the sovereign nation-state, mediated at least in theory by contract between rights-bearing, property-owning citizens. The Bourbon state labored long and hard to centralize its authority, modernize its bureaucracy, rationalize its economic policy, and dismantle a deep-running decentralized, customary, and contingent legal culture. Relative to its successes in other policy areas, the reform of legal practice was largely a failure.

The legal culture of republican Quito changed relatively rapidly in the 1810s and 1820s as a local manifestation of the Atlantic liberal revolution, even if republican government did not emerge overnight. Its contested emergence bore the marks of the specific trajectory of the Spanish political and legal heritage. That said, what resulted was still certainly the product of an Atlantic Enlightenment morphed into an Atlantic liberal revolution.[4] The tension between royalists and autonomists in the 1810s, prior to and then later coterminous with outright civil war, has obscured the extent to which liberal political and legal changes transformed the Spanish monarchy, including in the royalist camp. From the consolidation in 1809 of the *Junta Suprema Central* through the emergence of the Regency a year later, and on to the Cortes of Cádiz and the Cádiz Constitution of 1812, the global Spanish monarchy embraced political liberalism in the absence of King Fernando VII, even as local autonomist movements in the kingdoms of the Americas agitated for home rule. Thus, there were simultaneous political revolutions occurring on both sides of the Atlantic, and within the royalist forces in the Americas, that manifested as a sort of dueling popular sovereignties. As such, the dynamic of the 1810s was not exactly that of liberal/conservative or revolutionary/royalist as much as it was between contending visions of the locus of legitimate authority in the absence of a legitimate sovereign—residing either with peninsular officials and their designated imperial appointees, or in the capital cities of the kingdoms of the Americas. These concurrents transformed legal culture, as well as politics, in the kingdom and corregimiento of Quito, changes that accelerated further with the province's incorporation into Simón Bolívar's Gran Colombia in 1822.

It could go without saying that liberal ideas and republican governance did not appear whole cloth in 1808 with the invasion of the Iberian peninsula by the forces of Napoleon Bonaparte. Over the course of several decades, liberalism and enlightenment scientism percolated throughout the Atlantic world, carried to faraway corners including highland Quito. New forms of knowledge were disseminated by scientific missions like that of the French cartographer Charles Marie de la Condamine, who visited the region in the 1740s in an effort to measure the circumference of the globe at the equator; naturalist adventurers like Alexander von Humboldt, who traveled Mexico and South America from 1799 to 1804; as well as by both locally born quiteños and peninsular Spaniards who circulated the greater Spanish monarchy for educational, bureaucratic, and economic activities.[5]

Books propagating enlightenment ideas, many if not most of which were outlawed by the Spanish Inquisition, trafficked the Americas with regularity, carried surreptitiously by private citizens, priests, and bureaucrats alike.[6] There was, in fact, a tremendous circulation of both American and peninsular-born Spaniards in the ranks of the ecclesiastical and secular bureaucracies, as well as significant flows of information throughout the Atlantic.[7] These disseminations in the late-eighteenth and early-nineteenth centuries combined with local legal and political cultures to produce the hybrid conditions of the liberal revolution that swept the realm from 1808 to 1814.

This chapter details the confluence of global and local political developments in Quito during the first phase of liberal revolution. After a brief overview of the men and women who figured as precursors (and often participants) in Quito's revolutionary moment, this chapter turns to the events surrounding a pair of local ruling juntas in the city in 1809 and 1810. It follows Quito's concurrent participation in the liberal revolutions sweeping the Spanish monarchy from the moment of Fernando VII's abdication through his restoration. I will not narrate the entire process of the kingdom's incorporation into Bolívar's Gran Colombia, but rather focus on the period that birthed the dramatic shift in political and legal culture that was fully realized in the 1820s. As this chapter will confirm, the rise of a liberal republican legal culture actually dates to the crisis of royal authority in the early 1810s, rather than with Quito's liberation in 1822—and it held uncertain prospects for the vecinas of Quito's barrios.

THE GENERATION OF 1809

Early in the morning on August 10, 1809, the president of the Audiencia of Quito, Conde Ruiz de Castilla, was startled awake by an orderly, bearing a letter addressed, "From the Sovereign Junta to the Conde Ruiz, ex-president of Quito."[8] Ruiz's personal secretary reported that the conde then dressed himself and read the following,

> The present unsettled state of Spain, the total annihilation of the lawfully constituted authorities, and the dangers of the crown of the beloved Fernando VII and his domains falling into the hands of the tyrant of Europe, have impelled our trans-Atlantic brothers to form provincial governments for

their personal security, as well as against the machinations of some of their traitorous countrymen, unworthy of the name of Spaniards, as against the arms of the common enemy: the loyal inhabitants of Quito, resolved to secure to their legitimate King and Master this part of his kingdom, have established a sovereign junta in this city of San Francisco de Quito, of which, and by the command of his Serene Highness the President and the vocal members, I have the honor to inform your lordship, and to announce to you, that the functions of the members of the old government have ceased: God preserve your Lordship many years. Hall of the Junta in Quito, August 10th, 1809: Morales, Secretary of the Interior.[9]

Don Juan Dios de Morales was no stranger to the president. Morales was an American-born lawyer who had served, but been terminated, as a secretary in the government of Conde Ruiz de Castilla's predecessor, the popular François-Louis Héctor y Noyelle, Baron de Carondelet.[10] According to Stevenson, he had hoped to regain his position in the new government of Ruiz, but was passed over in favor of another young lawyer, Don Tomás de Arechaga, who had accompanied Ruiz from Peru. The insinuation of jealousy, while likely true as Arechaga and Morales became bitter rivals in the wake of the 1809 junta, underestimates the degree of political commitment that Morales brought to the revolutionary endeavor. He was a fervent liberal. Stevenson observed that Morales, "was possessed of a strong mind, had received a liberal education, and having been employed many years in the secretary's office, had obtained a knowledge of the affairs of the government and an insight into the intrigues of the Spanish court."[11] He was also one of a cadre of ambitious American-born men and women, reformers who sought liberal changes in response to the reform agenda of Bourbon absolutism. Born and raised in the second half of the eighteenth century, the reformers had only known the activist Bourbon state that set upon the Audiencia in the wake of the Rebellion of the Barrios, an experience they filtered through an increasingly liberal education that embraced enlightenment claims to the scientific foundation of knowledge and to liberal political economy.

The most famous of them all was Francisco Javier Eugenio de Santa Cruz y Espejo (1747–1795). Eugenio Espejo was the consummate enlightenment provocateur, who used polemic and satire, often pseudonymously, to circulate scathing social, educational, political, and economic critiques of late-colonial quiteño society. Espejo and his writings were made central to the nationalist historiography of Ecuador in the late-nineteenth century by Federico González Suárez, who, through both his multivolume history of Ecuador and his publication of an edited selection of Espejo's writings, placed Espejo at the center of the story that culminated with Ecuador's independence.[12] Espejo did not live to see quiteño independence, dying from complications of a jail term in 1795. Yet, as early as 1810 officials were blaming him for, or crediting him with, the rebellion that ultimately led to the formation of the nation-state of Ecuador. Astuto notes that in a letter dated November 17, 1810, the disputed Audiencia President Joaquín Molina wrote to the Regency's secretary of state that the 1809 conspirators in Quito "had utilized the seditious plans of a Quiteño named Espejo, who had died there some years before."[13] Writing in the early 1830s, Augustín Salazar y Lozano portrayed the period between 1809 and 1814 as the fulfillment the "oracle's" vision published some forty years earlier in the *Primicias de la cultura de Quito*, a direct allusion to Espejo.[14] His early writings tended to center on social and educational critique, rooted in his own experiences studying medicine at the Dominican college of San Fernando in the mid-1760s as well as civil and canon law at the University of Santo Tomás, where he was degreed in 1770. He was licensed to practice medicine in Quito in 1772, a career choice that may well have been influenced by the death of a younger brother in 1764 from smallpox. His publishing career began in 1779 with a pseudonymously published tract, *El Nuevo Luciano de Quito*, which satirically criticized Dominican education in the city. He followed this up with further criticism of education, including *Marco Porcio Caton* (1780), and the *Ciencia blancardina* (1780).[15] In 1781, a manuscript attributed to Espejo titled *El retrato de golilla* began circulating Quito. This time, the satirical eye was turned toward Carlos III and José de Gálvez, the consummate Bourbon reformer who was then serving as the head minister of the council on the Indies. Its publication would come back to haunt Espejo by the end of the decade, when he was called to task for it by the viceroy in Bogotá. In 1785, Espejo published what González Suárez considered to be his most important work, the *Reflexiones sobre . . . un método seguro para preservar a los pueblos de los viruelas*, which both criticized and corrected Quito's medical establishment on a plan to control the spread of smallpox in the city.[16]

Despite the importance of the work and its solicitation by the Audiencia, it was not well received by the medical community. Together with his caustic satirizations of the quiteño medical establishment, the hostility of the response to the *Reflexiones* prompted authorities to ask Espejo to leave Quito. Controversy followed him on his travels. A critique of the treatment of indigenous communities around Riobamba (*Defensa de los curas de riobamba*) sparked a series of defamation lawsuits and eight satirical letters (*Cartas riobambenses*) that pushed the limit of royal patience. In 1787, the president of the Audiencia had Espejo arrested and deported to Bogotá to face allegations of disloyalty of *El retrato de golilla*. It turned out to be a radicalizing experience for Espejo.[17] In Bogotá, Espejo met Francisco Zea and Antonio Nariño; he also, it would turn out, befriended Juan Pío Montúfar, a quiteño Marqués. In concert with this group of political radicals (Nariño was arrested in 1794 for translating *The Rights of Man* into a Spanish edition), Espejo's critical abilities increasingly turned to political economy.[18]

Returning from Bogotá, Espejo joined together with many of Quito's most elite residents to form the Society of Friends of the Country (*Sociedad de Amigos de País*), a group founded to advocate for economic and political renewal of the Audiencia. The economic societies of the Spanish monarchy played an important role in the emergence of an incipient public sphere of political-economic debate.[19] Quito's society was short-lived, but it fostered important developments to help establish a civil society in Quito. The city's first periodical, *Primicias de la cultura de Quito*, was established by the society, and edited by Espejo, though it lasted only seven issues.[20] The Society held its first meeting on November 30, 1791, at the old Jesuit College; at that meeting, members elected the president of the Audiencia, Don Luis Muñoz de Guzmán as head of the group. Quito's enlightened Bishop José Perez de Calama, reformer of the curriculum of the University of Santo Tomás, was chosen as director, with Espejo as the secretary. The list of original members included a number of individuals who joined the revolutionary cause in 1809 and 1810, including the Marqués de Selva Alegre, the Marqués de Villa Orellana, Don José Javier Ascusavi, Don Pedro Quiñones, and Don Antonio Tejada.[21] In fact, it was through the Society that Espejo's lineage to liberal revolution in Quito was best secured.

Juan Pío Montúfar y Larrea, named the second Marqués de Selva Alegre, was born in 1758 and was one of a number of titled nobility in the Audiencia who embraced political, economic, and social reforms in the name of king, religion, and homeland (*patría*). He was the son of two distinguished families. Juan Pío Montúfar y Fraso, the first Marqués de Selva Alegre, was a knight of the Order of Santiago and president of the Audiencia of Quito from the early 1750s through his death in 1761, when he was succeeded by Manuel Rubio de Arévalo. Juan Pío's mother was Doña Theresa Larrea, a native of the quiteña elites.[22] Along with his brother Pedro and son Carlos, Juan Pío was intimately involved with creole agitation for an improved political economy in the kingdom of Quito. He was a founding member, along with Espejo and Bishop Pérez de Calama, of the *Sociedad de Amigos de País*. Montúfar befriended Espejo in Bogotá, during the latter's sojourn there in 1788–1789 at the moment when Espejo's own politics were being radicalized through his friendships with Nariño and Zea.[23] Unlike Espejo, the Marqués de Selva Alegre had considerable resources to bring to bear on his reformist activism. At the time of his death, the appraisal of the Marqués's estate included four haciendas and a city-block-sized house in Quito. One of haciendas, named Chillo and located near Alangasí in the valley south and east of Quito, played an important role as a meeting place where much of the August 1809 conspiring took place. All told, the estate appraised at 124,093 pesos, 7 reales, with additional outstanding debts at 50,641 pesos, 4¾ reales.[24]

There was also José Mejía Lequerica, the illegitimate son of an Audiencia lawyer and a married quiteña, who was educated at the Colegio de San Fernando and later the Seminario de San Luis. In 1798, Mejía married Doña Manuela Santa Cruz y Espejo, the sister of Eugenio Santa Cruz y Espejo.[25] Mejía was well known for his erudition. Two years after his marriage to Doña Manuela, he obtained a chair in philosophy at San Luis, where he promoted the work of Copernicus, Kepler, Galileo, Francisco Suárez, and Descartes. He also was academically credentialed in medicine, and learned in civil law, botany, theology, and Latin. Mejía's combination of brilliance and commitment to progressive education brought on the ire of Quito's Dominican educational establishment. Just three years after attaining his chair in philosophy he was fired, which ultimately set him on a journey from Quito that would never see him return. In 1806, he left for Guayaquil and then Lima, and two years later he found himself in Spain where he became one of the Indies' most ardent liberal and defender in the Cortes of Cádiz.[26]

There was Captain Juan Salinas, a quiteño who rose in the ranks of the infantry in Panamá, and later returned to Quito where he served in the local garrison and became one of the core political conspirators. Dr. Don Jose Riofrio, the parish priest of Pintag in the Five Leagues of Quito, was a native quiteño who frequented Morales's home and came to loathe President Baron Carondelet.[27] There was Dr. Don Manuel Rodríguez de Quiroga, an attorney originally from Arequipa, who married a quiteña and whose temper led him to be fined and barred from arguing cases before the Audiencia during the presidency of Baron Carondelet. Stevenson reports that in response to this reprimand, Quiroga argued the tribunal was illegitimate, claiming, "the Regent and the Oidores had taken possession of their seats on the bench contrary to law, or held them contrary to justice; and he proved his assertions by stating the cases, quoting the laws, and citing the regulations of the tribunal." Stevenson continues, remarking, "This necessarily drew upon him the hatred of the members, and obliged him to leave the bar."[28] Quiroga's mind was thus honed in the technical arguments of the law that could be deployed to attack the legitimacy of Quito's political authorities.

Men were not the only participants amongst the Quito conspirators. Much of the actual work at establishing the first junta in Quito occurred at the home of Doñas Margarita and Manuela Cañizares. The salons (tertulias) that were held at Doña Manuela's house in El Sagrario were well-known meetings for political liberals. According to one letter writer who was close to the Cañizares family, Doña Manuela had a very close friendship with Quiroga.[29] There was Doña Manuela Santa Cruz y Espejo, the sister of Eugenio Santa Cruz y Espejo and wife to José Mejía Lequerica, whose correspondence with her husband was an important source of information on happenings in Spain. Agustín Salazar y Lozano account of 1809 specifically mentioned Doña María de la Vega, the wife of Juan Salinas, and Doña Rosa Sárate, wife of Nicolás de la Peña as well.[30] Manuela Sáenz, Quito's most famous female revolutionary, actually came of age politically in the tertulias and cafes of Lima, where she was taken when her

illegitimate peninsular father, Simon Saenz, left the Audiencia following his apprehension by the 1809 junta.[31] The names of these individual partisans associated with the generation of 1809 have been largely
preserved in association with revolutionary men. There are cracks
in the suppression of women's participation in events such as those
surrounding the events of 1809. We know, for example, that women
voted as vecinas and heads of household in the barrio elections to
choose representatives for the junta of 1809, even if the only names
preserved were those of Estefa Campuzano, Rosa Solano, Margarita
Orozco, and Manuela Solís.[32]

Morales and Quiroga, the core conspirators of Quito's liberal
reformers, announced their political leanings to Conde Ruiz de
Castilla shortly after his arrival to the city, if in slightly cryptic fashion. As part of the normal parades, festivities, and manifestations of
loyalty that occasioned newly arrived presidents and bishops, Morales
and Quiroga had produced a series of four plays for the Conde and
city's nobility. The quartet of pieces was performed by students
from the Colegio de San Fernando, and included *Cato*, the tragedies
Andromacha and *Zoraida*, and *Auraucana* [sic].[33] Stevenson noted
that these particular pieces seemed designed, "to inculcate a spirit of
freedom, a love of liberty, and principles of republicanism."[34] Liberal
and enlightenment ideas on legal, political, scientific, and economic
issues circulated the Audiencia of Quito for decades, despite the occasional futile attempt by crown officials to staunch their flow. The circumstances for their maturation finally burst forth in 1808 with the
French invasion of the Iberian kingdoms.

THE NAPOLEONIC CRISIS COMES TO QUITO

In early 1808, the Spanish crown was in crisis-level disarray. On
March 19, 1808, Carlos IV abdicated the throne, under pressure, to
his son, Fernando VII. Napoleon Bonaparte, angling to further cause
and profit from the instability of the Spanish throne, exploited the
weakness and in May 1808 forced Fernando VII to abdicate as well,
placing the royal family in exile at the French Château de Valençay. In
turn, Napoleon installed his brother, Joseph Bonaparte, on the Spanish
throne, precipitating a crisis of legitimacy that reached throughout the
global Spanish monarchy, as subjects in the kingdoms in Spain and the
Americas refused to recognize Bonaparte's authority.[35] Resistance to

the French ruler emerged immediately, and on May 2, 1808, Madrid rose up in revolt. Across Spain, local ruling committees (juntas) were established, dominated initially by the junta of Seville that refused to recognize the authority of the committee that Fernando VII had left in Madrid.[36] By September, the junta in Seville had ceded leadership to a single, national committee, the *Junta Suprema Central y Guvernativa de España e Indias* (Supreme Central Governing Committee of Spain and the Indies).[37]

As news of these events, from the abdication of Carlos IV through the formation of the Junta Central, filtered through Spain's American kingdoms, local subjects began to claim the same equal rights to home rule as those expressed by the local juntas of the peninsula. Word of Carlos IV's abdication officially arrived to the Audiencia in late July, four months after it had occurred.[38] The royal decree establishing the abdication was accompanied by a requirement to recognize and vow obedience to Fernando VII as the empire's "Natural Lord and King."[39] His reign was much shorter than the time needed for news of its commencement to traverse the empire, since the king had already abdicated two months before word of his ascension to office arrived. Restrepo reports that word of the events and a plea to secure the leadership of the Seville junta was sent from Seville to Bogotá on June 17, 1808. In response, on September 5, Viceroy Antonio Amar y Borbón held a public meeting at the viceregal palace to discuss the new situation, and to arrange a vow of loyalty to the Junta Suprema Central. The June 17 oficio from Seville was carried by Juan José Sanllorente, who was commissioned by the Junta Suprema to recruit support in New Granada. Some individuals present at the viceregal meeting expressed displeasure that the junta decided to name itself the Junta Suprema Central y Gubernativa de España e Indias without first consulting American Spaniards. Despite the point of pride, the assembled vowed support to Seville, and sent word further on to Popayán and Quito.[40]

As the Junta Suprema Central in Seville evolved into the Junta Suprema y Central, Amar y Borbón was ordered to circularize the viceroyalty with news of the abdications, the May 2 uprising, the formation of regional juntas, and the formation of the Junta Suprema Central, which he did on February 27, 1809.[41] The order was received in the Audiencia of Quito in March 1809, and indicated the political goal of the juntas and peninsular civil war as, "the defense of our Holy

Religion, . . . the restitution of the holy Person of our beloved King Fernando Séptimo [VII] and the Royal Family; and the liberty of the Homeland [patría]." This was the same formula adopted by the Quito junta some six months later. As Jaime Rodríguez has noted, peninsular reaction to the abdication of Fernando centered on regional polities, at the kingdom or Audiencia level. The formation of local juntas was justified under the authority of an old Spanish political principle that held that, in the absence of legitimate royal authority, sovereignty devolved to the people (*pueblo*).[42] The principle of ultimate popular sovereignty in the Hispanic world was long connected to a sense of communal justice (*equidad*) and customary rights (derecho vulgar) that defined the constellation of decentralized, contractual authority in the early modern Spanish monarchy. While this principle may have predated the early nineteenth century, the implications carried by its invocation in the wake of the spreading Atlantic liberal revolution were dramatically different from Quito's 1594 Rebellion of the Alcabalas, or 1765 Rebellion of the Barrios.

In a bid to secure the legitimacy of the Junta Central, local governments were instructed to hold public ceremonies marking the installation of the ad hoc government. As at moments of royal succession, the public ceremonies included cathedral and parochial Masses, the singing of the *Te Deum*, cabildo meetings, and public proclamations avowing obedience and fidelity to the duly appointed royal authorities.[43] Local acknowledgment of the junta was articulated on the basis of American claims to equal participation as part of the larger Spanish nation, such that the bishop of Cuenca articulated recognition of the junta as legitimated by its tie to the legitimacy of Fernando VII, who "ruled all of the [Spanish] Nation."[44] Though public displays of fidelity to the junta occurred during March in cathedrals and cabildos throughout the Audiencia, governing officials feared that instability on the peninsula would spill over to the Americas. Their fears were already realized with the discovery of a plot involving a number of the conspirators who were responsible for forming Quito's own Junta Suprema the following August. In late February 1809, two friars from the Order of La Merced, Fray Andrés Torresano and Fray Andrés Polo, reported to President Conde Ruiz de Castilla that they had been informed by Juan Salinas, then serving as captain of the Quito militia, of a plan to oust European Spaniards from Quito government and to replace them with officials elected from the city's "most respectable citizens."[45] Conde Ruiz de Castilla responded by opening a secret investigation under the authority of Oidor Felipe Fuertes Amar, the nephew of Santa Fé's Viceroy Antonio Amar y Borbón. Another European-born Spaniard, Pedro de Muños, was assigned as special secretary to Fuertes Amar, and it was Muños who took the statements of the conspirators, who were indeed the usual suspects of Quito conspirators in the early 1800s.

Juan de Dios Morales, Manuel Rodriguez de Quiroga, Juan Salinas, and Father José Riofrio were arrested, held at the church of La Merced, and questioned in secret as Muños and Fuertes Amar assembled their case. Stevenson noted that precautions for secrecy were taken by investigation—keeping the detainees incommunicado while "every inquisitorial practice was brought into action."[46] The conspiracy was conceived of on Christmas Day, December 25, 1808, at a secret meeting east of Quito near Alangasí at Hacienda Chillo, the country estate of Juan Pío Montúfar, Marqués de Selva Alegre. The meeting itself had grown out of an escalation of private conversations amongst the conspirators spurred by the arrival the previous August of Conde Ruiz de Castilla as president. At the meeting, plans were made to establish a Junta Suprema in Quito itself, in accord with the juntas of the various kingdoms in Spain. Juan Salinas's lack of discretion put only a temporary end to the conspiracy.[47]

In early April, Muños had prepared his report, and was readying the file to turn it over to Conde Ruiz de Castilla when the collected papers were stolen from him. Without the files, the case stalled and, according to Stevenson, "by a fortunate accident the plans of the government were frustrated, the prosecution ceased, and the prisoners were liberated."[48] Somehow, by further "fortunate accident," the papers of the investigation ended up in Quiroga's study, where he parsed and circulated their contents to interested parties. Meanwhile, an uneasy truce fell on the city. The incident further heightened tensions between local and European Spaniards, as Muños and Fuertes Amar were perceived by Quito's creoles as acting on behalf of peninsular interests. Muños himself was involved in a row over alcalde elections for 1809, when the cabildo of Quito broke with tradition and elected two American-born alcaldes, snubbing the European Spaniard Muños who had been alcalde de segundo voto in 1808.[49] Appointing Muños amounted to a political act as the tensions between European and creole Spaniards escalated to a level not seen since 1767.[50]

There was no more direct evidence of conspiracy in action between April and August, but this did not stop the rumor mill from continuing to grind as news of the abdication of Carlos IV, the accession and deposition of Fernando VII, and the emergence of juntas in Spain circulated and recirculated through the region.[51] In the process, Fernando VII became a proxy for expressions of competing political agendas. The fate of viceregal and Audiencia governance remained an open question in the absence of a legitimate royal sovereign. For liberals in Spain and the Americas, this opened a door to criticize standing royal officials couched as expressions of fidelity to the deposed and beloved Fernando. As Gilmore has noted, the legitimacy of governing authorities in the Andes at this point ultimately depended "upon the strength of tradition, upon inertia, and on their capacity to lead and administer to retain the consent of the governed."[52] In large part, this legitimacy hinged on royal officials' ability to maintain their privileged position as judicial authorities; royal sovereignty was justified through the mandate to justice and the adjudication of communal harmony. The perception that many of the appointed officials in the Americas were placed in power by Secretary of State Manuel de Godoy, who was blamed for the advent of French rule on the peninsula, jeopardized royal officials' claim to office.[53] Likewise, absent the body of an actual king, the viceregal positional claim to incarnate authority suffered real crisis.[54] Royal officials in the Americas were faced with both practical and theoretical challenges by the abdication of the throne and consolidation of the Junta Central. In Bogotá, Viceroy Amar y Borbón acted quickly to secure allegiance to his office and what he considered the still duly constituted authorities by recognizing the Junta Central in the name of Fernando VII, the Holy Catholic Faith, and the local patrías of the kingdoms under his administration.

Under pressure from American sources, the Junta Central was compelled to order the election of representatives to the government from the various overseas (*ultramar*) kingdoms. A decree from January 22, 1809, established the procedure by which the four viceroyalties and five captaincies general would elect officials to represent American interests in the junta. The decree stated,

> Considering that the vast and precious dominions which Spain possess in the Indies are not properly colonies or factories, such as those of other nations, but an essential and

integral part of the Spanish Monarchy . . . , [His Majesty] has chosen to declare . . . that the kingdoms, provinces, and isles which constitute the said dominions should have immediate national representation before his royal person and form part of the Junta Central . . . through their respective deputies. In order for this royal resolution to take effect, the viceroyalties of New Spain, New Kingdom of Granada, and Buenos Aires, and the independence captaincies general of the island of Cuba, Puerto Rico, Guatemala, Chile, Province of Venezuela, and Philippines are to each name an individual to his respective district.[55]

The Junta Central chose to speak with the voice of the king, inhabiting royal authority in the manner traditionally associated with the king's specially appointed and empowered officials of the viceroyalties and captaincies general of the empire. Ultimately, the plan for representation perpetuated the inequalities between peninsular and creole Spain, because the old kingdoms were allowed two representatives each while kingdoms in the Indies were allotted one each. The elections were to proceed through a series of steps that allowed no participation for the average plebeian of the barrios in the ultimate choice for representation. Each municipal council within the capital cities of the Americas was charged with electing three persons, one of whom was then chosen by lot for submission to a further election at the viceregal or captaincy general level. In keeping with tradition, the names of the three elected delegates were put together in a jar, with one to be pulled out by a young child. The selected name was forwarded to the viceroyalty, grouped together with all the region's delegates. From this group, three delegates were elected, with the final names chosen by the same process, to represent the viceroyalty in the junta.[56]

Thus, for the viceroyalty of New Granada, delegates were chosen from amongst those elected under this procedure by the municipal councils of the leading cities in the districts stretching from Cartagena to Loja. Guayaquil voted for delegates allotted to Lima, while Loja, Cuenca, Riobamba, Quito, Ibarra, Popayán, and Pasto all presented delegates to Santa Fé de Bogotá. The elections in Quito took place at a special meeting of the city council on June 9, 1809, during which the names of Carlos Montúfar, José Larrea y Jijón, and the Conde de Puñonrostro were nominated, all three of whom were Quito natives currently resident on the peninsula. José Larrea y Jijón's name was picked by the hand of a six-year-old boy. Elections occurred throughout the sierra during the month of June in the same manner. The process was repeated for the whole of the viceroyalty on September 16, 1809; three of the finalist delegates' names were placed in the jar with Cartagena's delegate, Antonio de Narváez selected.[57] That Quito participated in the elections, as elitist as they may have been, in the months prior to the August revolution indicates the extent to which political culture was transforming in the broader Spanish monarchy. Though these elections were not based on the popular vote, the move toward a broader sense of representative government marked a significant shift that only accelerated with the Regency, the Cortes of Cádiz, and the Cádiz Constitution of 1812. As Rodríguez argues, this revolution of the larger Hispanic world took place alongside of and in competition with the autonomist movements in the Americas, which Quito soon joined. Regardless of the saliency of local movements for home rule, the broader Spanish monarchy on both sides of the Atlantic was entering a period of liberal political revolution in 1808 and 1809. For the time being, that revolution was conveyed through vows of loyalty to King Fernando VII and the Junta Suprema Central.

Expressions of loyalty to the Junta Central by officials in Bogotá and Quito and municipal elections were not enough to quell the revolutionary rumor mill. The same month as elections for representation to the Junta Central in June 1809, an anonymous manuscript titled *Catecismo en que debe estar instruido todo fiel vasallo de F. 7.0* circulated the various jurisdictions of the viceroyalty originating from Quito.[58] The tract tapped into fears that royal officials appointed during the reign of Carlos IV were of suspect loyalties, and that Napoleon had his eye on actually invading the Americas. In response, it called on American subjects to declare independence from Napoleonic Spain and restore Fernando VII to his throne on this side of the Atlantic.[59] Rumors escalated that both viceregal and Audiencia governments were controlled by French sympathizers who would turn Quito over to Napoleon. The rumors culminated with word that a conspiracy was afoot in which European Spaniards in the Audiencia were planning on assassinating leading creole Spaniards on August 19, 1809. It was a powerful rhetorical combination: fealty to the king in the face of French aggression and a peninsular ineptitude caught up in obsequious devotion to the traitor Godoy. Morales, Quiroga, and Salinas used such justifications in establishing the junta of Quito and wooing the city's garrison.[60] It is likely, in fact, that either Morales or Quiroga was responsible for the (*Catecismo*).

FOUR HOURS OF REVOLUTION

Quito's revolutionary faction took advantage of increasing public discomfiture to finally hatch their conspiracy for home-rule on August 10, 1809. The central figures in establishing Quito's own Junta Suprema were the same conspirators arrested by Ruiz the preceding March: the Marqués de Selva Alegre, Captain Juan Salinas, Juan de Dios Morales, Dr. Don Manuel Rodriguez de Quiroga, and Dr. Don Jose Riofrio. Together with Don Mariano Villalobos and Don Antonio Ante, the conspirators solicited the public participation of many of Quito's leading citizens, including the Marqués de Villa Orellana, Bishop Joseph Cuero y Caycedo, Don Guillermo Valdivieso, the parish priest of San Roque Don Jose Correa, and members of the Quito garrison, amongst others. And indeed, support for the formation of a local ruling junta ran deep in the barrios.[61]

As an expression of that support, the collected citizenry (*vecendario*) of Quito signed a series of documents dated August 8 empowering representatives from each of the city's barrios to meet and elect the new junta. The documents selecting electors for the junta were signed by most of the vecino and vecina heads of household of the city—all the more impressive considering that the actual coup early in the morning on August 10 took the Audiencia authorities by some measure of surprise. Both women and men of the barrios signed the petitions.[62] Representatives were selected for the barrios of El Sagrario, San Sebastian, San Blas, Santa Bárbara, and San Marcos, marking a significant shift in the exercise of popular sovereignty, though there is no indication in the representations themselves exactly how individual representatives were chosen. In a letter to Don Jacinto Berjarno, Dr. Juan Pablo Arenas—university professor, lawyer, and conspirator—recounted that before August 10 the heads of household (*padres de familia*) of the city's barrios had chosen thirty-six representatives to form a Junta Suprema to represent Fernando VII, filling the void of magistrates whose function had ceased with the abdication.[63] In this case, given the presence of women's names on the petitions, padres de familia indicated heads of household, including those households headed by women in a continuation of the legal culture of government petition exercised in the preceding decades. These "voting rights," though, were short-lived, and by 1812, in the transition from vecina to *ciudadana,* or citizen in the modern sense of the term, women were no longer considered as bearers of any political citizenship rights. In addition to the barrios, representatives were appointed in the succeeding days by various corporate groups in Quito, including colegios, religious orders, merchants, lawyers, notaries, the local (i.e., American) nobility, and lower level bureaucrats. It is worth noting the heavy involvement of lawyers, attorneys, and notaries in forming the junta, particularly considering the judicial nature of the Spanish imperial state.[64]

As the barrios were selecting their representatives on August 8, a core group of conspirators met at the house of Don Javier de Ascásubi to plan their actions for the next few days. On the night of August 9, the thirty-six elected representatives of Quito's barrios met in semisecret at Manuela Cañizares's home in El Sagrario with the junta's lead conspirators, for a group totaling between forty-five and fifty individuals, to form the junta. According to one observer, the gathering's forty-five attendees included thirty plebeians, twelve nobles, and three ecclesiastics. The enthusiasm of all was aroused by an ample supply of chicha and aguardiente. The door was guarded, and passwords required, but for those who entered what followed was four hours of bloodless revolution, from the moment the meeting convened at 11 p.m. to the time they had taken control of the city barracks at 3 a.m. The details of the new government followed closely the plans that had been discussed in Chillo the preceding December.

Morales started the proceedings with a rousing speech that touched on the justificatory themes of the proposed junta's legitimacy. He began, "Beloved brothers and compatriots: Our Religion, our King, and our Homeland have called us together here that my feeble voice might inform you all of our present situation."[65] The present situation, Morales argued, pitted Quito's faithful subjects against European Spaniards (*chapetones*) in government who planned to turn the kingdoms of the Americas over to Napoleon and his French heretics who occupied all of Spain, a threat they must resist by "preserv[ing] themselves and this part of the Spanish dominion from the fate that awaited the rest."[66] He claimed furthermore that plans were afoot to "spill the blood" of some fourteen of Quito's leading citizens.[67] The speech, including the threat to creole Spaniards' lives, echoes the arguments put forth in the *Catecismo* that was circulating in June—only this time Quiroga made the impassioned plea that it was the time for action. In order to protect the kingdom of Quito from the seditious acts of Godoy's lackeys and French sympathizers, he enjoined the assemblage to form a provincial government in the name of Fernando VII, and to end chapeton rule.

At the end of his polemic, Morales turned the meeting over to Quiroga to further explain the plan for a new government. In the meantime, Captain Juan Salinas was dispatched to inform and recruit the Quito garrison. Salinas invoked the same formula to the troops that Morales had to the Cañizares audience—religion, king, patría. Reportedly, at some time shortly after midnight on the August 10, Salinas assembled the troops in the square facing the barracks and informed them that their "beloved King was a prisoner in France; expatiated on his sufferings; he told them that the existing governments in America were determined to deliver up the country to the common enemy, and concluded by asking them, whether they would defend their beloved Fernando, or become slaves of Bonaparte?"[68] One account states he said to them, "Brothers, Compañeros, [in the name of] Religion, the King, and the Patría! You all are vassals of our King Fernando VII and Christian Catholics. The Junta orders that we arrest the chapetones because they want to slit our throats and give us to France. ¡Viva el Rey! ¡Viva la Religión!"[69] The troops replied with resounding shouts of "¡Viva Fernando Séptimo [VII]! ¡Viva Quito!" Don Joaquin Saldumbide, head of Quito's cavalry regiment, delivered the same speech to his men, and recruited their support as well. Upon returning to the Cañizares house, Saldumbide and Salinas were instructed to administer an oath to the troops and set up guards outside the homes of everyone targeted for arrest by the junta. The new members of the Falange of Quito's Junta Suprema were made to repeat, "I swear by God and on the cross of my sword, to defend my legitimate King, Fernando VII; to maintain and protect his rights; to support the purity of the Holy Roman Catholic Church, and to obey the constituted authorities."[70]

While the troops were being recruited, Quiroga managed support for a new plan of government, formalized in an *Acta de instalación.*[71] The Acta began by proclaiming the cessation of all the functions of the city and province's current magistrature. This opening action highlights the judicial nature of the Spanish imperial bureaucracy. In nullifying the current government, the junta declared its judicial authority ended. But this judicial authority, resident in the kingdom's magistrates, would not be replaced by simply reconstructing a judiciary that possessed legislative and executive authority. Following the newly emergent political culture, the junta separated executive and judicial authority into two different entities—the Junta Suprema, and a senate (*senado*) made up of both a civil court and a criminal court.[72] The assembly "elected" the Marqués de Selva Alegre Juan Pío Montúfar as president, Juan de Dios Morales as secretary of state and war, Dr. Don Manuel Rodriguez de Quiroga as secretary of the treasury, and Dr. Juan de Larrea as secretary of justice and welfare. Don Vicente Alvarez was chosen as a voting secretary to the junta. The *Acta* also claimed that, because the junta was the legitimate representative of the Spanish monarchy, it should be treated as an entity as the manifestation of royal majesty.[73] In addition to these officers, Don Juan José Guerrero and Don Melchor Benebides were elected as representatives to the junta from Quito's cabildo. Barrio representatives were also elected (from amongst an apparently elite-only slate of potential candidates): for Santa Bárbara, the Marqués of Miraflores; for San Blas, Don Manuel Larrea; for San Roque, the Marqués de Villaorellana; for San Sebastian, Don Manuel Zambrano; and for San Marcos, Don Manuel Mateu y Aranda.[74] The junta accorded pomp and circumstance to its various individual members—the president should be addressed as "Serene Highness" (*Alteza Serenísima*), and ministers and voting members should be addressed as "Lords" (*Señoría*). This maintenance of title suggests the hybrid nature of Spanish liberalism as it was conceived of by Quito's revolutionaries— popular and constitutional, and yet monarchical and hierarchical, concerned with the appearance of authority. The anonymous letter writer of the "Memorias . . . en cinco cartas" saw this as an opportunity ripe for ridicule, characterizing the affair as "the omnipotence of forty-five barbarians, glutted on chicha and aguardiente, a complete Sovereignty, a Majesty more absolute than the Ottoman Empire [*Sublime Puerta*]."[75]

The senate was established as a judicial parallel to the junta, divided into two chambers headed by Don Javier Ascásubi as its governor. Ascásubi was to preside over a civil court with four judges and a state's attorney (fiscal). The criminal court was to be presided over by a regent (second in authority to the governor), to whom the assembly appointed Oidor Don Felipe Fuertes Amar in absentia. It is likely this appointment was a political overture to the Amar's uncle, Viceroy Amar y Borbón. The criminal court would also be staffed by four judges and a fiscal, as well as a protector de indios and an alguacil mayor.[76] The subordination of the criminal chamber to the civil chamber posits an interesting expression of legal priorities in which the maintenance of public safety would become subsidiary to the adjudication of property.

The deputies present at the Cañizares residence, together with representatives of the Cabildo and members of the new junta, declared their support for establishing this new system of government as an interim measure, representative of Fernando VII's legitimate sovereignty until that time that he would either regain the throne on the peninsula, or come to America to rule.[77] Even as the *Acta* was being finalized and printed, Salinas was deploying newly sworn troops throughout the city to execute arrest warrants on Audiencia ministers and bureaucrats identified as potential enemies of the junta. The troops were in place by 4 a.m.; as the sun rose two hours later on the saint's day of San Lorenzo, the arrests began. Conde Ruiz de Castilla was awakened with the news and taken into custody. He was joined by José Maria Cucalón, a secretary to the president and son of the governor of Guayaquil, Audiencia Regent and former Fiscal de lo Criminal José Merchante de Contreras, Oidor José Fuentes González Bustillos, Asesor Francisco Xavier Manzanos y Castillo, the mail administrator Don José Bergara, Ayudante Mayor Don Bruno Resua, Comandante Joaquín Villaespesa, and Don Simón Saenz y Vergara, the Collector of Diezmos and father of an illegitimate son, future revolutionary Manuela Saenz.[78]

Meanwhile, as early as 6 a.m. people began to gather in the main square of the presidential palace. The transfer of power was marked by a cannon salute and music from the Quito garrison's band. The junta posted announcements of its actions on corners throughout the city. A dispatch was sent to Juan Pío Montúfar at his hacienda Chillo, informing him of the successful conclusion of events over the night of August 9, as well as of his election as president of the new Junta Suprema de Quito. In what must have been a public relations action, the Marqués de Selva Alegre then made his way to Quito as a recruit of popular sentiment, rather than as a core conspirator. The concern with appearance, pomp, and circumstance fits well with Stevenson's characterization of the Marqués, about whom he stated, "As a public character Selva Alegre was extremely unfit; wavering and timid, wishing rather to reconcile the two parties than to support either; fond of show and parade, but frightened at his own shadow, as if it mocked him. At the gaze of the people he would, like a peacock, have allowed his gaudy plumage to fall to the ground; he would have endeavored to hide himself, or, as the most enthusiastic Quiteños expressed themselves, 'his shoes did not fit him.'"[79] Ever mindful of the need to legitimize the new government, the Marqués de Selva Alegre and his core advisors announced the convening of a cabildo abierto on August 16 to publicly ceremonialize the junta. With a continued eye to the plebeians in the barrios, the junta ordered that people in the city should burn lights in their windows for three days to illuminate the streets and the plazas, and music concerts were nightly at 7 p.m. On the final night, August 13, the junta attended Mass together at the Church of Carmen Alto, dressed in their most ornate affairs. The Marqués de Selva Alegre appeared in full livery of a knight of the military order of Carlos III. Stevenson recalled that the others wore, "scarlet and black; the two ministers were distinguished by large plumes in the hats; the corporation, officers of the treasury, and other tribunals, in their old Spanish uniforms, and the military in *blue*, faced with *white* instead of *red*, as heretofore" (emphasis original).[80]

All was not pomp and circumstance, though. The junta readied a series of public manifestos explaining the justifications for its actions. They also considered the tax, commercial, and security policies the junta should pursue. The central message communicated to the surrounding provinces, as well as to the Virreynatos of Santa Fé and Perú, expressed in the manifestos and in communications sent directly by the Marqués, was that the establishment of the Junta Suprema of Quito was a defensive maneuver intended to protect the interests of the patría in the face of French aggression and heresy and peninsular suspicion. "King, religion, and patria" was on everyone's lips.[81] Support outside Quito was immediately noticeable in its absence. This brought quickly to the fore the issue of public security, as Don Juan Salinas pressed to form and deploy three regiments of troops to protect the city from potential aggression radiating from Cuenca, Guayaquil, and Popayán, soon to be joined by Peru and

New Granada. Meanwhile, the junta almost immediately addressed an economic grievance that had its root in the 1760s, and ended the royal monopolies on aguardiente and tobacco.

On August 16, the city convened in what was now a veritable parade of cabildos abiertos called to express fidelity at word of each new of regime change—the ascension of Fernando VII, the invasion of Bonaparte, the Junta Central y Suprema, and now Quito's own. Members of the junta met in the main hall (*sala*) of the Convent of San Agustín together with representatives of the secular and ecclesiastical cabildos, the Alguacil mayor, ministers of the Audiencia, members of the military, representatives of the city's university and colegios, priests of the city's barrios, representatives of the religious orders, the college of lawyers, and merchants, as well as the administrators of royal tax collection all crowded together with the city's nobles and neighborhood vecinos. According to the minutes of the meeting, Quiroga, Larrea, and Morales all took turns addressing the assembled, reading the junta's manifestos and the *Acta de Instalación*. The junta reaffirmed its stance that the new government's actions would "conserve intact the Christian Religion, obedience to Sr. Don Fernando VII, and the happiness and welfare of the patría, important and necessary [actions] given the critical present circumstances, in which the common enemy of the Nations, Napoleon Bonaparte, sought to take over Spanish soil."[82] The junta solicited, and then received support for, the newly formed junta from the gathered individuals and representatives of Quito's economic, political, and legal corporations; these latter signed a notarized instrument to express their support. The week was capped off the following day with a public Mass, singing of the *Te Deum*, and swearing of allegiance to the junta, "in the presence of the image of Christ Crucified, Our Beloved Redeemer, and the Holy Saints." According to the *Acta del Cabildo Abierto* published on August 20, the actual oath sworn by all those present was as follows:

> We swear to Sr. Don Fernando VII as our Natural Lord and King and that we will adhere to the principles of the Junta Central, to never recognize the domination of Bonaparte nor to any other intrusive king. We swear to conserve in its unity and purity the Apostolic Roman Catholic Religion, into which by the loving-kindness of God we had the fortune to be born.

> And we swear to faithfully do all possible for the welfare of the Nation and patría, losing were it necessary for these sacred objects and the Constitution, every last drop of our blood.[83]

The oath carried within it the marks of the hybrid liberal political revolution emerging in the broader Spanish monarchy. Antonio Oleas, charged by the junta with transcribing and publishing the *Acta* of the cabildo abierto, continued the political sleight of hand by closing the document with the phrase, "By Royal Order," invoking the authority of the king traditionally manifest in the leading bureaucratic positions of the kingdoms of the Americas (viceroy, regent, captain general, president, and so on). The new junta traded on the public ceremonial practices of royal governance to shore up its legitimacy before the populace, but added to this performative tradition the gloss of a new, more popular sovereignty that equated, essentially, the blood of the gathered vecinos and vecinas with the life of a new constitutional order. The use of the term "constitution" is itself significant, since no formal constitutions had been written in or for the Spanish monarchy yet. Thus, the junta was portraying its own *Acta de instalación* as a constitutional document.

It was a triumphant week in Quito, as the new Junta Central marshaled broad support from the various corporations, social groups, and barrios of the city. The enthusiasm was short-lived, though, as the junta found itself quickly isolated. The solicited and anticipated support from the surrounding political jurisdictions did not materialize despite actions the junta felt would ameliorate potential flash points of protest. In the days after the cabildo abierto, Conde Ruiz de Castilla negotiated release with the Marqués de Selva Alegre, who offered his hacienda Chillo as a retreat for the Conde. Ruiz instead requested he be allowed to retire in house arrest at his estate in the commons land north of Iñaquito, to which the Marqués consented.[84] The junta also released Ayudante General Don José Cucalón, the son of the governor of Guayaquil, in a move seen as conciliatory toward the coastal capital.[85] The junta also sent emissaries to the surrounding jurisdictions, including Cuenca, Guayaquil, Riobamba, Guaranda, Latacunga, Ibarra and Otavalo, Pasto, Popayan, Bogotá, and Lima. They did not find many sympathetic ears.

Just two months after the publicly made vows of fealty to the new Junta Suprema of Quito, representatives were negotiating the return of power with Ruiz. Upon receiving news of the junta's for-mation, both the immediate surrounding districts and the viceregal governments in Bogotá and Lima formed an offensive stance against Quito. Guayaquil, under orders from Peru's Viceroy Abascal, block-aded coastal traffic to the interior and pulled together a militia to march against the capital; Cuenca did likewise. Abascal also sent a contingent of troops to Guayaquil, including Lima's mulatto regi-ment, which he intended to use to support the local militias. From the north, Viceroy Amar y Borbón ordered Pasto and Popayán to block-ade the Audiencia and organize armed resistance.[86] As in the 1760s, he also acted to bring troops to bear from Panamá. As the various groups of troops began to advance toward the city, the junta opened negotiations with Ruiz.

Selva Alegre was replaced by another local noble, Juan José Guerrero, conde of Selva Florida, as president of the junta. It was Guerrero who presented six terms of surrender to Ruiz on October 24, stipulating

I. That which has been constituted in Quito was done with no other object or design than the holy ends proposed from the beginning, the conservation of the Holy Faith, obedi-ence to the King our Lord Don Fernando VII, and the security of the patría, fearing it would be impressed and conquered by the wicked Tyrant of Europe Bonaparte, who notoriously desires to subjugate America. [That the Junta Suprema] will become a provincial Junta, subject and sub-ordinated to the Supreme and Central [Junta] of Spain and solely dependent on it, as is and has been recognized all along. . . .

II. That the Head and President of this [provincial junta] will be the same Excellent Señor Conde Ruiz de Castilla, who will direct and authorize the provincial Junta, as is done in the Kingdoms of Spain, who mandated [juntas] be estab-lished at the head of all Provinces. And since it was declared by Royal Ordinance that America is an integral part of the Spanish Monarchy, it is not irregular that Quito, as Capital of a Kingdom, participated in the prerogatives of [the king-doms] in Spain and has its own Junta just as do the capitals in Spain.

III. That in order to calm worries and public hatreds, neither Regente Don José Fuentes González Bustillo, Oidor Don José Merchante, Assessor don Francisco Javier Manzanos, don Simón Sáenz, don José Vergara, nor any retired Officials, all of whom disgust and offend the public opinion and the concept of the public, cannot be reinstated to their old functions and employment.

IV. That the Señor President, in agreement with the Junta, will make whatever modifications are esteemed opportune and convenient to the royal Judiciary naturally informing Señor Don Felipe Fuertes and Señor Don Tomás Arrechaga, who have not lost the estimation and trust of the public in any event.

V. That in the same manner the actions of the Junta as well as the individuals within it will be modified and tempered, as agreed upon earlier.

VI. That in no case or event will any action or harassment be made against any citizen, against his honor, life, nor interests, for [supporting the junta], which should all wait for resolution by the King, our Lord, to whom will be given the whole case.[87]

Conde Ruiz de Castilla accepted the terms offered by the junta and on October 28, 1809, he reentered the city and resumed his governing authority.

Quito's elite justified the formation of the ruling junta with an argument that harkened back to the jealousies and conflicts of the 1760s, but that was marked by the political innovations of fifty years of the Atlantic liberal revolution. In the absence of the king, local elites believed their ties of obedience to the peninsula were abrogated, as it were, as a result of Quito's standing as an independent kingdom within the broader Spanish monarchy. This juridical and bureaucratic argument was the foundation for home rule, and depended on the claim that no individual peninsular junta, aligned with an individual peninsular kingdom, could claim authority to rule over the king's other possessions. The quiteños were articulating political equality with the kingdoms of Spain, a claim ultimately recognized by the Junta Suprema Central. Furthermore, in the absence of the king those officials who derived their authority from his were no longer empowered, and thus were illegitimate.[88] This included the viceroys (literally, vice kings) of Santa Fé and Lima. As peninsular officials dominated imperial politics under the Bourbons, quiteños held European Spaniards in particular contempt for their colonial attitudes. In its manifesto, the junta explained, "the word criollo has been used as an insult on their lips."[89] The tensions between European and local Spaniards intensified in the coming years, no doubt heightened by a massacre of junta participants just one year after the revolution of Quito convened.

INTERREGNUM

The restoration of Conde Ruiz de Castilla ultimately carried a heavy price for both members of the junta and sympathizers with Quito's autonomists. Initially, it appeared Ruiz would respect the terms of surrender proffered by the conde de Selva Florida, but it was not to be. On the morning of November 8, Conde de Selva Florida returned to Quito from his estate at Iñaquito, holding a ceremony in the presidential palace during which representatives of the failed junta turned the collected archive of their rule over to the restored authorities. In the spirit of their agreement, Ruiz ordered the papers be burned, but instead they were kept by Fiscal Tomás de Arrechaga.[90] It was a fateful bit of disobedience. On December 2, 1809, after about a month of restored rule, troops sent from Peru finally arrived in Quito under the command of Don Manuel Arredonda. The presence of the troops proved to tip the scale in the direction of peninsular Spaniards seeking revenge for the acts of the preceding August. With the pacifying troops in place, Ruiz disbanded the Quito militia and consented, under pressure from Arrechaga, Oidor Fuertes Amar, and Arredonda, to reverse his position on punishment of the junta conspirators. Warrants were signed out on December 12 for both participants and sympathizers in the junta, dozens of whom were rounded up and incarcerated at the city's main barracks. Suspects of the regime were named in circulars sent to the surrounding region to alert royal officials. Among the list of those who escaped arrest was Manuela Cañizares.[91] The arrests immediately escalated tensions in the city. As Arrechaga compiled his dossier, royal troops kept peace in the city, but not without significant resentments. The relationship between the troops, many of them part of Lima's mulatto brigade, combined with Arrechaga and Arredonda's zealousness to keep a cloud of fear not only on the city, but particularly in amongst the prisoners in the barracks.

Writing the bishop of Quito from his incarceration sometime in July 1810, Rodriguez de Quiroga expressed real concern for his personal safety, writing he was afraid he would be murdered in jail.[92] His appeal to the bishop was an appeal for protection, seeking ecclesiastical support as a jurisdictional intervention. Quiroga was worried because he kept hearing rumors that the "ignorant and credulous population" of the barrios were spreading, rumors that stoked fear that the troops from Lima were planning to "sack the shops and houses" of the city. Quiroga heard the rumors from an officer of the troops, and watched from inside the barracks as the soldiery began making preparations for bloodshed.[93] Commander Don Fernando Basantes warned the troops from the patio of the barracks, in earshot of the prisoners inside, that "at the slightest provocation it all ends with us."[94] Quiroga and the others felt this was an immediate threat to their security. They worried that "whatever might happen with some drunk, or some other exterior thing, with which we poor, helpless and unarmed detainees, will be sold and exposed to be killed like dogs, without any court, without ruling."[95] Quiroga's fears were prescient.

The detainees were also protesting the judicial process brought against them. Arechaga turned his investigation over to Conde Ruiz de Castilla in May, along with recommendation of death for the core conspirators of the junta. Ruiz could have ended it then and there by ruling on the case, but he did not. Pressures mounted on him from Colonel Arredonda and from Arrechaga, who encouraged him to hand down the sentence. But Ruiz dithered, paralyzed, it seems, by the weight of a potential eighty executions. Rather than rule, he decided to forward the entire investigation to Bogotá and to the authority of Viceroy Amar y Borbón.[96] The task of transporting the case was assigned to Dr. Victor de San Miguel. On June 20, 1810, the detainees in the barracks penned a protest to Ruiz, asking for a chance to review the accumulated file, its charges, and its recommendations. They also protested the assignment of Dr. San Miguel on technical and polemical grounds.[97] They reiterated their position again the next day, not knowing if and when San Miguel had departed. Ruiz forwarded the petitions to Arrechaga as his fiscal, who unsurprisingly argued there were no legitimate impediments to San Miguel carrying the case to Bogotá, and that it should be done immediately. Ruiz relented to Arrechaga yet again, ruling on June 21 that San Miguel should take the case to Bogotá.[98]

Stevenson recalled that, with San Miguel on his way for Bogotá, many partisans of the junta who had escaped earlier detention returned to Quito, assuming the case was closed. Upon discovery, they immediately were arrested. Royal officials became suspicious of anyone entering the city, and began arbitrary detentions. The repercussions were immediate and,

> although [many of these individuals] were liberated after examination, the alarm flew from one place to another, so that none would bring their produce to market, and a consequent dearth of provisions began to be experienced in the city. This, instead of producing conciliatory measures for procuring them, enraged the Spanish soldiers, who committed several depredations, and the injured individuals through fear abstained from complaining to the officer or if they ventured to do it, they were insulted with the epithets of rebels, insurgents, and traitors.[99]

The tensions escalated until the afternoon of August 2, 1810. At around 2 p.m., in a bid to free the detainees held in the barracks, a handful of soldiers who were being held at the city presidio overtook their guard, along with their weapons and uniforms and proceeded across the square to the barracks. A scuffle began with the guard at the barracks, which, according to Stevenson was overheard by officers of the Lima troops that were supping at the presidential Palace on the plaza. The officers rushed out, saw the commotion across the square, and ordered the palace guard to open fire. Stevenson continues,

> This lasted about ten minutes when, all being silent, an officer ran to the barracks to inquire into the cause of the disturbance: on being informed of what had taken place, as well as that all was then safe, he returned with the report to his commandant, Arredonda. Another officer was immediately sent to inquire into the state of the prisoners, and he was briefly returned with the news, that they were all dead. Some had been shot during the uproar by the sentries placed over them, and many had been murdered by a zambo boy, one

of the cooks to the soldiers who had entered their cells, and dispatched them with an axe. Terror and consternation for a moment were visible in the countenances of the president and officers, when, on a sudden, the Spanish soldiers rushed from the barracks into the streets, shouting Revenge! Revenge! Our Captain is murdered. Scarcely was the alarm given, when the infuriated soldiers abandoned their posts, and running up and down the streets, murdered every individual they met with, without distinction either of age or sex: the drums in different parts of the city beat an advance, and murder and pillage raged in this horrid manner till three o'clock, all the officers standing on the esplanade of the palace, without making any effort to check the massacre: at length, the soldiers having expended their stock of cartridges began to return to the barracks, some of the so laden with plunder, that they had left their arms they knew not where.[100]

The barrios fought back, particularly those in San Roque, San Sebastian, and San Blas. The full toll of the carnage was not known till the next day. The city, stunned into silence, left some of the dead in the streets where they fell, while others were taken to various churches. On the morning of August 3, Don Juan José Guerrero, the remaining city's alcalde ordinario after the departure of San Miguel, made rounds of the hospital and churches to identify the dead. With a notary and two soldiers, he went San Agustín, la Merced, San Francisco, Santo Domingo, the cathedral of El Sagrario, and the colegio of San Buenaventura. The descriptions of the bodies testify to the intensity of the violence. People were shot at close range, and stabbed in the chest and face with bayonets and swords. Juan Salinas had bullet wounds in four places on his head as well as cuts across his chest. Manuel Rodríguez de Quiroga was shot and cut across the head by a saber. His unidentified female black slave was shot in the back. Don Juan Larrea had two bullet wounds in his head, and six significant cuts on his body. Salazar y Lozano recounted that Larrea's young wife, Doña Isabel Bou, was "hurt and drenched in her husband's blood . . . as he died at her feet."[101] Notary Atanacio Olea and Don Mariano Villalobos had head wounds severe enough that they were leaking brain matter ("con la tapa de los sesos fuera"). Doña N. Monge suffered unspecified bullet wounds. There were soldiers, carpenters, indigenous men, blacksmiths, musicians, and more amongst the dead.[102] Amongst the wounded survivors at the royal hospital was an eleven-year-old boy who suffered a saber blow to his hand and head.

The massacre permanently tainted the presence of the Lima troops in the city. Three days after the carnage, a cabildo abierto was called by Conde Ruiz de Castilla, who presided over the meeting along with the bishop and Colonel Arredonda. In the course of the meeting, Don Tomás Arrechaga and Colonel Arredonda were isolated by the remaining power brokers of the city. The bishop noted that the entire conflict was the result of Ruiz reneging on his promises to the outgoing junta. Arrechaga protested, and was rebuked to the point that Ruiz ordered he leave the meeting. Arredonda recognized his precarious position and observed "that he was fully convinced the government of Quito ought to rely on the loyalty of the Quiteños, and allow him to retire with the troops under his command."[103] There was immediate agreement, and the Lima troops began to withdraw from the city the next day.

THE JUNTA OF 1810

The tensions resulting from the massacre kept Quito on the brink of dissolution until Don Carlos Montúfar, son of the Marqués de Selva Alegre, arrived from the peninsula on September 12, 1810, bearing a commission from the Regency to reform a provincial junta. He quickly went about the business of organizing a new governing committee. As a conciliatory overture, Montúfar offered the presidency of the new body to Conde Ruiz de Castilla, who accepted the position. Other members of the new junta included Carlos Montúfar, his father the Marqués de Selva Alegre (as one of the few surviving members of the original junta), one representative each from the secular and ecclesiastical cabildos, two more clerics, two representatives of the city's vecinos, and one representative of each of the five barrios.[104] The resulting junta was designated as a Junta Superior, subservient to the Regency, as opposed to a Junta Suprema as it was named a year earlier, a title that claimed equality with the Junta Central in Spain.[105]

Early in its existence, the junta superior ordered the municipal council of Quito to participate in elections called for by the Junta Central before it ceded control to the Regency. On January 1, 1810, the Junta Central ordered the various capitals of the Spanish Empire to elect representatives to form national cortes. Each city council was to elect three individuals, from which one would be chosen for the cortes.[106] Quito did participate in this election cycle, which generally occurred in the provinces of the Americas toward the end of 1810 and in early 1811. On October 20, 1810, Montúfar ordered the municipal council to elect Quito's representative, an order that was fulfilled three days later. The names put forth were largely the same as those the year before. The council nominated José de Larrea y Jijón, the conde de Puñonrrostro, and José Fernández Salvador. As in June 1809, a child chose one name from a jar; this time the name chosen was that of the conde de Puñonrostro who, along with José Mejía de Lequerica, was already in Cádiz. After the selection, the council also appointed José Fernández Salvador to write instructions on behalf of Quito's interests to be delivered to the conde.[107] Thus, for the second time in as many years, Quito participated in indirect elections tied to the changing liberal political landscape in Spain.

Despite the formal approval of Spain granted to Carlos Montúfar, the validity of the new junta remained an open question for the viceregal authorities in Lima and Bogotá. Throughout the Bonaparte crisis, the viceroys in America rejected the need for ruling juntas in the kingdoms of the Indies because they believed they still carried the legitimate authority of Fernando VII that the House of Bourbon conferred in their original appointments. From Lima, Viceroy Abascal conspired to undermine any local expressions of sovereignty in the Andes. With Abascal's back channel support, the Regency in Spain changed its position on Quito after Montúfar had arrived, and named Joaquín Molina to assume the presidency of the old Audiencia. Molina, residing in Lima at the time, carried with him the support of Abascal when he arrived in Guayaquil on December 7, 1810, to assume control of the region.[108] Despite the military backing on offer, Molina was not able to proceed directly to Quito. Instead, he temporarily acted from bases of support in Guayaquil and Cuenca, plotting to again isolate Quito from the provinces. For its part, the people of Quito completely rejected the claims of Abascal and Molina. Popular ire toward representatives of the old regime continued to test the limits of the coalition Carlos Montúfar had forged. In a particularly ugly manifestation of these tensions, the bodies of former Audiencia Judge Fuertes y Amar and former Royal Mail Administrator José Vergara were left bloodied in the street, the victims of mob justice.[109] In October 1811, the junta removed Ruiz from the presidency and entered a period of more radical assertion of sovereignty.

In December 1811, a popular assembly was called in Quito to consider the future of the city, increasingly pressured by the forces of Molina to the south. The assemblage was moderated by Quito Bishop Cuero y Caycedo, who was serving also as president of the junta. The result of the meeting was the January 1812 proclamation of the Constitution of the Free State of Quito. Two separate proposals were considered to charter the new state. Both of them continued the fundamental proposition that Quito was an autonomous kingdom of Fernando VII, sovereign unto itself in his absence. Calixto Mirando, a priest from Ibarra, further proposed the new state should be governed by an indirectly elected senate composed of a president, vice president, four senators, a fiscal, and two secretaries. All were to be chosen for three-year terms by representatives of the barrios and the various corporate bodies of the state. The judicial operations of the state were to be separated from the political and bureaucratic functions through the formation of a tribunal of justice, composed of four judges, a fiscal, the protector of the Indians, an agent for civil cases, and the jailor and his subordinates. The presiding judge, chosen from the four, would carry the title "Governor of the Tribunal." Beneath the tribunal, which would act as an appellate court, a coterie of barrio and city magistrates would continue to function.[110] The assemblage opted for the second proposal offered by Dr. Miguel Rodríguez, which went further toward establishing a liberal, representative government. Rodríguez, similar to Miranda, reaffirmed both the sovereign nature of the quiteño state as well as its fidelity to Fernando VII, proclaiming,

> The State of Quito is and will be independent of any other State or Government as far as its administration and economy. . . . The form of Government will be popular and representative.

> In view of their long-standing love and constant fidelity given by the people to their former Kings, this State protests that it recognizes and will recognize as Monarch Señor don Fernando VII, who, free of French domination and secure from the influence of any friendship or relationship with the Tyrant of Europe, can rule without affecting this Constitution.[111]

The document went further to specify the new government would be divided into three coequal branches: executive, legislative, and judicial. The intention was clearly to establish a constitutional monarchy, and as such echoed the liberal constitution adopted on the peninsula later that year. Unlike the Spanish Constitution, which allowed for representation from all of the monarchy's kingdoms, including those in America, Quito endeavored to establish itself as a free, autonomous state whose only affiliation with Spain would be to a common monarch. Furthermore, the constitution that the delegates opted for moved away from social corporations as a basis for representation, and toward the individual.[112] The document was approved in February 1812, but the Free State of Quito was very short lived. On April 16, just two months later, opposition forces scored a major military victory against the Quito troops outside Cuenca. Shortly thereafter, reinforcements arrived in Guayaquil from Peru under the leadership of General Toribio Montes, who quickly departed for Guaranda in the highlands to stage his assault on Quito. By November, Montes was advancing north through the mountains. On November 7, the attack on Quito commenced, and just one day later, Montes triumphantly entered the city, which had been largely abandoned overnight. The Free State of Quito and any further activity toward home rule ended with retreat as Montes assumed the presidency of the old Audiencia.[113]

Montes faced a difficult task in restoring yet again royal legitimacy in the province of Quito. His position was complicated by the call for constitutional elections handed down by the Regency and the Cortes of Cádiz. His tack was to encourage the broadest male participation in municipal and provincial elections that he could. From his position as governor (*jefe político*), Montes ordered all of the jurisdictions of the newly coined Province of Quito (the old Kingdom of Quito) to make censuses in preparation for the elections ordered by the cortes. Initially, there was significant confusion relating to who should and who should not be counted as voting eligible.[114] Specifically, there were questions about indigenous people, religious vocation, legitimacy, literacy, and women. Montes ruled that, following the dictates of the new constitution, indigenous men who were not in servitude on a hacienda, illiterate citizens, and men of any birth status were to be counted as Spanish citizens, but women were not.[115] This shifted customary practices, which had long held that women who were heads of household had voting rights in community elections as vecinas. They had done this in the formation of the 1809 junta, as well as during the 1809 and 1810 elections. Montes, together with the Cádiz liberals, held that the new electoral system based voting rights on the individual, rather than the head of household. This was a revolutionary shift in political identification in the Spanish monarchy. As in other contract societies, the basic political unit of a constitutional Spanish monarchy would be the rights-bearing individual male citizen.[116]

The census was a first step preceding a series of three elections—municipal, provincial, and for representation in the cortes in Spain. When the censuses were finished, the old Kingdom of Quito qualified for five deputies for the new cortes. Following the census, a first series of elections were held for new constitutional municipal councils (*ayuntamientos constitucionales*) between September 1813 and January 1814. Rodríguez notes that, in the ayuntamiento elections for Quito, Toribio Montes explicitly supported the election of local elites, including former revolutionaries, as an overture to unity and peace in the wake of the previous years' upheavals.[117] In a manner extended from but similar to the selection of barrio junta representatives in 1809, individual male vecinos from each parish of the city chose electors who in turn appointed the magistrates, attorneys, and council members for the ayuntamiento. Thus, the elections still were indirect. Municipal elections were followed in August 1814 by elections for the formation of a provincial ruling committee (*diputación*) and for representatives to the cortes for the jurisdiction of Quito.[118] The diputación of the Province of Quito included a single representative each from Quito, Cuenca, Latacunga, Ambato, Riobamba, Loja, and Otavalo, as well as substitute members from Riobamba, Pasto, and Ambato.[119]

CONCLUSION

Thus the end of Quito's second ruling junta did not mean the end of liberal political practices in the city and the old kingdom. Montes continued the implementation of constitutional municipalities throughout the region following the new electoral system of the Cádiz Constitution of 1812. The end of Quito's experiment with home rule was a minor disappointment for the many contending liberal forces within the Spanish monarchy, forces that likewise flourished in the name of the king. Fernando VII's abdication and the French invasion of the peninsula largely unified the disparate kingdoms of the Indies and Spain as one Spanish nation (*nación español*), even if interpretations of the political implications of those events differed.[120] The unity of the Spanish world hinged on the continued legitimacy of Fernando VII in the eyes of his subjects. As discussed above, this resulted in repeated avowals of fidelity to the one legitimate king, including at moments when Spaniards and Americans were working to claim local, popular sovereignty in his absence. Everything was done in his name, which became an object of chimerical projection upon which liberals, royalists, and everyone in between cast their visions of fealty and authority. This included the Cádiz Constitution of 1812, which abrogated the Bourbon king's claims to absolute authority in favor of a constitutional monarchy in essence ruled by the Spanish parliament. Of course, when it was written, Fernando VII was still exiled in a French castle. In March 1814, the government of Joseph Bonaparte collapsed under continued Spanish resistance and the royal family was released from French custody. Fernando VII returned to Madrid to reclaim the throne. The rejoicing was short-lived, though, as the king was unable to adjust to the political realities forged in six years of resistance to Bonaparte, particularly the Cádiz Constitution of 1812. On May 4, 1814, less than two months after his return, Fernando abolished the constitution and disbanded the parliament, unwilling to share sovereignty. The action revealed a king different from the individual in whose name the juntas, parliaments, and anti-French resistance had been formed. It also spurred liberals to guerilla war with skills they had honed in the fight against the French. After six years of conflict, they were able to force Fernando's hand, and in 1820 he was forced to submit to the parliament and reinstate the Cádiz Constitution of 1812, out of which the new nation of Spain was born. The revanchist stance of Fernando VII likewise transformed the struggle in the Americas from one of home rule to outright independence, led in South America by the northern forces of Simón Bolívar and the southern forces of San Martín.

During the period 1809–1812, however, the struggle was not anticolonial, and neither independence nor modern statehood were on the horizon. Rather, local elites utilized political traditions such as the cabildo abierto and the ability of locals to resist the implementation of what was perceived as illegitimate use of authority to fashion a response to the political crisis sparked by Fernando VII's abdication.

As in the 1760s, this assertion to local participation stemmed from cultural and political principles of devolutionary power. Unlike the 1760s, however, the political understanding of sovereignty was on its way to a new governance regime. Thus, when the fantastical projections on the king were upended by the real actions of the real Fernando, the struggle moved beyond the traditional decentralism within the context of the Spanish monarchy and on to independence itself. For the future state of Ecuador, though, some outside help was required to get to that point.

CHAPTER FIVE

PRACTICE III

In the Name of King and Constitution

———•———

The competing legal agendas of quiteño autonomists and Spanish liberals had an almost immediate effect on legal operations in the city. The liberal revolution that swept the Spanish monarchy from 1808 to 1814 accelerated the long and contested slide in legal rights for the corregimiento's women, a slide that began with the Bourbons. The legal transformation tracked in a direction that was simultaneously politically modernizing and degrading to the legal interests of dominated corporate groups in society. The early constitutions, from the *Documento de Oro* to the Cádiz Constitution, dismantled fuero protections in the name of the equality of citizenry; they also removed protections that dominated groups used to help mitigate their domination. The interest in the rule of law, and the separation of judicial from executive or royal authority, marked the beginning of a shift away from status-based legality that began, at least in theory, during the first wave of liberal revolution.

This chapter will demonstrate that from the perspective of legal practice, the shift toward contract and liberal republican ideals that separated judicial practice from administrative, legislative, and executive power had an almost immediate effect on the legal resources available to Quiteña women. The status-based matrix that managed the array of legal positions available to defendants and plaintiffs was effectively reduced to the binary of citizen/noncitizen. The liberal commitment to the rule of law encouraged following its letter, and particularly the patriarchal strictures that existed in the old, and routinely ignored, codes. With those strictures unbound by customary practice and special rights, law became a tool of disfranchisement for individuals whose array of identities ultimately could not measure up to the political (and economic and racial and gender) standards of "citizen." In the short term, during the early 1810s women continued to pursue their customary rights by increasingly perpetuating the legal fiction of nonmarital status before the court. City and departmental magistrates increasingly sent women to verbal hearings, where they were charged to bring a "good man" (*hombre bueno*) to act as arbitrator along with the magistrate in mediation. The restoration of Fernando VII presented a lull in the liberal reformation of quiteño society. And yet, as this chapter will demonstrate, the many legal reforms that in the 1820s accelerated women's loss of legal status had their roots in the first wave of liberal revolution and the Napoleonic period.

EARLY LEGAL REFORMS

Though it took decades for the accumulated legal heritage of three hundred years of Spanish rule and customary practice to be fully transformed, already in the early days of the Free State of Quito, the Spanish Cortes, and the Cádiz Constitution of 1812, the legal culture of the empire was being reimagined by liberal revolution. In the 1811–1812 Quito Constitution, judicial power was already being segregated from executive and legislative power.[1] Article 45 of the document established,

> Supreme Judicial Power, as part of sovereign authority . . . will be exercised by the High Court of Justice in all cases and things stipulated by the Law with respect to the extinguished Audiencias and in regard to civil material and criminal disputes, save [those powers] reserved by this Constitution for the Executive and Legislative Powers.[2]

At the highest level, this shift in theory and practice was transformative, dismantling the hallmark structures of decentralized governance and its overlapping and competing jurisdictions of concentrated administrative and judicial power. The constitution, however, did not change this organization at the nonappellate level. The alcaldes ordinarios and other minor magistrates, such as those in the barrios, remained intact both as members of the city and as provincial-level bureaucracy. Ultimately, the new organization of judicial power at the Audiencia level remained theoretical since the Constitution of the Free State of Quito was essentially never enforced. It *was* representative, however, of the trends in law and legal culture sweeping the broader Spanish monarchy.

As the Free State of Quito was taking its first tentative steps toward reformulating the judicial system, Spanish liberals in the Cortes of Cádiz drove the empire farther into liberal revolution. The hallmark, from a juridical perspective, of Spanish and American liberalisms was the foundational principles of equality before the law for all citizens and the separation of powers into executive, legislative, and judicial arenas. This, of course, held significant implications for the organization of judicial authority in the empire. Title V of the Cádiz Constitution of 1812 established the guidelines for the administration of criminal and civil justice prior to Fernando VII's restoration, and again after the triumph of Spanish liberals with the reinstitution of the document in 1820. The first order of judicial business in Cádiz was to firmly detach the judiciary from executive and legislative administration, to establish a clear hierarchy of appeal, and to abolish the system of fuero rights that formed the basis of the traditional legal labyrinth:

ART. 242. The authority to apply the law in civil and criminal cases exclusively belongs to the courts.

ART. 243. Neither the Cortes nor the King may, in any circumstances, exercise judicial functions, advocate in pending cases, nor order terminated cases reopened.

ART. 245. The courts may not exercise any other functions than adjudication and executing judgments.

ART. 248. In common affairs, both civil and criminal, there will be only one fuero for all classes of people.

ART. 258. The civil, commercial, and criminal code will be the same for the whole monarchy, without prejudice to variations the Cortes may make for specific circumstances.

ART. 262. All criminal and civil cases will be concluded in the court within the territorial jurisdiction.

ART. 263. As determined by the law, all civil and criminal cases of the second and third instance will appertain to the high court associated with the lower court's jurisdiction.[3]

Privileges were established in Articles 249 and 250 for the limited preservation of ecclesiastical and military fueros, thus the constitution did not completely disband social corporations. What were disbanded were special jurisdictional rights at the municipal, regional, or kingdom level. The constitution further delineated rights for those accused of criminal offenses:

ART. 287. No Spaniard will be detained without there first being a summary investigation of the crime, which must, according to the law, qualify for corporal punishment and be accompanied by a judge's written order that notifies [the defendant] of the reason for imprisonment.

ART. 290. The detainee will be presented to a magistrate before being incarcerated. The magistrate will take the detainee's deposition, unless this is impossible, in which case the detainee will be incarcerated and a magistrate will take his deposition within twenty-four hours.

ART. 294. Possessions may be seized only when prosecuting crimes that involve financial penalty; [the seizure] will be proportionate to the amount that can be extended as penalty.

ART. 302. [Criminal] proceedings will move forward publicly, in the manner and form prescribed by the law.

ART. 303. Torture will never be used, nor compulsions.

ART. 304. Confiscation of property will not be imposed as a punishment.[4]

The enumeration of specific procedural rights and restrictions on state practice expressed a new understanding of legal subjectivity, as well as an attempt to curtail the exercise of arbitrary judicial power. There are two sides to this coin. The establishment of boundaries on both individual legal personhood and on state power simplified and clarified the judicial process. It also closed the avenues of mitigation that the old system provided with its contingency and imprecision. But that is not all: from the perspective of the legitimacy of state authority, the Cádiz Constitution of 1812 uncoupled royal authority from its traditional and privileged position as the ultimate arbiter and guarantor of justice and, by extension, communal harmony, capricious as that justice may at times have been.

IN MEDIATION

Locally, legal reforms based on the Cádiz Constitution of 1812 that had the most effect on practices related to the reconceptualization of the office and role of the alcalde. In the section on the administration of civil justice, Article 282 states, "The Alcalde of every town will exercise his office as a mediator [*conciliador*]; whomever seeks to petition over civil transactions [*negocios civiles*] or offense [*injurias*] should present themselves to the alcalde with this objective."[5] The following article further explains that the process of conciliation, monitored and directed by the alcalde, would be adjudicated by three men. In addition to the alcalde, the litigants were to bring with them "good men" (*hombres buenos*), men of reputation, to form a board of mediation. These three men would then hear verbal arguments from each of the litigants, and together proffer an "extrajudicial" conciliation. If the two parties agreed to the decision, the matter would end there. If not, the case could then be carried on in more formal and regular fashion.[6]

The inclusion of injurias, together with traditional contract disputes, as one of the two categories of offenses subjected to verbal conciliation was itself a shift in conceiving the type of offenses associated with the term. Injurias claims were largely, though not exclusively, restricted to public insults against reputation and person, and were traditionally filed as both criminal and civil complaints (*querellandome civil y criminalmente*), because the damages done by insult were considered to cause both criminal and civil harm. The move toward considering insult as a purely civil offense may well reflect the rise of the sense of contract as the basis for both legitimate governance and as the infrastructure for legal personhood. The contract theories of Atlantic liberalism held that the bases for governance and the means by which individuals engaged in mutual action, or litigated disputes over such actions, was through the willful participation of the property-carrying individual (in which the individual's self is defined as part of that property) contractually agreeing to cede his property in exchange for sociability, the protection of rights, and governing prerogatives.[7] Public insults, which threatened the reputation and contracting ability of the individual, came to threaten the civil status that afforded a citizen the ability to participate in political and economic society.

Verbal cases had been used within certain corporate entities prior to the Cádiz Constitution of 1812. For example, merchant disputes were often heard as verbal cases by commercial magistrates. We already have seen this in the January 1809 dispute between Doña Ygancia Sanchez and Don Antonio Ruiz over the bad shrimps. Prior to the involvement of Doña Ygnacia's husband, she and Ruiz took their quarrel to the local commercial magistrate for a verbal hearing. The practice, however, did not show up commonly amongst the general magistrature until 1812. The implementation of verbal cases for conciliation was very rapid. As in the case of establishing constitutional ayuntamientos, the legal reforms implied by the Cádiz Constitution of 1812 were already in practice in the Spanish Americas in 1813 and 1814. In Quito, the interpretation of the two categories included any number of contract disputes (loans, lands, houses, testaments) as well as injurias cases of both verbal and property damage. The practice accelerated from 1812 on, and in the 1820s was recodified under Gran Colombia (see Chapter 6). Our access to information about the early implementation of verbal conciliation is hampered when we look at the early 1810s. We know of the use of conciliation largely from moments when mediation failed or when cases were ordered by a magistrate to go to mediation rather than continuing as a traditional case; many seem to have continued in spite of the order to mediation.

For cases involving women as primary litigants, the recourse to verbal hearings patterned the emphases listed in the constitution. In 1812, when verbal cases began to show up regularly, there is a striking resemblance to the regular process of offering a verbal complaint to a magistrate, indicating the practice was not yet formalized but rather an extension of earlier judicial practices for less-formal complaints. That said, the cases ascribed the label verbal trial (*juicio verbal*), as opposed to verbal request or complaint (*pedimento verbal*), parallel the description in the constitution. In April 1812, Doña Juana Tavera, wife of a procurador from the pueblo of Pillaro, Don José Paz y Mino, pursued a verbal trial against her husband over 200 pesos she claimed he owed her from the sale of a house and in restitution of part of her dowry.[8] Paz y Mino appealed the verbal hearing to the city's alcalde ordinario claiming that she could not sue him in civil court, but that she should seek her recourse in an ecclesiastical venue and request the dissolution of their marriage if she wanted restitution of her dowry. Doña Juana, it seems, had abandoned Don José but was still seeking alimony support. He also provided a form delineating the monies and comestibles he had provided Doña Juana from June 20, 1810, through April 9, 1812, the period of her abandonment. A month later, in May 1812, Doña Ysabel Gordillo y Jibaja found herself in a verbal trial with Dr. Don José Ayala over a large, disputed silver plate. Doña Ysabel filed to recover the plate, which she claimed she had was owed as payment for more five months of personal service; in a verbal hearing the Audiencia ordered Don José to pay her 40 pesos in its stead. The verbal case was itself mentioned in a petition Doña Ysabel filed to force Don José's compliance with the earlier order.[9] Later that same month, Doña Maria Roman, a vecina of Quito, filed a complaint against Don Antonio dela Guerra for entering her room and stealing a number of household goods to sell for cash. The hearing resulted in a decision against Don Antonio, but did not result in his imprisonment.[10]

These cases from 1812 evidence the practice of verbal hearings prior to the innovations of the Cádiz Constitution. Notably absent, though, was the process of litigants naming an hombre bueno to represent their interests on a panel of arbiters, who appeared along with the alcalde. It did not take long before this innovation went into effect, and by early 1813, verbal cases were ordered according to the provisions and authority of the Cádiz Constitution. In part as a main marker for the shift to the new form of verbal case, the hearings were designated not simply as verbal trials, but as mediations or conciliations (juicio de conciliación). For example, in March 1813, widow Doña Mariana Ramires filed suit against Manuel Reynoso, an Indian belonging to the parish of San Roque, over a pair of silver lances (braceros) that Manuel had borrowed and then passed on to Don Ramon Borja. Doña Mariana's claim to the braceros, worth some 70 pesos, was upheld by the court, and the case quickly transformed into a dispute between Don Ramon and Manuel over returning the property to her. The judge ordered they "proceed to conciliation as provided by the Political Constitution of the Monarchy." He further ordered that, in conformation of the dictates of the law that Don Ramon and Manuel, through his representation by the office of defender of the Indians, should bring with them each an hombre bueno to the mediation to represent their interests.[11]

A few months later, in August 1813, Tomasa Arias, a married vecina of Quito, found herself sitting in the recogimiento of Santa Marta at the request of her husband, Eugenio Hidalgo. Hidalgo had had her detained in a complicated marital dispute in which Tomasa was requesting alimony and Hidalgo alleging abandonment. Tomasa petitioned the alcalde ordinario to order her release as well as financial support from a husband she declared was dedicated to her mistreatment. The magistrate ordered the case to conciliation, but before the hearing had occurred Eugenio Hidalgo skipped town with 4 pesos and a knife that belonged to Tomasa, and thus no outcome of the verbal case was recorded.[12] The case is notable for the predisposition of the magistrate to order a marriage dispute that hinged on abandonment and poor treatment (*mal vivir*) to conciliation, which marked a change from marital disputes discussed in chapters 3 and 4 of this work.

Evidence suggests that local magistrates interpreted the inclusion of injurias for verbal conciliation to encompass both physical and verbal offenses. For example, on August 3, 1814, Antonio Guacollante, an Indian resident of the pueblo of Cotocollao just north of the city, filed a petition on behalf of his adopted daughter, Rosa Tuña, who had been abducted and injured at the hands of Don Francisco Carcelen, patron of a neighboring hacienda.[13] Antonio submitted a petition directly to the president of the Audiencia, requesting the court intervene to stop the mistreatment of his adopted daughter.[14] He claimed that Don Francisco had shown up at Antonio's home in his absence and absconded with Rosa, whipping her in the process of taking her. Antonio's wife resisted the abduction together with Antonio who appeared during the fracas, and the two were treated brutally by Don Francisco and his men. The three were then carried to Don Francisco's hacienda where they were held for some time until Don Francisco released Antonio and his wife. In the two months that followed, Antonio claimed Don Francisco had arranged the marriage of Rosa Tuña to an old Indian, a marriage he could not approve. The stress of the situation had proven too much for Antonio's wife, who died, allegedly from grieving the treatment of her daughter Rosa. In response to all of these actions, Antonio petitioned the presidency for legal redress, requesting that the court at least fine Don Francisco and order him to leave Antonio's family alone, in peace. At the end of his petition, Antonio appended an explanation for why his petition was being submitted in circumvention of the protector de indios "as is customary," claiming that he had sought intervention of the protector, only to be rebuffed on repeated occasions. This final point became a note of significant controversy in the development of the case.

President Toribio Montes ordered the petition reviewed by the government's legal advisers, and ten days later ordered that the case be remitted to the city's first alcalde constitucional. The alcalde, Don Manuel de Larrea of 10 de Agosto fame, was first and foremost interested in establishing the final claim of Antonio's petition—that he had been repeatedly rebuffed by the protector de indios. Don Pablo Guevara, the current agent of the office of the protector, suggested that Antonio was being mendacious, and that in reality he was being manipulated by *pendolistas* who sought to undermine the honor and effectiveness of the protector's legitimate role as representative of Indians in need of legal redress.[15] It is likely that Don Pablo was in communication with Don Francisco Carcelen, because Don Francisco's own response to the allegations centered on the question of agitation by pendolistas seeking to foment revolutionary discontent amongst indigenous communities. Don Francisco protested,

> I, in defense of my good reputation, can offer Your Grace no better justification for these judicial messes than that they all have their origin in the abundance of pendolistas that have proliferated in this city, and who, in order to continue their fraud, go around seducing poor people . . . in order to slander Citizens of honor, charging them with the most indecent falsities causing damages [to one's reputation] both public and private.[16]

In response to the specifics of Antonio Guacollante's charges, Don Francisco offered that the girl in question, Rosa Diguai, was the daughter of an Indian who worked on, resided on, and belonged to his hacienda, and thus fell under his authority. Note that Don Francisco changed Rosa's surname from Tuña to Diguai. He also referred to her as a "young single Indian" [*yndiesita celibe*], which downplayed whether or not she was a minor from a legal perspective. Celibate or single were interchangeable terms that established a specific marital and legal status in a dispute. Don Francisco further argued that the death of Rosa's mother reinforced the need to remove Rosa from Antonio's purview. For what it is worth, Don Francisco made no apologies or explanations for the violence imputed by Antonio's complaint. It appears the court was not very concerned with it, either.

In response to these developments, Antonio Guacollante was compelled to appear in person to explain the source of his written petition, and why he had circumvented the protector de indios. On August 29, 1814, he appeared before Alcalde Larrea, the agent of the Protectoría Pablo Guevara, and Court Notary Francisco Ribadeneyra to explain under oath that he had been told by a soldier where to find someone to write a legal petition for him. The unnamed soldier directed Antonio to the plazuela of the San Francisco convent, where he was ushered into a room of one of the square's houses and met with a scribe who produced the petition for 4½ reales. This was a normal process for getting petitions written, and seems remarkable only to the extent that the individual involved was proactively petitioning the court *as* an Indian, but outside the office of the protector. It was much more common to find indigenous litigants petitioning the court simultaneously with their complaint and with a request for intervention by the protector de indios. Following this collection of information, Alcalde Larrea ruled on September 1, 1814, that the case should proceed to conciliation, with both parties appearing together with their hombre bueno for verbal adjudication. Additionally, Larrea ordered that the hombre bueno representing Antonio's interests on the mediation board must be chosen by an agent from the office of the protector de indios. Thus the case represented a number of significant realignments in judicial process; it also, unfortunately, ends without recording the outcome of the conciliation.

The injuries documented in the case filed by Antonio Guacollante were physical more than they were verbal. Guacollante was seeking redress for the abuse of his adopted daughter, as well as the physical mistreatment he and his wife experienced at the hands of Don Francisco Carcelen. The more likely scenario for injurias cases in mediation were verbal insults publicly hurled in moments of social tension. For example, just three days after Antonio filed his petition,

Don José Falconi complained to Alcalde Constitucional Larrea on August 6, 1814, against Joaquin Artudillo and his wife, Ygnacia Moreno, for insulting him and injuring his reputation with the most "indecorous words."[17] To be specific, Don José claimed that Ygnacia had called him a *runasambo* in the patio of a house where a transaction had soured between him and Ygnacia's husband.[18] In response to this public slight, Don José implored the alcalde to open a traditional investigatory case, and provided three witnesses to be deposed. On August 8 and 9, Larrea interviewed the witnesses—two men and one woman—concerning the altercation, and the circumstances that prompted the insult. His witnesses, however, were weak. Only one could fully endorse Don José's account, while the second had secondhand information, and the third, Doña Ana Giron, actually claimed she heard Ygnacia responding to Don José that her *husband* was *not* an "Indian or sambo." The magistrate was underwhelmed.

A few days later, Don José offered two more witnesses—eighteen- and fourteen-year-old boys. As minors, they were assigned a guardian, who then oversaw the questioning. Again, the testimony was weak. Both of the minors worked in the employ of Don José and their testimony extended the insult in a suspiciously consistent manner, as they claimed Ygnacia had not only called Don José an indio sambo, but also declared, "anyone with money [can claim to be] a nobleman. [Even still] Falconi is nothing but an Indian with money."[19] Alcalde Larrea must have been frustrated by the distraction and expense of time and effort. Based on the recommendation of his legal advisor (*asesor*) Dr. Don Pedro Jacinto Escobar, Larrea ordered on August 11, 1814, the dispute to conciliation with representation by two hombres buenos, but not with the most due speed. The trial apparently was not held until December 1, 1814, and the parties were not informed of the verdict until the following June. On June 3, 1815, Don José Falconi, Joaquin Astudillo, and Ygnacia Moreno were delivered the verdict from the juicio de conciliación, which found Joaquin and Ygnacia guilty of offending Don José but sentenced them only to court costs with a threat for much more severe treatment should they publicly insult someone again.

Sometimes, women represented their dependents in conciliation cases. Josefa Villacreses filed a complaint on September 7, 1814, before the alcalde constitucional for correction of verbal and physical abuses suffered by two of her children at a local bar (*estanquillo de aguardiente*) owned by Mariano Cueba.[20] Josefa was filing on behalf of her two sons, Ysidro and Manuel Sisneros, as their widowed mother. The two boys had gone to Maria Cueba's establishment to purchase a little liquor, but ended up playing a game of *palmo*, with Manuel, Juan, and Rosa Carrera—a father and his two children.[21] The game apparently took a bad turn at one point, resulting in the Carreras hitting Ysidro and Manuel with sticks and stones (*piedras y palos*). Under further investigation, the Alcalde Constitucional the Marqués de Solanda ordered, "In observance with the Sovereign Law of the Constitution, [the case] will proceed to a trial of conciliation, with each party naming for their part a good man." The alcalde's ruling marks one of the first instances I have found of the realignment of legal reasoning from dispensing the king's justice for communal harmony to enforcing the dictates of sovereign law. In the meantime, Rosa Carrera, who had been sequestered in the wake of the dispute, was ordered released. On September 17, the parties appeared with their representatives before the Marqués de Solanda. The notary recorded that, as a result of the verbal trial, the alcalde had found Manuel Carrera and his accomplices guilty, and ordered that he pay a 25-peso fine, as well as both the court costs and medical bills of Josefa's sons. Furthermore, the alcalde remarked that Manuel appeared to be "addicted to fighting," and that should he be found guilty of provoking tumults again he would be subjected to serious punishment.

Together, the *juicios conciliatorios* described above represent the beginning of a number of shifts that would come to fruition in the coming decades. The tendency to view *injurias* cases, including those that included significant violence, as civil disputes, and therefore property disputes, indicates the emergence of a new sense of a property-bearing citizenry, a shift that is the hallmark of the rise of contract as the basis of law, property, and sociability. It also appears that the court was increasingly concerned with funneling judicial resources through appropriate men, defined as "good men." For indigenous litigants, this meant a doubling down on restricting their representation to the office of the protector, whether desired or not. For women, the institution of the *juicio conciliatorio* increased their dependence on male representation. Even in cases where women filed or would customarily file independently, the process of conciliation required that they choose an *hombre bueno* to represent their interest in the mediation. The panel of three men, the judge plus each party's repre-sentative, pressured the parties to accept the panel's offer of media-tion, in the name of diminishing unnecessary litigation in the court system. Though the production of paper was curtailed, or potentially curtailed, by the advent of the juicio conciliatorio, the magistrature still oversaw the hearings, which took time. Thus, if nothing else, the normalization of mediation did change the process of male interven-tion in cases involving women.

ON REPRESENTATION

What, then, of licensure and representation data for the period of liberal revolution? For the five years 1810–1814, women were pri-mary participants in 134 of the cases documented by the office of the First Notary, a reduction from the 248 cases in the 1805–1809 sample (see Appendix III).[22] How do the numbers on male license and representation break down for these opening years of upheaval? Altogether, 179 individual women appeared as primary participants in the 134 cases for this five-year sample. Of those, 69.8 percent (n=125) appeared without license, 5.6 percent (n=10) presented license to the court, while 14.5 percent (n=26) were represented by their hus-bands or fathers. The remaining 10 percent were represented by a variety of men and women, carrying authority as attorneys, specially empowered representatives, or through the various legal offices of the crown designed to provide legal counsel for the poor, slaves, minors, or indigenous subjects.[23] Thus the general trends of the late colonial period held in the earliest years of the revolution. We still find close to 70 percent of female litigants ignoring license requirements, though the likelihood increased that a woman without license would claim no marital status before the court. From 1810 to 1814, 57.6 percent (n=72) of women filed or responded to complaints without noting their marital status, up from 52.9 percent (n=108) the five years pre-ceding, 47.5 percent (n=58) for the period 1785–1789, and 35 percent (n=7) for the period 1765–1769. This continued a trend in the samples of the late colonial period toward the legal fiction of women without marital status (not even as "single" or "celibate"). The new litigants without license were no more likely to be widows (21.6 percent, n=27) or religious (1.6 percent, n=2), but were less likely to be single (4.0 percent, n=5) than in the previous samples. They were also less likely to be married. Married women accounted for 15.2 percent (n=19) of nonlicensed litigants, down from 19.1 percent (n=39) the preceding five years, from 18.9 percent (n=23) from 1785 to 1789, and from 30 percent (n=6) from 1765 to 1769. The trend suggests an increasing sensitivity toward the legal expectation of license or male representation from married litigants, most often circumvented by omitting status from petitions.

Unlicensed legal actions by women still greatly outnumbered those made by women who presented permission from their husbands or were represented by them in court. As mentioned above, only ten women presented license to the court. It is notable that the number of women claiming license declined precipitously from the immediate five years preceding, during which twenty-four licenses were recorded. In part, it appears that the reduction is accounted for simply by an overall decrease in women's cases, since unlicensed acts were virtually halved as well. The decrease of licensed acts does not necessarily indicate a decrease in male control over women's legal resources. By comparison, the period 1810–1814 did witness a relative increase, or intensification of husbands and fathers representing women in court (see Appendix III). Fifty-nine female litigants utilized male representatives for the five years, though the majority of those representatives were attorneys, officials of the various protector offices (protector de indios, esclavos, and pobres), and third parties who carried power of attorney. These instances accounted for 56 percent (n=33) of representations, followed the same procedure regardless of the gender of the litigant, and were determined by nongendered corporate statuses of wealth, ethnicity, and privilege. Husbands and fathers represented women in 44 percent (n=26) of cases that had male representatives, which equated to 19.6 percent of all cases involving women as primary litigants in the sample. This was up from the five years previous, in which husbands and fathers combined for 38.8 percent (n=26) of cases involving male representation, and a mere 10.5 percent of total cases. Furthermore, as the information on juicios conciliatorios above suggests, the likelihood that cases filed by independent women would end up funneled into the innovative form of male representation embodied by the hombre bueno served to intensify male mediation of legal recourse.

Not all injurias cases were adjudicated at verbal trials. Sipriano Reynoso, a vecino of Quito and owner of a farm in nearby Chimbacalle, complained in mid-January 1810 of having been insulted publicly by an indigenous woman named Mercedes Umaso.[24] Mercedes was the legitimate wife of an indigenous man named Rafael Peres, and the two lived on a property in the neighborhood of Sipriano's farm. The proximity of their properties actually sparked the dispute: one of the Indian couple's pigs wandered onto Sipriano's land and was digging about in his grain stores. Sipriano claimed that when he informed the couple of this, Mercedes dressed him down with the most ugly of insults.[25] The couple also threatened that if he touched the animal again he would pay physically. Sipriano claimed the couple then pushed him to the ground, and hit him with clenched fists (*manos serrados*). Apparently, they did not stop with insults and blows for Sipriano, but also insulted the honor of his sister and niece, whom Sipriano characterized as honorable women—the first married, and the second her daughter, an honest virgin (*muger virgen*). Sipriano thus was filing a criminal and civil complaint on behalf of himself, his sister, and his niece. He also recruited individuals of status to support his claims and testify to the turpitude of Mercedes Umaso. The auxiliary parish priest of San Sebastian backed up Sipriano's claims, and wrote to the municipal alcalde that Mercedes in particular was a problematic person, always causing scandal and furor, disrespecting the "content citizens of [San Sebastian] who conduct themselves with esteem and decorum."[26] The alcalde ordered an investigation opened primarily against Rafael Peres, as if he were culpable for both his and his wife's actions. Unfortunately, the folio ended without the results of the investigation.

Sometimes, insults were part of the judicial complaint themselves. Three months after Sipriano's complaint, Doña Paula Cevallos complained to the municipal alcalde that Maria Dolores Gonzales was carrying on an illicit relationship with her husband, Don José Molina.[27] In petitioning, Doña Paula characterized herself as a vecina and merchant of Quito, and demeaned Maria Dolores as a common woman (*muger común*) and public prostitute (*pública meretriz*). Doña Paula complained that the relationship had ruined her marriage, leaving her and her legitimate children without support beyond the mercantile shop she managed in Quito. Five days prior to filing the complaint, Doña Paula's husband was surprised and caught with Maria Dolores, who was carried off to Santa Marta. This public scandal provoked the filing of the petition. From her cell in Santa Marta, Maria Dolores denied the allegations, stating that José Molina was found in her house, but that they were not even in the same room. His presence there was completely licit, she claimed. Furthermore, she claimed that the harsh words and actions of Doña Paula threatened the health of her soul and body, in part because they threatened her betrothal to Don Manuel Torres. The alcalde apparently believed her, because on March 26, 1810, he ordered her released from Santa Marta on the promise of future good conduct and with no further penalty. Interestingly, the court took no interest in the culpability of José Molina, a stance far different from the judicial activism of the 1780s and 1790s. During those years, officials regularly prosecuted and punished both parties of an adultery suit. It was also becoming increasingly rare to find adultery and illicit cohabitation suits. In the Criminales section of the archive, there are only three adultery cases from the corregimiento of Quito preserved for the years 1810–1814. Two of these cases were prosecutions of bigamy against one Bonifacio Velasco.[28] The third was an illicit cohabitation prosecution of Mariano Ceas and Antonia Prado.[29] By comparison, the preceding five years includes six prosecutions.[30] This was far down for the decades of the late eighteenth century, when, for example, the Criminales section of the Archivo Nacional del Ecuador, Quito, has sixty-six prosecutions from the city of Quito and the Five Leagues. Likewise, in the litigation preserved by the First Notary of Quito, sex crime allegations dropped dramatically. There were only four sex crimes prosecuted and recorded by the First Notary, all of which occurred in 1810.[31] In some cases, litigation that would have led to the investigation of sex crimes stuck instead to whatever the original offense was. Thus, in July 1814 a case of assault was brought against Maria Clara Mayquinga, an indigenous resident of the pueblo of Tumbaco east of the city, for assaulting her lover, Francisco Borja Toapanta.[32] The two had apparently lived together in long-term adultery, for years sharing a house on a hacienda owned by Don Juan José Laso, having abandoned their respective spouses. The new liberal governments of the 1810s and 1820s simply were not interested in policing domestic sexual behaviors in the way Bourbon governments had been.

Sex was not only of less interest to the state, it also played a decreasing role in the injurias suits involving women brought before the magistratura. In July 1810, Evaristo Valencia, a musician and soldier living in Quito, filed charges against Antonio Balladres, his two sisters, and José Hidalgo for verbally and physically abusing Evaristo's wife. They had publicly called her a "known thief" (*ladrona pública*), and then beaten her up in the street.[33] In September 1811, Don Juan Camino filed a complaint against Don Manuel Paredes who, in front of some shops near the Arco Magdalena, called and treated Don Juan's wife Doña Nicolasa dela Parra a *zamba*.[34] In May 1814, Ygnacia Roman was turned in for publicly abusing José Espindola in Guayllabamba just north of the city.[35] Ygnacia reeled off a string of slurs against José, calling him a "lying sambo, thief, cattle-rustler, and witch" (*picaro sambo, ladrón, quatrero, y brujo*). Finally, in September 1814, Doña Michaeyla Echeverria, a merchant in Quito, complained against Michaeyla Garson and her mother Ygnacia, for publicly insulting her by calling her a samba. Whereas harmful words in the late eighteenth century with women tended to emphasize their sexual honor, in the opening decade of the liberal revolution, race and economic reputation took precedence.

CONTRACTS

Economic reputation was still of key importance to women in the city, as they continued to operate as sources and consumers of credit. Indeed, as the political-economic justification for power moved increasingly toward a constitutional contract theory, credit worthiness was taking on a new import. Thus, women were caught in an increasingly delicate position as purveyors of credit in a milieu that increasingly challenged their customary capacity to make contracts. There is evidence in the First Notary litigation to suggest that this contradiction was overcome, much as the question of legal capacity was overcome, through the perpetuation of legal fictions. In this case, the legal fictions were not necessarily the omission of marital status in making contracts, but rather a tendency to more often use simple instruments to document loans.[36] It is difficult to judge the extent to which simple instruments were utilized by either male or female lenders, because they never showed up in the documentary record unless they were being contested. And because of that, it is also difficult to know whether simple instruments showed up in court more often because default was more common on simple instruments. Even still, anecdote in the First Notary suggests women were likely to use simple instruments to document loans, and the courts did uphold the contracts. The majority of pesos cases involving female litigants from 1810–1814 included simple instruments, and ranged from 15 to 1,480 pesos.[37] Simple instruments swore to the specifics of a loan in a fairly predictable format. Thus, from a case filed in early January 1810 the instrument reads,

> The Marqués of Villa Orellana and his son, the Dr. Don José Sanchez de Orellana, declare that with this instrument we are obligated to satisfy to my Señora Doña Francisca Hipalda 1,480ps among others that we have borrowed from the afore-mentioned Señora on this day from Don Miguel Ponse. The principal will be retired by the 15th of June of next year, 1809, along with interest of 6 percent, to which we oblige our assets. In Quito, 28th of April of 1808.[38]

The instrument was then signed by the Marqués and his son, and later appended to a complaint filed a year and a half later by Señora Doña Francisca against the Marqués. The two men had borrowed the money to pay for the son's marriage in Loja, but were late in repayment—no doubt the result of the instabilities they were involved with in the years following the loan. As was often the case, the collection of debt was complicated, and Doña Francisca had to garnish the rent of one of the Marqués' estates to collect her money.

Though few of the other pesos cases involved such substantial amounts, the pattern of the simple instruments was the same. In March 1810, Doña Maria Corrales, owner of a pulpería, filed suit against Don Domingo Flores, the governor of the indigenous community resident in the San Blas Parish of Quito. She presented the court with a simple instrument in which Flores together with his wife, Yduarda Araus, borrowed 40 pesos on October 8, 1802.[39] Because neither Flores nor his wife could write, the instrument was signed by a witness. By the time she took the couple to court, their outstanding debt was 53 pesos, 3 reales. In response to her complaint, the judge ordered the liquidation of Governor Flores's goods to repay the outstanding debt. It should be noted that, while Yduarda Arauz is present in the case and in the loan, as the legitimate wife of Domingo Flores, no marital status was mentioned in the instrument or throughout the case for Doña Maria Corrales. A few months later, in May 1810, Doña Nicolasa Romero filed suit against José Muirragui, the mayordomo of the city's poorhouse. She was attempting to enforce repayment of a debt of 24 pesos, 4 reales, the value of a container of wheat flour that José Muirragui had taken for the hospicio.[40] The judge ordered the instrument and Muirragui's signature validated, and while José agreed that the signature and debt were legitimate, he claimed the administrator of the poorhouse should repay the debt. The case was thusly resolved.

In May 1812, the courts enforced a simple contract signed by Doña Juana Bastidas, who had fallen behind in payment of a 430-peso debt that she owed Don Pablo Bascones.[41] In the accompanying instrument, Doña Juana claimed she was borrowing from Don Pablo on orders from her husband, Don Juan Luis Pazmiño, and under those orders that she was putting up her own estate as collateral for the loan. It is unclear from the documentation if Doña Juana felt coerced into the debt, and she accepted the obligation. That said, the inclusion of the phrase, "by particular order of my Husband," stands out in the instrument. Gender was used tactically in the pesos cases. In March 1813, Don Miguel Arevalo filed suit against Doña Mariana Moreno over 381 pesos she owed him for clothing used to stock her store.[42] In the early stages of the case, Doña Mariana was strikingly absent from the legal maneuvering. When she finally responded, she pled ignorance to the judicial procedure on account of being female, stating, "with respect to my being an ignorant woman, it is not my obligation to understand the course of an executive trial. . . . In such cases I am favored by the Law, as well as by my widowhood, sex, and by my not understanding and the notary not able to explain to me the rulings handed down."[43] For the remainder of the case, she maneuvered to discount Don Miguel's case and testimony, including demanding that his petitions be given as sworn testimony. The court ultimately ruled in her favor, and ordered Don Miguel Arevalo to pay part of the court costs.

In April 1813, Don Manuel Paredes borrowed 32 pesos from Doña Andrea Osirio, securing the money with a pair of emerald earrings.[44] Three years later, Doña Antonia Abad filed a petition with Oidor Merchante claiming that the emerald earrings in Doña Andrea's possession were hers. The original instrument made no mention of Doña Andrea's marital status, but when the provenance of the earrings came into question, Doña Andrea's husband filed on her behalf, and was ultimately successful in compelling Don Manuel to repay the loan. Finally, in September 1814, Don Jose Albuja filed suit to nullify a simple instrument his wife, Maria Mercedes Robalino, had signed with Doña Maria Herrera, a single vecina of Quito. Albuja petitioned, "And as it is prohibited by law and right for married women to be able to make a petition, it would be appropriate to order as null and of no value the instrument she signed."[45] More details on the arrangement were forthcoming with the response of Maria Herrera. She claimed the document was signed before Maria Mercedes was married to Albuja, and further that Maria Mercedes had only signed as a guarantor for her daughter in a case over the theft of a silver candelabra in which her daughter was accused. The daughter, Joaquina Albuja, had been arrested and freed based on this promise. Though Don Jose Albuja's argument was technically correct, the court still accepted the obligation.

Some of the strongest evidence that simple instruments formed a core mechanism for women's lending comes from testaments and petitions to be declared official destitute (*pobre de solemnidad*). For example, when Juana Flores, an indigenous women from Quito, died intestate in June 1810, she left behind a series of obligations, all in the form of simple instruments: (1) Don Manuel Velazquez owed her 60 pesos and a necklace; (2) Juan Montaquiza, an Indian from Chimbacalle, owed her for 68 pesos worth of pearl and gold jewelry; (3) Casimiro Lambarri and his wife Lorena Ramos owed her 6 pesos; (4) José Alvarado from Amaguaña owed her 36 pesos for a pair of earrings; (4) Petrona Criollo, an Indian, owned her 15 pesos and sundry items. She also had in her possession receipts for the rent on her tienda and others' loan obligations.[46] In July 1810, Doña Margarita Andrade appealed to the court for debt relief and declaration as a pobre de solemnidad, submitting an account of her outstanding obligations totaling 165 pesos, 5 reales. All but one of her creditors were women: Doña Barbara Paredez for 33 pesos, Ysabel Caserez for 25 pesos, Doña Ylaria Sanchez for 37 pesos, Antonia Salinas for 11 pesos, Juana Avilas for 10 pesos, 5 reales, and Don Joaquin Cadena for 30 pesos.[47]

These and other cases from the period 1810–1814 suggest the continued importance of legal fictions in both the legal and economic operation of the city at a time when the interpretation of law was becoming stricter.[48] The cases above suggest that the use of simple instruments was typical when women were involved in credit transactions. And likewise, simple instruments invariably omitted mention of the marital status of lenders and borrowers, unless a couple was borrowing money together. The practice of using simple instruments was not new to the revolutionary period, but the information above suggests that recourse to simple instruments escalated during the 1810s as a means to circumvent changing political-economic expectations of citizenship. It was exactly at the same moment that liberals in the Audiencia were disfranchising female heads of household of traditional voting rights. These conclusions, though, are largely suggestive, since women did continue to pursue their customary legal and economic rights within the context of changing royal authority. Thus, while authorities ruled that women would not participate in the elections of 1813–1814, they still did petition the government as part of corporate groups in spite of their gender. For example, in August and September 1818, the city's merchants filed a series of petitions protesting the cancellation of the nightly ronda on the order of the city's commercial magistrate.[49] It seems the magistrate was pressuring the merchants to pay a new tax to fund the duties and to form a new guardia mayor. In the process of reforming the ronda and determining by whom and how it would be paid for, groups of merchants and homeowners from various streets and locations within the city, such as the Portal and the Calle del Real Colegio de San Fernando, as well as the general corporation of merchants, submitted petitions on the process. All but one of the six petitions submitted included women, either through signatures in their hand or by witnesses for those who were illiterate. As in the case of the barrio petitions electing representatives to the 1809 junta, women's participation in the petitions is somewhat obscured. The petition from the Calle del Real Colegio only notes that there were witnesses for the women, but did not list the signatures, so it is difficult to know how many women in total were part of the petitions. Sixty-three men signed along with fifteen women, in addition to the unspecified number from the Calle del Real Colegio. In the petition from the shops on the Portal of the main square, four of the seven signatories were women. Thus, into the late 1810s women acted on their customary position as shop owners and homeowners to petition the government concerning the well-being of the barrios. That task was made more difficult after independence, with the wholesale rejection of custom and status as a basis for legal participation.

CONCLUSION

The era between 1808 and 1814 marked a period of hybridity and transition in the emergence of new legal and political forms of citizenship in the Spanish monarchy. That moment was put temporarily on hold with the restoration of Fernando VII in 1814. Almost immediately upon his return, the king invalidated many of the actions made in his name, and particularly the triumph that was the Cádiz Constitution of 1812. In August 1815, Toribio Montes circularized the province ordering the restoration of the municipal governments and its associated magistrature.[50] Accompanying the circular was a royal decree from December 28, 1814, ordering that the provinces of America dismantle the constitutional municipal councils and restore as quickly as possible the original office of the alcalde ordinario. The immediate concern was in tying back together executive, legislative, and judicial authority to the royal sovereign. But the reimagination of law and politics was a tide not so easily turned. The same year that Montes acted in obedience to reestablish the old judicial and political order, his subordinates were appealing to authority on a new footing. Thus, for example, when a conflict arose over a special tax to fix an asequia in Ambato, a town 120 kilometers south of Quito, the collector and alguacil mayor Don Apolinario Lopez Merino wrote to the constitutional municipality in terms of citizenship. Don Apolinario explained,

> I am not ignorant of the fact that all men are born the same with God, as well as together with us as men. One can view a man as based on three aspects, that is as Christian, as Rational, and as a citizen, and vassal.[51]

The three positions posited by the aguacil of a small town in the Andes were religious, natural, and national, even if the concept of citizen was modified with the recognition of vassalage. Don Apolinario wanted out of his responsibilities to collect the special tax, and justified his desire in terms of the appropriate behaviors and expectations of a citizen, "to conserve one's own person, one's House, one's interests, and one's credit."[52] To work to collect taxes from an uninterested population would detract from these commitments. It is not unusual to find a royal official trying to get out of an onerous responsibility.

It is, however, of note to find such an official deploying the concept of citizen (*ciudadano*) even before independence was realized. The question remained: who would be a citizen and who would enjoy full citizenship rights, including legal protections. The answer to that question would be contested through the 1820s, and would increasingly cede to male prerogative.

CHAPTER SIX

PRACTICE IV

In the Name of the Law

————

Final independence from Spain was not achieved until the Battle of Pichincha on May 24, 1822. At the time, Audiencia President Melchor Aymerich was finishing the process of reimplementing the electoral system of the restored Cádiz Constitution of 1812. In August 1820, Aymerich received word of Fernando VII's capitulation to liberal demands to restore the constitution.[1] In response, he ordered the publication and display of the constitution throughout the province of Quito, the restoration of the myriad constitutional municipal councils formed by the 1813–1814 electoral process, and a call to organize new elections. Aymerich, however, found himself leading a diminished province, under significant pressure from Bolívar's revolutionary forces in the north, San Martín's forces in the south, and rival quiteño factions in Guayaquil on the coast. The latter, recognizing the likelihood of encroachment from one or the other of the revolutionary forces, declared independence for the entire province in early October, naming José Joaquín Olmedo as president. Reaction in Quito to the announcement was mixed, in part, according to Rodriguez, because of Aymerich's promised electoral renewal. Other cities in the province soon followed Guayaquil's example—Cuenca (November 3), Machachi, Latacunga, and Riobamba (November 11), Ambato (November 12), and Aluasí (November 13).[2] Quito did not follow suit.

Despite the increasing chaos, Aymerich continued to pursue his electoral reforms through the next two years. In 1821, he commissioned

León Pereda de Saravia to review the electoral plan from 1813 and make suggestions to put it in effect again. Pereda de Saravia filed his report on August 1, 1821, detailing the results of the decade-earlier censuses, the number of ayuntamientos established in the jurisdictions of the province, their assigned numbers of delegates and electors, and so on.[3] One month later, the province was moving forward with naming parochial electors to restart constitutional governance.[4] Thus, even as the old kingdom of Quito was on the brink of liberation from Spanish governance, the resurgent Spanish liberal revolution was again under way.

The district of Quito, former kingdom and province of the global Spanish monarchy, first found independence from Spain as the third state of Simón Bolívar's unified Republic of Gran Colombia. The legal and juridical structures of the new province of Ecuador were already in the process of transformation when General Antonio José de Sucre liberated the territory, a process that continued through the 1820s as Ecuador morphed from a federated kingdom of the global Spanish monarchy into an independent nation-state in 1830. The legal changes that occurred during the Gran Colombian period marked an acceleration of the attack on special privilege and status rights in the Andes, a fulfillment of the liberal legal vision expressed in the Cádiz Constitution of 1812.

And it certainly was an attack on an array of special privileges—not just on the privileges of nobles and elites. Indeed, the move from status to contract, in the words of Henry Maine, was a maneuver against the whole complex of status-based legal privileges and obligations, a system that also had served the legal interests of dominated groups within Spanish American society.[5] This maneuver has been overlooked, to a certain extent, by perceptions of legal continuity across the independence divide. The new states of the Andes preserved the position of Spanish law in the new constitutional order of the early republic, as long as laws did not directly contradict the constitutional order, or until they were specifically repealed by new codes. Title X of the 1821 Colombian Constitution stated, "It is declared that all of the laws that until now that have been in force are in effect, as long as they do not directly or indirectly oppose this constitution or the laws and decrees issued by the Congress."[6] A May 13, 1825, law clarified for Gran Colombian courts the new hierarchy of law, which first privileged legislation of the new republican government followed in order by Spanish laws and decrees recognized by the Junta Central from 1808 onward, the *Recopilación de Indias*, the *Nueva Recopilación de Leyes de Castilla*, and the *Siete Partidas*. This codification of the concept of precedence, reminiscent of earlier attempts to make sense of the labyrinth of Spanish law, provided a veneer of legal stability in which old law codes, most specifically the thirteenth-century *Siete Partidas* and the sixteenth-century *Nueva Recopilación de Leyes de Castilla* were brought into the postcolonial order.[7] Traditional interpretations of this fact have emphasized this use of law, together with patriarchal familial structures and the social cohesion of Roman Catholicism, as fetters on the transition to modernity.[8] The contextualization of Andean independence in the broader Atlantic liberal revolution as discussed in the preceding two chapters challenges this interpretation.

This chapter will demonstrate that, from the perspective of legal practice, the shift to contract and liberal republican ideals that separated judicial practice from administrative, legislative, and executive power had an almost immediate effect on the legal resources available to dominated groups in quiteño society. The status-based matrix that managed the array of legal positions available to defendants and plaintiffs was effectively reduced to the binary of citizen/noncitizen. In the very short term, women, indigenous communities, poor mestizos, and free blacks tried to make the smooth transition to claiming equal citizenship rights under the law, and appeared before the judiciary appropriating the term citizen (*ciudadano* or *ciudadana*) in the same way they had used other status markers just years earlier. But these groups were ultimately disfranchised of traditional customary rights by the redeployment of Spanish law untempered by derecho vulgar. In the 1820s, magistrates increasingly referenced specific law, mostly from the *Siete Partidas* and the *Nueva Recopilación*, in adjudicating civil and criminal disputes. In fact, whereas judicial decisions in the colonial period were almost never justified but rather existed as expressions of sovereign will, magistrates increasingly explained their decisions, and employed the formula, "In the Name of the Republic, by authority of the Law" in adjudicating a dispute. This simple phrase sums up the significance of the shift in conceptions of sovereignty during the early republic: it was not the embodiment (in the form of the judicial official) of the king's will to justice and communal harmony (as messy as this often was), but rather the

will of the republican state, underwritten by the authority of codified law, that carried legitimacy. The magistrate was no longer the
personal incarnation of sovereign authority, but rather an official
whose legitimacy radiated from a separate political, executive, and
legislative authority that he did not simultaneously manifest. The
magistrate became a functionary of the law rather than the embodiment and dispensary of royal justice.

The liberal commitment to the rule of law encouraged following
the law's letter, particularly the patriarchal strictures that existed in
the old codes—strictures that were routinely ignored in the Spanish
period through the perpetuation of legal fictions. With those strictures unbound by customary practice and special rights, law became
a tool of disfranchisement for individuals whose array of identities
ultimately could not measure up to the political (and economic and
racial and gender) standards of "citizen." For the women of Quito,
the implications of this shift became increasingly clear across the
decade of the 1820s. Whereas they had once enjoyed a robust ability to participate in legal acts, as litigants and contract makers,
through the combined ambivalences of derecho vulgar and status
rights, their disputes, ability to make disputes, and protections from
certain forms of imprisonment were under attack. Married women
in particular experienced increased male representation and reduced
access to the courts in the 1820s. Protections, such as restrictions
against putting women in debtors' prison, were de facto, if not de
jure, lifted. And while inheritance law went unchanged, a decline in
dowry practice left women with less access to property.[9] Finally, in
a manner similar to the fundamental concept of Carole Pateman's
Sexual Contract, the emergence of a new, republican public sphere of
politics (engaged in by rights-bearing citizens) was predicated on the
simultaneous construction of a codified, private domestic sphere that
was restricted from police power.[10] Early republican rule-makers
constrained city officials on the ronda from entering peoples' homes,
and specifically from entering homes to interfere with domestic disputes. In so doing, they constructed a new private sphere of gender and sexuality beyond the state's control. The combination of
new law and unbound patriarchal tendencies within the old law
left women in a vulnerable legal position that was specifically the
product of republican legal culture, and its "equality" before the
"authority of the law."

The transformation of the judicial organization of the state was carried farther during Ecuador's eight years of inclusion in Gran Colombia. The superior court of the department of the south, the anchor of the province's reformulated judiciary, was installed in a ceremony on July 1, 1822.[11] Early in the Colombian period, in 1823, the offices of the barrio alcalde, police magistrate, and municipal notary were authorized to continue working.[12] Local jurisdictions were already establishing rules on policing, the ronda, and controlling vagabondage. Such instructions were invariably expressed in terms of ensuring public order and tranquility to ensure the exercise of the rule of law for the new citizenry.[13] On May 28, 1823, the provisional government issued its first police regulations (*reglamento de policia*), establishing a chief of police (*comisario general de policia*) charged with "attending to the security, health, and comfort of the community."[14] The contours of those responsibilities were further elaborated in 1825 with the publication of a more-detailed twelve-article set of police regulations.[15] The local 1825 reglamento de policia complemented a law passed by the national legislature on March 11, 1825, "on the organization and political and economic rules of departments and provinces."[16] The Colombian law was more broadly gauged, and, significantly, it established the limits of provincial and departmental governors as strictly executive offices, explicitly exempted from exercising judicial power.[17] The law also provided for the formation of an executive official at the municipal level, alcaldes at the city and parish levels, committees on sanitation, and a police force. The 1825 police regulations published in Quito applied this law to the specific needs of Quito, and placed the first municipal alcalde (*alcalde de primer voto municipal*) as the chief police magistrate in charge of the city's security, health, and welfare. In order to facilitate the administration of police duties, the city was divided into two sections—the *barrios de arriba* and the *barrios de abajo* (upper and lower neighborhoods), divided by a line from the former Jesuit church *La Compañia* to the plaza of the carnecería in Santa Bárbara. Each of the two sections of the city was assigned its own police commissioners, beneath which officers were assigned to two-to-three block sections of the parishes. The new structure greatly amplified the policing of the barrios, increasing the number of neighborhood officials from the post-1765 level of one magistrate per barrio. In addition to the officer corps, each section commissioner was allotted two ministers to serve as assistants.[18]

Day-to-day responsibilities for policing the city, under the new regulations, fell mostly on the block captains. The enumerated duties included the following:

1. To communicate to the municipal alcalde via the section commissioners the comings and goings of all foreigners in a block captain's sector.
2. To make and present a yearly census accounting for the inhabitants of each block by sex, age, profession, and "mode of life."
3. To inquire on the public lives and morals of their neighborhoods in order to correct vice, *"but without meddling to examine domestic behaviors."* [Emphasis added.]
4. To make sure not to permit vagabonds or people without work or destination. "As a consequence of this rule, all of the beggars of either sex must present themselves the first of each month in order to be examined to verify if they really are sick and old and too incapacitated to work, at which point they will receive from the magistrate a permit licensing them to beg."
5. To keep watch over the public peace, informing on any potential commotions.
6. To develop a registry of all the carpenters and masons living in the neighborhoods in case of fires.
7. To inform the owners of houses that pose a danger due to disrepair of a specific time period to fix the problems with their houses.
8. To remain vigilant of the cleanliness of the streets and plazas in their jurisdictions. To maintain the cleanliness of the streets, the officials were to oblige cooperation from shop owners; for the plazas, they were to seek help from the city's Indian governor (*governador de indígenas*).[19]

Additionally, the block captains were to quickly spread word of any disease outbreak, to clear the streets of abandoned dead bodies, to keep the aqueducts clear of debris, to clear the streets of hagglers and vendors selling simple foodstuffs (invariably indigenous women), and to make sure that gambling establishments were not admitting children or slaves or staying open too late at night.[20] The net of surveillance was cast wide, yet sexual activity was never explicitly mentioned among the objects of control. Block captains were charged with vigilant monitoring of public morals, but they were explicitly forbidden to intrude on domestic space.

In Article X of the regulations, public morality was defined to include injunctions against drunkenness and fighting. This was a significant departure from the sexual surveillance of the late-Spanish period, and recast the home as a private sphere to be shunned by state authorities, a private sphere that heretofore did not exist.[21] Article X's legality rested on the Gran Colombian "Law of 3 August 1824," which laid out the rules for the entrance and searching of homes in accordance with Article 169 of the Colombian Constitution.[22] Specifically, the law stated a home could be entered only in cases of (1) fire, (2) overhearing people in the midst of robbery, murder, rape, or other violent crime that put an individual at risk of losing life, (3) when a husband, father, mother, grandfather, brother, uncle, guardian, or other individual accompanies the police to retrieve his or her wife, child, grandchild, sibling, ward, or other minor that has been taken from their custody and is in a suspected house, (4) in order to arrest an suspect for a crime that carries corporal punishment, (5) to interfere with conspiracies against the government, (6) to stop counterfeiters, individuals stockpiling arms, or holding stolen goods, and (7) to examine the private correspondence and papers of an individual if those papers are kept in the house.[23] It is again remarkable the extent to which domestic affairs, both sexual and disciplinary, were exempted from the list. The state was still interested in certain types of intrusion, just not as Article X describes, "in meddling to examine domestic behaviors." The decreased state interest in monitoring sexual behavior did mean, as arrest statistics will testify, that women were not being detained by institutional authorities for moral behaviors at rates anywhere near those in the 1780s and 1790s. It also diminished women's judicial redress for their husbands' and partners' infidelities, mistreatments, and bad living. The removal of legal constraints on men's and women's private behaviors was bought at the price of removing a significant recourse for women to constrain male prerogatives.

To a large extent, evidence for the construction of a private domestic space in the control of social norms by the new police forces of the 1820s exists in its absence. People simply were not arrested for sexual behaviors or spousal mistreatment except in extraordinary circumstances. Thus, the bar of "public and notorious" was transformed by the new rules. It is unlikely that the type of relationships policed for decades simply disappeared. Rather, it is much more likely that relationships made "public and notorious" by an interested judiciary returned to their original form of publicity—neighborhood knowledge, rumor, and innuendo. There is evidence in the Criminal and First Notary files to suggest that citizens quickly used the new rules to prevent state intrusion into the domestic sphere, usually in the form of abuse of power complaints against various judicial and police officials.[24] In February 1825, Mariano Baca y Naranjo filed a complaint against Andres Ortega and Captain José Lana for violating his household at night and confiscating some bulls to collect on a court-ordered 25-peso fine.[25] Baca y Naranjo opened his complaint, "Of course the Judicial Authorities of any state should exercise [power] with the intention of rewarding merit and punishing crime, but it is never legitimate to abuse that invested power."[26] And what was this abuse of power? Andres Ortega and Captain Lana "violated, and defied late at night the security of [his] house," taking four bulls in the company of soldiers and sending them to the bullfighting ring in Latacunga.[27] For Baca y Naranjo, it was the jurisdictional usurpation of his home that he decried as most egregious.

In some of the complaints, state officials were not involved, though the reasoning was the same. The concern with maintaining domestic space, male representation of that space, and the increasing importance of tying legal argument to the specifics of the law are exemplified by the injurias case filed in May 1825 by ciudadana Jesus Nieto on behalf of her two natural daughters, Ygnacia Nieto and Maria Maldonado.[28] She claimed her daughters were the victims of both verbal and physical injuries resulting from the actions of ciudadana Teresa Reyes, who showed up with a group of "armed black men" (negros armadas) at the Nieto house one afternoon in a dispute over one of the household's servants. The servant had insulted Teresa Reyes on a "public street," prompting her to recruit judicial authorities and visit the Nieto home to arrest her. Throughout the case, her husband and an attorney that he hired represented Reyes. An attorney hired by their mother in turn, represented the young women. Thus, with both parties men intervened in representing the case. The extent of verbal and physical injuries suffered by the two women became of secondary concern in the course of the litigation, while the act of home invasion increasingly took center stage. Attorneys for both sides enlisted the *Siete Partidas*, the *Nueva Recopilación de Leyes de Castilla*, and Colombian law in making their cases. Older Spanish law was recruited to argue the intricacies of insult, assault, and the presence of armed men, but in the case of home invasion, the attorneys quibbled over the interpretation of national law. Thus, Fermin Cepada, representing the Nieto household, argued, "To enter the house of a Citizen under whatever pretense is an act in which, it is recommended, even the Public Authorities cannot engage in cases and under the formalities of the Law, without committing a crime. If one's own house is a sanctuary of security, respect, and repose for everyone, then it must be seen politically as a sacred place."[29] The choice of language is interesting. In Spanish legal tradition, the physical church played the role of sanctuary, a right that ecclesiastics jealously guarded even in protection of abominable crimes.[30] Thus Cepada was rhetorically constructing the household as a space beyond state intervention. Together, the attorneys for the two sides invoked nearly twenty specific laws from the *Siete Partidas*, the *Nueva Recopilación de Leyes de Castilla*, the constitution, and legislation to argue the gendered specifics of physical and verbal assault and its punishment, including whose wealth, and how much of it, can be accountable. In the end, Teresa Reyes was given a 50-peso fine for the twin criminal acts of physical assault and forcibly entering the Nieto house with a group of armed black men (who were themselves never charged in the fracas).

In August 1825, Joaquin Palacios of the Parroquia of Aloag filed a criminal complaint against his alcalde, José Nolibos, for a variety of abuses of power. Key amongst Palacio's complaints was the charge that Nolibos regularly invaded the homes of single and widowed women while out on the ronda to solicit "these poor women" for sex.[31] He also accused Nolibos of beating a scribe with a staff in the court while Palacios's wife was making a petition, of being drunk and abusive, and of arresting individuals for suspected adultery without reason. Palacio himself was accused of adultery by the alcalde for being found in the house of a widow named Josefa Surita. Nolibos apparently found Palacio in the home playing violin, and took the instrument as a form of chastisement. This led to a confrontation the next day, when Palacio returned to reclaim his violin and the alcalde, who was again drunk, beat him. Notably, Palacio's characterization of the alcalde's usurpation of authority involved the violation of homes where men were absent, targeting households that lacked the appropriate individual needed to demarcate private domestic space.

In February 1827, Dr. José Marzana, a quiteño professor of medicine, filed charges against the first alcalde of the Central district parish, Dr. Ygnacio Cardenas, for violating his household in a dispute that again radiated from the status of a servant living there.[32] Based on a complaint by Maria Mercedes Saenz, (also known as *La Cusquinga*), and ciudadano Segundo Arboleda, the alcalde issued a warrant to enter Marzana's house in the barrio of San Blas. Thus, the barrio alcalde of El Sagrario issued orders for a house outside his district. Saenz claimed a servant in the Marzana house belonged to her and should be returned. With the alcalde's order in hand, Saenz and Arboleda showed up with a troop of between eight and ten soldiers, entered the house, searched for the girl, and took her. According to Marzana, who apparently was not home at the time, his wife and the sundry members of the household were shocked and traumatized by the incident. In retelling the story, Marzana's petition centered on a series of arguments against the abuse of power that violated his house and home. First, he suggested it was irresponsible for an alcalde to take the uncorroborated word of Mercedes Saenz over the fate of a girl from Latacunga, an abuse that demonstrated a real lack of "zeal in [the alcalde's] love of Liberty, peace, and justice."[33] Marzana remarked that this lack of zeal for the rule of law led to the serious abuse of forcible entry into a citizen's home, an act he noted should not occur "unless certain circumstances happen under which the authorities should postpone the immunity of asylum that every Citizen has in his home."[34] This is essentially the same argument, two years on, as that deployed by Fermin Cepada on behalf of the Nieto household. The point of origin for the servant served as a basis for his second point—that the servant was from Latacunga, and rather than emancipate her Saenz simply took her into her own home. Third, Marzana claimed that the use of armed troops was irresponsible, since it so alarmed not just his own household, but also the entire neighborhood. Finally, Marzana argued that the warrant to enter his home was illegitimate as a usurpation of the barrio alcalde's jurisdiction.

In response, Maria Mercedes Saenz filed a petition claiming that she had a legitimate warrant issued by a legitimate judicial official, which she then took to an official of the city's guardia for help in its execution. It probably helped that Mercedes Saenz was the sister of the city's Comandante General José Maria Saenz. The guardia dispensed a group of soldiers to accompany her to the Marzana house, where she recovered her servant without resorting to violence.

The state's attorney sided with Dr. José Marzana. In his explanation, the fiscal pointed to two factors to critique the barrio alcalde's actions. First, he argued that before resorting to forcible entry of a "domestic asylum" (*asilo domestico*)—at night, in any jurisdiction, under whatever commission—a judicial authority should first have opened a case or attempted verbal conciliation between complaining parties. Second, based on information uncovered during investigation, the state's attorney decried that the servant was taken, with judicial order, by a known prostitute for employ in that profession.[35] Interestingly, the investigation did not spiral into the prosecution of Mercedes Saenz for prostitution, whatever the truth in those allegations. The issue was revisited in a second and longer discourse on the case, in which the state's attorney enumerated with specific reference to Spanish law on prostitution and Colombian law on home entry. The majority of the response was dedicated to the latter, citing the five specific circumstances enumerated in the "Law of 3 August 1824" on home invasion. Following the law, he suggested that the alcalde's support of Mercedes Saenz's request was an attack against, "the security of the individual, against the peace, and against the zones that all Citizens should enjoy under protection of the law."[36]

The judge in the case, Antonio Ante, followed his attorney's advice and condemned the violation of Dr. José Marzana's house, stating:

> The state attorney's exposition established with the most exact and exhaustive analysis of the appropriate law, the extensive evidence for a violation of the law of 3 August 1824, which addressed the protection of the sanctuary of a Citizen's house, and which decreed the cases and methods by which a home can be entered in respect to the public interest. By those reasons, and without repeating them with respect to his unwarranted acts, the Señor Alcalde Parroquial del Centro Dr. Ygnacio Cardenas is condemned in the name of the Republic

and by authority of the law . . . to a fine of 100ps to be paid according to the law to the Public Treasury, and also he is to pay for the costs incurred by Don José Antonio Marzano.[37]

Significantly, and despite the pleading of the state attorney, Judge Antonio Ante restricted the ruling to Dr. Ygnacio Cardenas, and ignored Mercedes Saenz's apparent involvement in illicit sexual activity. Regardless, it was a rough month for Ygnacio Cardenas, who found himself the object of a second abuse of power allegation in February 1827. Dolores Rivera wrote from Santa Marta prison that Cardenas had arrested her on unconstitutional terms over suspicion of a robbery, but without due process and investigation. The state attorney agreed.[38]

These cases, and others like them, document the process by which the law and the populace carved a private sphere out of the household.[39] In each of the cases, women's interests were subservient to and represented by men, most often their husbands. Male representation in forcible entry and abuse of authority cases takes on added significance when placed in the context of the changing locus of political identification in the 1820s. While the household played a role in the Spanish imperial system as the locus of communal political participation, it did so corporately. As such, in custom and practice, the head of the household (padre de familia) could be either male or female. There was no default assumption that the corporate position of household was an exclusively male space.[40] But the liberal revolution dismantled the standing of most corporations, the household included. Thus, the very public space and position of household was transformed by the liberal revolution into a gendered space of domesticity, excluded from the public realm of state intervention. And this shift was tied directly to the gendering of individual political citizenship. Women lost the customary right to act as political heads of household with the 1813–1814 elections, even as the vote was being extended to illiterate and indigenous subjects in both urban and rural parts of the province. In 1824, the Colombian government clarified that citizenship status indeed derived from the husband, stating, "through the headship of the husband, a wife and her minor children under age 21 are naturalized [as Colombians]."[41] This shift, from corporate to individual, from vecino to ciudadano, was analogous to the transformation of the household from corporate and thereby public space, to individual property and thereby private space. The effect was both stunning and relatively immediate.

COUNTING AND TAXING

The block captains, as noted above, were also responsible for maintaining and managing information in their jurisdictions as well as policing and maintaining order. They were to record the shifting populations of foreigners, the unemployed, and beggars, as well as to make a yearly census of permanent residents, broken down by sex, age, profession, and "mode of life" or public reputation. The desire to gather information on the city's inhabitants was part of the larger project to maintain and extend authority in the wake of the previous decade's instability. Groups that were counted included, among others, lawyers, merchants, nuns, street vendors, and others who owed municipal fees. In 1826, a count of practicing lawyers (abogados) in Quito yielded just twenty-three names.[42] Interestingly, each individual was evaluated in two categories: (1) moral and political conduct, and (2) observance of the constitutions and laws of the republic. For the first category, all thirty-three were rated as either "commendable" or "good," while in the second all but one individual were labeled "exact," the one remaining at "regular." The connection between moral and political conduct and faithfulness to the constitution and laws of the republic points to evolving notions of legality and justice. Faithfulness to the law, rather than to some communal sense of justice, became the modus operandi of the magistrature, as evidenced throughout the arguments and rulings of case files.

Such counts supplemented more generalized census data for each of the provinces of the new Department of Ecuador accumulated at the request of the government in Bogotá. Naming and numbering, whether as part of yearly neighborhood censuses or as part of more extensive provincial data taking, served the new government to enhance its ability to exercise fiscal authority. This had been the basis for extensive census taking in the final decades of Bourbon rule, often sparking violent local resistance.[43] In late 1825 and throughout 1826, the parishes of Ecuador engaged in the first full census of the republican period in fulfillment of an October 4, 1825, law by the provincial government in order to fulfill the dictates of Colombian Law of 11 March 1825.[44] Each parish counted men, women, slaves, births, deaths, and marriages, mines and metal deposits, houses (divided by type of roof: tile and straw), livestock, and agricultural products. I was able to locate the census of seven parishes in the old corregimiento of Quito: San Sebastian, Guayllabamba, Sambiza, Puembo/Pifo, Amaguaña, Aloasi, and Magdalena (Table 6.1). Though the sample includes only one urban parish, some interesting observations can be made. In the wake of more than a decade of on-again off-again civil war, women outnumbered men and more so in larger parishes than in smaller, and with the one exception of Guayllabamba. In fact, women accounted for 62 percent (n=3,338) of residents in the urban parish of San Sebastian. Unfortunately, the charts do not separate the broader categories by age or marital status, so it is impossible to determine fine demographic trends. That said, a high likelihood of female-headed households is supported by the overall distribution. The stats also indicate a high crude death rate (CDR) of 39.75 deaths per thousand. Though the CDR was definitely high, it was easily outpaced by an astonishing crude birth rate (CBR) of 93.2 births per thousand. The births counted were for all infants less than one year old in the parish at the time of the census. Again, without more specific age-related data on mortality, it is difficult to draw more significant conclusions. The parish with the lowest CDR by far in the sample was San Sebastian, the only urban parish, with a CDR of 14.5 deaths per thousand. San Sebastian was followed, in this order, by Aloasi, Sambiza, Amaguaña, Magdalena, Puembo/Pifo, and Guayllabamba; the latter had an astonishingly high CDR of 120 deaths per thousand. San Sebastian, with its overwhelming majority of female residents, had a CBR of 136.4 per thousand.

The provincial and municipal governments of Gran Colombia's Department of the South was more interested in gathering the information for tax and economic matters than for calculating death and birth rates. The new government was significantly in debt, and continually looking for new revenue sources. Social services in the city, ranging from street and light maintenance, to police duties, to the poorhouse, public schools, and the formation of the Committee of Philanthropy were serviced by municipal rents.[45] Sometimes government actions to raise revenue dovetailed with the liberal commitment to the principles of contract and private property, such as the 1823 bid to auction off the commons land to the north and south of the city.[46] Most of the revenue generation schemes were of the quotidian tax and

Table 6.1. Parish Census, 1825–1826

PARISH	MEN	WOMEN	SLAVES	NEW BIRTHS	DEATHS	NEW MARRIAGES
Sambiza	1086	1158	2	172	83	23
San Sebastian	2037	3338	260	733	78	55
Amaguaña	1638	1911	8	165	173	22
Aloasi	531	567		57	24	13
Puembo/Pifo	602	612	5	136	103	34
Magdalena	264	272		37	58	18
Guayllabamba	308	167	20	50	57	29
	6466	8025	20	1350	576	194

SOURCE: BAEP 7286 (4) 3, "ESTADO COMPRENSIVO," FOR EACH OF THE PARISHES LISTED ABOVE.

rent variety, but they often caused conflict nonetheless. In November 1823, Pedro Montúfar of second junta fame, requested relief from commercial taxes that he found onerous.[47] In predictable fashion he argued that special levies against the city's businesspersons (*comerciantes*) were unjust, and tyrannical in the form of the old Spanish rule they had fought so hard against. Montúfar also noted, though, that in the city's "lists," he was always "inscribed en the class of a simple Citizen," and thus should not be subject to merchant taxes. The lists could, then, highlight or obscure one's socioeconomic status.

The lists also provide a window into the gendering of commercial activity in the cities of the province. As a corollary to the demographics of city provisioning in Quito, a November 1828 census from Cuenca demonstrates similar gendering to historical food sales practices in the Audiencia reaching back to the seventeenth century. All sellers of goods, whether street-oriented vendors or large established merchants, were required to pay a monthly licensing fee or rent to the municipality. The registration rolls for the rents from November 1828 were divided into five categories (merchants, taverns and general stores, street vendors from the plaza mayor, gaming and cockfighting houses, and mills), and totaled 315 individuals who either had paid or still owed the tax (see Table 6.2).[48] Some clear trends emerge from the rolls. Men dominated the commercial houses of Cuenca, constituting fifty-two of the fifty-four individuals who paid or owed the fee of

Table 6.2. *Municipal Renters by Category, November 1828*

	COMMERCIAL MERCHANTS		TAVERNS AND GENERAL STORES		STREET MARKETING		GAMING AND COCKFIGHTING		MILLS	
	Paid	Owe	Paid	Owe	Paid	Owe	Paid	Owe	Paid	Owe
Men	26	16	59	25	3	0	4	4	7	6
Women	2	0	37	10	99	12	0	0	4	1
Total	28	16	96	35	102	12	4	4	11	7

SOURCE: BAEP 7287 (5) 2 "PADRÓN."

2 reales a month. Women maintained their Spanish-period presence as owners of taverns and pulperías, accounting for 36 percent (n=47) of those who paid or owed the tax. Women especially controlled street vending of foodstuffs. Of the 114 names on the street-marketer (*gatera*, a general term assumed to be female) list, only three were men! Interestingly, no ethnic data were provided on the rolls though many of the gateras carried explicitly indigenous surnames such as Paguay, Chuisaca, Changa, Quichimo, Pangol, Ynga, and Chimbo. The lack of ethnic data is of note because gateras were stereotypically indigenous women, in part due to the tax advantages they held as exempt from paying the alcabala, from the sixteenth century on.[49] The municipal rent records do indicate, though, that such exemptions disappeared with the removal of ethnic labels, since indigenous gateras were now paying municipal rents. A total of 165 women were listed on the rent rolls, representing 52.4 percent of those taxed, while providing good evidence that, in the early years of the republic, women continued to participate in the economic roles they traditionally occupied under Spanish rule.

POPULATING THE JAILS

Arrest statistics from the period, however, demonstrate that women also were subjected to economic punishments from which they traditionally enjoyed immunity. The jail statistics for the city of Quito from 1827 and 1829 hint that the new judicial arrangements were affecting women's access to legal resources already during the Gran

Colombian period (Table 6.3).[50] For both men and women, the statistics demonstrate a wholesale move away from morality enforcement, and toward property and debt vigilance. For female detainees, moral crimes accounted for only 6.4 percent (n=5) and 19.0 percent (n=11) of arrests for 1827 and 1829, respectively. Compare this to Bourbon-era detentions, in which moral arrests for female detainees averaged 29.1 percent in the late 1760s and rose to 54.4 percent in 1789. The same trends can be seen for male detainees as well. Raw detention numbers in 1827, with 404 individuals recorded on the books, were on par with the Bourbon era, though the gender division skewed increasingly toward men. Men accounted for 80.7 percent (n=326) and 74.0 percent (n=165) of arrests for 1827 and 1829, respectively. Compare this to the earlier data sets, in which male detainees averaged 57.7 percent for the late 1760s and 50.7 percent in 1789 when adjusted for tributaries. Did the reduction in arrests of women across all categories, and especially for moral crimes, in the Gran Colombian period signify a relaxation of surveillance and social control, even if temporary, in the postcolonial period?[51] It may have, but taken within the context of the police regulations of 1825, it is just as likely that the decrease in morality arrests represented a privatization of the disciplinary role previously played by the institutional authorities. Men and women ceased to be arrested for sexual activities as well. In 1827, three men were arrested on illicit sex charges, and only one woman was arrested for adultery for the whole year. In 1829 the numbers reversed, with two women and one man detained for sexual improprieties. Additionally, there were a handful of arrests aimed at encouraging married couples to live together.

Borchart de Moreno has noted a decline in arrests for drunkenness and other public improprieties, as well as a lack of reference to the ronda in the 1827 census stating, "In the early republican years . . . there were no prisoners listed as having been convicted of sexual crimes or offenses against public security and morals. There is no mention whatsoever of drunkenness, gaming, the abduction or hiding of women, rape, quarreling, or concubinage; nor is there any reference to 'rounding up.' Most prisoners were there not for crimes of violence, but for theft or debt."[52] The observation is not entirely correct. There were four arrests for sexual misconduct (adultery and concubinage were the terms used), as well as arrests for spousal abandonment, for just being poor, unemployed, or homeless (*vago*), for

Table 6.3. Arrests by Gender and Category, 1827 and 1829

GENDER	CATEGORY	1827	1829
Male	Debt	197 (60.4%)	86 (52.1%)
	Undetermined	2 (0.6)	4 (2.4)
	Moral Crime	12 (3.7)	18 (10.9)
	Property Crime	74 (22.7)	26 (15.8)
	Slavery Issues	8 (2.5)	15 (9.1)
	Violent Crime	33 (10.1)	16 (9.7)
	TOTAL MALE	326	165
Female	Debt	22 (28.2%)	11 (19.0%)
	Undetermined	3 (3.8)	7 (12.1)
	Moral Crime	5 (6.4)	11 (19.0)
	Property Crime	18 (23.1)	13 (22.4)
	Slavery Issues	8 (10.3)	7 (12.1)
	Violent Crime	22 (28.2)	9 (15.5)
	TOTAL FEMALE	78	58
TOTAL DETAINEES		404	223

SOURCE: AN/Q 1NJ 331 5°1°1827; 337 22°11°1829.

enticing and hiding an "innocent girl servant," soliciting a married woman, as well as women arrested at the request of various men. Furthermore, in the protection of public security, the 1827 rolls include fourteen individuals, six of them women, brought to the head municipal judge by the general police command of Quito for involvement in what they termed a "movement in San Sebastian." While it is certain that the number of arrests involved are miniscule in comparison to the 1760s to 1780s, they still were present in the city's jails. What is more important to note is the shift away from institutional enforcement of sexual norms and public morality. Absent the constraining power of institutional authorities, who took less interest in enforcing sexual morality, adjudication of these types of disputes likely moved to a newly formed private domestic sphere, to the detriment of women.[53]

There is further evidence within the arrest records to suggest that men subjected women to increasing physical control. Of the thirty-three arrests for violent crimes committed by men in 1827, 36.4 percent (n=12) had female victims. Two of the arrests were for murders, and the rest were for assaults. Fourteen of the remaining violent crime arrests were of group participants in two specific crimes—a murder in March 1827, and the tumult in San Sebastian in December 1827. Taking this into consideration, violent acts against women accounted for 57 percent of the violent crime arrests for the year, and for 33 percent of the murders. Similarly, in 1829 the six violent crimes carried out against women accounted for 37.5 percent of violent crime arrests. As a percentage of individual acts, violence against women accounted for 42.8 percent of violent crimes, including 66 percent of the year's murders. These statistics represent a real growth in arrests for violence against women in comparison with the closing decades of the eighteenth century. Violent crime on the whole was prosecuted at a higher rate than in the 1760s, but similar to the rate in the 1780s.

As mentioned above, arrests for violence in the 1820s were almost exclusively for very serious assaults and murders.[54] On January 5, 1827, José Antonio Sanchez "severely injured a woman's head." Asiencio Cachiguango fractured his mother's head, an act repeated one month later on June 30 against Escolastica dela Cruz by Miguel Quinayayo. On September 1, 1827, Come Chicho beat up a woman and cut off her hair. On September 11, 1827, Nicolas Hidalgo was taken into custody for cutting the lips of Juana Espinosa and cracking open his mother's head. (See more details on that crime below.) The severity of these assaults, placing their victims in mortal peril, suggests that the authorities monitored gendered violence only in the gravest of circumstances. It is likely that nominal assaults went unpunished and were placed within the domestic sphere that block captains, police officers, and magistrates shied away from. What is more, in the examples listed above that have identifying characteristics, the women who were victims of such egregious violence seem to be intimates of their assailants, or the violence seems to be directed at some sort of public humiliation (cutting off hair, slashing the face). From this perspective, the arrests could be read as evidence for an increase in physical control by individual men of their domestic space.

Beyond the entries in the jail censuses, the Criminal and First Notary case files testify in more explicit and in-depth terms the escalation of gendered violence in the 1820s. It seems, in fact, that the magistrature of the province was aware enough of an escalation of domestic violence to express at least rhetorical concern. In June 1826, hat-maker Calisto Mejia was arrested and sentenced for physically abusing his wife, Francisca Alarcon.[55] He was tried and convicted of beating her close to the point of death, the end of a long series of abuses that Francisca claimed had occurred throughout their nine years of marriage. The case was forwarded after definitive sentencing to for appeal to Ecuador's Superior Court.[56] On reviewing the case, the state attorney noted, "it is considered a husband's right to moderately discipline his wife, a limitation that indicates excessive [mistreatment] is criminal, and worthy of the censure of law. [. . .] Your excellency should take a measured reflection on the value of this class of men that treat their consorts with more ferocity than their animals, providing their sons a poor example, and insulting the respect due to the sacred bond of matrimony."[57] In issuing their verdict, the superior court judges concurred with the attorney's opinion, stating in their findings, "in line with that expressed by the state attorney, the abuse of women by rebuke and mistreatment has become far too common in this City, such that [the situation] demands appropriate remedies in order to maintain the public peace, and harmony between spouses."[58] Thus, in order to send a message to all husbands, the court ordered, "that administrating justice in the name of the Republic and by authority of the lay, Calisto Mejia be condemned to prison for two months in the public jail of this City, on the condition that in order to be released after those two months, he must give a guarantee to his wife that he will not harm her further."[59] The message to Quito's men was that they risked only two months incarceration for beating women close to the point of death.

It appears from the record that domestic abuse ran in the Mejia family. In early March 1828, an indigenous woman named Maria Ramos filed a complaint against her son-in-law Pedro Meija, Calisto's brother, for brutally beating her daughter.[60] According to the daughter, Maria Natividad Ramos, on the Monday night of the 1828 Carnival her hat-maker husband Pedro came home late, announced his intention to kill her, and proceeded to shower her with blows from "sticks, stones, fists, and kicks," and left her alone, "in the silence of the night with no assistance but God."[61] She was naked, beaten, and "bathed in blood," wandering the streets looking for help. Legal attention was slow in this case. Though the initial complaint and request for judicial inquiry was filed in early March, including at least one witness statement testifying to the incident, nothing happened until the end of July when Maria Natividad Ramos filed her own complaint against her husband. Beginning on July 31, 1828, First Municipal Alcalde Dr. José Javier Valdivieso took new witness testimony on Pedro Mejia's treatment of his wife. The three witnesses confirmed her account, and Maria Natividad requested again judicial intervention. On August 2, Valdivieso ordered the case to conciliation. The verbal hearing apparently never occurred. Two months later, Maria Natividad was appealing again to Valdivieso, asking for his August order to be enforced. The case ends there. Why the disjuncture in punishment and judicial will between these two cases? It is striking, given that the abusers were brothers. It is also striking that, in the case of Pedro Mejia, Maria Natividad found herself wandering the streets naked and bleeding, and still had difficulty marshalling neighborhood resources.

It took significant levels of violence to make it to the point of judicial intervention—violence that was almost, though not exclusively, men against women they knew well.[62] In September 1827, violence against intimates took a cross-generation tack, when Rita Merino denounced her son, Nicolás Hidalgo for assaulting her and for cutting the lips of a woman named Juana Espinosa, who lived in the Merino tienda and household.[63] In response, the barrio alcalde of San Sebastian opened an investigation of the charges, which held that a drunk and incorrigible Nicolás had entered his mother's tienda around eight o'clock in the evening, hit her, then entered the room where Juana was sleeping and set upon her with a knife, cutting her face with intent to kill her. The alcalde ordered Dr. José Antonio Marzana (of home invasion fame) to inspect Juana Espinosa's injuries, and he testified to a significant cut across her face, extending at an angle some four inches from nose to chin. At the time of his examination, a surgeon named Pedro Monrroy had already sewed up the wound. She also had other marks on her nose and head, as did Rita Merino. The injuries were confirmed by examination by a second surgeon. Nicolás Hidalgo was then arrested for the course of the investigation, and wrote from jail that he did not believe he had done the deeds on account of having been very drunk. Indeed, witnesses provided by Hidalgo testified that all of the parties involved had spent the day drunk and drinking, in celebration of the festival of San Nicolás, the son's saint's day. They backed up Hidalgo's claim that he was so drunk that he had passed out, and could not have assaulted anyone. They also noted that Juana

Espinosa was his "illicit friend," or lover (*amiga criminal*). As an alternative explanation, the witnesses claimed the two women had fallen in their drunken states, and hurt themselves on a doorframe or on the street. Incredibly, despite the testimony by the doctors certifying that Juana's wounds were the work of a "cutting instrument" (*instrumento cortante*), the barrio alcalde concluded with the witnesses that the women were responsible for their own injuries. He freed Nicolás Hidalgo after one week's stay in the city jail, and ordered,

> Considering that this complaint emanated from serious drunkenness, on the part of both the two female plaintiffs and the accused, they are given a serious warning to act better from here on out and abstain from their scandalous living in detriment to the public interest, and that furthermore they should give all due submission and obedience to their Parents.[64]

Alcohol was considered as a mitigating element in criminal prosecutions during the Spanish period. And again, in this case the magistrate followed the precedent by minimizing implications of sexual dalliance or gendered violence, while chastising the threat to public morality posed by excessive drunkenness.

Alcohol abuse did appear as a recurring theme in gender violence cases. In 1829, ciudadana Catalina Erazo filed simultaneous petitions with ecclesiastical and secular authorities over her husband's abusiveness.[65] She complained that, from the beginning of their marriage, Manuel Perez had provided her with "a most sad and pathetic life" (*una vida la mas lastimosa*). For the ecclesiastical venue, Manuel Perez's actions were characterized as "an inability to fulfill the obligations of a Christian man, without God or Religion."[66] She claimed that she bore the marks of his poor treatment on a "body filled with the signs of blows to the Head and Face." It seemed Manuel was particularly likely to beat her after consuming chicha. The bishop ordered the couple appear for a verbal hearing, and granted her request for a legal separation. Despite the ruling, Manuel Perez continued to harass her, so she filed a petition with the municipal alcalde; Catalina left out the commentary on Christian obligation and centered in on the criminality of his acts. Six months later, she was back again with the same complaint. Perez refused to recognize the separation, and continued to abuse her. Despite the repeated complaints, it was only when Perez brutally assaulted hat-maker and ciudadano José Cuello that he was detained, investigated, and sentenced to a short jail term.

Gender violence occasionally took on strange forms that carried a familiar ring to modern readers. In October 1827, Dr. José Feliciano Saenz, a professor of medicine at the university in Quito, was arrested for attempting to kill his wife and another woman with poison. Apparently, the good Doctor Saenz mixed arsenic in his wife's drinking chocolate, and in the horchata of a second woman.[67] In the case of his wife, the doctor mixed the chocolate drink while she was at Mass, leaving it for her later consumption. Saenz's motive for the attempted poisoning was apparently connected to his relationship with his mistress, Mercedes Loja. And it was the same Mercedes Loja who warned Francisca Garcia, her lover's wife, through their local priest of the plot to poison. In considering the sentence, the judges argued that the key question was the question of malicious intent to murder, following the dictates of Law 2, Title 31 of *Partida 7*, and then proceeded to cast doubt on the various witnesses. The deployment of the *Siete Partidas* brings to point the question of what law was most likely to be used in criminal and civil prosecutions. The gender violence and home invasion cases discussed above were much more likely to engage the *Siete Partidas* over any of the other codes listed as applicable under the Colombian Constitution. Interestingly, the ubiquity of the *Siete Partidas* upends, to a certain extent, the hierarchy of law established by the "Law of 13 May 1825," which placed the *Partidas* at the end of the list. And yet throughout criminal and civil litigation involving women, the *Partidas* were the most referenced. Why this fascination with such ancient law? The *Partidas* were the most restrictive of the corpus of Spanish Law with regards to women's legal personhood, and they also carried the harshest penalties for a variety of criminal activities—ranging from banishment to corporal and capital punishment.

As significant as these clues are for documenting the shifting legal culture of the early republican period and its impact on women's legal status, some of the starkest evidence in the arrest records for the removal of protective constraints long utilized by women in the interstices of male privilege came in the form of debtors' imprisonment. Interestingly, despite the perpetuity of Spanish law, provisions that prohibited imprisoning women for debts that were not incurred through criminal activities were routinely ignored. It seems that liberals were more attuned to reviving and enforcing restrictive elements of the Spanish legal inheritance over the protective elements, usually in the name of "equality" before the law as defined by a single fuero for all classes of people. The arrest rolls of the eighteenth century reflect the extent to which the ban on debtors' prison for women was respected. For the combined years 1767–1770 and 1789, only twenty-nine women out of 863 detained were held for debts, accounting for only 3.4 percent of arrests. By comparison, in 1827 and 1829, thirty-three women were detained for debts out of a total of just 136 detainees, or 24.2 percent of arrests.[68] Debts ranged from as small as 3 pesos, 4 reales, to as much as 100 pesos. These were small loans. There was some confusion regarding the law on detaining women for debt, and in July 1827, the magistrate making the jail census noted in the margin beside the entry for Maria Santos Arias, who was being held at the request of a creditor, that "A woman cannot be held for civil debts."[69]

It seems that the question of debt arrests for everyone was contested in the earliest years of the republic. As early as 1823, the issue of debtors' prison came before the magistrature. An August 1823 ruling reconfirmed the use of debtors' prison not only for liabilities resulting from criminal acts, but also for normal civil debts. The court stated, "The debtor who does not pay or have enough wealth in order to pay what he owes should be confined to prison. . . . The debtor confined to prison should work while there, providing for his needs with part of his wages deducted in order to cover his debts."[70] Lawyers had been arguing that debtors' prison was contrary to the constitution, and out of step with "the practices of Liberal and Civilized Nations." The court disagreed, and affirmed a belief that all unpaid debts were fraudulent, therefore making all debtors worthy of incarceration. While custom held that women were exempt from arrest for all noncriminal debts, this new line of interpretation made them vulnerable for arrest in civil cases as well. Despite moments of judicial admonition like that found in the 1827 jail census marginalia, women still found themselves in the recogimiento of Santa Marta for the charge. Indeed, it appears that by the end of the 1820s the proscription against arresting women for debt was being routinely ignored. The arrest of women for debt is significant because it demonstrates that, with the end of Spanish rule, the protections of women in Spanish law—protections that had provided a competitive advantage or some wiggle room for female litigants—began to be dismantled even as the strictures became more routinely enforced in the name of the law. What is more, women frequently found themselves in court over debts for loans, land and commercial transactions, and inheritance issues.

In fact, of the 133 cases involving women as primary litigants for the five years 1825–1829 preserved by the First Notary, 66.2 percent (n=88) were disputes over some form of debt contract (house or land sales, straight loans, uncollected testamentary debts, or animal sales).[71] On the question of representation, the case set from 1825–1829 suggests continuities across the revolutionary period. In comparison to the years of Bourbon rule, and in line with the revolutionary period of 1809–1814, married women continued to experience a decreased ability to assert self-representation in legal issues. From 1825 to 1829, questions of legal representation were interpreted through increasingly literal interpretations of the strictures of the *Siete Partidas* in particular. Licensure data from the First Notary 1825–1829 case set suggests the continued perpetuation of the no-status legal fiction coterminous with a decline of licensure and escalation of male representation of married women (see Appendix III). The period carried approximately equivalent numbers as that of 1809–1814, with 182 primary female litigants in 133 cases. For the case set, 65.9 percent of women self-represented, men represented 28.6 percent (n=52), and 5.5 percent of women presented license to the court. In cases where men represented women, those women rarely hired their own attorneys, but rather were represented by their husbands, sons, fathers, or other specially empowered third parties at a rate higher than had been available a decade before. Licensed acts and representation by husbands, fathers, and other nonattorney third parties together accounted for 23.6 percent (n=53) of cases, but male representation accounted for 66.7 percent of married women's actions. Of those remaining married women who acted without representation or license, three had absent husbands, and another six were engaged in litigation against their own male relatives.[72]

Together, women who claimed no marital status, invariably invoking the social-political moniker "citizen," or who were single or widowed, dominated, with 81.7 percent (n=98) of the nonlicensed litigation. Following the letter of the Spanish legal labyrinth, widows and single women of majority age would never have had an expectation of license, or even necessarily of male representation. The seventy-two no-status citizens, though, continued to fall into a nether world of legality. By appealing to the status of citizen instead of positing a potentially conflicting marital status, women continued to engage the practice of perpetuating the legal fiction of status-less litigants. As in the 1810s, women continued to pursue legal resources in an atmosphere of increasing restriction in which the range of positions from which to appeal were narrowing.

SEEKING CONCILIATION

Also as in the 1810s, it was not simply debt, but many other types of women's legal disputes that were being shuffled through the system of mediation. The process for conciliation during the early republic was governed initially by the "Organic Law of Judicial Power of 11 May 1825," which established the responsibilities of the array of judicial officials, from the Supreme Court (*Alta Corte*) down to parish magistrates, lawyers, and notaries.[73] Authority in verbal and conciliation cases was placed primarily under the municipal magistrates, though parish magistrates had a role as well. Article 153 established the municipal magistrate's primary judicial function as the verbal adjudication of civil and injurias cases:

> The municipal alcaldes will exercise the following judicial functions in their cantons: 1. To act, in disposition with parish alcaldes, as court-appointed conciliators in civil and injurias cases; 2. to hear, in disposition with parish alcaldes, the verbal trails of minor injurias complaints that carry light punishments; 3. To hear, in disposition with other judges of first instance and parish alcaldes, unopposed judicial procedural formalities; 4. To hear in first instance minor cases valued between 100ps and 400ps; 5. To hear verbal appeals in second instance of minor cases originally heard by parish alcaldes.[74]

Article 155 defined parish alcalde responsibilities as the same as those listed above for the municipal magistrate, with the exception of the second instance appeal. Having established the requirement for verbal trials and conciliation, two days later the legislature passed its first civil procedure law, with the "Law of 13 May 1825," which included instructions for juicios de conciliación.[75] Chapter 2, Article 3 of the "Law of Civil Procedure," determined that most forms of first-instance litigation—civil, military, and ecclesiastical—should go through mediation prior to filing a formal suit. This included, for example, divorce, injurias, contract disputes, and the like. Article 4 of that law exempted from verbal hearing any cases involving the national treasury, municipal rents, cases involving whole communities, minors, intestate estates, chaplaincies, multiple creditors, debtors who were a flight risk, or cases concerned with establishment of estate inventories.[76] Procedure held that a municipal or parish alcalde should conduct the mediation at the home of the dispute's plaintiff, or at the defendant's home with permission of the plaintiff. Conciliation could be requested by verbal or written complaint, and the parties involved could appoint representation for the hearing. The magistrate was instructed to listen to both parties, and consider any documents they might present in attempts to find an amicable mediation. At the end of the hearing, the magistrate was also instructed to record the outcome in a book entitled, *Conciliation Decisions*.[77] Notably, the role of the hombre bueno was mentioned in the law only in cases heard by parish alcaldes that exceeded 25 pesos in value. This was a significant change from the 1810s.[78]

Statistics for juicios de conciliación for the second half of the 1820s demonstrate interesting trends for women's participation and representation in the petty cases sent to conciliation. To get a glimpse at mediation practice, I have compared complete sets of verbal trials for the years 1825 and 1827–1829. Unfortunately, the extant books do not come from one single jurisdiction, but rather from the First Municipal Alcalde (1825), the Second Municipal Alcalde (1828 and 1829), and the Second Parish Alcalde of the Central District (1827).[79] Two of those jurisdictions were citywide, and the inclusion of the parish data makes for an interesting comparison. The books include 332 litigants who submitted to conciliation. On average across the four years, men accounted for 62.7 percent (n=208) of those litigants. Though men dominated the litigant count, women were involved in the vast majority of the disputes—66 percent (n=33) of the cases in 1825, 72 percent (n=18) in 1827, 64 percent (n=29) in 1828, and 39.4 percent (n=13) in 1829. As those numbers hint, though, women constituted a declining percentage of litigants across the four years (see Table 6.4). At the municipal level, female litigants declined from 42.6 percent (n=46) in 1825 to 23.0 percent (n=17) over the period, while total litigants remained relatively stable. This trend is confirmed by the INJ case set, which saw conciliation cases decline from 29.2 percent (n=7) to 15.2 percent (n=5) of cases involving women as primary litigants.[80]

When women appeared in mediation, they were much more likely to appear as plaintiffs, particularly at the parish level. On average, 57.7 percent (n=71) of female litigants were plaintiffs for the four years (see Table 6.4). Thus, given the higher rates of cases involving women, we can observe that juicios de conciliación were not only more likely to involve women, but were more likely to involve women making complaints. From a representational perspective, the initial participation of women in cases depended on the venue. At the municipal level, women appeared for their verbal hearings with higher rates of male representation than in previous decades (see Table 6.7). In the Central parish cases, rates of self-representation were inordinately higher than previous trends. In part this may be the result of the comparative pettiness of the claims adjudicated there, as well as the increased likelihood that litigants were from outside of the city proper. Licenses for making legal acts were almost completely absent from the records. The exception was 1828, when one litigant presented license in a loan

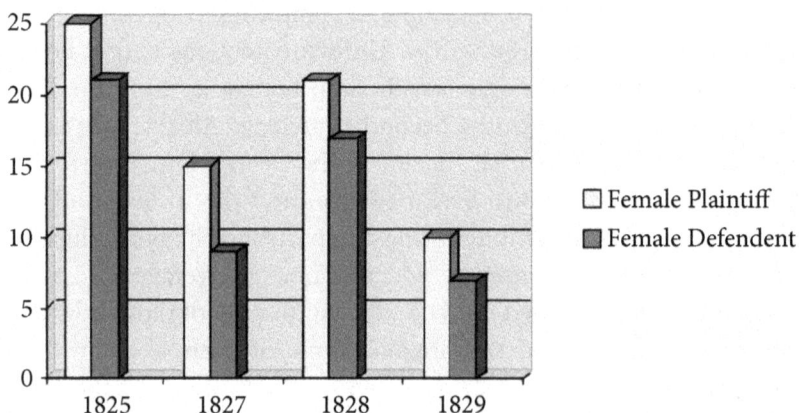

Table 6.4. Female Litigants, Juicios Verbales, 1825–1829
SOURCE: ANE/Q INJ 323, 25-1-1825; 331 27-1-1827; 333, 18-1-1828; 340 1829.

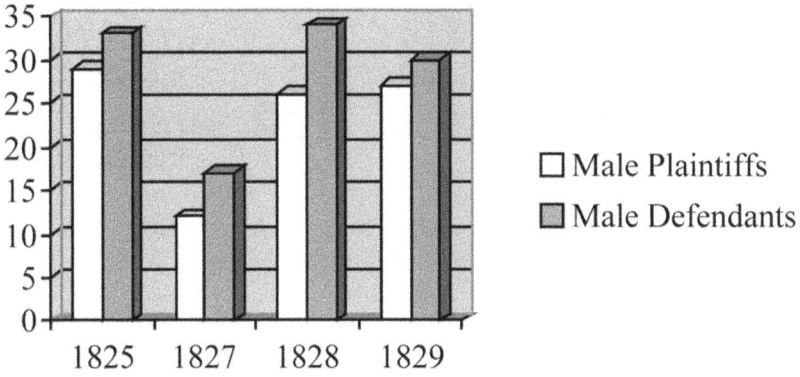

Table 6.5. Male Plaintiffs and Defendants, Juicios Verbales, 1825–1829

SOURCE: ANE/Q 1NJ 323, 25≠1≠1825; 331 27≠1≠1827; 333, 18≠1≠1828; 340 1829.

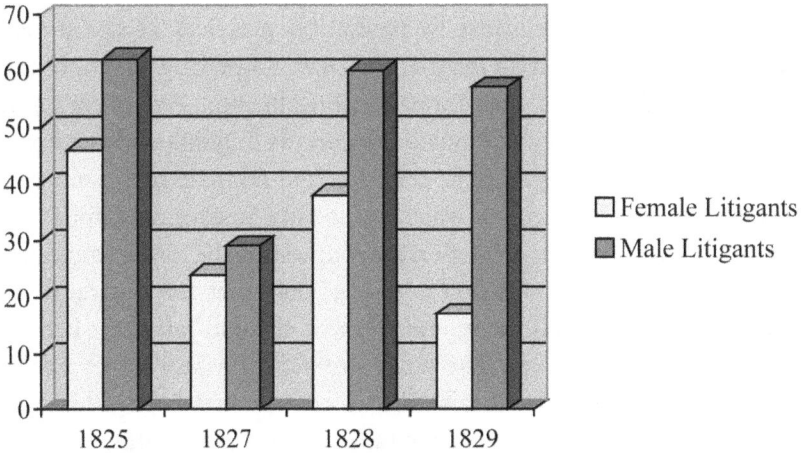

Table 6.6. Total Male and Female Litigants, Juicios Verbales, 1825–1829

SOURCE: ANE/Q 1NJ 323, 25≠1≠1825; 331 27≠1≠1827; 333, 18≠1≠1828; 340 1829.

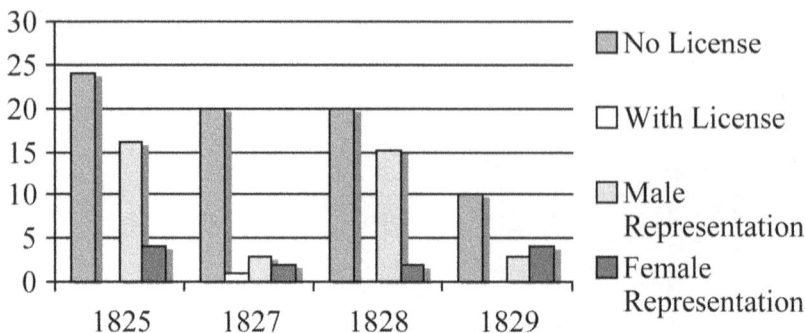

Table 6.7. Female Representation, Juicios Verbales, 1825–1829
SOURCE: ANE/Q 1NJ 323, 25ʳ1ʳ1825; 331 27ʳ1ʳ1827; 333, 18ʳ1ʳ1828; 340 1829.

dispute. The practice of the 1810s of bringing an hombre bueno to the case to form a tribunal with the magistrate was unevenly enforced. In the municipal-level conciliations from 1825 and 1828, the involvement of hombres buenos is never mentioned. In the 1829 cases, only two cases mentioned the presence of hombres buenos, one a dispute over a cattle sale between Juan Mansano and Carlos Caloastrano, and the other over mutual insult allegations between Señora Mercedes Aspiaso and Juan Albuja.

This is in stark contrast to mediation practices at the parish level. In the Central parish records for 1827, 68 percent (n=17) of the cases recorded the participation of hombres buenos. Five of the eight remaining cases in 1827 did include women as litigants without hombres buenos. Of those, though, only one had no male representation for her case. On February 3, 1827, ciudadana Susana Asia appeared before alcalde Joaquín dela Berrara requesting he order musician Mariano Reyes Badillos pay off a 78-peso debt that was outstanding. It seems Susana needed the money because she had fallen far behind in her ecclesiastical taxes. The judge ordered Mariano to pay at the rate of 2 pesos per month, with the agreement that half of his payments go directly to pay her church taxes (*tercio*) at the cathedral. The other cases lacking the participation of hombres buenos but involving women saw other forms of male representation. Ciudadanos Mariano and Josefa Pazmiño together sued ciudadana Melchora Ruiz for 16 pesos, 4½ reales on February 16, 1827. Three months later, on

May 11, 1827, municipal council member Manuel Carrion appeared with power-of-attorney for his mother, Señora Margarita Quiñones, in a dispute with Torivio Valencia over some jewelry and 60 pesos. On December 4, 1827, ciudadano Juan Arrova brought his legitimate wife, Petrona Flores, before the parochial magistrate in an attempt to mediate their broken marriage. The judge encouraged Petrona to return to her husband and live a normal married life, but she would have none of it. Recognizing that conciliation was not possible, he admonished her to pursue a legal separation from the ecclesiastical courts. Finally, ten days later on December 14, 1827, dela Berrera heard the complaint of indigenous Justo Ynquerres against Mariana Cañizares over 94 pesos he claimed she owed him as the underwriter of a loan made to another Indian, Manuel Sanches. Neither of the parties appeared, but rather both were represented by lawyers. Interestingly, when the court made its decision, the notary informed Mariana Cañizares's brother, Don José Cañizares, of the outcome.

Outside of these few cases, the remaining verbal trials held by the Second Parish Magistrate of the Central District involved the participation of hombres buenos in the same manner as that prescribed by the Cádiz Constitution of 1812. Significantly, of the four available samples of verbal trials, the parish jurisdiction had both the largest percentage of women litigating without male representation and the largest usage of the hombre bueno rule. Though 83 percent (n=20) of women acted without male representation, either on their own or with other women as representatives, all but one of those cases involved hombres buenos. Thus, even though self-representation rates and the lack of licensure suggest the maintenance of independent female legal agency, the inclusion of hombre bueno representation at the lowest court level established an inescapable encroachment of men into women's legal disputes. Given the higher rates of female litigation at the juicio de conciliación level, the reformed legal system of the republican era thus surreptitiously degraded women's independent legal status.

What more, then, do we know of these women shuffled into the juicio de conciliación system and what types of litigation were they involved in? The overwhelming majority of cases heard in the verbal system were contract disputes over uncollectible loans, and rental agreements gone afoul. At the municipal level, loans, rents, inheritance, land, and house sales accounted for 86.7 percent (n=111) of the cases. The remaining cases divided between disputes over water, slaves, animals, jewelry, a dowry, and insults. Unlike in the 1810s, injurias cases were rare in the verbal courts, accounting for only two of the 128 cases in the samples 1825, 1828, and 1829. Loan disputes also led to the 1827 Central parish records, accounting for 60 percent of claims. As at the parish level, many of the remaining cases involved property disputes, including cases over wine, cattle, jewelry, a knife, and crystal. The parish records also included one assault case, one insult case, and two marital disputes. The most striking difference between the parish and municipal levels, though, was the size of the contested monetary amounts. For the Central, pesos cases that noted the contested amount averaged 60 pesos, with the smallest case at 15 pesos. In contrast, at the municipal level the stakes were much, much higher. In 1825, pesos cases averaged just over 793 pesos, with the smallest contested amount 100 pesos and the largest 4000 pesos! In 1828, the average was just over 976 pesos, ranging from 80 up to 3976 pesos.[81] Finally, for 1829, reported amounts averaged only 262 pesos, ranging from 18 to 1428 pesos. The *Libro* for 1829 also included a dispute over 40 ounces of gold that Coronel Nicolas Barcones had lost in a game of dice to ciudadano Vicente Calisto. Barcones claimed Calisto was using a fixed die (*dado falso*), a fact that was substantiated by numerous witnesses. Barcones requested the magistrate revoke a bank draft in Calisto's possession on account of his dishonesty, and the court so ordered.[82]

Other information about the litigants involved in the two venues further suggests economic class divisions, particularly for women. At the end of the mediation, all of the parties involved signed their names to the record if they were literate. If a litigant did not know how to sign her name, this was noted in the document by the notary, and a witness, invariably a man, signed on her behalf. Thus, the cases provide information on the most basic level of literacy. As with the amounts involved in credit disputes, literacy rates suggest that litigants at the municipal level, both male and female, were more educated. At the municipal level, male litigants were almost guaranteed to know how to write. On average, 91.6 percent of male litigants (n=163) were able to sign their own names for the years 1825–1829. For the same period, 58.8 percent of female litigants (n=62) were functionally literate. At the parish level, male rates of literacy remained high, though the opposite was the case for women. For the Central parish in 1827, only 27.3 percent (n=6) of women could sign their name. The remaining 72.7 percent required witness signatures on their hearings. By contrast, 80.6 percent (n=25) of men involved in verbal cases in the Central were able to sign for themselves, a rate lower than at the municipality but still a vast majority. Thus, women who found themselves in municipal verbal trials were more than twice as likely as those at the parish jurisdiction to be able to write their names.

Status claims were markedly different for both venues relative to the late Spanish period. The predominant status claim for women in verbal cases was that of citizen (*ciudadana*). Use of the term citizen in all types of legal petitions and actions emerged almost immediately with the transition to the State of Ecuador in Bolívar's Gran Colombia, quickly replacing the terms doña and vecina. It is worth noting that the term vecina, much like mujer (woman and wife), carried a double meaning—as citizen and as resident. In claiming the status vecina in legal actions, women were putting themselves not only in a physical place, but also making a claim to judicial participation. Judicial power was not separated from political power in the Spanish monarchy, and as such the claim to vecina was a political claim as well. The term was also immediately dispensed of after independence, in favor of the modern term for citizen, *ciudadana*. This term no longer carried the same implications of place, but did initially indicate women's proactive claim to both judicial and political rights. In contrast, doña had been a term purely of social status that carried no intrinsic legal power, but rather marked one's social honor. Its dispensation, in favor of either ciudadana or señora, reflecting the marriage status of the complainant, signified a shift in republican notions of honor. The use of ciudadana was a contestation of writing women out of political participation, a process that began with the elections of 1813–1814. It also represented a period of hybridity, where participants in the new political culture of republicanism, which separated the political and judicial spheres, were operating under old assumptions of the nature of judicial power. After 1830, as the liberal system was consolidated, though, women ceased to refer to themselves, or be referred to as ciudadana, and became simply señora. The vecina, whose position in the corporate structures of the old regime carried an array of political, social, and legal implications, was morphed into the citizen, whose claims were narrowed to a legal claim from the outside of a political category, into the señora whose position was purely social.

The full independence of Ecuador furthered the reorganization of governance and legal culture initiated in the 1820s. This reorganization had its analogous effect on social authority in the newly formed nation. Most notably, on the political level instability ruled as Ecuadorian affairs of state were subsumed in the intrigues of caudillos, monarchists, liberals, conservatives, and regional struggles for which nineteenth-century Spanish America is renowned.[83] The causes and effects of the instability of postcolonial government have long been of interest to historians of the period. Gender relations have formed a core element of recent analyses of social and political dislocations in Spanish America in the nineteenth century as historians have proffered a formulation arguing that, in the absence of secure and steady governance, Spanish American societies turned to the family and the church for social stability. Inherited religious institutions and patriarchal social forms, it is argued, were brought forward from the colonial period as a bulwark against the social, economic, and political insecurities of the postcolonial landscape. These fetters, it is further argued, served to mutate Spanish American modernity, preventing the full realization of its emancipatory potential. The gendering of Spanish America's malformed modernity depended on an absolutist model of gender domination as a colonial legacy, updated or modernized for the new discursive conditions of republican virtue and honor. In the words of Caulfield, Chambers, and Putnam, "In theory, liberals sought to abolish what they considered the outmoded concept of birthright as the legitimate foundation of authority, replacing it with notions of representative forms of government and judicial equality. In practice, most of them were equally or more concerned with establishing modern, generally capitalist, forms of social control without destroying existing social hierarchies."[84] The research presented in this book suggests that this framework for interpreting the presence of patriarchal gender relations in the nineteenth century may be based on a fundamentally mistaken assumption. If, in the case of gendered domination, social authority was formed through a matrix of legal, economic, and cultural constraints that flowed in both directions, providing agency for dominated as well as dominating groups, then the problem of patriarchy in the modern period becomes a problem internal to the dynamics of modernity. It is likely that scholars have been caught up in nineteenth-century nationalist discourses, much as characterizations of the treatment of indigenous populations by the Spanish were long colored by the black legend as it was reformulated in postcolonial portrayals of the Indian. Liberal and conservative renderings of colonial gender relations clearly articulated a system of absolute gender control that was alien to their foremothers, at least in the corregimiento of Quito.

In the course summary to his 1975–1976 Collège de France lecture series "Society Must Be Defended," Michel Foucault posited, "rather than privileging the law as manifestation of power, we would do better to try to identify the different techniques of constraint that it implements."[85] In the context of this quote, Foucault's concern was to move the study of power away from the universal subject whose interactions with social power was mediated by universally endowed "rights." It may seem strange to quote a dismissal of the potency of law as power at the end of a book that has sought to painstakingly document the way in which women used the law. Though Foucault's desire was to deconstruct the juridical subject and remove discussions of power from the constitution of some form of natural, legal rights, his encouragement to look beyond the concept of law as power fits well with what I have gleaned from the thousands of instances of litigation encountered in this project. Indeed, the image of legality derived from the final decades of Spanish rule in the corregimiento of Quito suggests that law served primarily as both techniques and tactics of constraint.

There were, without question, patriarchal tendencies within the Spanish legal inheritance that sought to restrict women's access to both legal and economic resources through the mediation of men. This was one vector of constraint impelled by the law, but that same legal inheritance contained within itself protective tendencies that worked to prevent the consolidation of authority and, as a result, that also constrained patriarchal privileges. These tendencies, embodied in customary practices, jurisdictional wrangling, and judicial discretion, decentralized power relations within the Spanish monarchy. In the arena of the court, these tendencies also included legal protections against debtors' prison or alienation of dowry wealth, equitable and partible inheritance, the same access to free legal representation for poor, minor, or indigenous women as that afforded to men, and, most important, the customary practice of accepting the ability of women of all ethnicities and marital statuses to make legal acts before the many judicial officials of the corregimiento. Despite legal proscriptions on women's use of the legal system, Quito's magistrates routinely accepted their presence in both civil and criminal actions. At a certain point, exceptions become normative, and this appears to be the case in gendered legal status for the corregimiento of Quito.

Part of the juridical construct Foucault was struggling against was the tendency to see legal identities as classificatory and determinative. The construct of "rights" ascribed subjectivity to citizens through the legal system's power to classify individuals as within or without of the body of juridical acceptability. The Spanish legal inheritance clearly operated on a different principle, though its dismantling during the liberal revolution began to move exactly toward that form of classification. The particular legal subjectivity present in any given suit during the Spanish period was contingent on circumstances. Gender was one node among many along a spectrum of options available for litigants to accentuate or play down the given tactical necessities of the moment. Law and legal representation were techniques of dispute resolution that sought to exploit the intricacies of the judicial labyrinth to constrain the other party. Most surprising, perhaps, was the extent to which the judiciary responded.

This is not to suggest that women in Spain's America experienced parity or equality. Just as indigenous communities were clearly subordinated, so too were women, but the constraints implemented by the judicial form worked in both directions—against the centralization of power in the hands of the dominating, as well as toward subordination of the dominated. It must be noted, as well, that the experience of these constraints was differentiated by other nodes along the spectrum of identities to which individuals could appeal. Wealthy women were much more likely than poor women to make contracts, pursue debtors, sue their husbands over dowry issues, and generally be involved in property disputes. Even so, poor women or indigenous women *were able* to access legal resources with crown-provided legal counsel. Marital status could be employed to seek protection, for example, from a spouse's creditors or in an attempt to invalidate legal acts made outside the purview of a husband's tutelage. Marital status could also be blatantly ignored.

Women were much more likely than men to be subject to domestic violence, which appeared to be tolerated to a certain extent. It is difficult to judge the extent to which domestic violence went unpunished, though it is likely the vast majority of instances did. Women sued their husbands in both ecclesiastic and secular venues for domestic violence and other mistreatments. Likewise, from the 1760s to the 1790s, women's bodies experienced an inordinate amount of sexual surveillance. These gendered differentiations, however, did not constrain the customary means by which women (or men) approached the adjudication of accusations. As with legal status, the terms of criminal prosecution were open to interpretation. The meaning of words such as scandalous, notorious, and public as well as marriage and adultery were contested, and carried with them popular as well as institutional interpretations.

In both the civil and criminal arenas, the many hundreds of instances of litigation analyzed in this book attest to a wide variety of legal acts engaged in by women independently and acceded legitimacy by bureaucratic and judicial officials, even when said officials may personally have favored patriarchal authority. These legal acts included signing contracts, loaning and borrowing monies, witnessing notarial acts, making testaments and bequeathing property, alienating property, testifying as witnesses in criminal proceedings, filing criminal charges, defending criminal accusations, filing civil suits, and defending civil actions. In the closing decades of Spanish rule, Bourbon officials attempted to undo the customary structure of authority in Quito in favor of new, institutional values of paternal authority and filial obedience, to use the terms of Saether.[86] Whatever their success in other arenas of imperial bureaucratic and economic administration, the Bourbon era never completely remade quiteño understandings of legality and justice because they were unable to diminish or sidestep the role of customary practice in the operation of the legal system. In Quito, customary practice ceded to women a measure of economic and legal independence. In those instances where the gender rights of male prerogative were pursued in court, they were pursued for perceived tactical advantage. They also were often rebuffed. In the opening chapter to this book, I posited using the definition of patriarchy developed by Sousa, which describes patriarchy as a system, "in which (1) authority is invested in the eldest male; (2) a woman has no individual legal status and, therefore, cannot order testaments, witness legal documents, or legally represent herself in court; (3) a woman has no individual economic status and, therefore, cannot own property or carry out economic transactions without approval of her legal guardian (usually either her father or her husband); and, (4) a woman's identity is derived from her association with the family patriarch (either her husband or her father)."[87] There is clear evidence in the judicial records of the closing decades of Spanish rule in Quito that this description of patriarchy is not applicable. Women had customary legal status, and made all sorts of legal acts in that status. Women had customary independent economic status, and formed a significant phalanx in the city's petty credit and commercial sectors. From this base of economic and legal identity, women in Quito were able to defend against arbitrary male privilege.

Social authority, it seems, mirrored the customary organization of judicial, bureaucratic, and economic authority despite the best efforts of the Bourbon era to change the organization of authority from the top down. The flexibility and contingency of the system enabled women to constrain the patriarchal tendencies within the law, as well as, to a certain extent, within quiteño society itself. Special rights, rather than simply serving the interests of a moribund nobility, combined with customary practice to limit male prerogative. Because this situation derived from deep structural and cultural realities, characterizing the situation simply as resistance to patriarchy denies the systemic nature of the relationship. And yet, with the rise of republican liberalism in the 1810s and 1820s, social authority began to change with the formulation of a new organization of judicial, bureaucratic, and economic authority that favored the citizen, the male citizen, as an individual, contracting his property, including the private domestic domain under his control, in the name of the republic, and by authority of the law. This vision was exclusionary of women, and, though contested, was consolidated in the years after Ecuador's full independence from Gran Colombia.

APPENDIX I

Occupations in the Santa Bárbara Padrón, 1768

Table A.1

OCCUPATION	TOTAL	IM	IF	BM	BF	NM	NF
Lawyer (*abogado*)	2					2	
Magistrate (*alcalde*)	2					2	
Royal Standard Bearer (*alférez real*)	1					1	
Sugar vendor (*azucarero*)	2	1				1	
Bricklayer (*albañi*)	2	2					
Master barber (*maestro barbero*)	1	1					
Carpenter (*carpintero*)	5	3				2	
Farmhand (*chacarero*)	4					4	
Produce grocer (*chagro*)	5		1		2		2
Linen clothier (*damasquero*)	1	1					
Administrator of the liquor monopoly (*estanco real*)	1					1	
Blacksmith (*herrero*)	5					5	
Indian servant (*huasicama*)	1	1					
Laborer (labrador)	2					2	
Teacher (*maestro de escuela de niños*)	1					1	
Grammar teacher (*maestro de gramática*)	1					1	
Merchant (*mercader*)	4					4	
Musician (*músico* or *guitarrero*)	3					3	
Notary (*notario* or *notario mayor*)	2					2	
Worker (*obrero*)	1					1	
Copyist (*oficial plumario*)	2					2	
Canteen (*ollero*)	6					2	4
Bread baker (*panadero*)	1					1	

OCCUPATION	TOTAL	IM	IF	BM	BF	NM	NF
Master painter (*maestro pintor*)	1					1	
Painter (*pintor*)	1					1	
Master silversmith (*maestro platero*)	1					1	
Silversmith (*platero*)	2					2	
Town crier (*pregonero*)	1	1					
Clothes presser (*prensadora*)	1						1
Ecclesiastic (*presbítero*)	4					4	
Grocer and general merchant (*pulpero*)	7	1				4	2
Rope maker (*reatero*)	3	1				2	
Rosary vendor (*rosariero*)	1					1	
Sexton (*sacristan*)	3	1				2	
Master tailor (*maestro sastre*)	3	1				2	
Tailor (*sastre*)	14	1				13	
Chair maker (*sillero*)	2					2	
Hatter (*sombrerero*)	2					2	
Weaver (*tejedor*)	9	9					
Ají (hot pepper) vendor (*vendadora de ají*)	1		1				
Street vendor (*vendedor en las calles*)	1					1	
Cobbler (*zapatero*)	10	9				1	

SOURCE: "PADRÓN DE SANTA BÁRBARA" (1978).

I = Indian; B = Black or Mulatto; N = No ethnicity; M = Male; F = Female

APPENDIX II

List of Adulterous Couples
from the Pueblo of Chillogallo, 1790

1. Antonio Fernandez lives in illicit commerce with Maria Zevallos, wife of Francisco Ypes, who has been absent for many years. The accomplices have been reprimanded, but they have not been reformed.

2. Marcos Poso, husband of Baltasara Jurita, lives in adulterous commerce with Manuela Soria, single woman. A judicial process is under way, and they been jailed. However, he abandoned his wife to pursue his relationship.

3. Bernardo Vega, single, lives in adulterous commerce with Visenta dela Cruz, wife of Josef Fernandez, who has repudiated his wife for her liberties from a prior occasion. They have been reprimanded but have not reformed, and with notable [. . .] when they were discovered by the husband *infraganti* the two accomplices proceeded to mistreat him with words as well as physically.

4. Januario Rosero and Baltasara Jurita, both married, live in adulterous commerce having abandoned their consorts, taken together freely in their bad living. They have been reprimanded. . . .

5. Josef Dias and Maria Juana Jurita, singles. They have children, but do not want to redeem them.

6. Vicencio Perez and Magdalena dela Cruz, which they are able to remedy, or abandon along with their accomplices.

7. Xavier Salazar and Fulgencia Fernandez, singles. A judicial process is being pursued by the Señor Alcalde don Gomez de la Thorres.

8. Antonio Salazar and Eugenia Garzes, singles. They were reprimanded that one of the two should leave the area because there is an impediment to changing their station.

9. Teracio Zeballos and Agustina Cusinfuilla, married, are involved in illicit commerce, usurping the rights of their spouses.

10. Domingo Vargas y Gregoria Perez, married, have lived in adulterous commerce many years. They have been prosecuted, but have not reformed. To the detriment of their spouses, the relationship continues.

11. Mauricio Salazar, husband of Leonora Villafuerte, lives in illicit commerce with Ygnacia Pullas, single, in the detriment of his wife.

12. Gregorio Leon and Maria Lomas it's said they are in adulterous commerce, in detriment to their consorts, but are living [with their spouses].

13. Asencio Villafuerte and Petrona Cuya, married, as with those named in the above clause, live with their spouses, but also live as accomplices in illicit commerce.

14. Lorenso Ortiz, husband to Juana Cajamarca, is in involved illicit commerce with Thoribia Chuasangil, wife of Pasqual Atapuma. They are living with their consorts, but proceed in this poor state.

15. Pedro Garces, husband of Maritna Fernandez, lives in adulterous commerce with Petrona Mantilla, wife of Josef Ortuño. They have been reprimanded. The man was tried and punished, but they have not reformed.

16. Manuel Ortiz, husband of Juaquina Xacome, lives in illicit commerce with Cecilia Choasangil, single, who could leave the area.

17. Pasuqal Piñeda, husband of Ana Pilcosisase, is involved in illicit commerce with Nicolasa Cuya, single. The man lives with his wife.

18. Antonio Pillajo, Indian, married to Melchora Pilla, has lived a long time in illicit commerce with Juaquina Albarado, to the detriment of his spouse.

19. Josef Llivi, single Indian, lives in a bad condition with Manuela Chucquillamora, single. They are able to remedy the situation [through marriage].

20. Visente Miranda and Manuela Chimbo, single Indians, live in a deplorable condition and are capable of remedying it.

21. Thomas Alvares and Cathalina Salazar are involved in illicit commerce. They are single, and have offspring but do not want to redeem them.

22. Juan Lopez, a married Indian, lives in a deplorable state with Maria Conya, single, in detriment to his spouse.

23. Mariano Tello and Antonia Chicayzo, residentes of Saguanche, live in illicit commerce. They have been prosecuted, but have not reformed. [A marginalia indicates the two married.]

24. Tiburcion Paez and Maria Candelaria live in illicit commerce, also in Saguanche. They are single, and could remedy the situation.

SOURCE: AN/Q CR 137, 19*VII*1790, "DOSSIER FORMED THROUGH THE ACTIONS OF THE PEDANEO OF THE PUEBLO OF CHILLOGALLO FOR THE INVESTIGATION OF SUBJECTS WHO LIVE DISUNITED FROM THEIR WIVES."

APPENDIX III

Licensure Totals, 1765–1829[1]

Table A.2. License Claims by Status, 1765–1769, 1785–1789, 1805–1809

YEAR	RELIGIOUS	MARRIED	MARRIED, HUSBAND ABSENT	MARRIED, SEPARATED	JUDICIAL GRANT	TOTAL
1765	0	1	0	0	0	1
1766	0	1	0	0	0	1
1767	0	1	0	0	0	1
1768	0	0	0	0	0	0
1769	0	0	1	0	0	1
TOTAL	0	3	1	0	0	4
1785	0	2	1	0	0	3
1786	1	3	0	0	0	4
1787	2	5	0	0	0	7
1788	0	3	0	0	0	3
1789	0	8	0	0	0	8
TOTAL	3	21	1	0	0	25
1805	0	6	0	0	1	7
1806	0	2	0	1	0	3
1807	0	6	0	0	0	6
1808	0	5	0	0	1	6
1809	0	2	0	0	0	2
TOTAL	0	21	0	1	2	24
TOTAL ALL YEARS	3	45	2	1	2	53

Table A.3. License Claims by Status, 1810–1814, 1825–1829

YEAR	RELIGIOUS	MARRIED	MARRIED, HUSBAND ABSENT	MARRIED, SEPARATED	JUDICIAL GRANT	TOTAL
1810	0	3	0	0	0	3
1811	0	1	1	0	0	2
1812	0	1	0	0	0	1
1813	0	0	0	0	0	0
1814	0	4	0	0	0	4
TOTAL	0	9	1	0	0	10
1825	1	2	0	0	0	3
1826	0	3	0	0	0	3
1827	0	1	0	0	0	1
1828	0	1	0	0	0	1
1829	0	2	0	0	0	2
TOTAL	1	9	0	0	0	10
TOTAL ALL YEARS	1	18	1	0	0	20

Table A.4. Litigants Without License by Status, 1765–1769, 1785–1789, 1805–1809

YEAR	RELIGIOUS	MARRIED, SEPARATED	MARRIED, HUSBAND ABSENT	MARRIED	SINGLE	NO STATUS	WIDOW	TOTAL
1765	0	0	0	3	0	2	1	6
1766	0	0	0	0	2	1	1	4
1767	0	0	1	0	0	2	1	4
1768	0	0	1	1	0	1	1	4
1769	0	0	0	0	0	1	1	2
TOTAL	0	0	2	4	2	7	5	20
1785	1	0	0	3	2	14	13	33
1786	0	0	0	6	0	7	6	19
1787	0	2	1	3	2	12	8	28
1788	0	0	0	1	1	7	3	12
1789	0	0	0	7	0	18	5	30
TOTAL	1	2	1	20	5	58	35	112
1805	1	1	0	8	1	27	9	47
1806	0	0	0	7	1	26	11	45
1807	0	0	0	8	3	23	13	47
1808	0	0	6	0	2	18	7	33
1809	1	0	1	8	5	14	3	32
TOTAL	2	1	7	31	12	108	43	204
TOTAL ALL YEARS	3	3	10	55	19	173	83	336

Table A.5 *Litigants Without License by Status, 1810–1814, 1825–1829*

YEAR	RELIGIOUS	MARRIED, SEPARATED	MARRIED, HUSBAND ABSENT	MARRIED	SINGLE	NO STATUS	WIDOW	TOTAL
1810	1	0	0	5	2	14	7	29
1811	0	0	1	0	1	19	4[2]	25
1812	1	0	0	3	1	9	3	17
1813	0	0	1	8	0	13	7	29
1814	0	0	0	1	1	17	6	25
TOTAL	2	0	2	17	5	72	27	125
1825	0	0	0	2	1	12	4	19
1826	1	0	0	4	2	18	5	30
1827	0	0	0	3	1	21	3	28
1828	0	0	2	6	0	15	3	26
1829	1	0	1	2	4	6	3	17
TOTAL	2	0	3	17	8	72	18	120
TOTAL ALL YEARS	4	0	5	34	13	144	45	245

Table A.6 Women Represented by Men in Litigation, 1765–1769, 1785–1789, 1805–1809

YEAR	HUSBAND	HUSBAND FOR BOTH	FATHER	ATTORNEY	GENERAL PROTECTORATE	THIRD PARTY	TOTAL
1765	0	0	0	2	0	1	3
1766	0	0	0	1	0	1	2
1767	0	0	0	0	0	0	0
1768	0	0	0	0	0	0	0
1769	1	0	0	0	0	0	1
TOTAL	1	0	0	3	0	2	6
1785	0	0	1	3	0	1	5
1786	0	1	1	1	0	0	3
1787	2	0	2	2	1	2	9
1788	3	1	0	1	2	1	8
1789	3	2	2	7	2	6	22
TOTAL	8	4	6	14	5	10	47
1805	5	0	0	3	3	1	12
1806	4	3	2	5	4	0	18
1807	6	1	0	4	4	2	17
1808	2	1	0	5	2	1	11
1809	1	1	0	3	2	2	9
TOTAL	18	6	2	20	15	6	67
TOTAL ALL YEARS	27	10	8	37	20	18	120

Table A.7 Women Represented by Men in Litigation, 1810–1829

YEAR	HUSBAND FOR WIFE	HUSBAND FOR BOTH	FATHER	ATTORNEY	PROTECTORES (INDIOS, ESCLAVOS, POBRES)	THIRD PARTY	TOTAL
1810	3	2	1	0	3	2	11
1811	1	0	3	3	1	4	12
1812	1	2	1	3	2	1	10
1813	3	1	1	0	3	2	10
1814	2	4	1	2	5	2	16
TOTAL	10	9	7	8	14	11	59
1825	4	0	1	0	0	4	9
1826	2	4	0	0	4	4	14
1827	1	2	0	2	2	1	8
1828	2	3	0	0	2	2	9
1829	9	1	0	0	1	1	12
TOTAL	18	10	1	2	9	12	52
TOTAL ALL YEARS	28	19	8	10	23	23	111

NOTES

INTRODUCTION

1. The title of this book makes an obvious overture to R. Douglas Cope's *The Limits of Racial Domination: Plebeian Society in Colonial Mexico City, 1660–1720* (Madison: University of Wisconsin Press, 1994). There is a certain utility in noting the similarities between the very messy racial social order of the Spanish Empire and the hardening of that system in the late-eighteenth and early-nineteenth centuries.

2. *Vecina* is the feminine equivalent of the masculine *vecino*, which indicated a man's membership in the local citizenry (*vecinidad*). For more on early modern Spanish conceptions of citizenship, see Tamar Herzog, "Early Modern Spanish Citizenship: Inclusion and Exclusion in the Old and New World," 205–25 in John Smolenski and Thomas J. Humphrey, eds., *New World Orders: Violence and Authority in the Colonial Americas* (Philadelphia: University of Pennsylvania Press, 2005).

3. AN/Q 1NJ 46, 3-vi-1768. Spelling conventions were not set in the eighteenth century. In the orthography of names, I have chosen to remain faithful to the original documents, opting to use the most common version of an individual's name as presented at the time.

4. AN/Q 1NJ 46, 3-vi-1768.

5. The endeavor to historicize indigenous interactions with Spanish authorities, particularly through the courts, legal practices, and the political office of the indigenous chief (*cacique*), have a long presence in the literature, beginning with Charles Gibson, *The Aztecs Under Spanish Rule: A History of the Indians of the Valley of Mexico, 1519–1810* (Stanford, CA: Stanford University Press, 1964). See also, among many others, James Lockhart, *The Nahuas After the Conquest: A Social and Cultural History of the Indians of Central Mexico, Sixteenth through Eighteenth Centuries* (Stanford, CA: Stanford University Press, 1992); Karen Powers, *Andean Journeys: Migration, Ethnogenisis, and the State in Colonial Quito* (Albuquerque: University of New Mexico Press, 1995); Frank Salomon, "Indian Women of Early Colonial Quito as Seen Through Their Testaments," *Americas* 44, no. 3 (January 1988): 325–41; Karen Spalding, *Huarochirí: An Andean Society Under Inca and Spanish Rule* (Stanford, CA: Stanford University Press, 1984); Steve J. Stern, *Peru's Indian Peoples and the Challenge of Spanish Conquest: Huamanga to 1640* (Madison: University of Wisconsin Press, 1982); Kevin Terraciano, *The Mixtecs of Colonial Oaxaca: Nudazahul History, Sixteenth through Eighteenth*

Centuries (Stanford, CA: Stanford University Press, 2004); and Charles F. Walker, *Smoldering Ashes: Cuzco and the Creation of Republican Peru, 1780–1840* (Durham, NC: Duke University Press, 1999). For two recent works that investigate intersections of gender and ethnicity, see Kimberly Gauderman, *Women's Lives in Colonial Quito: Gender, Law, and Economy in Spanish America* (Austin: University of Texas Press, 2003); and Jane Mangan, *Trading Roles: Gender, Ethnicity, and the Urban Economy in Colonial Potosí* (Durham, NC: Duke University Press, 2005). For an interesting study of African experiences with many of the same processes, see Herman Bennett, *Africans in Colonial Mexico: Absolutism, Christianity, and Afro-Creole Consciousness, 1570–1640* (Bloomington: Indiana University Press, 2003); Sherwin K. Bryant, "Enslaved Rebels, Fugitives, and Litigants: The Resistance Continuum in Colonial Quito," *CLAR* 13, no. 1 (2004): 7–46; and Kris Lane, "Captivity and Redemption: Aspects of Slave Life in Early Colonial Quito and Popayán," *The Americas* 57, no. 3 (2000): 225–46.

6. The continuing presence of functioning and record-producing institutions amidst the conflicts spanning the late colonial period and the civil wars and tumults of the independence period confirms the observation of James Lockhart on the emergence of civil society in a sixteenth-century Peru wracked by conflict and war, "that to a certain extent basic development is compatible with war, political chaos, and bad governors." Lockhart, *Spanish Peru, 1532–1560: A Social History*, 2nd ed. (Madison: University of Wisconsin Press, 1994), 6. The very language of justice began to change during the independence period in Quito, just as the meanings and symbols changed, and new litigation continued to be filed. By comparison, the number of cases filed before the First Notary of Quito averaged approximately 86 per year for the decade 1780–1790, 140 per year for the decade 1805–1815, and 93 per year for the decade 1820–1830, as compiled in AN/Q 1NJ boxes 72–120, 219–85, 306–45.

7. By judicial form, I mean to indicate the actual physical form used to submit petitions, document actions, make declarations, notate transactions, and so on, as well as the discursive form in which the documents were produced. There was a remarkable discursive continuity across the variety of acts that have entered the written record, encapsulated in the judicial form.

8. For descriptions of the decentralized nature of Spanish rule, see Clarence H. Haring, *The Spanish Empire in America* (New York; Harcourt Brace, 1975 [1947]); John Leddy Phelan, *The Kingdom of Quito in the Seventeenth Century: Bureaucratic Politics in the Spanish Empire* (Madison: University of Wisconsin Press, 1967); Phelan, *The People and the King: The Comunero Revolution in Colombia, 1781* (Madison: University of Wisconsin Press, 1978); Phelan, "Authority and Flexibility in the Spanish Imperial Bureaucracy," *Administrative Science Quarterly* 5 (1960): 47–65; Richard Kagan, *Lawsuits and Litigants in Castile, 1500–1700* (University of North Carolina Press, 1981); Charles R. Cutter, *The Legal Culture of Northern New Spain, 1700–1810* (Albuquerque: University of New Mexico Press, 1995); Ruth MacKay, *The Limits of Royal Authority: Resistance and Obedience in Seventeenth-Century Castile* (Cambridge: Cambridge University Press, 1999); Helen Nader, *Liberty in Absolutist Spain: The Sale of Habsburg Towns, 1516–1700*

(Baltimore: Johns Hopkins University Press, 1993); J. B. Owens, *"By My Absolute Royal Authority": Justice and the Castilian Commonwealth at the Beginning of the First Global Age* (Rochester, NY: University of Rochester Press, 2005); Gauderman, *Women's Lives in Colonial Quito*, 12–29; and Alejandro Cañeque, *The King's Living Image: The Culture and Politics of Viceregal Power in Colonial Mexico* (New York: Routledge Press, 2002). Most recently, the *HAHR* published a special forum on issues of taxation, negotiation, and wealth redistribution in the Indies. See the forum on "Bargaining for Absolutism," in *HAHR* 88, no. 2 (2008): 169–245, and particularly the lead article, Alejandra Irigoin and Regina Grafe, "Bargaining for Absolutism: A Spanish Path to Nation-State and Empire Building," *HAHR* 88, no. 2 (2008): 173–209.

9. Owens, *"By My Absolute Royal Authority,"* 1–4.

10. Witness, for example, Bianca Premo, *Children of the Father King: Youth, Authority, and Legal Minority in Colonial Lima* (Chapel Hill: University of North Carolina Press, 2005), 10, which holds that patriarchy provided the organizing principle and legal framework for the whole range of social relations mirrored on the legitimate position of the "Father King." See also Steve Stern, *The Secret History of Gender: Women, Men, and Power in Late Colonial Mexico* (Chapel Hill: University of North Carolina, 1995).

11. Owens, *"By My Absolute Royal Authority,"* 2.

12. John Lynch, *Bourbon Spain, 1700–1808* (Oxford: B. Blackwell, 1989). In Lynch's introduction, his critique of the state of Spanish politics and economics at the opening of the eighteenth century reproduces the language of decline, inefficiency, and irrationality that the Bourbons used to justify centralization of power in the monarchy.

13. Patricia Seed led the way in questioning absolutist models of gender relations for the early period in her study of marriage choice, *To Love, Honor, and Obey in Colonial Mexico: Conflicts over Marriage Choice, 1574–1821* (Stanford, CA: Stanford University Press, 1988). Seed concluded that the penetration of capitalist markets combined with a secularization of marriage authority to undermine the church's ability to patriarchal authority over marriage choice. She therefore dates the emergence of patriarchy in early Latin America in the late eighteenth and early nineteenth centuries. Other contributions that question patriarchy, if not directly then implicitly, include Kimberly A. Gauderman, *Women's Lives in Colonial Quito;* Salomon, "Indian Women of Early Colonial Quito"; Lisa Mary Sousa, "Woman and Crime in Colonial Oaxaca: Evidence of Complementary Gender Roles in Mixtec and Zapotec Societies," in Susan Schroeder, Stephanie Wood, and Robert Haskett, Eds., *Indian Women of Early Mexico* (Norman: University of Oklahoma Press, 1997); and Stephanie Wood, "Matters of Life at Death: Nahuatl Testaments of Rural Women, 1589–1801," 165–82 in Schroeder, Wood, and Haskett. The Spanish historiography largely ignores the term, but has tackled the issue often in concert with questioning the particularities of the Mediterranean honor/shame complex rooted in twentieth-century anthropological literatures. See, for example, Allyson Poska, "When Love Goes Wrong: Getting out of Marriage in Seventeenth-Century Spain," *Journal of Social History* 29.4 (1996): 873–82; Allyson Poska, *Women and Authority in Early Modern*

Spain: The Peasants of Galicia (Oxford: Oxford University Press, 2005); Allyson Poska, "Elusive Virtue: Rethinking the Role of Female Chastity in Early Modern Spain," *Journal of Early Modern History* 8:1–2 (January 2004), 135–46; and Scott Taylor, "Credit, Debt, and Honor in Castile, 1600–1650," *Journal of Early Modern History* 7:1–2 (January 2003), 8–27; and Helen Nader, ed., *Power and Gender in Renaissance Spain: Eight women of the Mendoza Family, 1450–1650* (Baltimore: Johns Hopkins University Press, 2004). For Brazil, see Muriel Nazzari, *Disappearance of the Dowry: Women, Families, and Social Change in São Paulo, Brazil (1600–1900)* (Stanford, CA: Stanford University Press, 1991); Nazzari, "Parents and Daughters: Change in Dowry Practice in São Paulo (1600–1770)," *HAHR* 70.4 (1990): 639–65; and Linda Lewin, "Natural and Spurious Children in Brazilian Inheritance Law from Colony to Empire: A Methodological Essay," *Americas* 48.3 (1992): 351–96. Jane Mangan maintains the use of the term "patriarchy" in her study of colonial Potosí with a certain measure of skepticism, using the term to indicate a situation in which "men [were] dominant in controlling power and resources," but allows women room to maneuver in both economic and legal contexts. For many, use of the term "patriarchy" to designate gender inequality remains par for the course. See for example, Stern, *Secret History*. Stern explains women's ability to utilize structural mitigations of male authority as the "pluralization of patriarchs" (p. 100–101). The model is likewise ubiquitous in modern studies, particularly modern period studies' portrayals of the colonial period. See, for example, Silvia Arrom, *The Women of Mexico City, 1790–1857* (Stanford, CA: Stanford University Press, 1985); Susan Besse, *Restructuring Patriarchy: The Modernization of Gender Inequality in Brazil, 1914–1940* (Chapel Hill: University of North Carolina Press, 1996); Sueann Caulfield, *In Defense of Honor: Morality, Modernity, and the Nation in Early Twentieth-Century Brazil* (Durham: Duke University Press, 2000); Sueann Caulfield, Sarah C. Chambers, and Lara Putnam, eds., *Honor, Status, and Law in Modern Latin America* (Durham: Duke University Press, 2005); Sarah C. Chambers, *From Subjects to Citizens: Honor, Gender, and Politics in Arequipa, Peru, 1780–1854* (University Park: Penn State University Press, 1999); Elizabeth Dore and Maxine Molyneux, eds., *Hidden Histories of Gender and the State* (Durham: Duke University Press, 2000); Christine Hünefeldt, *Liberalism in the Bedroom: Quarrelling Spouses in Nineteenth-Century Lima* (University Park: Penn State University Press, 2000); and Erin O'Connor, "Widow's Rights Questioned: Indians, the State, and Fluctuating Gender Ideas in Central Highland Ecuador, 1870–1900," *The Americas* 59:1 (July 2002): 87–106. In the cases listed above, modern historians accept wholesale the a priori assumption of patriarchal gender relations in the early period, and thus explain "modern" patriarchy as an updating of colonial social relations. Outside of the Brazilian cases, this assumption is invariably built on the uncritical acceptance by modernists of Sylvia Arrom's portrayal of the late colonial gender regime. Elizabeth Dore has noted the difficulties of broad-stroke applications of the patriarchal model for the nineteenth century due to the prevalence of female-headed households. Elizabeth Dore, "The Holy Family: Imagined Households in Latin America History," chapter in Dore, ed., *Gender Politics in Latin America: Debates in Theory and Practice* (New York: Monthly Review Press, 1997): 113.

14. Judith Butler, *Gender Trouble: Feminism and the Subversion of Identity* (New York: Routledge, 1999), 173.

15. Sousa, "Woman and Crime in Colonial Oaxaca," footnote on 395.

16. Judith Bennett, *History Matters: Patriarchy and the Challenge of Feminism* (Philadelphia: University of Pennsylvania Press, 2006). Bennett decries skepticism in women's and gender history over the universality of patriarchal domination as evidence of presentism, depoliticization, and co-optation of feminist history as it has gained a foothold in academia. As an antidote, she posits that reviving patriarchy as a metacategory of analysis and renewing the historical search for the origin of female domination will return feminist history to its formerly privileged position within women's and gender studies (2–4).

17. Ibid., 56.

18. Gauderman, *Women's Lives in Colonial Quito*, 12. For the objects of her criticism, see Richard Boyer, *Lives of the Bigamists: Marriage, Family, and Community in Colonial Mexico* (Albuquerque: University of New Mexico Press, 1995); Jenny Londoño, *Entre la sumisión y la resistencia: Las mujeres en la Audiencia de Quito* (Quito, Ecuador: Ediciones Abya-Yala, 1997); Luis Martín, *Daughters of the Conquistadors* (Albuquerque: University of New Mexico Press, 1983); Irene Silverblatt, *Moon, Sun, Witches: Gender Ideologies and Class in Inca and Colonial Peru* (Princeton, NJ: Princeton University Press, 1989); and Stern, *Secret History*, among others.

19. Gauderman, *Women's Lives in Colonial Quito*, 13–14. Marysa Navarro makes a similar argument for dissembling the artificial theoretical construct of marianism, positing in its stead, "feminist scholarship should be grounded in the cultural, geographic, and historical specificity of gender arrangements." Marysa Navarro, "Against *Marianismo*," in Rosario Montoya, Leslie Jo Frazier, and Janis Hurtig, eds., *Genders Place: Feminist Anthropologies of Latin America*, 257–72 (New York: Palgrave, 2002), 257.

20. For patriarchy as women's exclusion from political power, see Mangan, *Trading Roles*. Exclusion from political power is indeed a necessary but not a sufficient condition for the particular form of patriarchal male domination, particularly in light of the poststructuralist insight into the articulation of power throughout social and cultural forms. Bianco Premo responded to Gauderman's critique of the ahistoricity, or transhistorical deployment of patriarchy by expanding Stern's four-part definition of the category "as a system of social relations based on male control of women's sexuality and labor, male superiority over women, elder/father authority, and political rule based on the family model" to also include the importance of age, household authority, and political governance. Premo, *Children of the Father King*, ff. 265. She argues, "Patriarchy, then, was a political ideology that transcended even if it often implicated gender. And because authority in the colonial Spanish American household contained gendered, racial, and generational dimensions simultaneously, patriarchy could never be rigid or stable. Its encompassing nature . . . meant that mothers as well as fathers, and female slave masters as well as priests, could exert control over others based on socially constructed notions of that natural familial authority entailed, even if only momentarily and conditionally" (Premo, 10).

21. Stern, *Secret History*. A similar argument is made in a different context by Herman Bennett, who sees both free and slave Afro-Mexican uses of the legal system as generative of creole consciousness rather than as a predictable and structural feature of Spanish imperial legality. H. Bennett, *Africans in Colonial Mexico*, 2–4.

22. Sousa, "Women and Crime in Colonial Oaxaca."

23. A fuero was a special legal charter or set of privileges granted to various polities by the crown. Groups with such charters included, for example, members of the military or clergy, as well as citizens of many of the kingdoms ruled by the crown of Castile. For example, Basques could request their cases be heard before the senior judge (*juez mayor*) of Vizcaya, even if they were arrested in the New World. As Kagan has noted, the many fueros "created . . . a web of jurisdictional refuges which many used to escape prosecution and to delay proceedings in the king's courts." Kagan, *Lawsuits and Litigants*, 30.

24. Carole Pateman, *The Sexual Contract* (Stanford, CA: Stanford University Press, 1988).

25. Terry Eagleton, *The Functions of Criticism* (New York: Verso, 2005), 9.

26. I recognize that none of these forms constituted total systems, with wholly integrated and successfully implemented state forms, ideologies, and so on. They were, though, ideal forms or foundational expressions of guiding principles of political organization. As such, they provide a more compelling modality for analysis than, say, state forms that became notoriously weaker across the period of study even as claims to political and social power became more absolute. I would argue, in fact, that the centrality of the state and state formation in recent scholarship relies on an artificial relationship between state and society, a divide dependent on Gramscian concepts of consent and coercion that bisects society into the acting and the acted-upon. Governance, instead, looks to parallels between the ideals of governing, the logic behind bureaucratic organization, and the constitution of the informal authority of social relations. This opens a door to investigating gendered power relations by going beyond official rhetoric to *how* power was established.

27. Under the influence of Michel Foucault, recent work on legal culture in Latin America has centered almost exclusively on the evolution of criminality, the codification of criminal law, and the emergence of modern forms of punishment. I wish to expand the concept of legal culture to include legal acts in all their variety, notarial, civil, and criminal in order to have a fuller understanding of the role of law and the relationship of individuals to legality. This is even more important in light of the dramatic alteration of the legal order in the period following independence. On criminality and the law, see Carlos Aguirre and Robert Buffington, eds., *Reconstructing Criminality in Latin America* (Wilmington, DE: Scholarly Resources, 2000); Carlos Aguirre and Charles Walker, eds., *Bandoleros, abigeos y montoneros: Criminalidad y violencia en el Perú, siglos XVIII–XIX* (Lima: Instituto de Apoyo Agrario, 1990); Víctor Tao Anzoátegui, "Ordenes normativos y prácticas socio-jurídicas: la justicia," in *Nueva historia de la nación argentina*, vol. 2 (Buenos Aires: Planeta, 1999), 283–315; and Ricardo D. Salvatorre, Carlos Aguirre, and Gilbert M. Joseph, eds., *Crime and Punishment*. Interesting works that touch on issues of legal culture

outside criminal justice include Jeremy Adelman's investigation of commercial codes and the legal construction of capitalism in Argentina, *Republic of Capital: Buenos Aires and the Legal Transformation of the Atlantic World* (Stanford, CA: Stanford University Press, 1999); Laura Benton, *Law and Colonial Cultures: Legal Regimes in World History, 1400–1900* (Cambridge: Cambridge University Press, 2002), particularly chapters 1, 2, and 6; Robert Jackson, ed., *Liberals, the Church, and Indian Peasants: Corporate Lands and the Challenge of Reform in Nineteenth-Century Spanish America* (Albuquerque: University of New Mexico Press, 1997); Mark Thurner, *From Two Republics to One Divided: Contradictions of Postcolonial Nationmaking in Andean Peru* (Durham, NC; London: Duke University Press, 1997); and Walker, *Smoldering Ashes*.

28. *Real Audiencia* literally translates as Royal Audience; the body was considered the physical manifestation of the king's presence and judicial will. For more on the notion of royal embodiment in Spanish American rule, see Cañeque, *The King's Living Image*, particularly Chapter 1.

29. "Padrón de Santa Bárbara en 1768," *Museo histórico* 56 (1978): 93–122.

30. Minchom notes that the percentage of female-headed households rose even higher in the parish, to 58.2 percent in 1831. Martin Minchom, *The People of Quito, 1690–1810: Change and Unrest in the Underclass* (Boulder, CO: Westview Press, 1994), 149.

31. "Padrón de Santa Bárbara," 94–95, 97–98.

32. Minchom makes the suggestion that the organization of space in the corregimiento produced a Spanish-mestizo urban center surrounded by increasingly rural, and increasingly Indian, parishes leading into an Indian hinterland. Minchom, *The People of Quito*, 11. This conception of ethnic space reinforces an association between urbanity and Hispanization and the rurality with authentic Indianness that is both an overly restrictive and reductionist means of conceiving ethnic identity.

33. Minchom, *The People of Quito*, 11, 47.

34. Francisco Silvestre, *Descripción del reyno de Santa Fé de Bógota* (Bógota: Ministerio de Educación Nacional, 1950 [1789]): 19.

35. Ibid., 28–29.

36. Juan Romualdo Navarro, "Idea del reino de Quito," in Manuel Miño Grijalva, ed., *La economía colonial: Relaciones socio-económicas de la Real Audiencia de Quito* (Quito: Corporación Editora Nacional, 1984), 111–66.

37. There are more than seven thousand cases archived in 1NJ for the period 1765–1835. The volume of cases available within the alternating decades was still overwhelming. The case set was further culled within the chosen decades based on gender and geography. Cases were restricted to Quito and the Five Leagues. Additionally, I attempted to collect all cases involving women as primary litigants, as well as occasional representative suits that did not involve women at all. Selected cases were then digitally photographed for later analysis. This brought the total number of cases analyzed from 1NJ to a manageable number.

38. Sir Henry Sumner Maine, *Ancient Law: Its Connection with the Early History of Society, and its Relation to Modern Ideas* (London: 1861), 170.

1. The Bourbon period officially began with the end of the War of Spanish Succession in 1716, but intensive attention to reform of the American kingdoms was not given until the 1760s in the wake of the Seven Years War. The period of so-called Bourbon reforms, then, arrived in Quito in the mid-1760s with the new fiscal policies discussed in this chapter, and continued through the end of the century. For a broader discussion of the Bourbon reforms as they affected the northern Andes, see Christiana Borchart de Moreno, *La Audiencia de Quito: Aspectos económicos y sociales (siglos XVI–VIII)* (Quito: Abuya Yala/Banco Central, 1998), 299–322; Allan J. Kuethe, "The Early Reforms of Charles III in the Viceroyalty of New Granada, 1759–1776," in *Reform and Insurrection in Bourbon New Granada and Peru*, ed. John R. Fisher, Allan J. Kuethe, and Anthony McFarlane, 19–40 (Baton Rouge: Louisiana State University Press, 1990): Allan J. Kuethe, *Military Reform and Society in New Granada, 1773–1808* (Gainesville: University of Florida Press, 1978); and Rosemarie Terán Najas, *Los proyectos del imperio borbónico en la real audiencia* (Quito: Abya-Yala/TEHIS, 1988).

2. On the laborious process of establishing the viceroyalty of New Granada and Quito's participation in that process, see Terán Najas, *Los proyectos de imperio borbónico*, particularly Chapter 1. See also Anthony McFarlane, *Colombia Before Independence: Economy, Society, and Politics under Bourbon Rule* (Cambridge, UK: Cambridge University Press, 1993), 187–207. On Río de la Plata, see Ricardo Lesser, *Los Orígenes de la Argentina: Historias del Reino del Rió de la Plata* (Buenos Aires: Editorial Biblos, 2003).

3. Though no visitador was ever appointed to investigate the viceroyalty as a whole, in 1778 Juan Francisco Gutiérrez de Piñeres was appointed regent and visitor general (*visitador general*) for the Audiencia of New Granada, an investigation that lasted until 1783. For more on Gutiérrez de Piñeres' reform policies, see McFarlane, *Colombia Before Independence*, 208–27.

4. Kuethe "The Early Reforms of Charles III," 29–30.

5. The Rebellion of the Barrios, so called because insurrectionary activities radiated out of the city of Quito's various popular parishes, or barrios, has received extensive attention in the historiography of late colonial Quito. Colonial Quito was divided into seven parishes, or barrios: El Sagrario, San Roque, San Sebastian, San Marcos, San Blas, Santa Bárbara, and Santa Prisca. For descriptions of the barrios in the eighteenth century, see Martin Minchom, *The People of Quito*, 22–27. The rebellion occurred in two stages: first with a riot the night of May 22, 1765, and then with the more generalized insurrection that began on the night of June 24. Traditionally, the rebellion has been placed within a nationalist discourse as a predecessor of independence. See, for example, Carlos de la Torre Reyes, *La revolución de Quito del 10 de agosto de 1809, sus vicisitudes y su significación en el proceso general de la emancipación hispano-americano* (Quito: Talleres Gráficos de Educación, 1961), 147–54; and Federico González Suárez, *Historia general de la república del Ecuador*, Vol. 2 (Quito: Casa de la Cultura, 1970 [1892]), 1121–37. For more recent analyses of the rebellion, including reconstruction of the events of May

and June, see, among others, Anthony McFarlane, "The Rebellion of the Barrios: Urban Insurrection in Bourbon Quito," Fisher, Keuthe, and McFarlane (1990): 197–254; Minchom *The People of Quito*, 222–34; Kenneth Andrien, "Economic Crisis, Taxes and the Insurrection of 1765," *Past & Present* 129 (1990): 104–31.

6. On tax burden in Quito and Guayaquil during the late eighteenth century, Kenneth Andrien writes, "Despite the decline in textile manufacturing in the north-central highlands, taxpayers in the Quito district paid twice as much in per-capita taxes as the English colonists in North America. The amounts paid in Guayaquil dwarfed anything collected in the thirteen English colonies. In fact, the per-capita tax burden in Guayaquil reached nearly twice the amounts paid in England itself, which reputedly had the highest tax levies in Western Europe. By the late colonial period, the reforms of [Audiencia President] García Pizarro had created a state fiscal apparatus as powerful and exploitative as any in the world" (Andrien, "The State and Dependency," 178). The level of taxation is all the more impressive within the context of economic decline experienced in the Audiencia during the period. Kenneth Andrien, "The State and Dependency in Late Colonial and Early Republican Ecuador," in *The Political Economy of Spanish American in the Age of Revolution, 1750–1850*, ed. Andrien and Lyman Johnson, 169–96 (Albuquerque: University of New Mexico Press, 1994).

7. González Suárez, *Historia general*, 1120.

8. Rubio de Arévalo's career in Quito was marred by a 4,000-peso fine and eight-year suspension beginning in 1747, the result of a bureaucratic squabble with a former president of the Audiencia. Mark A. Burkholder and D. S. Chandler, *Biographical Dictionary of Audiencia Members in the Americas, 1687–1821* (Westport, CT: Greenwood Press, 1982), 302.

9. Andrien, "Economic Crisis," 107–8. A voluminous literature exists on Quito's obraje sector. On the economic troubles and trends involving obraje production and the Audiencia, particularly relating to the reform effects of the Bourbons, see Kenneth Andrien, *The Kingdom of Quito, 1690–1830: The State and Regional Development* (Cambridge: Cambridge University Press, 1995); Borchart de Moreno, *La Audiencia de Quito*, especially sections 3 and 4, 227–362; and Robson Brines Tyrer, "The Demographic and Economic History of the Audiencia of Quito: Indian Population and Textile Production, 1600–1800" (PhD diss., University of California at Berkeley, 1976).

10. Andrien, "Economic Crisis," 109.

11. Ibid., 110.

12. González Suárez, *Historia general*, 1105–8; Minchom, *The People of Quito*, 224. For a firsthand account of the quakes, see P. Bernardo Recio S. J., Vol. 2, Biblioteca Misionera, *Compendiosa relación de la cristianidad de Quito*, Garcia Goldaraz S. J., P. Carlos (Madrid: Consejo Superior de Investigaciones Científicas/Insituto Santo Toribio de Mogrovejo, 1957 [1773]): 379–86.

13. Archivo Municipal de Quito (AMQ), *Actas de Cabildo*, 10-ix-1764, 9-x-1764, 18-x-1764; Archivo Nacional del Ecuador/Quito (AN/Q) Gobierno 22, 19-i-1765. See also "Relación sumaria de las dos sublevaciones de la pleve de Quito," *Boletín de la academia nacional de historia* XV, 42 (1937): 102.

14. For a more extensive description of the responsibilities of the various juris-dictions, see the encyclopedic Haring, *The Spanish Empire*, 110–65.

15. AMQ, *Actas de Cabildo*, 1764.

16. Juan de Velasco, *Historia del reino de Quito en la America meridional*, ed. by Alfredo Pareja Diezcanseco (Caracas: Biblioteca Ayacucho, 1981 [1789]), 334.

17. Andrien, "Economic Crisis," 121.

18. The following discussion is based on the cache of documents collected as the "Expediente seguido por los Jueces de Real Hacienda Contador Cristobal Vicente Calderón y Tesorero Salvador Sánchez Pareja para el remate de Estanco de Aguardientes de Quito y sus cinco leguas, según las propuestas del Abogado Licenciado Melchor de Rivadeneyra," ANQ, Fondo Especial (FE) box 21, vol. 59 (1764), doc. # 2608. All quotes are from this document unless otherwise noted. See also McFarlane, "The Rebellion of the Barrios," 203–4; and Andrien, "Economic Crisis," 121–22.

19. AN/Q FE 2608, 1–2.

20. Ibid., 1.

21. Ibid., 4, 8.

22. AMQ, *Actas de Cabildo*, 25-i-1764.

23. AN/Q, FE 2608, 9.

24. Ibid., 19–21.

25. Andrien, "Economic Crisis," 120.

26. Quoted in McFarlane, "The Rebellion of the Barrios," 207.

27. Andrien has found that at the time of Dias de Herrera's appointment receipts in Quito were one-third of their levels in Bogotá for the alcabala and the aguardiente monopoly, despite the cities being of similar size. "Economic Crisis," 120.

28. Phelan, "Authority and Flexibility," 59. Quoted in Gauderman, *Women's Lives in Colonial Quito*, 17.

29. Dias de Herrera reported on the pasquinades to Messia dela Zerda in a December communiqué. The viceroy ordered an investigation and punish-ment of the responsible parties. In March 1765 he reiterated this earlier order in a dispatch to the Audiencia. FE 22.60 (1765), 2631, 5-iii-1765, AN/Q.

30. "Relación sumaria," 102.

31. Ibid.

32. AMQ, *Actas de Cabildo*, 19-x-1764.

33. Ibid., 19-x-1764.

34. Ibid., 23-x-1764.

35. Ibid., 7-xi-1764.

36. For more on the cabildo abierto, see Haring, *The Spanish Empire*, 159–61. For the revolt against the imposition of the alcabala in the 1590s, see Bernard Lavalle, "La rebelión de las alcabalas," *Revista de Indias* 44 (1984): 141–201. The following discussion draws on the records of the assembly in AMQ, *Actas de Cabildo*, fojas 128–55. Additionally, McFarlane offers an overview and political interpretation of the meeting

based on documents compiled in Spain. McFarlane interprets the event as an expression of a "constitutional conflict" based on perceived political rights of representation associated with the elites. McFarlane, "The Rebellion of the Barrios," 205–17. I argue that this interpretation is too proscriptive, confining the debate over fiscal reform to the realm of political rights. Rather, the cabildo abierto and the bureaucratic fight represent a much larger and more significant struggle between opposing cultural logics with associated understandings on the legitimate organization of authority across society, both formal and informal.

37. AMQ, *Actas de Cabildo*, 14-xi-1764.

38. Ibid., 14-xi-1764.

39. Ibid., 135.

40. Ibid., 136. Emphasis in original.

41. Ibid., 1764, 137.

42. Ibid., 1764, 139–40. Cañeque has argued that the discourse of wretchedness formed an essential discourse in the development of Spanish colonialism, particularly in developing a colonial identity for the indigenous subjects in the Americas. Interestingly, he finds that the association of wretchedness or miserableness with Indians was largely an association with the Indian as alien to urbanity, and that the responsibility of crown agents was to civilize and protect indigenous populations. *The King's Living Image*, Chapters 6–7.

43. AMQ, *Actas de Cabildo*, 1764, foja 143.

44. Phelan, *The People and the King*, xviii.

45. McFarlane, "The Rebellion of the Barrios," 217.

46. Andrien, "Economic Crisis," 122.

47. McFarlane, "The Rebellion of the Barrios," 210.

48. AN/Q, Gobierno 5, 19-i-1765.

49. AN/Q, Estancos 4, 11-v-1765.

50. Navarro was the only native quiteño serving on the Audiencia; he served with three other American-born Spaniards: Luis de Santa Cruz, Gregorio Ignacio Hurtado de Menoza, and Felix de Llano, all from Lima. Two European Spaniards were members of the council as well: President Manuel Rubio de Arévalo and Fiscal José de Cistue, in his seventh year of service in Quito. McFarlane states the removal of Llano weakened the antireform position because Llano had worked to roadblock the implementation of policy. Subsequent events did show Navarro to be loyal to viceregal wishes, a position that problematizes simple equations between loyal Europeans and rebellious creoles. Navarro was eventually rewarded for this loyalty with a position on the Audiencia court of Santa Fé de Bogotá, a position he assumed at the end of 1773. McFarlane, "The Rebellion of the Barrios," 206, 219. Burkholder and Chandler, *Biographical Dictionary*, 232–33. The following two sections draw heavily on McFarlane's reconstruction of the events of May and June as found in the AGI in Sevilla, as well as on documents from AN/Q and AMQ that he did not use, and the published primary sources.

51. McFarlane, "The Rebellion of the Barrios," 219; "Relación sumaria," 103.

52. Recio, *Compendiosa relación*, 518.

53. Ibid. Recio's characterization was, "Porque contaban los descontentos y creían los más sencillos, mayormente los indios, temblosos que de todo se había de pagar." In Minchom's reconstruction of the city's demographic profile during the late eighteenth century, he presents a picture of a city bifurcated by ethnicity, with the barrios of Quito proper inhabited by mestizos and the surrounding corregimiento the abode of Indians. This characterization misses the daily mixing in the city's streets of Indian hawkers, tradespeople, and so on, and likewise reproduces a false dichotomy that equates hispanization with urbanity and Indianness with rurality. This underlying assumption has led to a certain equivalence between the Quito plebe with contemporary European crowd actions, a portrayal shared by Minchom, MacFarlane, and Andrien. For more on the role of Indians in the city's daily economic life, see Gauderman, *Women's Lives in Colonial Quito*, 92–123. For comparison in other Andean contexts, see Leo Garafalo, "The Ethno-economy of Food, Drink, and Stimulants: The Making of Race in Colonial Lima and Cuzco" (PhD diss., University of Wisconsin-Madison, 2001); and Mangan, *Trading Roles*.

54. McFarlane, "The Rebellion of the Barrios," 220.

55. González Suárez, *Historia general*, 1127.

56. Recio, *Compendiosa relación*, 518.

57. Minchom notes that one account of the uprising places San Roque as the originating center of the riot, converging first at the Plaza de Santo Domingo, then moving to San Sebastian, and finally congregating in Santa Bárbara. Minchom, *The People of Quito*, 224–25.

58. Velasco, *Historia del reino*, 335; "Relación sumaria," 103.

59. González Suárez, *Historia general*, 1127.

60. McFarlane, "The Rebellion of the Barrios," 221.

61. González Suárez, *Historia general*, 1128; McFarlane, "The Rebellion of the Barrios," 221; Recio, *Compendiosa relación*, 518; "Noticias de los movimientos de Quito en el año de 1765," *Museo histórico* 9 (1951): 37.

62. McFarlane, "The Rebellion of the Barrios," 222.

63. "Relación sumaria," 104; Recio, *Compendiosa relación*, 520; González Suárez, *Historia general*, 1129; McFarlane, "The Rebellion of the Barrios," 222–23.

64. McFarlane, "The Rebellion of the Barrios," 228.

65. Ibid., 225–28.

66. "Relación sumaria," 104.

67. McFarlane, "The Rebellion of the Barrios," 229.

68. González Suárez, *Historia general*, 1140.

69. "Sublevación de Quito en protesta por la aduana y los estancos, 1765," *Museo histórico* 2.7 (1951): 29; "Noticias de los movimientos de Quito," 37.

70. Recio, *Compendiosa relación*, 521.

71. AMQ, *Actas de Cabildo*, 1765, foja 170.

72. The figures on European Spaniard participation come from "Relación sumaria," 114–15.

73. "Noticias de los movimientos," 39; McFarlane, "The Rebellion of the Barrios," 229.

74. "Noticias de los movimientos," 38–39; "Relación sumaria," 106; McFarlane, "The Rebellion of the Barrios," 230; Minchom, *The People of Quito*, 226.

75. "Noticias de los movimientos," 39; "Relación sumaria," 107; McFarlane, "The Rebellion of the Barrios," 231.

76. Izquierdo's own account of the evening and the loss of his house can be found in "Noticias de los movimientos," 40–42. The account forms part of a petition in which the merchant was asking for grace in the repayment of 15,000 pesos of debt obligations he was having trouble meeting. See also "Relación sumaria," 107. On the destruction of Solano dela Sala's house, see his petition to be relieved of his duties as alguacil, filed with the Audiencia on July 4, 1765. Solano dela Sala claimed he was targeted because he had ordered his servants, slaves, and weaponry be used to quell the city in the preceding May riots. See AN/Q, FE 22.60, 2637.

77. The first phrase comes from González Suárez, *Historia general*, 1130. The second was reportedly said by Mariano Alvarez Monteserín according to the testimony of Agustín Cruz, a soldier of the palace guard, and is found in "Sublevación de Quito," 34.

78. Recio, *Compendiosa relación*, 524.

79. Ibid., 525.

80. Ibid., 528.

81. Ibid., 523–29.

82. "Noticias de los movimientos," 43–44.

83. Recio, *Compendiosa relación*, 530.

84. Ibid., 531.

85. *Relación sumaria*, 110; McFarlane, "The Rebellion of the Barrios," 234.

86. "Noticias de los movimientos," 44. A list of all the resident and non-resident European men present in Quito during the June uprising, their marriage status, positions within the bureaucracy (where applicable), and whether or not they participated in fighting the insurgents can be found in "Relación sumaria," 114–15.

87. "Noticias de los movimientos," 44.

88. AN/Q FE, 22.60, 2637.

89. McFarlane, "The Rebellion of the Barrios," 238.

90. Ibid., 238–40.

91. AN/Q Estancos 4, 11-v-1765. Members of the cabildo present included Francisco Maria de Larrea Zurbano (alcalde ordinario), Mariano Alvares Monteserin (alcalde ordinario and interim alguacil mayor), Francisco Borja y Larraspura (interim alferez real and procurador general of the cabildo), Xavier Sanchez de Orellana (alcalde provincial), Thomas de Bustamente Zeballos (alguacil mayor of the municipal jail), Sebastian de Salvzedo y Oñate (*alcalde de aguas*), Joseph Gomez Lazo dela Vega (*fiel executor*), Juan Antonio Domingo y Friere (*regidor perpetuo*), Joseph de Alias y Clerque (regidor del depositorio general), and Don Joachin Gutierrez (*procurador general de menores*). These men would ultimately form the core of royal government in Quito until the restoration of the Audiencia, and then would play significant roles through the close of the decade.

92. AN/Q FE 22.60, 2638.

93. Ibid., 2641.

94. Ibid., 2649.

95. Ibid., 2651.

96. Ibid., 2647.

97. McFarlane, "The Rebellion of the Barrios," 245.

98. Recio, *Compendiosa relación*, 531.

99. AN/Q Gobierno 22, 6-ix-1766.

100. Ibid.

101. González Suárez, *Historia general*, 1141–42. For Diguja's appointment to the office of president, see AN/Q FE 24, vol. 66, 2873, 26-iv-1768.

102. AN/Q, Estancos 5, 28-i-1767.

103. AN/Q, Alcabalas 5, 8-iii-1768.

104. José Antonio Garcia y Garcia, ed., *Relaciones de los vireyes del nuevo reino de Granada, ahora Estados Unidoes de Venezuela, Estados Unidos de Colombia y Ecuador* (New York: Hallet and Breen, 1869): 93–94.

105. AN/Q, FE 24, vol. 67, 2894, 2-ix-1768.

106. AN/Q, FE 33, vol. 91, 3515.7, 4-ii-1774, and 3515.12, 17-iii-1774.

107. AN/Q FE 32, 3400.9, 16-viii-1773; 3400.10, 16-viii-1773; 3400.11, 3-ix-1773. For the use of the tobacco factories in criminal sentencing, see Chapter 2.

108. See Andrien, "The State and Dependency," 172.

109. Garcia Leon was a native of Granada, and moved his way up the bureaucratic chain on the peninsula before receiving his appointment as regent and president of the Audiencia. During the period of his presidency, his brother Ramon served as governor of Guayaquil. From his regency in Quito, Garcia Leon was elevated directly into the Council of the Indies in 1784. Burkholder and Chandler, *Biographical Dictionary*, 133. On the unrivaled nature of taxation in the Audiencia, see Andrien, "The State and Dependency," 178.

110. Alvaro Jara and John Jay TePaske, *The Royal Treasuries of the Spanish Empire in America*, Vol. 4, *Eighteenth-Century Ecuador* (Durham, NC: Duke University Press), 123–64.

111. Burkholder and Chandler, *Biographical Dictionary*, 164. Hurtado de Mendoza, a *limeño*, purchased a supernumerary appointment to the Audiencia for 20,000 pesos in 1750. In 1753, he served as interim fiscal. In 1775, his position was finally promoted to numerary judge. The other members of the council during the period 1775–1795 lived in Quito only during their appointments, and then moved on to other bureaucratic positions in the empire. The longest serving of the ministers was Isidro de Santiago Alvear y Arrunduaga, who was brought in to the court in the wake of the rebellion along with Serafín Veyan y Mola and José Ferrer dela Puente in an attempt to switch over leadership of the council. Santiago Alvear served almost twenty years, until his death in 1785.

112. For more on fiscal policy and the development of fiscal machinery in the closing decades of the colonial period, see Andrien, "The State and Dependency," 171–83; Andrien, *The Kingdom of Quito*, 190–210; and Robinson Tyrer, "The Demographic and Economic History of the Audiencia

of Quito: Indian Population and Textile Production, 1600–1800" (PhD diss., University of California at Berkeley, 1976).

113. For more on the surveillance of the barrios, see Chapter 2.

114. See for example the census of the parish of Santa Bárbara performed by barrio magistrate Manuel de la Lastra, "Padrón del barrio de Santa Bárbara en 1768," *Museo historico* 56 (1978): 93–122. It should be noted that Manuel de la Lastra was a European Spaniard who had participated in the defense of the royal palace during the insurrection, only to later become the first barrio alcalde, and then a member of the cabildo and ordinary magistrate. This alone points to a realignment of elite interests against the popular sectors of the barrios in the years following the rebellion. For more on Lastra's activities as a magistrate, see Chapter 2.

115. AN/Q FE 28, vol. 76, 3140.23 2-vii-1771; 3131.3 17-vi-1771. For more on the troubles caused by the survey in the central sierra, see Segundo E. Moreno Yánez, *Sublevaciones indígenas en la Audiencia de Quito: Deside comienzos del siglo XVIII hasta finales de la colonia*, 3rd ed. (Quito: EDIPUCE, 1985): 131–51.

116. Moreno Yánez, *Sublevaciones indígenas*, 152–223. For more on the demography of Villalengua's census, see Tyrer, "Demographic and Economic History," 57–60.

117. This is not, of course, true for the rest of the Andean world. The 1780s witnessed a dramatic escalation in agitation, from the Comunero Revolt in the north, south to Pasto, and into the Andean heartland with Tupac Amaru and Tupac Katari. See among many, many others, Phelan, *The People and the King;* Rebecca Earle Mond, "Indian Rebellion and Bourbon Reform in New Granada: Riots in Pasto, 1780–1800," *HAHR* 73, no. 1 (1993): 99–124; Sergio Serulnikov, *Subverting Colonial Authority: Challenges to Spanish Rule in the Eighteenth-Century Southern Andes* (Durham, NC: Duke University Press, 2003); Steve J. Stern, ed., *Resistance, Rebellion, and Consciousness in the Andean Peasant World, 18th to 20th Centuries* (Madison: University of Wisconsin Press, 1987); and Walker, *Smoldering Ashes,* chapters 1–2.

118. The numbers for 1767–1770 are from AN/Q 1NJ 45 1767, "Visita de los que están en la carcél publica y Sta. Marta." The numbers from 1789 are compiled from 1NJ 107, 16-i-1789, "Quaderno de Visitas de las Carceles, publica y de Sta Marta, hechas por los SS Prest.e y Oydores de esta Real Aud.a en el presente año de 1789." It should be noted that the entries for tribute detainees do not list individual names, so it is entirely possible that the number of individuals is less than 186 since some could be holdovers from week to week. The entries from 1789 are

16 October— 11 *yndios*	24 October— 12 *yndios*	31 October— 9 *yndios*
7 November— 15 *yndios*	14 November— 20 *yndios*	21 November— 12 *yndios*
28 November— 13 *yndios*	5 December— 16 *yndios*	12 December— 19 *yndios*
19 December— 13 *yndios*		

All of the detainees were apprehended at the request of the office of royal tribute. It can be assumed from the sources that the detentions in both periods were indigenous men residing in the corregimiento of Quito. Interestingly, the arrests all occurred from October through December, while customary practice involved twice-yearly payments of tribute in June and December.

119. For discussion of the declarations of mestizo, see Alexia Ibarra Dávila, *Estrategias del mestizaje: Quito a finales de la época colonial* (Quito: Abya-Yala, 2002); Minchom *The People of Quito*, 159–80; and the special issue of *Quitumbre* 9 (1995), entitled "Los mestizos en la sociedad colonial."

120. "Decreto de 1764 sobre normatives para declarcion de mestizos," *Quitumbre* 9 (1995): 119–21. This document, transcribed in the special issue of *Quitumbre*, was included in the litigation of Tomás Pazmiño, AN/Q Mestizos 8, 15-iii-1791. As further evidence for the lack of official interest in delineating the ethnic status of individuals who were neither Indian or black, the arrest rolls from the Quito jails for 1767–1770 and again in 1789 never use ethnic terms for anyone except those determined to be Indian, black, or *pardo*. Out of the 2,177 individuals who appeared in the jail rolls for those years, the word mestizo is never used, with *blanca* appearing once.

121. AN/Q 1NJ 89, 21-v-1785.

122. Tributary status carried with it exemption from the vast majority of other Spanish taxes, including the alcabala.

123. AN/Q 1NJ 87, 28-ii-1785. Emphasis in original.

124. "Tramite legal para declatoria de mestizaje," *Quitumbre* 9 (1995): 122.

CHAPTER TWO

1. AN/Q, 1NJ 88, 17-iii-1785. Thomasa Cusallos contra Mariano Thena and Rosa Muños.

2. Literally, "¡Putabieja, alcagueta, traqueada!"

3. Literally, "¡Puta, adultera, descasadora!"

4. Jane Mangan has found for Potosí that women, and particularly indigenous women, played a significant role in the urban economy as sources of credit through pawnshops run out of their pulperías and chicherías. Mangan, *Trading Roles*, 106–33.

5. Borchart de Moreno has noted that, during the period, insults directed toward women almost always impugned their sexual behavior, while insults directed toward men most often suggested thievery and dishonesty. Christiana Borchart de Moreno, "Words and Wounds: Gender Relations, Violence, and the State in Late Colonial and Early Republican Ecuador," *CLAR* 13.1 (2004): 137. She interprets this tradition as placing women in the private sphere, and men in the public. This chapter will argue, however, that during the closing decades of the eighteenth century particularly, sexual behavior by both men and women was a topic of decidedly public concern, for both institutional and informal authorities. Both women's and men's bodies were brought under direct public surveillance, belying any supposed separation of public and private gendered spheres. The observation is likewise confirmed by the very public economic presence

and actions of women in the streets of Quito, as indicated by a wide range of documents. For more on insults to honor, Chambers, *From Subjects to Citizens;* Lyman L. Johnson and Sonya Lipsett-Rivera, eds., *The Faces of Honor: Sex, Shame, and Violence in Colonial Latin America* (Albuquerque: University of New Mexico Press, 1998); Stern, *Secret History;* and Ann Twinam, *Public Lives, Private Secrets: Gender, Honor, Sexuality, and Illegitimacy in Colonial Spanish America* (Stanford, CA: Stanford University Press, 1999).

6. While fallout from the Rebellion of the Barrios provides an immediate context for Quito's increased surveillance of moral and sexual behavior, the actions of the city's judges follow a more generalized trend during the reign of Carlos III. Throughout the Spanish Empire, Carlos III's reign witnessed a dramatic increase in policing morality, by the church as well as by the state. See, for example, Michael Scardaville, "(Habsburg) Law and (Bourbon) Order: State Authority, Popular Unrest, and the Criminal Justice in Bourbon Mexico City," *The Americas* 50, no. 4 (1994): 501–25; and Lee Michael Penyak, "Criminal Sexuality in Central Mexico, 1750–1850" (PhD diss., University of Connecticut, 1993). For an example of church activism, see Kathy Waldron, "The Sinners and the Bishop in Colonial Venezuela: The *Visita* of Bishop Mariano Martí, 1771–1784," in *Sexuality and Marriage in Colonial Latin America,* ed. Asunción Lavrín, 156–77 (Lincoln: University of Nebraska Press, 1989).

7. For a full definition and description of the bureaucratic and judicial offices of imperial administration, see José M. Mariluz Urquijo, *El agente de la administración pública en Indias* (Buenos Aires: Insituto Internacional de Historia del Derecho Indians; Instituto de Investigaciones de Historia del Derecho, 1998); Enrique Ruíz Guiñazú, *La magistratura Indiana* (Buenos Aires: Facultad de Derecho y Ciencias Sociales, 1916); and Haring, *The Spanish Empire.*

8. For more on the differing training and responsibilities of the two, see Victor M. Uribe, "The Lawyers and New Granada's Late Colonial State," *Journal of Latin American Studies* 27, no. 3 (1995): 517–49.

9. On declarations of solemn poverty, see Cynthia Milton, *The Many Meanings of Poverty: Colonialism, Social Compacts, and Assistance in Eighteenth-Century Ecuador* (Stanford, CA: Stanford University Press, 2007), 65–97.

10. See, for example, AMQ, *Actas de Cabildo,* 1-i-1765, among the many years catalogued in the *Actas.* For the first election of barrio alcaldes, see AMQ, *Actas de Cabildo,* 2-i-1768. See also Tamar Herzog, *La administración como un fenómeno social: La justicia penal de la ciudad de Quito (1650–1750)* (Madrid: Centro de Estudios Constitucionales, 1995), 59–82.

11. For procedural overviews of prototypical criminal litigation and templates in the primary legal literature, see Villadiego, *Instrucción política, y práctica judicial, conforme al estilo de los consejos, audiencias, y tribunales de corte, y otros ordinarios del reyno, utilissima para los governadores, y corregidores, y otros jueces ordinarios, y de comission, y para los abogados, escrivanos, procuradores, y litigantes* (Madrid: en la Oficina de Antonio Marin), 58–93, 477–85; Joseph Juan y Colom, *Instrucción juridica de escribanos, abogados y jueces ordinarios de juzgados inferiores,*

2nd ed. (Madrid, 1795 [1736]), 200–203; Cutter, *Libro de los principales*, 29–70; Juan Sala, *El litigante instruido ó el derecho puesto al alcance de todos: Compendio de la obra del Doctor D. Juan Sala que se enseña en las universidades de España* (Mexico: UNAM, 1978 [1870 edition of 1792 work]), 189–249, 359–74. For secondary literature examinations, see Charles R. Cutter, *The Legal Culture of Northern New Spain, 1700–1810* (Albuquerque: University of New Mexico Press, 1995), 109–38; Colin M. MacLachlan, *Criminal Justice in Eighteenth-Century Mexico: A Study of the Tribunal of the Acordada* (Berkeley: University of California Press, 1974), 21–25; Asunción Lavrín, "Sexuality in Colonial Mexico: A Church Delimma," in *Sexuality and Marriage in Colonial Latin America*, 69–73 (Lincoln: University of Nebraska Press, 1989).

12. Asucnión Lavrín, "Introduction: The Scenario, The Actors, and the Issues," in *Sexuality and Marriage in Colonial Latin America*, 1–43 (Lincoln: University of Nebraska Press, 1989), 1–4, 8–9; and Lavrín, "Sexuality in Colonial Mexico," 62–71.

13. Gauderman, *Women's Lives in Colonial Quito*, 55–63.

14. In Cutter, *Libro de los principales rudimentos*, 38, the instructions for investigating a statutory rape victim involved the physical examination of the victim by two midwives and a surgeon to ensure virginity had been lost. For sodomy investigations, the book councils that the man's body should be investigated through the insertion of a surgeon's tool or a chicken egg to determine if he had engaged in anal sex. The text says, "se reconoserlo es con vn instrum.to que traheen los ciruxanos, y no habiendolo con vn huebo de Gallina que sea largo el qual se le pone en el ojo de atraz, y se sume."

15. The following section is based on the weekly censuses of the city jails for 1767, 1768, 1769, and January to July 1770. The three and a half years are relatively complete, but deterioration of the manuscript prevents drawing any absolute conclusions. A section of approximately five centimeters of the bottom of much of the manuscript is missing. That said, the general trends in the records hold up. The censuses for the three years are found together in AN/Q Primer Notaría Juicios, 45, 1767, "Visita de Carceles."

16. Borchart de Moreno, "Words and Wounds," 132, has dated the dramatic increase in detentions to the 1780s, the period with the most rigorous application of Bourbon reforms. Numbers of detainees were actually higher in the late 1760s than in the 1780s, though. Michael Scardaville has documented increased community policing in the case of Bourbon Mexico City. Scardaville found an increased interest in "proactive" policing of crimes like "vagrancy, illegal gambling, property crimes, and drink-related offenses" that ultimate led to "a ten-fold increase in the number of arrests and trials, the vast majority involving the urban poor, between the early 1780s and the late 1790s." Scardaville, "(Habsburg) Law and (Bourbon) Order," 512. For more on the women's jail, the recogimiento de Santa Marta, see Maria Isabel Viforcos Marinas, "Los recogimientos, de centros de integración social a cárceles privadas: Santa Marta de Quito," *Anuario de estudios Americanos* 50, no. 2 (1993): 59–92.

17. The earlier figure is from Borchart de Moreno, "Words and Wounds," 132.

18. Literally, "el cuidado de los delitos y pecados publicos." Herzog, *La administración*, 94–95. The Audiencia again made the request to appoint

barrio magistrates at the January 2, 1768, meeting of the municipal council. AMQ, *Actas de Cabildo*, 2-i-1768. This time the office took permanent hold.

19. The terms "pardo," "mulato," "negro," and "esclavo" variously appear as ethnic descriptors in individual entries, while detention most often related to slave–master relations.

20. In reference to the Pasto disturbances, Rebecca Earle Mond quotes President Regent Garcia de Leon y Pizarro writing in July 1781, "The degree of fear and terror has reached inexplicable proportions." Mond, "Indian Rebellion and Bourbon Reform," 99. That same year, Garcia Pizarro opened three separate investigations into suspected sympathizers with the Tupac Amaru rebellion. The first investigation targeted Francisco Borja de Amburnala, a cacique from Latacunga. The second investigated an anonymous broadsheet published in Cuenca that was critical of the local government. The third pursued a number of questionable public statements made by Franciscan Fray Manuel Corrales in Ibarra. None of these investigations yielded much in the way of serious evidence of support or planning for a Tupac Amaru–style uprising in the Audiencia, but they do suggest a certain level of terror and fear influencing the institutional authorities. BAEP 7339 (57) 3, "Ymbentaroi de varios expedientes seguidos pr el Sor Dn [Don] Josef Garcia de Leon y Pizarro, Presidente, Regente, y Visitador Grāl de estas Provincias en los años de 1778, "hasta el de 1783" contra algunos sujetos de ellas por sospechas de Ynfidelidad."

21. Borchart de Moreno, "Words and Wounds," 131–32.

22. The following discussion is based on AN/Q 1NJ 107, 16-i-1789. The manuscript is entitled "Quaderno de visitas de las carceles publicas y Sta Marta, hechas por los SS Pres.te y Oydores de esta Real Aud.a en el presente año de 1789." As with the earlier census, the entries are incomplete due to deterioration of the document, which for the first thirty pages is missing approximately five centimeters off the top.

23. The emergence of poorhouses in Spanish America was a late eighteenth-century development. The poorhouse is not the same as debtor's prison. Debtors could be imprisoned in any number of places, including the ospicio. The ospicio was more of a half-way house, and could include poor people convicted of any number of offenses. For comparison in Mexico, see Silvia Arrom, *Containing the Poor: The Mexico City Poor House, 1774–1871* (Durham, NC: Duke University Press, 2000). See also Milton, *The Many Meanings of Poverty*, 153–90.

24. In the case of Peru, Carlos Aguirre dates the emergence of the modern penitentiary system to the 1850s, much delayed from its eighteenth-century origins in Western Europe. Aguirre argues the realization of a modern penitentiary reform in Peru, defined as "their transformation in regimented institutions for the rehabilitation of prisoners through a strict therapy consisting of mandatory silence and segregation, obligatory work, religious counseling, and constant, total surveillance," was first delayed and then never fully engaged, in large part due to colonial legacies of racial and class disparity and privilege that prevented according criminals the citizenship rights that underpin prison reform. Carlos Aguirre, *The Criminals of Lima and Their Worlds: The Prison Experience, 1850–1835* (Durham, NC: Duke University Press, 2005), 1–4. Interestingly, the prosecution and

punishment of sexual crimes in the 1780s and 1790s in Quito found judicial officials experimenting with many of the goals and methods of the modern penitentiary, minus the construction of actual panopticons. As will become clear, there was a movement away from corporal punishments for sexual crimes specifically, and toward the type of disciplinary, reformatory punishment associated with the modern penitentiary.

25. AN/Q, CR 61, 23-iv-1770, "[N]otorio concubinato y Osado Orgullo con que á procedido."

26. Lastra used the term *"amancebamiento,"* which the *Libro de los principios* defined as a single man and single woman living and sleeping together "in one bed and house [causing] scandal in the Republic and Neighborhood," a charge that could be brought either through denunciation or official investigation. Charles R. Cutter, transcription and Estudio preliminar, *Libro de los principales rudimentos tocante a todos juicios, civil, criminal y exectuvio: Año de 1764* (Mexico: UNAM, 1994), 37. The *Libro* distinguishes between amancebamiento and *adulterio*, but does not include the term *"concubinato."* In the Quito judiciary, all three terms appear for illicit relationships involving at least one married partner, with concubinato far and away the most common. Concubinato tends to be used as illicit cohabitation, akin to amancebamiento, though at times married people are accused of concubinato as well.

27. "[P]ara que se conosca su enmienda."

28. "[A]prehendidos en el actual delito en que estavan con total escandalo y libertad, a segurados de un quarto subterraneo, para burlar, escondiendose en el Zelo y Vigilancia dela Justicia."

29. "Ygualm.te es cierto el d.ro que no hay Adulterio, quando no hay violacion del Lecho Conjugal."

30. "En estas circunstancias el lecho de su Muger abandonado mas años que yó la conociera; no se puede llamar conjugal, pues esta denominacion la traé dela cohabitacion."

31. "[E]n vista qe no podia culparme Merino dela division de su matrimon.o ni dela prostitucion de su Muger, ni para condenar de Adulterio una amistad q. no fue causa de aque desastres, q. le precedieron . . . ; ni podra ser tan culpable un hombre que conoce á una Muger Casada libre de la Sugecion, y respecto de Marido abandonada de él."

32. "[E]s bien sabido por todos los derechos, Municipal, Canonico, y civil, que paraque el consorte varon, tenga su accion, y derecho de acusar a su muger en el delito de adulterio, es necessario que aya cumplido exactamente con las obligaciones de Marido honrrado, esto és, confiriendole á la muger, los alimentos y besturario . . . que assi mismo, haya sido de arreglada conducta en sus costumbres, para el mejor buen exemplo de la muger, y que esta le haya disfrutado áquel amor, y buen tratamiento, que se requiere paraque mutuamente sea correspondido."

33. The cases are AN/Q, CR 57, 11-v-1768, "Querella criminal de doña Catalina Moreno contra Alonso Fenix y Flores"; CR 59, 4-iv-1769, "Querella criminal contra don Manuel Cabezes, escribano receptor de la Audiencia, iniciada por su esposa doña Petrona Rosero, por la sustraccion de sus bienes y por haberla abandonado desde hace cinco meses"; CR 61, 23-iv-1770, "Causa criminal seguida por Alexo Merino contra su esposa Francisca Naranjo por concubinato con Javier Sansoya"; CR 66, 13-ix-1771, "Causa

criminal contra Ramon Balverde y Martina Chavez, por adulterio"; and AN/Q 1NJ 43, 7-ii-1765; 54, 1-x-1773.

34. AN/Q, 1NJ 43, 7-ii-1765, "[M]andado que entregace sin executa la criatura tenidose este paraqe se paro del concubinato por combeniente por haberlo desobedecido . . . que si dieselo menor causa derregular la o de bolber al concubinato, será puesta en pricion, y sele sequiera el castigo que afiance la enmiendo."

35. AN/Q, 1NJ 54, 1-x-1773, "Autos criminales contra Bacilio Thorres y Petrona Ortuño por concuvinato apedimto de Josefa Escobar."

36. AN/Q, 1NJ 44, 5xi-1766. The relationship is characterized as an estrupo, which indicates the violation of a virgin (*doncella*). It does not appear that the crime has to be one of force. In this case, Ana's age was likewise never mentioned, with only the status word vecina available to place her socially.

37. AN/Q, CR 120, 28-i-1785, "Querella criminal de Maria Ximines contra Josef de Leon por estrupo de su hija menor de edad."

38. The phrase used was "niña doncella." The use of the word "niña" emphasized Francisca's youth to the point of a prepubescent characterization.

39. For another example of a case being dismissed because of an extrajudicial arrangement, see 1NJ 141, 27-iv-1794, "Criminales contra Antonio Borja por estrupo."

40. AN/Q CR 135, 12-xii-1788, "D.n [Don] Mariano Yepes contra D.n [Don] Juan Subra p.r extrupo combado"; and CR 161, 11-iv-1795, "D.a [Doña] Agustina Galaxia contra Ramon Ximenes por el estrupo de su hija." In both cases, the judge ordered the defendants arrested and their wealth embargoed based on the complaint and initial prueba, but neither case includes a definitive sentence. See also AN/Q 1NJ 108, 26-iii-1789, "D.n [Don] Joaquin Chamorro contra los prosedimientos de Manuel y Mariano Jacome y toda su familia, y referiendoel hecho que stando depostada una hija de me parte en el Monasterio de Conceptas a cuasa del estrupo que con ella se cometio por Manuel Jacome."

41. AN/Q 1NJ 94, 2-v-1786, "Autos criminales seguidos por querella, y Pedm. to de Geronimo Ruiz contra Josef Segura pr el delito de haver corrompido á Angela Ruiz."

42. "[P]or el castigo del delito y exemplo de otras."

43. AN/Q CR 152, 1-xii-1792, "Causa criminal de Antonio Pazmiño contra Ventura Hidalgo, por estrupo a su hija Maria Pazmiño." "*Moso vago.*" Rueben Zahler has argued that in the early years of the Venezuelan Republic, *vago* emerged as the male-gendered equivalent of the female prostitute (*puta*), indicating someone without honor, "a threat to society and the very opposite of good republican citizenship." Reuben Zahler, "Bums, Vice, Poverty, and Honor in the Early Venezuelan Republic, 1821–1835," paper presented at the *AHA*, Philadelphia, PA, January 8, 2006. As Borchart de Moreno, "Words and Wounds," 134, has noted, the traditional male-gendered insult of the colonial period was thief, to go along with the female whore. Vago, it seems, begins to appear in the 1780s, as both an insult and a prosecutable crime. See, for example, AN/Q CR 115, 17-iii-1785, "Autos seguidos por el alcalde del barrio de San Sebastian d.n [Don] Luis Alvares y Canisares, contra Marcos Flores y Luisa Tapia,

vesino deesta Ciudad, por el Delito de Adulterio y Vago." The combination of crimes condemned Flores to two years in the royal tobacco factory of Quito, a sentence reduced to six months on appeal. Luisa Tapia was not incarcerated.

44. AN/Q 1NJ 134, 4-xii-1792, "Criminales seguidos por querella propuesta pr Rafaela Gonzales contra Pedro Velastigui pr haver estrupado a Bernarda Bargas."

45. The order is mentioned by the alcalde of San Sebastian in AN/Q CR 116, 18-v-1785, "Autos . . . por el Alaclde de Barrio de Sn Sevastian contra Joaquin Chavarria y Melchora Frayre por adulterio." "Alcalde de la Parroquia de San Sebastian en observancia de lo mandado por el Superior Govierno, y Auto publicado en forma de Bando para que se corrijan los Pecados publicos mediando su obligacion." I have been unable to locate the actual text.

46. The text of the Pragmatic is available in Konetzke, *Colección de documentos*, vol. III, no. 1, 406–12, along with further clarifying orders, 438–43, 465–69, 509–10, 527–28, 623–25, 670–71, 759–66. The extensive clarifications were the result of continual conflicts of both interpretation and implementation, stretching on for more than twenty years.

47. For the implementation of the Pragmatic generally, see Steinar A. Saether, "Bourbon Absolutism and Marriage Reform in Latin Colonial Spanish America," *Americas* 59, no. 4 (2003): 475–509; for Mexico, Patricia Seed, *To Love, Honor, and Obey in Colonial Mexico: Conflicts over Marriage Choice, 1574–1821* (Stanford, CA: Stanford University Press, 1988), 200–215; for Buenos Aires, Susan Socolow, "Acceptable Partners: Marriage Choice in Colonial Argentina, 1778–1810," 209–52, in Lavrín, "Sexuality in Colonial Mexico."

48. Saether, "Bourbon Absolutism and Marriage Reform," 476. Emphasis in original.

49. AN/Q 1NJ 90, 9-viii-1785.

50. Of course, the cases collected in 1NJ do not represent all of the ordinary magistrate prosecutions during the period. However, as a note of comparison to the stats from 1765 to 1774 for the same two sections of the archive, the trend is both obvious and surprising. The Audiencia clearly took a greater role in first-instance prosecutions.

51. AN/Q CR 117, 4-vii-1785, "Recurso de Josef Joaq.n de Alarcon con Micayla Valles su Muger, sobre su mal vivir." *Mala vida* has traditionally been interpreted as "abuse of power by one spouse," and usually as a feminine accusation, the result of a husband's abuse of his responsibilities to provide material sustenance, or of inordinate physical abuse or sexual daliance, whether within or outside the marriage bed. Lavrín, "Introduction," 20–21. See also Boyer, *Lives of the Bigamists*, 128–32, 158–60. I would suggest that mala vida/mal vivir were not terms tied to the abuse of power as much as they were an accusatory linguistic trope. The meaning was neither so fixed nor so gendered as much as it was an imputation of the defendant's public moral character. When women in Quito wished to indict their husbands' abuse of power, they generally used the phrase *mal tratos* or *maltratamientos* (mistreatments), rather than mala vida.

52. Spying by the patrols went beyond the confines of Quito, and adultery cases predicated on such activities were appealed to the Audiencia from

Ibarra, Ambato, Riobamba, Cuenca, Babahoya, Puerto Tumaco, and Guayaquil. On the use of spying and informants in particular, see the case from Cuenca, AN/Q CR 120, 20-ii-1786, "Informe del alcalde ordinario de Cuenca a la Audiencia sobre dos casos distintos de amancebamiento."

53. AN/Q CR 120, 6-ii-1786, "Autos criminales seguidos contra Miguel y Fernando Lagos, y Petrona Ayala sobre adulterio."

54. "[D]esnubos bajo una misma Covija unidos los Cuerpos como si fueran de Matrimonio, siendo corta la distancia, de donde se hallava dicho su marido con el Suelo."

55. For example, AN/Q CR 123, 26-viii-1786, "Autos seguidos por el Alcalde ordinario contra D.n [Don] Fran.co Xavier Ascasubi y D.a [Doña] Thomasa Domingues sobre concubinato"; and CR 141, 16-vi-1790, "Doña Mariana Flor dela Bandera por falsa ynforme de Juaquina Enrriquez sobre adulterio con José Chagaray." In yet another instance, local officials from Yaruqui in the valley east of Quito refused to comply with arrest orders issued by the president regent in a case brought by a husband against his wife. For two years, the offenders remained at large. It eventually came to light that the denouncing husband was well known for his own philandering, physical abuse, and eventual abandonment of his wife. Malicious denunciations did not have to be false, and adulterous relationships were not necessarily condemnable. CR 112, 19-i-1785, "Autos seguidos p.r Fernando Sumiga contra Fernando Estrella, y Ana Valberde, muger de dho Fernando Sumiga, pr el delito de concubinato."

56. For example, AN/Q CR 114, 22-ii-1785, "Expediente formado por Maria Josefa Suares, contra Manuel Manrique su Marido y Maria Yturrabalde, so.e concubinato en que se han mantenido estos."

57. AN/Q CR 128, 9-vii-1787, "Autos criminales contra Vis.te, Felipe, y Lorenzo Basques Alban y Palis por haber insultado al Alcalde de San Sebastian y Ministros de Justicia."

58. See, for example, AN/Q CR 128, 16-v-1787, "Autos seguidos pr el alcalde de San Sebastian contra Manuel Chavarria por concubinatio, condenado al Real Fabrica de Tabaco un año"; CR 129, 13-ix-1787, "Autos seguidos pr el Alclade de Barrio de Sn Sebastian contra Maria Yepes alias la Chunchulli pr Alcagueta y Amansebamiento"; and CR 134, 1-xii-1788, "Seguidos pr Alcalde ordinario Mariano Maldonado contra Mariana Rodriguez Beto y Pedro Arcos pr ylicita correspondencia."

59. AN/Q CR 133, 13-viii-1788, "Sumaria sobre averiguas la mala conducta y versacion de d.n [Don] Fran.co Ortis e Ceb allos en el oficio de Theniente del Barrio de San Sebastian, a serca de las extrociones, y exacciones de dineros que les ha irrogado a SS vecinos, con ptretxto de multas y carcelajes."

60. AN/Q CR 112, 14-i-1785, "Autos seguidos contra D.n [Don] Josef de Mena, por varios acrehedores, pr el delito de haverles pedido con fraude, y de engaño varias halajas, y empeñado, ó vendidolas pr mantener escandaloso concubinato con Manuela Martines."

61. Chiriboga was widowed from Josef de Mena's father, and claimed the authority of Patria Potestad, or paternal authority, and therefore the right to represent his legal interests in court. The petition was accepted in due course. The traditional interpretation of Spanish law has been that neither

guardianship nor Patria Potestad were transferable to a widowed woman. See Sylvia M. Arrom, *The Women of Mexico City, 1790–1857* (Stanford, CA: Stanford University Press, 1985), 57–58, 69–70.

62. AN/Q CR 143, 19-viii-1790, "Expediente formado a respresentac.n del Pedaneo del Pueblo de Chillogallo p.a averiguar los sujetos que viven desunidos de sus Mugeres."

63. AN/Q CR 129, 29-vii-1787, "Autos criminales seguidos por el Alcalde de San Marcos contra Josefa Lara and Manuela Palis por el delito concubinato yncestuoso"; and CR 132, 10-v-1788, "Autos seguidos sobre el feo, y abominable Delito de el Crimen nefando de Sodomia contra natura, que se le atribuye haver cometido á Custodio Legendres, con varios Muchachos." Interestingly, the case of lesbianism was labeled as incestuous adultery only on its cover page. Inside, the two women were variously attributed with the crimes of sodomy, illicit friendship, and illicit concubinage.

64. AN/Q CR 132, 10-v-1788.

65. Ibid.

66. Ibid. "[C]omo si fuera su Dama." The trope appears in sodomy prosecutions under a variety of guises, including "como si fueran hombre y muger" (as if they were man and woman/wife); "como se trata una muger" (as one would treat a woman/wife); and in this instance, "como si fuera su dama" (as if he were his lady). The word *muger* can be translated as woman or wife, though in the judicial setting of the eighteenth century it invariably indicates the latter. For more on these phrases, see Zeb Tortirici, "Heran Todos Putos": Sodomitical Subcultures and Disordered Desire in Early Colonial Mexico," *Ethnohistory* 54, no. 1 (Winter 2007): 45–46.

67. AN/Q CR 132, 10-v-1788.

68. Ibid.

69. AN/Q CR 132, 20-vii-1787.

70. Female same-sex prosecutions were rare in Spanish America, which might explain the discomfort evident in characterizing the relationship. The front page lists the crime as "concubinato incestuoso," while inside the file the relationship is generally called an illicit friendship. It may be that the language at the magistrate's disposal fell short in providing an adequate descriptor for women involved in same-sex activity. As such, the label of sodomy here refers not to sexual penetration, but rather to the sexual activity of two persons of the same sex.

71. For other examples of sexual prosecutions radiating from neighborhood patrols, see AN/Q CR 114, 22-ii-1785, "Expediente formado por Maria Josefa Suares, contra Manuel Manrique su marido y Maria Yturrabalde, sobre concubinato en que se han mantenido estos"; AN/Q CR 120, 6-ii-1786, "Autos criminales contra Miguel y Fernando Lagos, y Petrona Ayala sobre adulterio"; AN/Q CR 123, 26-viii-1786, "Autos seguidos por el Alcalde ordinario contra D.n [Don] Fran.co Xavier Acusabi y D.a [Doña] Thomasa Domingues sobre concubinato"; AN/Q CR 141, 16-vi-1790, "Doña Mariana Flore dela Bandera or falsa ynforme de Juaquina Enrriquez sobre adulterio con José Chagaray."

72. AN/Q CR 129, 29-vii-1787, "[Q]ue los hombres a sus concubinas ó mancebas."

1. The phrase comes from the boilerplate language used to begin a petition to the court, usually constructed as "Como mas haya lugar en derecho, parezco ante V. M. y Digo."

2. Villadiego, *Instrucción política*, 42, states, "nor can a woman be imprisoned for debt, as long as it did not proceed from a crime, and she cannot renounce this privilege." Villadiego also notes that individuals cannot be imprisoned for someone else's debts (including wives for their husbands' debts), unless the individual is acting as a third-party debt guarantor.

3. AN/Q, Civiles 41.16, 11-i-1809, "Expediente acerca de un contrato de 16 arrobas de camarones hecho por dn [Don] Antonio Ruiz, a da [Doña] Ygnacia Sanchez."

4. "La muger, durante el Matrimonio sin licencia de su Marido, como no puede hacer *contrato alguno*, asi mismo no se puede apartar, ni desistir de ningun contrato, que á ella toque, . . . ni estár en juicio haciendo, ni defendiendo, sin la dicha licencia de su marido." Emphasis in original.

5. "El punto de Dro. es inadaptable, por que nada mas obrio que la validacion delos contratos que celebran las mugeres casadas, que exercitan publicamente el oficio de negoicantes à presencia del Marido, por que se supone su conocimiento con tanta mas fuerza quanto los hechos explican mejor que las palabras los sentimientos del asimismo. De esta clase es la muger de Santiana pues tiene quatro Tiendas con sus Factores tratando, y contratando sin intervencion del marido. Por esto es que ella sola comparecio al Jucio verbal en que salio condenada, presensiando la declaracion de los testigos, que de pusieron à favor del contrato. . . . Lo cierto es que el conocio este mui bien y aora por escparse del complimiento del contrato sale openiendo la incapacidad de su Muger para poder contratas."

6. "Vistos: siendo publico y notorio que Da [Doña] Ygnacia Sanches, contrata porsi sola en Tienda publica, y q.e su Marido dn [Don] Jose Santiana lo confiesa en su Escrito deloque se deduse su permiso para negociar francam.te y ratiabicion delos contratos en el Comercio: en cuya caso sesa el pribilegio otras mugeres casadas, respecto de seer este en obsequiò delos maridos . . . se declara sin lugar el reclamo de nulidad opuesta contra la de terminac.n verbal, qe dio este Juzgado nosolo con prebio y cierto conocim. to deser Mercadera publica al dha da [Doña] Ygnacia, sino tambien dela buena calidad delos quatro quintales de Camaron.s tendidos conla excepcion de una arroba . . . y dela regularidad de su precio abiendo prosedido para todo en virtud de prueba de testigos abiles que al efecto produjo el demandante."

7. Cutter, *Legal Culture*, 31.

8. Ibid., 34.

9. On the definition of derecho vulgar, see Cutter, *Legal Culture*, 34.

10. Phelan, "Authority and Flexibility," 55. As an example of duplication, a murder in the corregimiento of Quito of the late eighteenth century could be investigated and prosecuted by any one of four authorities: an alcalde of the court of the Audiencia, an alcalde ordinario, the corregidor, or an alcalde of the Santa Hermandad.

11. Kagan, *Lawsuits and Litigants*, 32, 34.

12. Phelan, "Authority and Flexibility," 60.

13. Cutter, *Legal Culture*, 34, 41.

14. For example, Basques could request their cases be heard before the juez mayor of Vizcaya, even if they were arrested in the New World. Kagan, *Lawsuits and Litigants*, 29. On the fuero militar, see I. A. A. Thompson, *War and Government in Habsburg Spain, 1560–1620* (London, 1976), 45–48. As Kagan has noted in the case of Castile, the many fueros "created . . . a web of jurisdictional refuges which many used to escape prosecution and to delay proceedings in the king's courts" (30).

15. On the genealogy of Castilian law, see Kagan, *Lawsuits and Litigants*, 21–31; and M. C. Mirow, *Latin American Law: A History of Private Law and Institutions in Spanish America* (Austin: University of Texas Press, 2004), 12–18.

16. Kagan, *Lawsuits and Litigants*, 31.

17. Patricia Seed led the way in questioning absolutist models of gender relations for the Habsburg period in her pioneering study on marriage choice, *To Love, Honor, and Obey in Colonial Mexico*. Seed demonstrated that in cases of prenuptial marriage, supplicants were often able to contravene the wishes of disapproving parents by exploiting the willingness of the church to uphold willful marriage. Seed concludes, though, that the church's ability to undermine patriarchal authority waned as the secular bureaucracy gained the upper hand with the Bourbon *Pragmática* on marriage in 1776. For more on marriage and law, see Arrom, *Women of Mexico City*, 57, 59; Gauderman, *Women's Lives in Colonial Quito*, 22–27; the uneven essays in Lavrín, *Sexuality and Marriage*; and Daisy Rípodas Ardanaz, *El matrimonio en Indias: realidad social y regulación jurídica* (Buenos Aires: Conicet, 1977). On legal function and practice of the dowry and inheritance during the Habsburg period, see Gauderman, *Women's Lives in Colonial Quito*, 30–41; Eugene H. Korth and Della M. Flusche, "Dowry and Inheritance in Colonial Spanish America: Peninsular Law and Chilean Practice," *Americas* 43, no. 4 (April 1987): 395–410; Asunción Lavrín and Edith Courturier, "Dowries and Wills: A View of Women's Socioeconomic Role in Colonial Guadalajara and Puebla, 1640–1857," *HAHR* 59, no. 2 (May 1979): 280–304; Salomon, "Indian Women of Early Colonial Quito."

18. Arrom, *Women of Mexico City*, 53; Korth and Flusche, "Dowry and Inheritance," 396–97.

19. Gauderman, *Women's Lives in Colonial Quito*, 92–123.

20. The following section relies primarily on three manuals: Juan y Colom, *Instrucción juridica;* Villadiego, *Instrucción política;* and Cutter, *Libro de los principales.*

21. On the renewal of notarial and legal literatures in the eighteenth century, see José Bono y Huerta, "Los Formularios Notariales Españoles de los Siglos XVI, XVII y XVIII," *Anales de la Academia Matritense del Notariado* 23:1 (1981), 311–12. Thanks to Kathryn Burns for directing me to this reference.

22. Kagan, *Lawsuits and Litigants*, Chapter 1.

23. For more editions of Villadiego, see, for example, "Alonso de Villadiego Vascuñana y Montoya, Instruccion Politica, y Práctica Judicial, Conforme al Estilo de los Consejos, Audiencias, y Tribunales de Corte, y Otros

Ordinarios del Reyno, Utilissima para los Governadores, y Corregidores, y Otros Jueces Ordinarios, y de Comission, y para los Abogados, Escrivanos, Procuradores, y Litigantes" (Madrid: en la Oficina de Antonio Marin, 1766).

24. Chad Thomas Black, "Between Prescription and Practice: Governance, Legal Culture, and Gender in Colonial Quito, 1765–1830" (PhD diss., University of New Mexico, 2006); and Chad Thomas Black, "Between Prescription and Practice: Governance, Legal Culture, and Gender in Quito, 1765–1830," *Colonial Latin American Review* 16, no. 2 (2007): 273–98. I mistakenly attributed this work to Alonso Villadiego due to a typographical error in my original citation. That simple error cascaded into not recognizing the work was a newer edition of Villadiego's classic 1612 work. I appreciate Kathryn Burns's keen reading eye for recognizing Villadiego's prose, and catching the mistake which I am correcting here.

25. Many of these works are available through http://books.google.com and from the excellent digital collection of the Universidad Autónoma de Nuevo Leon at http://cd.dgb.uanl.mx. Joseph Berni y Catalá, *Instrucción de alcaldes ordinarios, que comprehende las obligaciones de estos y del amotacen* (Madrid: Ministerio para las Administraciones Públicas, Secretaria General, 1988 [1763]); José Febrero, *Liberia de escribanos, é instrruccion juridical theorico practica de principiantes*, 3 vols. (Madrid: Oficina de la Viuda de Marin, 1790); Francisco Antonio de Elizondo, *Práctica universal forence de los tribunals de España y de Indias*, 4th ed. (Madrid, 1792, and an early edition in 4 volumes in Madrid: Joachin Ibarra, Impresor de Cámara, 1779); Conde de la Cañada, *Observaciones practicas sobre los recursos de fuerzo: Modo y forma de introducirlos, continuarlos, y determinarlos en los tribunales superiors* (Madrid: Imprenta Real, 1793); Juan Sala, *Ilustración del derecho real de España*, 3 vols. (México: Imprenta de Arizpe, 1807–1808); Gabriel de Monterroso y Alvarado, *Práctica criminal y civil* (Valladolid: 1566 and Madrid: 1609). Juan de Hevia Bolaños's *Curia philipica*, in two volumes, was republished as *Curia philipica, primero y segundo tomo* (Madrid: J. Doblado, 1778), and again as *Curica philipica, primero y segundo tomo* (Madrid: Oficina de Ramon Ruiz, 1797). See also Pedro de Castro, *Defensa de la tortura y leyes patrias que la establecieron* (Madrid: Miguel Escribano, 1778); Manuel de Lardizábal y uribe, *Discurso sobre las penas contrahido á las leyes criminales de España, para facilitar su reforma* (Madrid: Joachim Ibarra, Impresor de Camara, 1782); Ignacio Jordan de Assso and Miguel de Manuel y Rodriguez, *Instituciones del derecho civil de Castilla*, 2 vols. (Madrid: Imprenta Tomás Alban, 1802), and trans. Lewis F. C. Johnston (London: A. Strahan, 1825).

26. Cutter, "Estudio Preliminar," 16, in *Libro de los principales rudimentos*.

27. Bernardino Bravo Lira, "El derecho indiano y sus raíces europeas: Derecho común y propio de Castilla," *Anuario de historia del derecho Español* 58 (1988): 63. Quoted in Cutter, "Estudio Preliminar," 16, in *Libro de los principales rudimentos*.

28. Juan y Colom, *Instrucción juridica*, 2. "El Derecho es una arte buena y equitativa, y sus preceptos vivir honestamente, no dañar á otro, y dar à cada uno lo que es suyo."

29. Ibid., 2–3.

30. Ibid., 18–25.

31. Ibid., 32–34.

32. Ibid., 32.

33. Ibid., 61.

34. Ibid., 61.

35. See Chapter 2.

36. See note 18 above.

37. "[D]e reputarse el marido y la muger matrimoniados por una misma carne y cuerpo . . . deve ser la cabeza de este cuerpo el marido, y donde él quisiere ha de morar la muger, como su subdita." Juan y Colom, *Instrucción juridica*, 66. Juan y Colom verifies this assertion by attributing it to law 27, title 3, book 7 of the *Recopilación*.

38. Juan y Colom, *Instrucción juridica*, 66. "Y si fuere hidalga, y casáre con hombre que no lo sea, debe ser pechera mientras viviere su marido, pero despues de su muerte volverá á gozar de los pirivlegios de hidalga."

39. Juan y Colom, *Instrucción juridica*, 66–67. "Y al marido se le concede por todos Derechos, y por la *ley* 7. *tit.* 11 *partid.* 4. el gobierno y administracion, asi de sus bienes, como de los de su muger." The legal precedent for this comes from *Partida* 4, as stated by Juan y Colom. There remains, though, the question of enforcement and degree. To what degree did husbands control their wives' estates? And was this control immutable? In a later chapter, Juan y Colom concedes the right of a woman to protect her dowry from bad administration. Juan y Colom, *Instrucción juridica*, 82. Likewise, Villadiego allows that control was not absolute, and women could sue for the return of their property in cases where they feared their husband's administration risked impoverishment. For more on the intricacies of women's property and Castilian law, see Gauderman, *Women's Lives in Colonial Quito*, 31–47.

40. Juan y Colom, *Instrucción juridica*, 67.

41. Ibid., 68–69. "Y aunque la muger no puede ponder demanda ni acusacion criminal al marido por delito que le pueda sobrevenir infamia ò pena corporal, si no es por el de ofendida Magestad, segun la *ley* 5. *tit.* 2. *partida* 7. se pratíca generalmente en todos Tribunales admitirse la querella de la muger contra el marido en causa graves, pero no de las ligeras."

42. Dowry and other property brought into the marriage are dealt with in Juan y Colom, *Instrucción juridica*, Chapter 3, 69–90. Issues relating to profits are treated in Chapter 4, 91–99.

43. Ibid., 130. "La muger casada, cometiendo adulterio, pierde su dote, arras y bienes gananciales y deben aplicarse al marido." The *arras* were property given as a gift to the woman by her husband upon entering marriage. Exceptions to the penalty include occasions where the woman was forced to commit adultery or where her husband turned out to be Jewish, Muslim, or a heretic (131).

44. *Las siete partidas del Rey Don Alfonso el Sabio*, Tomo III, Partida IV, Título XVII, Ley I (Madrid: Lope de Vega, 1972 [1807]): 96–97.

45. Juan y Colom, *Instrucción juridica*, 113.

46. Ibid., 117–18.

47. Ibid., 120.

48. Ibid., 121.

49. Ibid., 122–23.

50. Villadiego, *Instrucción política*, 2: "[S]e puede intentar en una de cinco maneras: contra el reo su presencia, ò en su rebeldìa, ò en la ausencia, ò siendo à difunto, ò por caso de Corte."

51. Ibid., 2.

52. Ibid., 3. "Y si el actor es hijo de familia, o menor, que tenga curador, o muger casada, no pueden paracer en juicio sin licensia de su padre, curador, o marido; y assi ha de pedir licencia qualquier de ellos al principio de la demanda, ò peticion primera para ellos."

53. The legal minority of women has been claimed often in the literature on early Latin America; this claim is usually based on a misreading of Arrom. See Gauderman *Women's Lives in Colonial Quito*, 12, 137; Boyer, *Lives of the Bigamists*; and Arrom, *Women of Mexico City*, 57–58.

54. Petitions included in this section vary widely, and include such templates as general phrases utilized in every suit (opening phrases, ways to address the court, closing phrases, and so on), married women in the absence of their husbands, accusations of contempt, requests for restitution, interrogation of witnesses, appeals to the Audiencia, requests for defendants to be jailed, requests by creditors to embargo the assets of a debtor, appointment of a legal guardian, requests by married women that their fathers give them a dowry, requests for the release of the assets of an individual who died intestate, proper petition for a woman whose husband has mistreated her, requests by natural children for alimony, requests to investigate one's parentage to legitimate one's personhood, and so on.

55. Villadiego, *Instrucción política*, 330.

56. See for example, Villadiego, *Instrucción política*, "Muger casada en ausencia de su marido," 349; "Demanda por caso de Corte por una viuda," 356; "Pide yerno la dote de su muger al suegro," 376; "Pide una muger viuda, que le herederos de su marido le dè su dote," 376; "Pide la muger legitima los bienes de su marido, que murió abintestato, sin hijos," 380; "Demanda y querella de muger contra su marido, de malos tratamientos," 383; "Pedimiento de la hija natural sobre alimentos," 401.

57. Villadiego, *Instrucción política*, 3.

58. Ibid., 349. The maravedi was the smallest denomination of Spanish coinage. Thirty-four maravedis equaled one peso.

59. For examples of religious women granted ecclesiastic license, see AN/Q 1NJ 47, 10-ix-1770, "La Reverenda Madre San Ygnacio Romero religiosa, demanda cantidad de pesos a D.n [Don] Juan Fran.co Rivadeneyra"; 1NJ 93, 18-i-1786, "Juicio ordinario que sigue el procurador Manuel dela Parra a nombre de Sor Maria Jasienta de la Precentas.n Barba, relig.a dela Concep.n contra la posehedora dela haz.da de Turubamba, que fue de D.n [Don] Nicolas Barba, por 650 ps. que este tomó con hipoteca de ella, al 5 por ciento"; 1NJ 101, 6-x-1787, "Expediente relativo à la demanda que sigue la Madre Rosalia dela Visitacion y Moreno religiosa del Monasterio dela Concep.n contra la testamentaria de Dn [Don] Salvio Balladares, sobre el encargo de una puerca y el procreo de doce serdos." As a corrallary, for an example of a loan made by a male confraternity (*cofradía*)

under license from the bishop, see AN/Q 1NJ 44, 3-ii-1767. In another interesting twist, Josefa Aguirre, a single woman, requested ecclesiastical license for Dr. Francisco Xavier Suares Alava, the local priest of the pueblo of Aloag, to participate in a contract dispute she had engaged against married couple Mariana Ballejos and Jose de Luna. For examples of license being granted to a soldier to testify in a criminal proceeding, see 1NJ 111, 3-9-1789, "Criminales seguidos pr Margarita Espinosa contra D.a [Doña] Sebastiana Olais, sobre injurias," a case brought by Margarita Espinosa, a married woman, without her own license; and 1NJ 230, 26-iii-1806, "Antonio Garcia contra Antonia Morales, sobre injurias," a case brought by a husband on his wife's behalf.

60. AN/Q 1NJ 53, 22-xii-1772.

61. AN/Q 1NJ 87, 7-i-1785.

62. AN/Q 1NJ 101, 6-xii-1787, "Querella de Manuela Gomes contra el Then. te Cobrador de Tributos pr unas perlas."

63. AN/Q 1NJ 223, 10-vi-1805, "Memoria y razon de los bienes muebles pertenecientes a D.a [Doña] Mariana Paez y Coleti, que se hallan en el Asiento de Otavalo, en poder de D.n [Don] Gregorio Ocampo."

64. AN/Q 1NJ 103, 4-iv-1788.

65. "[P]remisa lo necessario."

66. AN/Q 1NJ 107, 16-i-1789, "Criminal contra Fran.co Xavier Garzon por concubinato."

67. AN/Q 1NJ 227, 12-xii-1805.

68. The judge's ruling stated, "Esta parte consulte esta Querella con Letrado, y proponga conforme a derecho respecto de que la muger no puede Querella el adulterio." Technically, the judge's ruling was correct for the context of secular court. See Arrom, *Women of Mexico City*, 65. Twenty years earlier, judges openly ignored the rule. One of the customary means around the restriction was for the wife to simply denounce her husband for publicly scandalous behavior, which was then investigated de oficio. As demonstrated in Chapter 4, spousal prosecutions for adultery were regularly filed by both men and women.

69. AN/Q 1NJ 234, 22-ix-1806.

70. See, for example, AN/Q 1NJ 110, 13-viii-1789, "Ysavel Vermudes contra Francisco Donoso y Josefa Navate de Segura por el temerario acesinato que han cometido contra mi marido." Donoso and Navate stabbed her husband fourteen times, but he lived. Ysavel then filed on his behalf, "premisa la licencia." Also, AN/Q 1NJ 111, 12-x-1789, "Expediente criminal relativo á la causa que sigue Agueda de Leon por su marido, contra el negro Manuel esclavo de Don Simon Saenz por heridas."

71. See, for example, AN/Q 1NJ 99, 10-v-1787, "Autos criminales seguidos contra Manuel Ysquierdo sobre aber formado un escrito denigrativo con el Jues." The case was pursued by Francisca Biscaino of the village of Pugilli on behalf of her husband Domingo Espinar, who was the subject of the injurious letter. Notably, there was no mention of license or consent in this case. Also, in AN/Q 1NJ 244 8-ii-1808, Doña Eulalia Ramirez, wife of the absent Don Cebilio Xaramillo, represented him in the adjudication of a tax dispute over lands he owned in the village of Machache, south of Quito.

72. For the estrupo cases, see AN/Q 1NJ 94, 2-v-86; 100, 2-vii-1787; 100, 4-vii-1787; 108, 26-iii-1789; and 231, 7-vii-1806.

73. AN/Q 1NJ 44, 22-i-1767.

74. AN/Q 1NJ 100, 17-ix-1787, "Criminales seguido por Agustina Araus, vecina de esta ciudad, contra Vetnura Tomasa, y Luisa dela Zenda, por unos golpes dados á Nicolasa Bales y Arauz."

75. AN/Q 1NJ 10-vi-1788.

76. For inheritance and dowry cases, see AN/Q 1NJ 109, 14-v-1789, "Expediente sobre pretender el menor Yldefonso de Albuja, como hijo de Don Manuel de Albuja y Jacinta Villacis su legitima muger, ser uno de los herederos del yntestado Dr Dn [Don] Nicolas Albuja Presbytero"; and 1NJ 238, 27-ii-1807. For protection of a son from an abusive employer, see AN/Q 1NJ 241, 1-ix-1807, "Criminales seguidos por Da. [Doña] Petrona Mogollon contra Bernardo Ruyloba, de oficio Platero." For protection from an abusive royal official, see 1NJ 221, 5-iii-1805, "Expediente criminal seguido pr Da [Doña] Narsisa Duarte, contra el Teniente del Quinche Dn [Don] Manuel Oñate, por los exesos executado en Da [Doña] Juaquina Baraona y Duarte su hija."

77. AN/Q 1NJ 52, 2-vi-1772.

78. AN/Q 1NJ 230, 17-v-1806.

79. "[D]e que las obligaciones que tengo otorgadas, son nulas, por haverlas hecho sin intervencion de mi Marido, y contener manifiesta usura."

80. In addition to the current case, see, for example, AN/Q 1NJ 99, 15-vi-1787, in which Don Sebastian Nuñes, his wife Doña Ysabel Ponce, Don Josef Ponce, and his wife Doña Maria Calle y Vega borrowed 375 pesos from Doña Maria Mena. Before proceeding with the transaction, the two women verbally requested license from their husbands in the presence of the notary; AN/Q 1NJ 222 29-iii-1805, in which Doña Maria Bermeo, a vecina of Quito, sued Doña Josefa Coloma and Don Luis Gazia over a house sale in San Sebastian; and AN/Q 1NJ 251, 4-iii-1809, in which Don Josef de Leon and his wife Doña Ana Jiron together borrowed 500 pesos from Don Jose Moreno de Paz. In each of these cases, the act of licensure was proffered verbally in front of the notary recording the legal act.

81. AN/Q 1NJ 55, 12-iv-1774, "Autos criminales contra Maria Ortiz y Ygnacia Paredes, por perdimiento de respeto a la Justicia Juez de el Sor alcalde ordinario Dn [Don] Pablo de Unda y Luna."

82. The 8-peso debt was owed by Mariano Baca to Josef Marsilla, who was himself being prosecuted for 563 pesos he owed to six different women. AN/Q 1NJ 115, 18-v-1790. The 5,000-peso debt was amassed by Doña Josefa Sotomayor, who was forced to sell her very valuable home to cover the obligation. AN/Q 1NJ, 12-viii-1786.

83. AN/Q 1NJ 88, 17-iii-1785.

84. AN/Q CR 108, 14-i-1785, "Autos seguidos contra D.n [Don] Josef de Mena, por varios acrehedores, pr el delito de haverles pedido con fraude, y de engaño varias halajas, y empeñado, ó vendidolas pr mantener escandaloso concubinato con Manuela Martines."

85. AN/Q 1NJ 90, 16-vi-1785, "Quaderno de alhajas y ropas que han estado en poder de rafaela y juntam.to ha sido consumiendo mi ama como consta por el mismo quaderno."

86. A *corbacha* was a whip made from a bull's penis. In the course of litigation, Yepes and his witnesses continually referred to the defendant as Antonia la Corbacha, while she referred to herself as Doña Antonia Perez, merchant of Quito.

87. AN/Q 1NJ 91, 5-ix-1785.

88. AN/Q 1NJ, 28-vii-1790, "Criminales. Expediente de recurso interpuesto por Antonia Peréz alias la Corbacha de las providencias dadas por el Alcalde Ordinario á pedimiento de Don Jose Freyles en la demanda sobre el robo de unas alhaxas."

89. AN/Q 1NJ 115, 18-v-1790.

90. "[P]or acaecimientos desfortunas y contratiempos que he padecido, de forma que diariamente he experimentado quebrantos y perdidas en las negociaciones que he llevado."

91. AN/Q 1NJ 223, 28-vi-1805, "Lista de los sugetos que han de contribuir para el empedio y reparo dela Calle larga de San Sebastian que sale ala Cruz de Piedra."

92. AN/Q 1NJ 89, 21-v-1785.

93. AN/Q 1NJ 99, 25-vi-1787.

94. AN/Q 1NJ 17-x-1785.

95. AN/Q 1NJ 106, 24-xi-1788.

96. AN/Q 1NJ 7-ix-1786.

97. AN/Q 1NJ 254, 27-vi-1809, "Expediente executivo seguido por Ventura Guzman, Yndia, contra Don Julian de Echeverria, por cantidad de pesos."

98. "D.a [Doña] Ventura Guzman Vecina de esta Ciudad, de estado celive."

99. "Ventura Guzman, Yndia vecina de esta Ciudad ante V. conforme a Dro. Paresco y Digo."

SECTION II

1. Quoted in Jaime Rodríguez O., *The Independence of Spanish America* (Cambridge, MA: Cambridge University Press, 1998), xv–xvi.

CHAPTER FOUR

1. There is a long historiography in Spanish, on the period 1808–1814 that began as early as the 1820s. The first works established the nationalist line of interpretation, obsessed with delineating both heroic and duplicitous actions of the revolutionary participants. The Ecuadorian literature also, in good nationalist form, tended to present the autonomist movements as independence movements from their inception, and often, erroneously, as the first proclamation of independence in the Spanish Empire. See William Bennet Stevenson, *Relación histórica, de la conspiración y revoluciones que tuvieron lugar en Quito desde el año de 1808 hasta 1810* (Guayaquil: Imp. de la Nación, 1884 [1825]); José Manuel Restrepo, *Historia de la revolución de Colombia* (Librería Americana, 1827); Antonio Salazar y Lozano, *Recuerdos de los sucesos principales de la revolución de Quito . . .* (Quito: Imprinta y encuadernación nacional, 1910 [1831]); Manuel de Jesús Andrade, *Próceres de independencia: Índice alfabético de sus nombres con algunos bocetos biográficos*

(Quito: Tip. y Encuadernación de la Escuela de Artes y Oficios, 1909); Angel T. Barrera, *Inciativa de la independencia en Sud-América* (Quito: Imprenta Nacional, 1909); Roberto Andrade, *Historia del Ecuador*, Vol. 1–3 (Guayaquil: Reed and Reed, 1934); Isaac Barrera, "La Revolución de Agosto," *Boletín de la academia de historia* (July/Dec. 1944): 320–26; Gabriel Cevallos García, "El 10 de Agosto y Nosotros," *Anales de la universidad de cuenca* 15: 3–4 (1959): 423–48; Alfredo Ponce Ribadeneira, *Quito, 1809–1812: Según los documentos del Archivo Nacional de Madrid* (Madrid: A. Ponce Ribadeneira, 1960); Manuel Maria Borrero, *La revolución de Quito, 1809–1812* (Quito: Editorial Espejo, 1962); de la Torres Reyes, *La revolución de Quito;* José Gabriel Navarro, *La revolución de Quito de 1809* (Quito: Instituto Panamericano de Geografía e Historia, 1962); Demetrio Ramos Pere, *Entre el plata y Bogotá: Cuatro claves de la emancipación Ecuatoriana* (Madrid: Ediciones Cultura Hispanica, 1978); Jorge Salvador Lara, ed., *La Revolución de Quito, 1809–1822: Según los primeros relatos e historias por autores extranjeros* (Quito: Corporación Editora Nacional, 1982). For more recent works, those that are critical of the nationalist heroic line, see Claudio Mena Villamar, *Quito rebelde (1809–1812)* (Quito: Abya-Yala, 1997); and, most importantly, Jaime E. O. Rodríguez, *La revolución política durante la época de la independencia: El reino de Quito, 1808–1822* (Quito: Universidad Andina Simón Bolívar: Corporación Editora Nacional, 2006). For works in English, see Robert Gilmore, "The Imperial Crisis, Rebellion, and the Viceroy: Nueva Granada in 1809," *Hispanic American Historical* 40, no. 1 (1960): 1–24; Michael Hamerly, "Selva Alegre, President of the Quiteña Junta of 1809: Traitor or Patriot?" *HAHR* 48, no. 4 (1968): 642–53; Minchom, *The People of Quito;* and Rodríguez, *The Independence of Spanish America*. Finally, for a full bibliography of work on Ecuador's independence period (1809–1830) published through the mid-1990s, see Michael T. Hamerly, *Bibliografia histórica del Ecuador*, Vol. I, Periodo Nacional, available online at http://www.ecuatorianistas.org/bibliographies/hamerly/ec9.html, which includes 352 citations. Accessed March 19, 2009.

2. Arlene J. Diaz, *Female Citizens, Patriarchs, and the Law in Venezuela, 1786–1904*, vol. *Engendering Latin America* (Lincoln: University of Nebraska Press, 2004), 111, 132–33. Diaz argues that the "continued use of the Siete Partidas prolonged the rights and privileges of the padres de familia over their dependents in the new republic. It also allowed the family to be treated as the private property of the padre de familia, sheltered and protected by a different set of rights in which these men held the authority and the state should not intervene. As one male litigant put it, 'public authority commences only where the husband's authority does not reach'" (111). In the next two chapters, I will argue that this represented not a continuation of colonial practices, but rather an innovation implemented through a legal culture unbridled by derecho vulgar. Additionally, the concept of padre de familia was transformed in the years between 1809 and 1814 to exclude female heads of household in ways it did not in the eighteenth century.

3. A growing body of work on indigenous communities in the nineteenth century is demonstrating that the end of special protections afforded indigenous communities by colonial law was ultimately destructive to those

communities. In many cases, indigenous communities fought to maintain the tribute-for-land equation that was the cornerstone of the institutional and juridical Indian under Spanish rule, even while struggling to gain citizenship rights in the new republican states of the region. It was, it seems, much more a postcolonial development (with roots in the Bourbon period) that saw Indians and indigenous communities broadly reduced to peonage without the subsistence support of legally recognized communal lands and ethnic leadership. For the Andes, see Andrés Guerrero, *Curagas y Tenientes políticos: La ley de costumbre y la ley del estado (Otavalo 1830–1875)* (Quito: Editorial El Conejo, 1990); Andrés Guerrero, *La semántica de la dominación : El concertaje de Indios.* (Quito: Ediciones Libri Mundi, Enrique Grosse-Luemern, 1991); Tristan Platt, "Liberalism and Ethnocide in the Southern Andes," *History Workshop Journal* 17 (1984): 3–18; Tristan Platt, "The Andean Experience of Bolivian Liberalism, 1825–1900: Roots of Rebellion in 19th-Century Chayanta (Potosí)," in *Resistance, Rebellion, and Consciousness in the Andean Peasant World, 18th to 20th Centuries*, ed. Steve J. Stern, 280–323 (Madison: University of Wisconsin Press, 1987); Tristan Platt, "Simón Bolívar, the Sun of Justice and the Amerindian Virgin: Andean Conceptions of the Patría in Nineteenth-Century Potosí," *Journal of Latin American Studies* 25, no. 1 (1993): 159–85; Thurner, *From Two Republics to One Divided;* Mark Van Aken, "The Lingering Death of Indian Tribute in Ecuador," *The HAHR* 61, no. 3 (1981): 429–59; and Walker, *Smoldering Ashes.* For the double effects of ethnic and gender domination in the postcolonial period, see Deborah E. Kanter, "Native Female Land Tenure and Its Decline in Mexico, 1750–1900," *Ethnohistory* 42 (1995): 607–16. For more on the gendered effects of the independence period, see Chambers, *From Subjects to Citizens;* Sarah C. Chambers, "Private Crimes, Public Order: Honor, Gender, and the Law in Early Republican Peru," in *Honor, Status, and Law,* ed. Caulfield et al.; Rosanna Barragán, "The 'Spirit' of Bolivian Laws: Citizenship, Patriarchy, and Infamy," in *Honor, Status, and Law,* ed. Caulfield et al.; and Diaz, *Female Citizens, Patriarchs, and the Law in Venezuela.*

4. On the Spanish Enlightenment, see Richard Herr, *The Eighteenth Century Revolution in Spain* (Princeton, NJ: Princeton University Press, 1958); Arthur P. Whitaker, *Latin America and the Enlightenment* (Ithaca, NY: Cornell University Press, 1961); Alfred Owen Aldridge, *The Ibero-American Enlightenment* (Urbana: University of Illinois Press, 1971); John Lynch, *Bourbon Spain, 1700–1808* (Oxford: Basil Blackwell, 1989), especially Chapter 7; Teresa Ann Smith, *The Emerging Female Citizen: Gender and Enlightenment in Spain* (Berkeley: University of California Press, 2006); Joaquín Álvarez Barrientos, François Lopez, and Inmaculada Urzainqui, *La república de las letras en la España del siglo XVIII* (Madrid: Consejo Superior de Investigaciones Científicas, 1995); and most recently, Gabriel Paquette, *Enlightenment, Governance, and Reform in Spain and its Empire, 1759–1808* (New York: Palgrave McMillan, 2008). It is worth noting that in many circles the Spanish Enlightenment is still considered so peripheral as to be completely ignored, as in the recent collection edited by Francis Cogliano and Susan Manning, *The Atlantic Enlightenment* (Burlington, VT: Ashgate Publishers, 2008), which mentions Spain only

in passing through the circulation of *Don Quixote* in North Atlantic countries.

5. On the Condamine expedition and its exploration of the Amazon, see *Colloque International "La Condamine": Paris, 22–23 Novembre 1985, Museum national d'histoire naturelle* (Mexico: IPGH, 1987); Charles-Marie de la Condamine, *Relation abrégée d'un voyage fait dans l'intérieur de l'Amérique Méridionale* (Paris: Veuve Pissot, 1745); Charles-Marie de la Condamine, *Viaje a la América Meridional*, 4th ed, edited by Federico Ruiz Morcuende (Madrid: Espasa-Calpe, S. A, 1962); Florence Trystram and A. Darío Lara, *Diálogo con las estrellas: Relación de la prestigiosa expedición de tres científicos franceses a sudamerica y de las aventuras que le siguieron (1735–1771)*, 2nd ed., vol. 8 *Colección Luna tierna*; (Quito: Campaña Eugenio Espejo por el Libro y la Lectura, 2002). Jorge Juan and Antonio Ulloa were a part of the Condamine expedition and based their secret royal report on the need for enlightened government to deal with social, economic, and political problems in South America on their observations during this trip. On Juan and Ulloa, see Jorge Juan and Antonio Ulloa, *Discourse and Political Reflections on the Kingdoms of Peru: Their Government, Special Regimen of Their Inhabitants, and Abuses Which Have Been Introduced Into One and Another, With Special Information on Why They Grew Up and Some Means to Avoid Them*, edited by John Jay Tepaske (Norman: University of Oklahoma Press, 1978); Jorge Juan and Antonio de Ulloa, *Noticias secretas de America* (Buenos Aires: Ediciones Mar Oceano, 1953); Kenneth J. Andrien, "The Noticias Secretas de America and the Construction of a Governing Ideology for the Spanish American Empire," *Colonial Latin American Review* 7 (1998): 175; Jorge Juan and Antonio de Ulloa, *Relación histórica del viaje a la America meridional* (Madrid: Fundación Universitaria Española, 1978). On Humbolt, see Alexander von Humbolt, *Political Essay on the Kingdom of New Spain* (New York: 1966 [1811]). On the circulation of enlightenment and liberal ideas in Spanish America, see Anthony McFarlane, "Identity, Enlightenment and Political Dissent in Late Colonial Spanish America," *Transactions of the Royal Historical Society*, 6th Ser., vol. 8 (1998): 309–35; Antonio Lafuente, "Enlightenment in an Imperial Context: Local Science in the Late-Eighteenth-Century Hispanic World," *Osiris*, 2nd Ser., Vol. 15, *Nature and Empire: Science and the Colonial Enterprise* (2000): 155–73; José Luis Peset, "Enlightenment and Renovation in the Spanish University," in *Universities and Science in the Early Modern Period*, ed. M. Feingold and V. Navarro-Brotóns, 231–39 (Amsterdam: Springer, 2006); Juan Carlos Arias Divit, *Las expediciones científicas españolas durante el siglo XVIII* (Madrid: Instituto de Cultura Hispánica, 1958); Thomas F. Glic, "Science and Independence in Latin America (with Special Reference to New Granada)," *HAHR* 71, no. 2 (1991); and Victor Uran Uribe, *Honorable Lives: Lawyers, Family, and Politics in Colombia, 1780–1850* (Pittsburgh, PA: University of Pittsburgh Press, 2000), 437–39.

6. The Inquisition updated its lists with some regularity. See, for example, *Indice de los libros prohíbidos, compuesto del índice último de los libros prohibiods y mandados expurgar hasta fin de diciembre de 1789 por el Señor Inquisidor General y señores del Supremo Consejo de la Santa General Inquisición, de los suplementos del mismo, que alcanzan hasta*

25 de agosto de 1805, y ademas de un Index Librorum Proibitorum Juxta Exemplar Romanum Jussue SS. D. N. Editum Anno MDCCCXXXV, en el que van intercalados en su respectivos lugares los prohibidos hasta fin de 1842 (Madrid: Imprenta de D. José Felix Palacios, 1844). And of course, the list is well populated by tracts of the Enlightenment, including the anticipated Rousseau, Montesquieu, Voltaire, Diderot, Kant, Hume, Smith, Hobbes, Locke, and more. It seems the Holy Office was very up-to-date on political writing in the Atlantic World. Reconstructed libraries from the late-eighteenth and early-nineteenth centuries reveal that works of the Enlightenment traveled far and wide. See, for example, Harry Berstein, "A Provincial Library in Colonial Mexico, 1802" *HAHR* 26, no. 2 (1946): 162–83; "Inventario de la biblioteca perteneciente a don Francisco de Ortega, 15 de noviembre de 1790," Appendix I in Ricardo R. Caillet-Bois, *Ensayo sobre el Río de la Plata y la Revolución Francesa* (Buenos Aires, 1929); and I. A. Leonard, "A Frontier Library, 1799," *HAHR* 23, no. 1 (1943): 21–51. Finally, the bibliographic work and correspondence of Quito-born Antonio de Alcedo demonstrates the extent to which an Atlantic-world class of lettered men knew of and shared each others' works. See Antonio de Alcedo, *Bibliotheca Americana: Catálogo de los autores que han escrito de la América en diferentes ydiomas y noticia de su vida y patría, años en que vivieron, y obras que escribieron*, 2 Vols., prologue by Jorge A. Garces G. (Quito: Imprenta Municipal, 1964); José de Onis, "Alcedo's Biblioteca Americana," *HAHR* 31.1 (1951): 530–41; and Chares E. Ronan, "Antonio de Alcedo: His Collaboratos and His Letters to William Robertson" *The Americas* 34, no. 3 (1978): 490–501.

7. In researching the events surrounding the August 2, 1810, massacre recounted below, I stumbled on a press report of the massacre, albeit factually challenged, in the December 10, 1810, edition of *The Scots Magazine and Edinburgh Literary Miscellany*, tucked amongst letters to the editor, descriptions of small towns in Scotland, and a reprint of Humboldt's account of his travels in Mexico, in a section titled "Historical Affairs" that included brief comments on political develops in countries around the Atlantic and European world. The account of the massacre was itself based on information that appeared in "the New York papers." It is startling to realize the speed with which news traveled from Quito to New York to Edinburgh, only slightly slower than information was transiting between Quito and Seville. "Historical Affaires: South America," *The Scots Magazine and Edinburgh Literary Miscellany*, 72 (Edinburgh: Archibald Constable, 1810): 943.

8. William Bennett Stevenson, *A Historical and Descriptive Narrative of Twenty Years Residence in South America*, Vol. III (London: Hurst, Robinson, and Co. 1825), 11.

9. Ibid.

10. Carondelet was born in Flanders, and served a long career in the Spanish bureaucracy. Prior to his presidency in Quito (1799–1807), he served most of the 1790s as governor of Louisiana, where he was preceded, among others, by Antonio Ulloa and Alejandro O'Reilly, both lions of Bourbon reformism. As president of the Audiencia, the baron was a staunch advocate for quiteño political autonomy, resisting any bureaucratic reforms that diminished the province's status as a kingdom, and championing its promotion to a captaincy general. Though this was never successful, Rodríguez

claims it did endear him to the creole elite. For more on Carondelet, see Rodríguez, *La revolución política*, 63; Thomas Marc Fiehrer, "The Baron de Carondelet as Agent of Bourbon Reforms: A Study of Spanish Colonial Administration in the Years of the French Revolution," 2 Vols. (PhD diss., Tulane University, New Orleans, LA, 1977); and Carlos Manuel Larrea, *Baron Luis Héctor de Carondelet: El vigesimonono presidente de la real audiencia de Quito* (Quito: Corporación de Estudios y Publicaciones), 1968. On Carondelet in Louisiana, see Ned Sublette, *The World that Made New Orleans: From Spanish Silver to Congo Square* (Chicago: Chicago Review Press, 2008): 163–76.

11. Stevenson, *A Historical and Descriptive Narrative*, 3.

12. In his *Historia general de la República del Ecuador*, Tomo 3 (Quito: 1892), González Suárez deemed Espejo "the most enlightened creole, without doubt, present in the colony" (González Suárez, *Historia general*, 1275). The first public edition of Espejo's writings was published as Francisco Xavier Eugenio de Santa Cruz y Espejo, *Escritos de Doctor Francisco Javier Eugenio Santa Cruz y Espejo: Pulibandse a expensas de la ilustre municipalidad de Quito con un prologo y notas del director de la "Sociedad ecuatoriana de estudios historicos,"* 3 Vols., ed. Federico González Suárez and Jacinto Jijon y Caamano (Quito: Imprenta municipal, 1912–1923). A new edition is available as Federico González Suárez and Carlos Escudero Paladines, eds., *La obra de Espejo* (Quito: Campaña Nacional Eugenio Espejo por el Libro y la Lectura, 2006). For more editions of his writings, see Espejo, *Primicias de la cultura de Quito*, edición fascimilar (Quito: 1947); Espejo, *Obra educativa*, ed. Philip Astuto (Caracas: Biblioteca Ayacucho, 1981); Leopoldo Benítez Vinueza, ed., *Precursores* (Puebla, Mexico: J. M. Cajica, Jr., 1960), 127–342; and most recently, Carlos E. Freile Granizo, ed., *Cartas y lecturas de eugenio Espejo* (Quito: Banco Central, 2009). The best biographical work remains Philip Astuto, *Eugenio Espejo: reformador ecuatoriano de la ilustración (1747–1795)* (Mexico, DF: Fondo de la Cultura Económica, 1968). In anticipation of the two-hundredth anniversary of Ecuadorian independence, there is a resurgence in works on Espejo. In addition to Freile's work above, see Plutaro Naranjo and Rodrigo Fierro-Benítez, eds., *Eugenio Espejo: su época y pensamiento* (Quito: Corporación Editora Nacional, 2008); and Carlos Palidanes Escudero, *Eugenio Espejo: estudio, selecciones, y notas* (Quito: Campaña Nacional Eugenio Espejo por el Libro y la Lectura, Corporación Editora Nacional, Universidad Andina Simón Bolívar, 2007).

13. Philip L. Astuto, "A Latin American Spokesman in Napoleonic Spain: José Mejía Lequerica," *The Americas* 24, no. 4 (1968): 336.

14. The *Primicias de la cultura de Quito* was the publication of Quito's local Sociedad de Amigos del País, founded by Espejo and other leading members of quiteño society in the early 1790s. See Espejo, *Primicias de la cultura de Quito*, and more below.

15. These writings are available in Espejo, *Obra educativo*.

16. The whole title is *Reflexiones sobre la utilidad, importancia, y conveniencia que propone don Francisco Gil, Cirujano del real Monasterio de San Lorenzo y su sitio, e individuo de la Real Academia Médica de Madrid, en su disertación físico-médica, acerca de un método seguro para*

preseravar a los pueblos de las viruelas. It is available in Benítez Vinueza, *Precursores*, 131–96. See also Astuto, *Eugenio Espejo*, 60–61.

17. Ibid., 61–63.

18. Ibid., 62–63.

19. See R. J. Shafer, *The Economic Societies in the Spanish World (1763–1821)* (Syracuse, NY: Syracuse University Press, 1958); and *Las reales sociedades economicas de amigos del país y su obra* (San Sebastian: Patronato "José Maria Quadrado," 1972).

20. Shafer, *The Economic Societies*, 176.

21. For the full list of participants, see González Suárez, *Historia general*, 1278.

22. Ponce Ribadeneira, *Quito, 1809–1812*, 45; Hamerly, "Selva Alegre," 643.

23. Astuto, *Eugenio Espejo*, 62–63.

24. BAEP 7285.1, "*Plan que manifiesta el cumulo de los bienes que quedaron por muerte del Sr Marquis de Selva Alegre.*"

25. Astuto, "A Latin American Spokesman," 354.

26. Ibid., 355–56.

27. Stevenson, *A Historical and Descriptive Narrative*, 8.

28. Ibid., 5.

29. In late August 1809, Don Manuel Parra y Oramas wrote in a letter to Don Francisco Oramas concerning the implications of the junta on a pending case in which Don Manuel was representing the interests of Don Francisco that the revolutionaries were intimates of the Cañizares household, and reminded Don Francisco that Margarita Cañizares was the great-granddaughter of their aunt, one Doña Margarita Oramas. He felt that this boded well for their litigation, because Quiroga in particular had an "intimate friendship with the household, and that which he could not do with Manuelita, he would not do with anyone." Parra y Oramas felt this strengthened their case in the way that complicated patron–client relationships could. Andrade, *Historia del Ecuador* (1934), 749–50. "Dicho Dr. Quiroga tiene íntima amistad en al casa, y lo que no hiciere por Manuelita, no hará por nadie."

30. Salazar y Lozano, *Recuerdos de los sucesos*, 14–15. In predictable fashion, Salazar y Lozano credits the two women for their beauty and sacrifice in all manner connected to their husbands.

31. On Manuela Sáenz, see Pamela S. Murray, *For Glory and Bolívar : The Remarkable Life of Manuela Sáenz, 1797–1856* (Austin: University of Texas Press, 2008); and Sarah C. Chambers, "Republican Friendship: Manuela Saenz Writes Women into the Nation, 1835–1856," *HAHR* 81, no. 2 (May 2001), http://www.jstor.org/stable/c114510.

32. Andrade, *Historia del Ecuador* (1934), "Poderes dados por los vecinos de los diferentes barrios de la ciudad de Quito para nombrar Representantes a la Junta Suprema gubernativa," 421.

33. Stevenson, *A Historical and Descriptive Narrative*, 1. He does not specify beyond these names. It is likely that the plays were Joseph Addison's *Cato* (1713); Jean Racine's *Andromache* (1667); Nicasio Álvarez de Cienfuego's *La Zoraida* (1798); and a dramatic adaptation of Alonso de Ercilla y

Zuñiga's epic poem, *La Araucana* (1569). Interest in *La Araucana* was revived in the eighteenth century when Voltaire included a discussion of the epic in his essay on poetry. See Voltaire, *An Essay Upon the Civil Wars of France, Extracted From Curious Manuscripts. And Also Upon the Epick Poetry of the European Nations, From Homer Down to Milton. The Fourth Edition, Corrected. To Which Is Now Prefixed, a Discourse on Tragedy. By the Same Author.* (London: N. Prevost, and Comp., 1731), 65–69.

34. Stevenson, *A Historical and Descriptive Narrative*, 1.

35. Rodríguez, *The Independence of Spanish America*, 50–51; John Lynch, *The Spanish American Revolutions, 1808–1826*, 2nd ed. (New York: Norton, 1986), 35–36; Astuto, "A Latin American Spokesman," 356–57.

36. Gilmore, "The Imperial Crisis, Rebellion, and the Viceroy," 4–5.

37. Rodríguez, *The Independence of Spanish America*, 59. For more on the formation of the Junta Central in Sevilla, see Angel Martinez de Velasco, *La formación de la junta central* (Pamplona, Spain: Ediciones Universidad de Navarra, 1972).

38. BAEP 7823 (1) 1, "Josef Manuel Flores to Presidente don Diego Antonio Nieto," 20-vii-1808. The official arrival date of the news to Bogotá and the viceroyalty of New Granada was June 11, 1808, though it is likely on both accounts that the news made it to the interior faster through personal correspondence with American-born Spaniards (*criollos*) living in the peninsula. Gilmore, "The Imperial Crisis, Rebellion, and the Viceroy," 3.

39. BAEP 7823 (1) 1, "Josef Manuel Flores," "nuestro Rey Sor Natural."

40. Restrepo, *Historia de la revolución de la república de Colombia*, 4–5.

41. Gilmore, "The Imperial Crisis," 5.

42. Rodríguez, *La revolución política durante la época de la independencia*, 40–41. See also, Mónica Quijada, "From Spain to New Spain: Revisiting the *Potestas populi* in Hispanic Political Thought," *Mexican Studies/ Estudios Mexicanos* 24.2 (Summer 2008): 185–219.

43. In a letter to Intendant Governor Melchor Aymerich, the bishop of Cuenca reported on March 19, 1809, having held Mass in conformity with a October 7, 1808, order. The royal order arrived in Cuenca on March 13, 1809, and likely was in Quito a few days earlier. BAEP 7283 (2) "Andres Obpo de Cuenca to Sor Gov.or Intendente Dn [Don] Melchor Aymerich," 19-iii-1809. See also, AGI ESTADO 72 N 63, "Presidente de Quito acusa recibo Real Orden," 21-iii-1809, in which Conde Ruiz de Castilla acknowledges to the secretary of state, Don Pedro Cevallos in Sevilla, the receipt of a 1-xi-1808 report on the abdications, the Napoleonic invasion, and installation of the Junta Suprema Central as well as Quito's fulfillment of royal decrees recognizing the new government. Oidor Fuertes Amar also mentions the reception, in Quito, of a representative of the Junta Suprema Central and fiestas demonstrating support for king, religion, and patría in deference to the junta in his letter to Peru's Viceroy Abascal in September 1809. The letter is reproduced in Andrade, Historia del Ecuador (1934), 451–46.

44. BAEP "Andres . . . que manda a toda la Nación."

45. Stevenson, *A Historical and Descriptive Narrative*, 6.

46. Ibid. Andrade reports that Montúfar was arrested alongside Morales, Quiroga, Salinas, and Riofrío, though it is unlikely Stevenson would have missed noting this, given his opinion of the Marqués. Andrade, *Historia del Ecuador* 2nd Ed. (Quito: Corporación Editora, 1982), 182–83. In his letter to Viceroy Abascal, Fuertes Amar portrays the legal process as targeted primarily against Salinas, with the others, including Montúfar and Captain Nicolás de la Peña, as codefendants. Andrade, *Historia del Ecuador* (1934), 446. Fuertes Amar noted that the case was unable to establish anyone's complicity.

47. Andrade, *Historia del Ecuador* (1982), 182–83.

48. Stevenson, *A Historical and Descriptive Narrative*, 7.

49. Gilmore, "The Imperial Crisis," 8.

50. Fuertes Amar's account of the investigation and Muños's botching of it can be found in Andrade, *Historia del Ecuador* (1934), "Oficio del Oidor Fuertes al Virrey Abascal," 17-ix-1809, 447–49.

51. Stevenson, *A Historical and Descriptive Narrative*, 9.

52. Gilmore, "The Imperial Crisis," 7.

53. Royal officials were placed in a precarious situation by competing claims from the pro-French Madrid Junta, the more popular, liberal, and revolutionary Seville Junta, and the crown prince and princess, all of whom sent agents and communiqués to the kingdoms of the Americas soliciting support. Gilmore, "The Imperial Crisis," 4.

54. For viceregal authority as incarnate authority, see Cañeque, *The King's Living Image*, 27–29.

55. "Real Orden de la Junta Central expedida el 22 de enero de 1809," in *Filiación histórico del gobierno representativo Argentino*, ed. Julio V. González, 2 vols. (Buenos Aires: Editorial "La Vanguardia," 1937–1938): I:267, trans. and quoted in Rodríguez, *The Independence of Spanish America*, 60.

56. Rodríguez, *La revolución política*, 65–67; Rodríguez, *The Independence of Spanish America*, 59–64. For more on the 1809 elections, see also Virginia Gueda, "The First Popular Elections in Mexico City, 1812–13," in *The Evolution of the Mexican Political System*, ed. Jaime E. O. Rodríguez (Wilmington: Scholarly Resources, 1993), 45–48; and Nettie Lee Benson, "The Elections of 1809: Transforming Political Culture in New Spain," *Mexican Studies/Estudios Mexicanos* 20, no. 1 (2004): 1–20.

57. Rodríguez, *La revolución política*, 67–68.

58. Gilmore, "The Imperial Crisis," 8.

59. Ibid.

60. One anonymous contemporary recalled a pasquinade posted on the morning of August 10 proclaiming the junta as remedy for the political crisis defined by "finding our beloved Fernando a prisoner of the Tyrant Napoleon, the Nation occupied by the French, the Junta Central dissolved, and Quito governed by suspect men, inept, lackeys of Godoy, who are scheming to deliver to the usurper [Joseph Bonaparte]." AGI Estado 72 n. 64 "Papeles diversos sobre la Revolución de Quito," Letter number 2 of the "Memoria de la Revolución de Quito en cinco cartas escritas a un amigo. 25-x-1809."

61. Not everyone, of course, supported the junta. The author of the "Memoria . . . en cinco cartas" described the 1809 junta as "seventy five days of dark tempest" (setenta y cinco dias de una negra borrasca). Estado 72 n. 64, "Papeles," "Memoria . . . en cinco cartas," Letter, 125-x-1809.

62. Copies of the petitions can be found in Andrade, *Historia del Ecuador* (1934), "Documento 3. Poderes dados por los vecinos de los diferentes barrios de la ciudad de Quito para nombrar Representantes a la Junta Suprema gubernativa," 417–27. Andrade's transcriptions came from the personal archive of Colombia's independence chronicler José Manuel Restrepo. Unfortunately, Andrade expurgated the vast majority of the signatures. As a result, there is only a hint at the participation of women— the petition for San Marcos includes the names Estefa Campuzano, Rosa Solano, Margarita Orozco, and Manuela Solís, amongst a few men. It is the only petition that includes women's names, but in each case Andrade notes that many signatures have been left off. The net effect, of course, is to hide the participation of women in political action. Minchom, *The People of Quito*, 244, portrays the Junta of 1809 as an inherently conservative and temporary transfer of power because of the heavy involvement of the Quiteño elite, going as far as to argue, "This was a strictly conservative transfer of local authority, assured by aristocratic influence in the military. Structurally, the new government was the old Audiencia under a new name." This portrayal neglects the process of choosing electors engaged in by the Barrios as well as the apparent broad support that accompanied the establishment of the new government.

63. Arenas wrote, "en atención a haber cesado en sus funciones los magistrados actuales, por las presentes circunstancias de la nación, procedieran a nombrar representantes por la ciudad, y varios que compusieran una Junta Suprema, representativa del señor Don Fernando Séptimo." Andrade, *Historia del Ecuador* (1934), "Arenas a Bejerano," 727.

64. For more on lawyers and independence in New Granada, see Uribe, "The Lawyers and New Granada's Late Colonial State," 517–49; Victor M. Uribe, "Kill All the Lawyers!: Lawyers and the Independence Movement in New Granada, 1809–1820," *The Americas* 52, no. 2 (1995): 175–210; and Uran Uribe, *Honorable Lives*.

65. AGI, Estado 72 n. 64, "Memoria . . . en cinco cartas," Letter 1.

66. Stevenson, *A Historical and Descriptive Narrative*, 13.

67. AGI, Estado 72 n. 64, "Memoria . . . en cinco cartas," Letter 1, "derramar la preciosa Sangres de catorce Quiteños de los mas Ylustres."

68. Stevenson, *A Historical and Descriptive Narrative*, 13–14.

69. Estado 72 n. 64 "Memorias . . . en cinco cartas," Letter 1.

70. Stevenson, *A Historical and Descriptive Narrative*, 14.

71. The Acta is reproduced in Andrade, *Historia del Ecuador* (1982), 188–90.

72. Andrade, *Historia del Ecuador* (1982), 189.

73. Ibid., 188. Appointment to office was expressed in the Acta as the assembly stating, "elejimos y nombramos" (we elect and name).

74. AGI Estado 72 n. 64, "Memorias . . . en cinco cartas," Letter 1.

75. Ibid. "[L]a ominpotencia de quarenta y cinco Barbaros repeltso de Chicha y Aguardiente una Soberania completa, una Magestad . . . mas absoluta q la de la Sublime Puerta."

76. Andrade, *Historia del Ecuador* (1982), 189–90.

77. Ibid., 188.

78. AGI, Estado 72 n. 64, "Memorias . . . en cinco cartas," Letter 1.

79. Stevenson, *A Historical and Descriptive Narrative*, 16. This last observation did not make it into the Spanish edition of Stevenson's book, *Relación histórica de la conspiración y revoluciones*, 10.

80. Stevenson, *A Historical and Descriptive Narrative*, 16. Wearing plumes in one's hat became an almost instant fashion statement, leading letter writers who wished to curry favor with the junta to request friends and family members send any plumes that could be found to Quito. See letters in Andrade (1934), "Arenas a su hermana chepita," 732; "Parra y Oramas a Fran.co Oramas," 748–49; and "Joaquin Yerovi a Pedro Camacho," 745.

81. See Ponce Ribadeneira, *Quito, 1809–1812*, "Manifiesto del Pueblo de Quito," 142–44; "Manifiesto de la Junta Suprema de Quito al Público," 136–42; "Manifiesto de la Junta Suprema de Quito a América," 157–58; and "Oficio del Marqués de Selva Alegre al Ayuntamiento de Popayán," 139.

82. Ponce Ribadeneira, *Quito, 1809–1812*, 148. "Acta de cabildo abierto celebrado en Quito el 16 de Agosto de 1809 en la sala capitular de San Agustín."

83. Ponce Ribadeneira, *Quito, 1809–1812*, 149. "Juramos al Sr. D. Fernando VII como a nuestro Rey y Señor Natural y juramos adherir a los principios de la Junta Central de no reconocer jamás la dominación de Bonaparte ni a la Rey alguno intruso; juramos conservar en su unidad y pureza la Religión Católica, Apostólica, Romana, en que por la misericordia de Dios tuvimos la felicidad de nacer, y juramos fielmente hacer todo el bien posible a la Nación y Patría, perdiendo, si necesario fuere por esos sagrados objetos, la última gota de nuestra sangre y por la Constitución."

84. The exchange of letters between the Marqués and the Conde are documents 12–16 in Ponce Ribadeneira, *Quito, 1809–1812*, 146–48. The exchange took place August 17–18, 1809.

85. "Garces a Herrera Campuzano," 20-viii-1809 in Andrade, *Historia del Ecuador* (1934), 734.

86. Ponce Ribadeneira, *Quito, 1809–1812*, 33–39. See also, Marío Herrán Baquero, *El virrey don Antonio Amar y Borbón: la crisis del régimen colonial en la Nueva Granada* (Bogotá: Banco de la República, 1988).

87. "Oficio del Conde de Selva Florida, D. Juan José Guerrero, Presidente de la Junta Suprema de Quito, al Conde Ruiz de Castilla," in *Quito, 1809–1812*, ed. Ponce Ribadeneira, 180–81.

88. "Oficio del Marqués de Selva Alegre al Ayuntamiento de Popayán," in *Quito, 1809–1812*, ed. Ponce Ribadeneira, 142.

89. "Manifiesto del Pueblo de Quito," in Ponce Ribadeneira, *Quito, 1809–1812*, ed. Ponce Ribadeneira, 142.

90. Stevenson, *A Historical and Descriptive Narrative*, 18.

91. Andrade, *Historia del Ecuador* (1934), "Lista de los sujetos que de público y notorio se sabe concurrieron e intervinieron en la resolución y disposición de la Junta constituida el 10 de Agosto del presente año," 467–69. A second list, compiled toward the end of December 1809 identified 92 individuals as participants in the Junta that were rounded up in the arrests. Andrade, *Historia del Ecuador* (1934), "Lista de los sujetos," 792–99. An additional 129 individuals were identified as wanted in a third list of conspirators that was circulated. Andrade (1934), "Lista de los sujetos q' faltan que apresar, y son comprendidos en la revolución de 10 de Agosto del año proximo pasado," 840–45.

92. Andrade *Historia del Ecuador* (1934), "Clamor del Dr. Rodriguez de Quiroga al Opisbo," 469–73. The letter is not dated, but Quiroga states he is writing after seven months of incarceration.

93. Ibid., 470–71. "El resultado fue, que puesto en movimiento todo el Quartel, preparados cañones, la soldadesca sobre las armas, cargados los fusiles, ordenada la caballería y dispuesto todos, llenos de un involuntario furor y saña, a derramar sangre y llenar de cadáveras la ciuadad."

94. Ibid., 471. "A la menor novedad se acabase con nosotros."

95. Ibid., 471. "[D]e lo que se sigue que por cualquiera borrachera, por cualquiera novedad exterior, en que no tenemos la menor parte ni culpa los pobres desvalidos e inermes presos, estamos vendidos y expuestos a ser asesinados, como perros, sin forma judicial, sin sentencia."

96. Stevenson, *A Historical and Descriptive Narrative*, 22.

97. Andrade, *Historia del Ecuador* (1934), "Los presos quiteños se oponen al viaje de San Miguel," 930–36.

98. Ibid., "Insiten los presos," 936–37; "Negativa de Aréchaga," 937–38.

99. Stevenson, *A Historical and Descriptive Narrative*, 26–27.

100. Ibid., 27–28.

101. Salazar y Lozano, *Recuerdo de los sucesos*, 86. "La Joven Doña Isabel Bou, fue también herida y empapada en la sangre de su marido . . . Don Juan larrea y Guerrero habiendo este caído muerto á sus pies."

102. Andrade, *Historia del Ecuador* (1934), "Examen de cadáveres," 474–79.

103. Stevenson, *A Historical and Descriptive Narrative*, 31–33.

104. Ponce Ribadeneira, *Quito, 1809–1812*, 71–72.

105. Rodríguez, *La revolución política*, 75.

106. Ibid., 74.

107. Ibid., 75.

108. "Oficio del Virrey del Perú a D. Carlos Montúfar, 22-x-1810," in *Quito, 1809–1812*, ed. Ponce Ribadeneira, 217.

109. Ponce Ribadeneira, *Quito, 1809–1812*, 81.

110. "Proyecto de constitución para el Reino de Quito elaborado por el Canónigo D. Calixto Miranda, Dignidad de Maestraescuela de la S. I. Catedral," in *Quito, 1809–1812*, ed. Ponce Ribadeneira, 271–73.

111. Quoted in *Quito, 1809–1812*, ed. Ponce Ribadeneira, 102.

112. This shift was emblematic of political changes occurring in both Spain and the Americas. Rodríguez, *The Independence of Spanish America*, 73.

113. Ponce Ribadeneira, *Quito, 1809–1812*, 107–10.

114. Rodríguez, *La revolución política*, 82–83, 104–6.

115. Ibid., 107. Members of indigenous communities in the remnants of the old *república de indios* qualified for voting rights, along with indigenous individuals living in urban settings. Indigenous men who were *conciertos*, a form of peonage, attached to specific haciendas were not given voting rights because the Cádiz Constitution exempted domestic servants from political citizenship.

116. Ibid., 82.

117. Ibid., 84–85.

118. The original electoral plan is reproduced as Appendix I in Rodríguez, *La revolución política*, "Plan de elecciones de Diputados en cortes, y de Provincia (1813)," 217–24.

119. Rodríguez, *La revolución política*, 87–88.

120. Rodríguez, *The Independence of Spanish America*, 52.

CHAPTER FIVE

1. *Documento de oro*, 24.

2. Ibid.

3. BAEP 7342 (60), 7 "Constitución política de la Monarquía española, 1812," 33–34. See also "Constitución de Cádiz de 1812," http://www.cervantes virtual.com/servlet/SirveObras/02438387547132507754491/index.htm (accessed March 23, 2009).

4. BAEP 7342 (60), 7 "Constitución política de la Monarquía española, 1812," 37–38.

5. "Constitución política de la Monarquía española, 1812. Promulgada en Cadiz á 19 de Marzo de 1812" 81. Available at http://www.cervantesvirtual .com/servlet/SirveObras/c1812/12260843118006070754624/index.htm (accessed March 31, 2009).

6. Ibid.

7. Pateman, *The Sexual Contract*, 5–6.

8. AN/Q 1NJ 266, 6-iv-1812.

9. AN/Q 1NJ 267, 14-v-1812.

10. AN/Q 1NJ 267, 25-v-1812.

11. ANQ/E 1NJ 270, 29-iii-1813, "Da [Doña] Mariana Ramires contra Manuel Reynosa."

12. AN/Q 1NJ 271, 5-iii-1813.

13. AN/Q 1NJ 277, 3-viii-1814.

14. In the opening petition, Antonio refers to Rosa Tuña as his adopted servant girl (*criada adoptiva*), an appellation that points to the circulation of children in Spanish America. For the remainder of the petition, he refers to her as his daughter (*hija*). Often, children taken into a home, male or female, were considered charges of the family while also serving that family as apprentices and the like. See Laura Shelton, "Like a Servant or Like a Son: Circulating Children in Northwestern Mexico (1790–1850)," in *Raising an Empire: Children in Early Modern Iberia and Colonial Latin America*, ed. González and Premo, 219–37 (Albuquerque: University of New Mexico Press, 2007). In this case, Rosa was the daughter of Antonio's

wife by another man, who was reportedly a resident of the hacienda of Francisco Carcelen.

15. *Pendolista* literally meant one who worked by the pen, the same as a *plumero*, but not as an officially recognized scribe. The term, though, also carried negative connotations in Castilian as a synonym for swindler, imposter, liar (*embustero, trapacista*).

16. AN/Q 1NJ 277, 3-viii-1814, "Yo en defensa de mi buena opinion, no puedo menos que recomendar a la justificacion de V. que todos estos enrredos judiciales, tienen origin de la furiosa muchedumbre de Pendolistas, queseha levantado en esta ciudad, y para mantener sus vicios, andan seduciendo a las personas miserables . . . para calumniar a los Vecinos de honor, levantandoles las falsedades mas groseras con daño tanto publico, como privado."

17. ANQ/E 1NJ 277, 6-viii-1814.

18. The term *runasambo* is a compound of *runa*, the Kichwa term for man or person, and *sambo* or *zambo*, a person of mixed indigenous and African descent.

19. "[Q]e el qe tenia plata era Cavallero, y qe Falconi era Yndio con plata."

20. AN/Q 1NJ 277, 7-ix-1814.

21. In Old English, the game of palmo was called span-farthing. The object of the game was for players to toss coins, marbles, or some other marker, attempting to land less than a palm's width from an opponent's marker, or from a neutral marker placed against a wall. See Alice Bertha Gomme, *The Traditional Games of England, Scotland, and Ireland*, Vol. 2 (London: David Nutt, 1898), 210.

22. ANQ/E 1NJ, boxes 255–78.

23. The numbers do not line up exactly with the charts in Appendix III because women who petitioned with or without license and later appointed attorneys, officials, or others to represent them are counted twice. Likewise, women representing their husbands or others are not included in the representation counts in the charts.

24. AN/Q 1NJ 256, 12-i-1810, "Expediente promovido pro Sipriano Reynoso contra Rafael Peres y su muger Mercedes Umaso por injurias."

25. "[P]usó a lo de mi a entablar riña perfecta pr medio de las negras injurias."

26. "Mercedes Umaso Yndia muger letigima de Rafael Peres, causando una esadalosa e intolerable inquietud, faltando respeto de los Vecinos Feligreses de dicha Parroquia que se manejan con decoro y estimacion."

27. AN/Q 1NJ 256, 20-iii-1810, "Paula Cevallos contra Maria Dolores Gonzales pr concubinato."

28. AN/Q CR 217, 20-iii-1810, and CR 222, 14-vi-1814, "Criminal seguido contra Bonifacio Velasco por doble matrimonio."

29. CR 219, 19-ix-1812, "Contra Mariano Ceas y Antonia Prado pr concuvinato."

30. AN/Q CR 201, 22-iii-1805, "Autos con Mariano Albarez sobre rapto y seduccion de Da [Doña] Maria Dolores Paredes"; CR 203, 5-x-1805, "Contra Joseph Antonio Polo sobre estrupo"; CR 203, 7-v-1805, "Rosalia Cando contra Asencia Morales pr ilicito comercio con su marido"; CR

204, 25-iv-1806, "Contra Narciso Argote pr Ladron y Tereza Alberes su Concubina y receptadora"; CR 209, 12-iii-1807, "Contra Flora Arentales pr concubinato con Mariano Xaramillo y prostitucion publica"; CR 209, 25-iv-1807, "Pr Da [Doña] Manuela Mendosa contra el Rexid.r Dn [Don] Manuel delas Eras pr haber estrupado a su hija Da [Doña] Maria Mercedes Garcia"; CR 213, 22-iii-1808, "Contra Jose Delgado pr doble matrimonio y Catalina Ramis pr haver testificado de su solteria"; CR 213, 3-vi-1808.

31. In addition to the case of Doña Paula discussed above, an insult case between Visenta Moncayo and Da [Doña] Leonor Francisco y Guerrero centered on allegations by Vicenta that Doña Leonor's daughter was having an affair with Vicenta's husband (ANQ/E 1NJ 258, 2-vi-1810). Doña Luisa Alarcon filed a petition with court requesting intervention into her husband's continued habitation with a single woman named Petrona Aroca (ANQ/E 1NJ 258, 19-vi-1810). Finally, Manuela Soria filed suit against her husband for material support, and alleged adultery with various women as well. This case originally was adjudicated verbally, but two weeks after it ended Manuela approached the court again over her husband's incorrigibility (ANQ/E 1NJ 259, 10-ix-1810).

32. AN/Q 1NJ 277, 27-VII-1814, "Auto Cabeza de Procesos sobre haberlo herido Maria Clara Mayquinga a Fran.co Borja Topanta."

33. AN/Q 1NJ 258, 5-vii-1810, "Expediente criminal promovido pr Evaristo Valencia contra Antonio Balladres, sus dos hermanas, y José Hidaldgo sobre injurias."

34. AN/Q 1NJ 264, 6-ix-1811.

35. The petition by José Espindola is included as the last two pages of an unrelated series of petitions in ANQ/E 1NJ 276, 13-v-1814.

36. Simple credit instruments are loan documents signed by lenders, borrowers, and sometimes witnesses, but are not formally notarized. Notarized instruments, recorded in the ledger of one of the city's official notaries, were often referred to as *escrituras*, or deeds.

37. The cases under consideration were described as pesos cases, and as such were usually unspecified monetary loans. They do not include conflicts over house- or land-sale contracts. Some of the information on loans comes from testamentary details, though I have not included cases that were primarily over inheritance issues.

38. AN/Q 1NJ 256, 8-i-1810, "Expediente executibo seguido pro la Sra Da [Doña] Fran.ca Ripalda contra el Marques de Villa Orellana y su hijo el Dr Dn [Don] José Sanchez, por cantidad de pesos."

39. AN/Q 1NJ 256, 13-iii-1810.

40. AN/Q 1NJ 257, 21-v-1810.

41. AN/Q 1NJ 269, 28-vii-1812.

42. AN/Q 1NJ 270, 15-iii-1813, "Executivos de Dn [Don] Miguel Arevallo contra Da [Doña] Mariana Moreno por cantidad de ps."

43. "Respeto de ser yo una Muger ignoranta, qe no es de mi obligacion de saber los tramites de un Juicio executivo . . . y favoresiendome en estos casos las Leyes, tanto por mi vihudes, mi sexso, y el de no saber ni avermelo hecho entender el Escribano las providencias libradas."

44. AN/Q 1NJ 270, 7-iv-1813.

45. AN/Q 1NJ 277, 19-ix-1814, "Y siendo prohibido por leyes y derechos qe las mugeres casadas lo puedan hacer sup.co se digne mandar sede pr nulo, y de ningun valor el ynstrumento otorgado."

46. AN/Q 1NJ 258 13-iv-1810, "Testamentaria de Juana Flores Yndia quien murio abintestado el 13 de Junio de 1810." See also 1NJ 261 25-ii-1811, for the case of Mariana Rodriguez, a shop owner who died intestate in February 1811. Her case included numerous simple instruments as well. Also, 1NJ 278 6-x-1814, "Expediente seguido pr Da [Doña] Tomasa Tovar contra Da [Doña] Magdalena Cortes pr cantidad de ps provenientes de la Hacienda de Pusuqui."

47. AN/Q 1NJ 258 5-vii-1810. See also 1NJ 260, 12-ii-1811, which includes the enumerated debts of Sebastiana dela Cruz, who owed 178 pesos, 6 reales to a series of four women for mules she had bought from them; and 1NJ 265, 10-ii-1812, "Principales y reditos resulta dever Dn [Don] Miguel de Almeyda a D. Jose de Salazar y a su muger legitima Da [Doña] Fran.ca de Soria."

48. In addition to the cases discussed above, see AN/Q 1NJ 260, 29-xii-1810, "Da [Doña] Mariana de Olais por su marido Dr Dn [Don] Antonio Ante contra Dn [Don] José Maria Ruiz"; 1NJ 260, 24-i-1811, "Da [Doña] Joana Checa con Dn [Don] Eugenio Espinosa"; 1NJ 264, 31-viii-1811, "Da [Doña] Feliciana Suares contra Manuel cardenes pr un cantidad de pesos"; 1NJ 266, 8-iv-1812, "Expediente seguido pr Dn [Don] José Paz y Mino pr demanda de su Muger Da [Doña] Juana Tavera"; 1NJ 267, 14-v-1812, "Expediente de Da [Doña] Estefania Salazar contra Dn [Don] Manuel Salazar pr Cantidad de pesos"; 1NJ 267, 20-v-1812, "Da [Doña] Mariana, Da [Doña] Margarita y Da [Doña] Leonor Mosquera contra Josefa de Sna Sacram.to"; 1NJ 271, 11-vi-1813, "Expediente executibo seguido contra Juan Jph Zalasar pr da [Doña] Josefa Ayllon pr haberla queriendo cobrar a esta falsamente cien ps."; 1NJ 272, 27-vii-1813, "Dn [Don] Alexandro Garzon y su Muger Da [Doña] Rita Gordon con Dn [Don] Juan Josef Garson"; 1NJ 274, 6-xii-1813, "Doña Juaquina Cañizares con Dr Dn [Don] Victor de San Miguel"; 1NJ 275, 8-iii-1814, "Da [Doña] Mariana Baquero contra Pedro Proaño por cantidad de pesos"; and 1NJ 276, 22-iv-1814, "Da [Doña] Joaquina Cañizares contra Dn [Don] Jose Gortayre pr cantidad de pesos."

49. AN/Q 1NJ 277, 12-viii-1814, "Expediente formado por los Yndividuso del Comercio de esta Ciudad sobre la Creacion de guarda Mayor y reglas que deben observarse."

50. BAEP 7284 (2) 7-viii-1815, "Torivio Montes al Sr Alcalde Ordinario de la Villa de Zaruma." "Que en las Provincias de America se restalbesca el sistema guvernativo, economico, y de administracion de Justica que regia antes de que se publique en ellas la Constitucion formada por las llamadas Cortes para que V. la haga notoria en el distrito de su mando, y en su punctual cumplimm.to disponga la pronta restitucion de los Alcaldes Ordinarios que existian quando se estableció el cavildo Constitucional, y que igualmente sean repuestos todos los demas funcionarios del Cuerpo municipal antiguo."

51. BAEP 7284 (2) "Dn [Don] Apolinario Lopez Merino al Y. C. de Ambato." "No ignoro q todo hombre ancio pa con dios consigo mismo, y para con

nostoros los hombres. Mirado el hombre bajo estos tres aspectos se le mira tambien como Cristiano, como Racional y como ciudadano, y vasallo."

52. BAEP 7284 (2) "Dn [Don] Apolinario Lopez Merino al Y.C. de Ambato." "Quien podrá negar que las incumbencias de conserbar la propia persona, su casa, sus intereses, sus creditos."

CHAPTER SIX

1. Rodríguez, *La revolución política*, 196.

2. Ibid., 196–97.

3. Pereda de Saravia's report is reprinted as Appendix II in Rodríguez, *La revolución política*, 225–32.

4. For example, Cuenca named electors in early September. BAEP 7285 (3) 2-ix-1821, "Viva la Constitución. Expediente relativo al nombram.to de Electores de Parroquia."

5. Maine, *Ancient Law*, 170.

6. "Constitución de la República de Colombia (1821)," *Cuerpo de leyes de la república de Colombia* (Caracas: Universidad Central de Venezuela, 1961), 23.

7. "Ley de 13 de Mayo," *Cuerpo de leyes*, 352. Diaz, *Female Citizens, Patriarchs, and the Law in Venezuela*, 5–6, 142. Diaz argues that this codification of colonial law "allowed that class, race, and gender distinctions formed the primary basis for determining people's rights in courts." Furthermore, she states, "The use of colonial legislation gave continuity as well as legitimacy to Venezuelan judicial institutions" (142). The assertion neglects the real changes in context and force with which the most restrictive of colonial laws were enforced after independence.

8. Recent expressions of this perspective can be found in Caulfied et al., *Honor Status, and Law*, particularly the editors' introduction, "Introduction: Transformation in Honor, Status, and Law over the Long Nineteenth Century," 1–26; Elizabeth Dore, "One Step Forward, Two Steps Back: Gender and the State in the Long Nineteenth Century," in *Hidden Histories of Gender*, ed. Dore and Molyneux, 3–32; Elizabeth Dore, *Myths of Modernity: Peonage and Patriarchy in Nicaragua* (Durham, NC: Duke University Press, 2006); Arrom, *Women of Mexico City;* Susan Besse, *Restructuring Patriarchy: The Modernization of Gender Inequality in Brazil, 1914–1940* (Chapel Hill: University of North Carolina, 1996); Sueann Caulfield, *In Defense of Honor: Sexual Morality, Modernity, and Nation in Early Twentieth-Century Brazil;* Chambers, *From Subjects to Citizens;* Christine Hünefeldt, *Liberalism in the Bedroom: Quarreling Spouses in Nineteenth-Century Lima* (University Park: Pennsylvania State University Press, 2000); and Erin O'Connor, "Widow's Rights Questioned: Indians, the State, and Fluctuating Gender Ideas in Central Highland Ecuador, 1870–1900," *The Americas* 59, no. 1 (July 2002): 87–106. In the cases listed above, modern historians accept wholesale the a priori assumption of patriarchal gender relations in the early period, and thus explain "modern" patriarchy as an updating of colonial social relations. The argument of colonial fetters preventing development is not new to the literature on nineteenth-century Latin America. It was the centerpiece of arguments over the nature of the region's political economy

reaching back to the 1920s in the writings of José Carlos Mariátegui and extending through the transition to capitalism debates of the 1970s and 1980s. See, for example, José Carlos Mariátegui, *Siete ensayos de interpretación de la realidad Peruana*, Colleción obras completas, vol. 2 (Lima: Empresa Editora Amauta, 1969 [1928]); Andre Gunder Frank, *Capitalism and Underdevelopment in Latin America;* Ernesto Laclau, "Feudalism and Capitalism in Latin America," *Politics and Ideology in Marxist Theory* (London: NLB, 1977); and Stanley J. Stein and Barbara Stein, *The Colonial Heritage of Latin America.* For a generalized critique of the argument of the fetter in the emergence of capitalism, see Ellen Meiksins Wood, *The Origins of Capitalism* (New York: Monthly Review Press, 1999), 4–8.

9. For more on the decline of dowry practice throughout see Latin America in the late eighteenth and early nineteenth centuries, see Muriel Nazzari, *Disappearance of the Dowry: Women, Families, and Social Change in São Paulo, Brazil (1600–1900)* (Stanford, CA: Stanford University Press, 1991); C. D. Deere and M. León, "Liberalism and Married Women's Property Rights in Nineteenth-Century Latin America," *HAHR* 85, no. 4 (2005): 653–54; and Christine Hünefeldt, "Las dotes en manos Limeñas," in *Familia y vida privada en la historia de Iberoamérica,* ed. Pilar Gonzalo and Cecilia Rabell, 255–87 (Mexico, DF: Colegio de México, 1996).

10. Pateman, *The Sexual Contract,* 10–11.

11. BAEP 7285 (3) 3, "Acta de instalación."

12. BAEP 7286 (4) 1, "Yndice de los Bandos y Decretos dictados por la Yntendencia y Comandancia General del Departamento con expresion de fechas, y del jefe que los mandó publicar." The referenced order was dated 25-i-1823.

13. See, for example, the 1822 instructions on controlling vagabonds in Loja handed down by Governor Pio de Valdivieso Torres in BAEP 7285, (3) 3, 3-xii-1822.

14. BAEP 7286 (4) 1, "Yndice de los bandos y decretos dictados por la Yntendencia y Comandancia General del Departamento." The referenced order was dated 28-v-1823, and used the terms, "cuidar la seguridad, salubridad, y comodidad del vecindario."

15. BAEP 7286 (4) 5, "Reglamento de Policia, 1825."

16. "Ley de 11 de Mayo: Sobre la organización y régimen politico y económico de los departamentos y provincias," *Cuerpo de leyes de la república,* 274–86.

17. Ibid., 277.

18. BAEP 7286 (4) 5 "Reglamento de Policia, 1825."

19. Ibid.

20. In December 1829, a group of men and women from the barrio of San Roque wrote to the municipality to complain that an open acequia was flooding and damaging their streets and houses. They complained specifically that the juez de policia, as the officer in charge of the block police, had neglected his duties in fixing the problem. Five of the twelve homeowners that signed the petition were women. BAEP 7287 (5), 1 3-xii-1829.

21. There is a certain slippage between the way political theorists, following Reinhart Koselleck, Carl Schmitt, and, in particular Jürgen Habermas, and feminist scholars have used the terms public and private. On the one hand, the term public indicates a sphere of communication, criticism, and political engagement that emerged in the late eighteenth century in civil society in opposition to the privatized politics of European absolutism. The public sphere was a product of bourgeois political, intellectual, and market activism in spaces of the home, street, and village that were nominally private, but that stood in opposition to the reason of state. Thus, according to Dena Goodman, the perception of the public sphere as existing in opposition to the private in the epoch before the nation state was a "false opposition" (Dena Goodman, "Public Sphere and Private Life: Toward a Synthesis of Current Historiographical Approaches to the Old Regime," *History and Theory* 31.1 [1992]: 1). For feminists, the terms public and private have long indicated a divide between the domestic sphere and the rest of the world—economic, political, and cultural. It is, in a sense, an attempt to critic or invert of the cult of domesticity. This divide makes dialogue difficult between the two conceptions, even more so for the eighteenth century when, for Habermas, the concept of public was emergent but not yet secure. Latin American scholars have largely utilized the feminist conception of public/private, tied to the maintenance of the supposed Mediterranean honor code, that posited enclosure and domesticity as ideological ideals for women, cloistered from the world of the market, the court, the street, and politics writ large. I am invoking a bridge between the two. Following Habermas and Goodman, I would suggest that private and public are anachronisms for the eighteenth century, prior to a real cult of domesticity as well as a genuine and immutable divide between public and private realms gendered as male and female and firmly controlled by men alone. In Ecuador, following the French model, those categories were established and ossified during the age of liberal revolution. For more, see Jürgen Habermas, *The Structural Transformation of the Public Sphere: An Inquiry into a Category of Bourgeoise Society*, trans. Thomas Burger (Cambridge, MA: MIT Press, 1989); Goodman, "Public Sphere and Private Life," 1–20; Jean L. Cohen and Andrew Arato, *Civil Society and Political Theory* (Cambridge, MA: MIT Press, 1994), 117–76, 201–54. For an excellent overview of the emergence of the political public sphere in Spanish America, see for example, Victor M. Uribe-Uran, "The Birth of a Public Sphere in Latin America During the Age of Revolution," *Comparative Studies in Society and History* 42.2 (2000): 425–57; and Rafael Rojas, *La escritura de independencia: El surgimiento de la opinion pública en México* (Mexico: Taurus/CIDE, 2003). Carol Pateman forms a sort of bridge between the two camps. See Pateman, *The Sexual Contract*, 10–11, where she locates the emergence of the public sphere in the legal theory of the contract, and places women as both part of and separate from civil society. For feminist uses of public/private and critiques of Habermas see, for example, Joan Landes, *Women and the Public Sphere in the Age of the French Revolution* (Ithaca, NY: Cornell University Press, 1988); Carol Pateman, "Feminist Critiques of the Public/Private Dichotomy," in Pateman, *The Disorder of Women: Democracy Feminism, and Political Theory*, 118–41 (Stanford, CA: Stanford University Press, 1989); Nancy Fraser, "Rethinking the Public Sphere: A Contribution to the Critique of

Actually Existing Democracy," in *Habermas and the Public Sphere*, ed. Craig Calhoun, 109–42 (Cambridge, MA: MIT Press, 1992); and Amanda Vickery, "Golden Age to Separate Spheres? A Review of the Categories and Chronology of English Women's History," *The Historical Journal* 36.2 (1993): 383–414.

22. "Ley de 3 de Agosto 1824: Que señala los casos en que debe ser allanada la casa de un colombiano," *Cuerpo de leyes de la república*, 260–61.

23. Ibid., 260.

24. Of course, not all abuse of power charges against officials hinged on the invasion of domestic space. For example, see AN/Q 1NJ 323, 25-ii-1825, "Seguidos pro Angelo Tipan Yndigena de la Parroquia de Pintac contra Manuel Coyago, pr haverlo herido y acuzarlo de varias Estafas ue hace en el Pueblo a pretexto de ronda," in which Angelo Tipan complained against the local Indian alcalde, Maneul Coyago, for assault and for abusing the ronda, acting as if he had authority beyond that of an indigenous alcalde and extorting the community. The complaint, made by an Indian against an Indian, carried with it racialist overtones relative to the limits of authority.

25. AN/Q CR 241, 9-ii-1825.

26. Ibid., "Que desde luego la Autoridad Judicial en qualquier estado Politico debe exerserse con direccion a premiar el merito, y castigar el delito; pero nunca es lisito hacer un abuso de aquella autoirdad depositada."

27. Ibid., "[B]ulneró, y atropelló muy tarde de la noche la seguridad de mi casa."

28. AN/Q CR 242, 14-vi-1825, "Ciudadanas Maria Maldonado é Ygnacia Nieto contra la C. Teresa Reyes, sobre injuries reales y verbales."

29. Ibid. "Allanar la casa de un Ciudanado cuales quiera que sea es un acto tan recomendable, que ni las mismas autoridades publicas lo pueden hacer en los casos y con las formalidades de la ley, de lo contrario cometen un crimen. Si la casa propria es el asilo de la seguridad, respeto, y reposo de cada uno, y si sele debe mirar en lo politico como un lugar sagrado."

30. See, for example, Zeb Tortorici, "Heran Todos Putos: Sodomitical Subcultures and Disordered Desire in Early Colonial Mexico," *Ethnohistory* 54 (2007): 36, where a man caught in the act of sodomy in 1604 sought sanctuary and was protected by his local parish church.

31. AN/Q 1NJ 325, 23-viii-1825, "Criminales seguidos por Joaq.n Palacios de la Parroqu.a de Aloag, contra el Alcalde de ella Ciudadano José Nolibos pr mala bersación en su empleo y otro motives representados en la querella." "[Y] el bolverse a las Casas de estas Pobres Mugers, a solicitar la Malicia y dormir con ellas, á q.e un hombre de ese orror puede ser Jues, no puede ser."

32. AN/Q CR 246, 22-ii-1827, "El Dr. José Marzana con la C. Maria Mercedes Saenz."

33. Ibid., "[F]alta de cello en el amor de la Libertad, de la paz y de la justicia."

34. Ibid., "El hallanamiento de una casa, sin qe ocurar áquellas circunstancias en que la autoridad deb posponer la inmunidad del asilo qe cada c. tiene en su havitación."

35. Ibid., "El fiscal dice; que un allanam.to con fuerza armada executado en el asilo domestico de noche, en agena jurisdic.n, y pr comis.n conferida a la misma parte sin qe hubiere precedido el tramite conciliatorio ni jucio alguno, y sin otro objeto que el qe Mercedes Saenz ramera publica recupiran una muchacha de menor edad que tenia a su servicio."

36. Ibid., "[D]e la seguridad individual, de la quietud, y de las zonicas que debe gozar todo Ciudadano vajo la proteccion de leyes."

37. Ibid., "Autos y vistos: la esposicion fiscal estampada con el mas exacto y prolijo examen de lo obrado, estensamente manifiesta la infraccion de la lei de 3 de Agosto del año 14 [de la independencia] qe dirijida a protejer el asilo de la casa de un ciudadana, decretó los casos, y modo con qe en obseguio de un interes publico, podia ser allanada. Por tanto, omitiendo repetir el pr menor del atentado cometido pr el Sr. Alc.e Parroquial del Centro Dr Ygnacio Cardenas, á nombre de la Republica, y por autoridad de la ley, se le condena a dho Sr Alc.e . . . en la multa de 100ps aplicados segun la ley al Tesoro publico; igual.mte se le condean en las costas causadas al Don José Antonio Marzana."

38. AN/Q CR 246, 17-ii-1827.

39. For more cases dealing with complaints on forcible entry, the ronda, and abuse of power, see AN/Q 1NJ 339, 17-vii-1829, in which José Tigsi, an indigenous resident of the pueblo of Nono northwest of Quito, filed suit against the parish alcalde of Nono for illegally entering his home and harassing his wife, Manual Amaquiña. Also, AN/Q CR 242, 19-iv-1825, in which ciudadana Narcisa del Pino filed a complaint against ciudadana Antonia Lopez for entering her house, armed with a sword, with plans to kill Pino for publicly engaging in adultery with Lopez's husband. In this case, the court was again more concerned with armed entry than with sexual dalliance. Also, in CR 250, 4-xi-1828, "Expediente seguido pr el C. José Portalansa, marido legitimo de Mariana Rueda, sobre allanamiento que hicieron du su Casa y injurias."

40. While Spanish law made no specific mention or designation of household head as exclusively male, Portuguese law did. See Deere and León, "Liberalism and Married Women's Property Rights," 647.

41. "Ley de 3 de Agosto de 1824: Por el que se declara qe las viudas é hijos de extrangeros, que hayan muerto con derecho á obtener cara de naturaleza, obtenga esta," *Cuerpo de leyes de la República*, 259. "[E]n cabeza del marido quedan naturalizados la muger y sus hijos menores de 21."

42. BAEP 7286 (4) 6, "Ynforme de Abogados de la capital de Quito que presenta su Municipalidad al Sr. Yntend.te del Departamento," 11-iv-1826. See also Juan de Ascaray, "Abogados de la Real Audiencia de Quito," *Boletín del Archivo Nacional de Historia* 8, no. 13 (1964): 29–45.

43. The various liberal governments of the 1810s engaged in similar information collection. As noted in the previous chapter, this included census-making for electoral, as well as tax, purposes. See, for example, AN/Q 1NJ 255, 5-i-1810, "Expediente que contiene la orden del Exmo. Señor Diptuado de éste Reyno, sobre que se dén pr éste Ylustre Ayuntamiento las noticias qe se solicitan por el Plan." In the 1810s, indigenous communities were more likely to participate than in the Bourbon period in hopes of establishing new constitutional municipalities. In contrast, census-making in the late-eighteenth century often led to local revolts. On those revolts

in the Audiencia of Quito, see Mond, "Indian Rebellion and Bourbon Reform," 99–124; and Yánez Moreno, Segundo, *Sublevaciones indígenas en la Audiencia de Quito: Desde comienzos del siglo XVIII hasta finales de la colonia*, 3rd ed. (Quito: Ediciones de la Universidad Católica, 1985).

44. The provincial decree and the Colombian law are mentioned in BAEP 7286 (4) 3, "Estado comprensivo á la Parroquia de Sambiza, con arreglo al decreto del Sup.mo gobierno de 4 de Octubre del año de 1825."

45. "Ley de 11 de Abril 1825: Sobre establecimiento, inversion y administración de rentas municipales," *Cuerpo de leyes de la república*, 307–14.

46. "El coronel Vicente Aguirre transcribe al Cabildo un Decreto sobre remate de tierras y ejidos," 18-iv-1823, 70, in *Colección de Oficios y Documentos dirigidos por las autoridades del departamento de Quito al cabildo, 1823–1826*, Gustavo Chiriboga C., trans. (Quito: Imprenta Municipal, 1972).

47. BAEP 7286 (4) 1, 4-xi-1823.

48. BAEP 7287 (5) 2, "Padrón ó Apuntamiento que manifiesta el Administrador de Rentas Municipales a los SS. de la Junta Administrativa con arreglo al que sele pasó por dhos SS. de lo producido en el mes de Nov.e del presente año."

49. Gauderman, *Women's Lives in Colonial Quito*, 92–123.

50. The following discussion is based on the jail censuses for 1827 and 1829 collected by the First Notary. The 1827 census covers the whole year, from January to December, while the 1829 folio begins the week of March 7, 1829, and covers the following eleven months through the week of February 6, 1830. In both cases, the counts are not 100 percent complete due to deterioration of the manuscript and the occasional missing page, but the trends analyzed remain robust. AN/Q 1NJ 331, 5-i-1827, "Año de 1827. Cuaderno de Visita de Carceles y Santa Marta que empieza desde 5 de enero de dho año"; AN/Q 1NJ 337, 22-ii-1829, "Año de 1829. Cuaderno de Visita de Carceles y Santa Marta que empieza desde 7 de marzo de dho año."

51. The jail censuses for 1834 and 1845 contain very similar profiles of criminal enforcement to the late 1820s. The trends appear to change, however, in the 1850s during the presidency of Gabriel Garcia Moreno, ardent conservative and Catholic. The 1853 jail census looks more like 1789 than the 1820s, and contains a significant number of arrests for prostitution, vagrancy, drunkenness, gambling, adultery, and concubinage. For 1834, see AN/Q 1NJ 355, 1833; for 1845, 1NJ 387, 4-i-1845, "Vicita de la Carcel y Santa Marta"; and for 1853, see 1NJ 412, 8-i-1853, "Cuaderno de vicita de Carcel del año de 1853."

52. Borchart de Moreno, "Words and Wounds," 133.

53. It could be argued that this is a retreat by the state back to the confines present before the Bourbon state took new initiative to control the sexual behavior of its subjects. I would suggest that the evidence points to a new conception of public/private that did not exist under Habsburg rule either, a conception of public/private tied to property and contract that was innovative of the republican era.

54. For gendered murders, see also AN/Q CR 241, 29-i-1825, "Sentencia pronunciada en la causa que se ha seguido al Religioso Belemita Fray Manuel de Santa Maria pr la muerte que dio a Juana Parra"; CR 243, 21-i-1826, "Causa seguida contra Juan toasa pr la muerte de Dolores Aulla"; and the attempted murder in CR 248, 17-x-1827, "Criminales seguidos de oficio contra el Doctor José Feliciano Suarez, profesor de medicina por el crimen de haber proyectado en venenar a su muger legitima Francisca Garcia."

55. AN/Q 1NJ 327, 13-ii-1826, "Criminales seguidos de oficio contra el Sobredero Calisto Mexia por haverle dado de palos à desoras de lanoche à su Muger legitima Fra.ca Alarcon, de cuyos resuls se halla agonisante."

56. AN/Q CR 244, 15-vi-1826.

57. Ibid., "[Q]ue al marido se le considera condro a corregir moderadam.te a su Esposa, y esta misma limitac.n prueba qe el exceso lo hace criminal, y digno de la animadvercion de la ley. [. . .] V. E. debe graudarlas con refleccion a la valuaria de esta clase de gentes que tartan a sus consortes con mas ferosidad que a las bestias dando a sus hijos un pecimo ejepo, é insultando el repeat debida al sagrado vinculo del matrimonio."

58. AN/Q CR 244, 15-iv-1826, "VISTOS con lo expuesto por el Sr Fiscal; el abuso de increpar y maltratar a las Mugeres, se ha hecho tan comun en esta ciudad que ya exige remedios oportunos par amantener el sosiego publica, y la armonio con los consortes."

59. Ibid., "[Q]ue administrando justicia a nombre de la republica, y por autoridad de la ley, condenado a Calisto Mejia a pricion de dos meses, en la carcel publica de esta ciudad, con declaración de que apra slir depues de ellos, ha de dar fianza a satisfaccion de su muger de que no la ofendera."

60. AN/Q 1NJ 334, 1-iii-1828.

61. Ibid., "[A]matar con Palos, Piedras, golpes de mano, y patadas. . . . entre el silencio de la noche sin mas auxilio que le de Dios."

62. There are cases in the record of female on female and male on male violence that have gendered overtones, conflicts over gendering insults, or sexual suspicions that ended in physical confrontations. See, for example, AN/Q 1NJ 324, 2-vii-1825, "Criminales seguidos pr Juan Espinosa, Manuel Escobar, y Maria Trinidad Tiran contra C. Francisco Javier de la Guerrra sobre haber estropeado"; 1NJ 324, 11-viii-1825, "Criminales seguidos por Maria Calbachi, contra José Molina, su muger, y mas socios por la azonada que hisieron"; 1NJ 327, 1-ii-1827, "Criminales seguidos por el C. Felipe Cadena pr su muger legitima C. Dolores Paredes contra la C. Maria Proaño por roturas de cabeza." For an example of female on male violence, see AN/Q CR 245, 19-viii-1826, "Causa seguido de oficio contra Trindad Moranduz pr heridas q dió a Narciso Leon."

63. AN/Q 1NJ 332, 12-ix-1827, "Criminales seguidos de oficio contra Nicolás Hidalgo por denuncia echa de qe le havia puestos manos violentas a su Madre Rita Merino, y haver cortado los labios a Juana Espinosa."

64. Ibid., "[C]onsiderando qe estas quejas han emanado de la suma embriagues qe han tenido las querellosasy el acusado, se le apercibe seriam.te, tenga major comportac.n en lo succesibo, absteniendose de vivir escadalosam.te con perjuicio de la vindicta pública, y que asi mismo debe tener la mayor sumicion y obediencia a sus Padres."

65. AN/Q 1NJ 339, 11-vii-1829.

66. Ibid., "[É]ste no sabe que coas es cumplir con las obligaciones de hombre cristiano, sin Dios, ni Religion."

67. AN/Q CR 248, 17-x-1827, "Causa seguida contra Dr. José Feliciano Saenz, Profesor de Medicina por el crimen de haber proyectado envenenar a su muger legitima Francisa Garcia."

68. By the middle of the nineteenth century, women were still being held regularly for debts. In 1845, 15.1 percent of female arrests were for debt, most often for rents owed the municipality. In 1853, debt arrests for women rose back up to 25.5 percent of total female arrests. AN/Q 1NJ 387, 4-i-1845, "Vicita de la Carcel y Santa Marta"; for 1853, see 1NJ 412, 8-i-1853, "Cuarderno de vicita de Carcel del año de 1853."

69. "La muger no puede ser presa pr. deuda civil."

70. AN/Q Civiles 50, 19-viii-1823, "El deudor que no paga ni manifiesta bienes bastantes para satisfacer deve sér reducido á pricion. . . . El deudor reducido á pricion debe trabajar dentro de ella, facilitandosele todos los medios, y una parte de sus ganancias debe deducirse para el cubierta de sus deudas."

71. The numbers are taken from AN/Q 1NJ 323–40, through categorizing each case to which women were primary parties.

72. See, for example, AN/Q 1NJ 332, 12-ix-1827, in which a woman filed against her son; 1NJ 332, 27-x-01827, in which Maria Tomasa Cargua filed suit against her husband's lover, Rosa Erosco (who was also married); 1NJ 327, 2-ii-1826, in which Luisa Delgado sparred with her husband over the proceeds of a house sale; 1NJ 327, 13-ii-1827, "Criminales seguidos contra el Sombredero Calisto Mexia por haver dado de palos a desores de la noche a su muger legitima Francisca Alarcon"; 1NJ 327, 27-ii-1827, in which Rosa Miranda sued her husband, Ramon Miranda, for alimony; and 1NJ 334, 1-iii-1828, in which a woman filed against her son-in-law.

73. "Ley de 11 de Mayo de 1825: Orgánica del Poder Judicial," *Cuerpo de leyes de la república*, 334–52. The *Ley orgánica* covered a tremendous number of officials, from appellate judges to court secretaries, jailers, the state attorney (fiscal), the registrar of documents, tax judges, attorneys, as well as the variety of subaltern magistrates (*juez letrado, alcalde municipal, alcalde parroquial*, and so on).

74. "Ley de 11 de Mayo de 1825," *Cuerpo de leyes de la república*, 349–50.

75. "Ley de 13 de Mayo de 1825: Arreglando de procedimiento civil de los tribunals y juzgados de la República," *Cuerpo de leyes de la república*, 353–55. This is the same law that established the hierarchy of national and Spanish law.

76. "Ley de 13 de Mayo de 1825," *Cuerpo de leyes de la república*, 353.

77. Ibid., 353–54.

78. Ibid., 355.

79. This discussion compiles the cases listed in AN/Q 1NJ 323, 25-i-1825, "Juicios de Conciliación"; 1NJ 331, 27-i-1827, "Libro de actas del Alcalde 20 Parroquial del Centro del año de 1827"; 1NJ 333, 18-i-1828, "Libro de actas de juicios de conciliación que lleva el Sor Alcalde segundo Miguel Carrion qe empiesa hoy 1 de enero de 1828"; and 1NJ 340, 1829, "Libro de juicios verbales pa el año de 1829."

80. In the 1NJ case set for 1825–1829, cases with women as primary litigants that mention or were sent to conciliation were 29.2 percent (1825), 29.4 percent (1826), 16.7 percent (1827), 17.9 percent (1828), and 5.2 percent (1829) per year.

81. In the entry for 8-x-1828, ciudadano Joaquin Benancio Alvares Ramires laid claim to the astonishing sum of 160,000 pesos on behalf of the estate of Doña Tomasa Vellian and from the estate of Doña Victoriana Losa via her heirs. The judge threw the case out, though, because Ramires could not substantiate the sum with even a single document. I excluded this amount from the calculation. AN/Q 1NJ 333 "Libro de actas," 8-x-1828.

82. AN/Q 1NJ 340, 1829 "Libro de juicios verbales," 5-viii-1829.

83. See Linda Alexander Rodriguez, *The Search for Public Policy: Regional Politics and Government Finances in Ecuador, 1830–1940* (Berkeley: University of California Press, 1985); Ana Gimeno Gómez, *Una tentativa monárquica en América: El caso Ecuatoriano* (Quito: Centro de Investigación y Cultura, Banco Central del Ecuador, 1988); Ralph Haskins, "Juan José Flores and the Proposed Expedition against Ecuador, 1845–1847," *HAHR* 27, no. 3 (1947): 467–95; and Mark Van Aken, *King of the Night: Juan José Flores and Ecuador, 1824–1864* (Berkeley: University of California Press, 1989). By comparison, for Colombia see James E. Sanders, *Contentious Republicans: Popular Politics, Race, and Class in Nineteenth-Century Colombia* (Durham, NC: Duke University Press, 2004).

84. Caulfield et al., *Honor, Status, and Law,* 1.

85. Michel Foucault, *"Society Must Be Defended": Lectures at the Collège de France, 1976–1976* (New York: Picador, 2003), 266.

86. Saether, "Bourbon Absolutism and Marriage Reform," 476.

87. Sousa, "Women and Crime in Colonial Oaxaca," 395.

APPENDIX III

1. The following tables are derived from tabulating licensure claims for all women who were primary litigants (defendants or plaintiffs) in 1NJ 43–47, 87–112, 220–78, and 323–40. In instances where loan instruments were incorporated, the license status was included in the litigation count. A total of 793 cases were analyzed, with 27 from the period 1765–1769, 169 for 1785–1789, 248 for 1805–1809, 178 for 1810–1814, and 171 for 1825–1829.

2. In 1811, one of the widows presented herself to the judge as a widow now in a second marriage. She is counted as a widow because she was litigating as a widow and as guardian of the children from her first marriage. ANE/Q 1NJ 263, 17-viii-1811.

BIBLIOGRAPHY

ABBREVIATIONS IN BIBLIOGRAPHY

AGI Archivo General de las Indias (Seville, Spain)
AMQ Archivo Municipal de Quito
AN/Q Archivo Nacional del Ecuador, Quito
BAEP Biblioteca "Aureliano Espinosa Pólit"
AHR *American Historical Review*
CLAR *Colonial Latin American Review*
HAHR *Hispanic American Historical Review*
LARR *Latin American Research Review*

ARCHIVAL SOURCES

Series consulted at the AN/Q:
  Criminales (CR)
  Civiles
  Estancos
  Fondo Especial (FE)
  Gobierno
  Matrimoniales
  Primer Notaría—Juicios (1NJ)

I have referenced National Archive manuscripts by the series, box number, date, and manuscript title (where available). I have not noted folio and folder numbers, because these often change with archival rearrangements. In the case of the FE, which are bound volumes, I have provided the volume and document number.

Series consulted at the AMQ:
  Actas de Cabildo

The *Actas de Cabildo* are bound volumes of the proceedings of the municipal council of Quito, and are divided in the archive by year. I have noted the volume as well as the actual municipal council meeting date.

Series consulted at the AGI:
  Estado

The ministry of culture of the Spanish government has made an increasing number of sources from its archive system available through its web portal, http://pares.mcu.es/. For this book, I used the portal to consult documents relevant to the Audiencia of Quito in Estado Cajas 52–55 and 72–74.

Manuscripts of the BAEP:
  The manuscript collection of the BAEP has been microfilmed onto seventy rolls of film. For this project, I consulted rolls 1–7 and 56–60. The manuscripts in the collection range across the secular and religious spectrum, including litigation, correspondence, and notarial papers. Individual documents on the rolls have not been catalogued, numbered, or paginated. Likewise, individual rolls are not necessarily temporally sequential or topically organized. Though Saint Louis University filmed the collection, the set consulted for this project resides at the Heard Library at Vanderbilt University. BAEP manuscripts are notated by the original St. Louis roll number, the Vanderbilt roll number, the roll section number, and document title and date wherever possible (BAEP 7823 [1] 1 Josef Manuel Flores to Presidente don Diego Antonio Nieto 20-vii-1808).

PUBLISHED PRIMARY WORKS

Abreu y Bertodano, Joseph Antonio de. 1746. *Derecho público de la Europa, fundado en los tratados concluídos hasta el año de 1740*. Madrid: Peralta.

Alcedo, Antonio de. 1964. *Bibliotheca Americana: Catálogo de los autores que han escrito de la América en diferentes ydiomas y noticia de su videa y patría, años en que vivieron, y obras que escribieron*. 2 vols. Prologue by Jorge A. Garces G. Quito, Ecuador: Imprenta Municipal.

Alfonso el Sabio. 1972/1807. *Las siete partidas del rey Don Alfonso el sabio*. 3 vols. Madrid: Lope de Vega.

Assso, Ignacio Jordan de, and Miguel de Manuel y Rodriguez. 1802. *Instituciones del derecho civil de Castilla*. 2 vols. Madrid: Imprenta Tomás Alban.

Assso, Ignacio Jordan de, and Miguel de Manuel y Rodriguez. 1825. *Instituciones del derecho civil de Castilla*. 2 vols., trans. Lewis F. C. Johnston. London: A Strahan.

Biefeld, Jakob Friedrich. 1767. *Instituciones politicas: Obra en que se trata de la sociedad civil, de las leyes, dela policía, de la real hacienda, del comercio y fuerzas de un estado, y en general, do todo quanto pertenece al gobierno*. 6 vols., trans. Domingo dela Torre y Mollinedo. Madrid: Imprenta de G. Ramirez.

Berni y Catalá, Joseph. 1988 [1763]. *Instrucción de alcaldes ordinarios, que comprehende las obligaciones de estos y del amotacen*. Madrid: Ministerio Para las Administraciones Públicas, Secretaria General Técnica.

Caicedo, Manuel José. 1960. "Viaje imaginario por las provincias limítrofes de Quito." In *Cronistas de la independencia y de la república*, 29–111. Puebla, Mexico: J. M. Cajica Jr.

de Callières, François. 1778. *Tratado de la ciencia del mundo, y de las noticias utiles para la conducta de vida.* Madrid: Imprenta de Blas Román.

Castro, Pedro de. 1778. *Defensa de la tortura y leyes patrias que la establecieron.* Madrid: Miguel Escribano.

Chiriboga C., Gustavo. 1972. *Colección de oficios y documentos dirigidos por las autoridades del departamento de Quito al cabildo, 1823–1826.* Quito, Ecuador: Imprenta Municipal.

Condamine La, Charles-Marie de. 1745. *Relation abrégée d'un voyage fait dans l'intérieur de l'Amérique Méridionale.* Paris: Veuve Pissot.

Condamine La, Charles-Marie de, and Jean Godin de Odonais. Edited by Federico Ruiz Morcuende. 1962. *Viaje a la América Meridional.* Madrid: Espasa-Calpe, S. A.

Conde de la Cañada. 1793. *Observaciones practicas sobre los recursos de fuerzo: Modo y forma de introducirlos, continuarlos, y determinarlos en los tribunales superiors.* Madrid: Imprenta Real.

"Constitución de la Monarquia Española. Promulgada en Cádiz á 19 de Marzo de 1812." http://www.cervantesvirtual.com/servlet/SirveObras/02438387547132507754491/index.htm.

Cuerpo de leyes de la República de Colombia. 1961. Caracas: Universidad Central de Venzuela.

Cutter, Charles R. Transcription and "Estudio preliminar." 1994. *Libro de los principales rudimentos tocante a todos juicios, civil, criminal y exectuvio: Año de 1764.* Mexico: UNAM.

"Decreto de 1764 sobre normatives para declarcion de mestizos." 1995. *Quitumbre* 9: 119–21.

Díaz de Valdepeña, Hernando. 1544. *Suma de notas copiosas muy sustanciales y compendiosas.* Toledo: Hernando Diaz and Juan de Medina.

Documento de oro: Constitución del estado de Quito, 1811–1812. 1913. Quito, Ecuador: Editorial Casa de Ernesto Menga.

Duchesne, Jean Baptiste Philipoteau. 1782. *Compendio de la historia de España.* Trans. José Francisco de Isla. Madrid: En la oficina de Hilario Santos Alonso.

Elizondo, Francisco Antonio de. 1779. *Práctica universal forence de los tribunals de España y de Indias.* 4 vols. Madrid: Joachin Ibarra, Impresor de Cámara.

Elizondo, Francisco Antonio de. 1792. *Práctica universal forense de los tribunals de España y de Indias.* 4th ed. Madrid: Oficina la Viuda e Hijo de Marín.

Febrero, José. 1790. *Liberia de escribanos, é instrruccion juridical theorico practica de principiantes.* 3 vols. Madrid: Oficina de la Viuda de Marín.

Garcia y Garcia, José Antonio, ed. 1869. *Relaciones de los vireyes del nuevo reino de Granada, ahora Estados Unidos de Venezuela, Estados Unidos de Colombia y Ecuador.* New York: Hallet and Breen.

Genovesi, Antonio. 1785–1786. *Lecciones de comercio, ó, bien de economía civil.* 3 vols. Madrid: Joachin Ibarra.

González Suárez, Federico, and Carlos Escudero Paladines, eds. 2006. *La obra de Espejo.* Quito, Ecuador: Campaña Nacional Eugenio Espejo por el Libro y la Lectura.

Hevia Bolaños, Juan de. 1778. *Curia philipica, primero y segundo tomo.* Madrid: J. Doblado.

Hevia Bolaños, Juan de. 1797. *Curica philipica, primero y segundo tomo.* Madrid: Oficina de Ramon Ruiz.

"Historical Affaires: South America," 1810. *The Scots Magazine and Edinburgh Literary Miscellany.* Vol. 72. Edinburgh: Archibald Constable: 943.

Humbolt, Alexander von. 1966/1811. *Political Essay on the Kingdom of New Spain.* New York.

Indice de los libros prohíbidos, compuesto del índice último de los libros prohibiods y mandados expurgar hasta fin de diciembre de 1789 por el Señor Inquisidor General y señores del Supremo Consejo de la Santa General Inquisición, de los suplementos del mismo, que alcanzan hasta 25 de agosto de 1805, y ademas de un Index Librorum Proibitorum Juxta Exemplar Romanum Jussue SS. D. N. Editum Anno MDCCCXXXV, *en el que van Intercalados en su Respectivos Lugares los Prohibidos Hasta fin de 1842.* 1844. Madrid: Imprenta de D. José Felix Palacios.

Juan, Jorge, and Antonio Ulloa. 1978. *Discourse and Political Reflections on the Kingdoms of Peru: Their Government, Special Regimen of Their Inhabitants, and Abuses Which Have Been Introduced Into One and Another, With Special Information on Why They Grew Up and Some Means to Avoid Them.* Trans. John Jay Tepaske. Norman: University of Oklahoma Press.

Juan, Jorge, and Antonio de Ulloa. 1953. *Noticias Secretas De America.* Buenos Aires, Argentina: Ediciones Mar Oceano.

Juan y Colom, Joseph. 1795 [1736]. *Instrucción juridica de escribanos, abogados y jueces ordinarios de juzgados inferiores.* 2nd ed. Madrid.

Konetzke, Richard, ed. 1962a. *Colección de documentos para la historia de la formación social de Hispanoamérica, 1493–1810,* Vol. III, No. 1. Madrid: Consejo Superio de Investigaciones Científicas.

Konetzke, Richard, ed. 1962b. *Colección de documentos para la historia de la formación social de Hispanoamérica, 1493–1810,* Vol. III, No. 2. Madrid: Consejo Superio de Investigaciones Científicas.

Lardizábal y Uribe, Manuel de. 1782. *Discurso sobre las penas contrahido á las leyes Criminales de España, para facilitar su reforma.* Madrid: Joachim Ibarra, Impresor de Camara.

Mercado, Thomas de. 1569. *Tratos y contratos de mercaderes y tratantes.* Salamanca: M. Gast.

Mercado, Thomas de. 1571. *Suma de tratos y contratos de mercaderes.* Sevilla: En casa de Hernando Dias.

Monterroso y Alvarado, Gabriel de. 1566. *Práctica criminal y civil.* Valladolid: F. Fernandez de Cordova.

Monterroso y Alvarado, Gabriel de. 1603. *Práctica criminal y civil.* Madrid: Pedro Madrigal.

Muratori, Lodovico Antonio. 1782. *Reflexiones sobre el bueno gusto en las ciencias, y las artes.* Trans. Juan Sempere y Guarinos. Madrid: Publisher unknown.

"Noticias de los movimientos de Quito en el año de 1765." 1951. *Museo Histórico* 9: 37–51.

Olmeda y Leon, Joseph de. 1771. *Elementos del derecho público de la paz, y de la guerra*. Madrid: Viuda de Manuel Fernandez.

"Padrón de Santa Bárbara en 1768." 1978. *Museo histórico* 56: 93–122.

Pérez Calama, José. 1997. *Escritos y testimonios*, ed. Ernesto dela Torre Villar y Ramiro Navarro de Anda. Mexico: UNAM.

Pinton, Joseph. 1760. *Compendio historico de la religion: Desde la creacion del mundo hasta el estado presente de la Iglesia*. Madrid: Viuda de Esquero.

Ponce Ribadeneira, Alfredo, ed. 1960. *Quito 1809–1812: Según los documentos del Archivo Nacional de Madrid*. Madrid: Imprenta Juan Bravo.

Recio S. J., P. Bernardo, 1957 [1773]. *Compendiosa relación de la cristianidad de Quito*. Vol. 2 *Biblioteca Misionera*, ed. P. Carlos and Garcia Goldaraz S. J. Madrid: Consejo Superior de Investigaciones Científicas/Insituto Santo Toribio de Mogrovejo.

"Relación sumaria de las dos sublevaciones de la pleve de Quito." 1937. *Boletín de la Academica Nacional de Historia* XV (42–45): 102–16.

Restrepo, José Manuel. 1827. *Historia de la revolución de Colombia*. Paris, France: Librería Americana.

Ripia, Juan de la. 1692. *Practica de testamentos y modos de subceder*. Pamplona: publisher unknown.

Sala, Juan. 1978 [1792]. *El litigante instruido ó el derecho puesto al alcance de todos: Compendio de la obra del Doctor D. Juan Sala que se enseña en las universidades de España*. Mexico: UNAM.

Sala, Juan. 1807–1808. *Ilustración del derecho real de España*. 3 vols. Mexico: Imprenta de Arizpe.

Salazar y Lozano, Antonio. 1910 [1831]. *Recuerdos de los sucesos principales de la revolución de Quito*. Quito, Ecuador: Imprinta y encuadernación nacional.

Santa Cruz y Espejo, Francisco Xavier Eugenio de. 1912–1923. *Escritos de Doctor Francisco Javier Eugenio Santa Cruz y Espejo; pulibandse a expensas de la ilustre municipalidad de Quito con un prologo y notas del director de la "Sociedad Ecuatoriana de estudios historicos,"* 3 vols., ed. Federico González Suarez and Jacinto Jijon y Caamano. Quito, Ecuador: Imprenta municipal.

Santa Cruz y Espejo, Francisco Xavier Eugenio de. 1947. *Primicias de la cultura de Quito*. Edición fascimilar. Quito, Ecuador: Imprenta Municipal.

Santa Cruz y Espejo, Francisco Xavier Eugenio de. 1981. *Obra educativa*, ed. Philip Astuto. Caracas, Venezuela: Biblioteca Ayacucho.

Solano de Luque, Francisco. 1738. *Idioma de la naturaleza: Con el qual enseña al medico, como ha de curar con acierto los morbos agudos*. Cádiz, Spain: Geronymo de Peralta.

Stevenson, William Bennett. 1825. *A Historical and Descriptive Narrative of Twenty Years Residence in South America*. Vol. III. London: Hurst, Robinson, and Co.

Stevenson, William Bennett. 1884. *Relación histórica, de la conspiración y revoluciones que tuvieron lugar en Quito desde el año de 1808 hasta 1810*. Guayaquil, Ecuador: Imprenta de la Nación.

"Sublevación de Quito en protesta por la aduana y los estancos, 1765." 1951a. *Museo Histórico* 2 (7): 25–37.

"Sublevación de Quito en protesta por la aduana y los estancos, 1765." 1951b. *Museo Histórico* 3 (8): 16–31.

Trystram, Florence, and A. Darío Lara. 2002. *Diálogo con las estrellas: Relación de la prestigiosa expedición de tres científicos Franceses a Sudamérica y de las aventuras que le siguieron (1735–1771).* 2nd ed. Quito, Ecuador: Campaña Eugenio Espejo por el Libro y la Lectura.

Ulloa, Antonio de, and Jorge Juan. 1978. *Relación histórica del viaje a la América Meridional.* Introduction and ed. José P. Merino Navarro and Miguel M. Rodríguez San Vicente. Madrid: Fundación Universitaria Española.

Velasco, Juan de. 1981 [1789]. *Historia del reino de Quito en la America meridional,* ed. Alfredo Pareja Diezcanseco. Caracas: Biblioteca Ayacucho.

Villadiego, Alonso de. 1747 [1612]. *Instruccion politica, y practica judicial, conforme al estilo de los consejos, audiencias, y tribunales de corte, y otros ordinarios del reyno.* Madrid: publisher unknown.

Villadiego, Alonso de. 1766. *Instruccion politica, y práctica judicial, conforme al estilo de los consejos, audiencias, y tribunales de corte, y otros ordinarios del reyno, utilissima para los governadores, y corregidores, y otros jueces ordinarios, y de comission, y para los abogados, escrivanos, procuradores, y litigantes.* Madrid: en la Oficina de Antonio Marin.

Voltaire. 1731. *An Essay Upon the Civil Wars of France, Extracted From Curious Manuscripts. And Also Upon the Epick Poetry of the European Nations, From Homer Down to Milton. The Fourth Edition, Corrected. To Which is Now Prefixed, a Discourse on Tragedy. By the Same Author.* London: N. Prevost, and Comp.

SECONDARY WORKS

Adelman, Jeremy. 1999. *Republic of Capital: Buenos Aires and the Legal Transformation of the Atlantic World.* Stanford, CA: Stanford University Press.

Adorno, Rolena, Hernan Vidal, Walter D. Mignolo, and Patricia Seed. 1993. "Commentary and Debate." *LARR* 28 (3): 113–52.

Aguirre, Carlos. 2005. *The Criminals of Lima and Their Worlds: The Prison Experience, 1850–1835.* Durham, NC: Duke University Press.

Aguirre, Carlos and Robert Buffington, eds. 2000. *Reconstructing Criminality in Latin America.* Wilmington, DE: Scholarly Resources.

Aguirre, Carlos and Charles Walker, eds. 1990. *Bandoleros, abigeos y montoneros: Criminalidad y Violencia en el Perú, Siglos XVIII–XIX.* Lima, Peru: Instituto de Apoyo Agrario.

Aldridge, Alfred Owen. 1971. *The Ibero-American Enlightenment.* Urbana: University of Illinois Press.

Álvarez Barrientos, Joaquín, François Lopez, and Inmaculada Urzainqui. 1995. *La República de las letras en la España del siglo XVIII.* Madrid: Consejo Superior de Investigaciones Científicas.

Alexander Rodriguez, Linda. 1985. *The Search for Public Policy: Regional Politics and Government Finances in Ecuador, 1830–1940.* Berkeley: University of California Press.

Alonso, Ana María. 1995. *Thread of Blood: Colonialism, Revolution, and Gender on Mexico's Northern Frontier.* Tucson: University of Arizona Press.

Anderson, Benedict. 1983. *Imagined Communities*. London: Verso Press.

Andrade, Manuel de Jesús. 1909. *Próceres de independencia: Índice alfabético de sus nombres con algunos bocetos biográficos*. Quito, Ecuador: Tip. y Encuadernación de la Escuela de Artes y Oficios.

Andrade, Roberto. 1934. *Historia del Ecuador*. Vol. 1–3. Guayaquil: Reed and Reed.

Andrien, Kenneth. 1990. "Economic Crisis, Taxes and the Insurrection of 1765." *Past & Present* 129: 104–31.

Andrien, Kenneth. 1994. "The State and Dependency in Late Colonial and Early Republican Ecuador." In *The Political Economy of Spanish American in the Age of Revolution, 1750–1850*, ed. Andrien and Lyman Johnson, 169–96. Albuquerque: University of New Mexico Press.

Andrien, Kenneth. 1995. *The Kingdom of Quito, 1690–1830: The State and regional development*. Cambridge, UK: Cambridge University Press.

Andrien, Kenneth J. 1998. "The Noticias Secretas De America and the Construction of a Governing Ideology for the Spanish American Empire." *CLAR* 7 (2): 175–92.

Arias Divit, Juan Carlos. 1958. *Las expediciones científicas Españolas durante el siglo XVIII*. Madrid: Instituto de Cultura Hispánica.

Arrom, Silvia. 1985. *The Women of Mexico City, 1790–1857*. Stanford, CA: Stanford University Press.

Arrom, Silvia. 2000. *Containing the Poor: The Mexico City Poor House, 1774–1871*. Durham, NC: Duke University Press.

Ascaray, Juan de. 1964. "Abogados de la Real Audiencia de Quito." *Boletín del Archivo Nacional de Historia* 8 (13): 29–45.

Ashcroft, Bill, Gareth Griffiths, and Helen Tiffin. 1998. *Key Concepts in Post-Colonial Studies*. New York: Routledge Press.

Astuto, Philip. 1968. *Eugenio Espejo: Reformador ecuatoriano de la Ilustración (1747–1795)*. Mexico, DF: Fondo de la Cultura Económica.

Astuto, Philip L. 1968. "A Latin American Spokesman in Napoleonic Spain: José Mejía Lequerica." *The Americas* 24 (4): 354–77.

Barrera, Angel T. 1909. *Inciativa de la independencia en Sud-América*. Quito, Ecuador: Imprenta Nacional.

Barrera, Isaac. 1944. "La Revolución de Agosto." *Boletín de la Academia de Historia*. July/Dec.: 320–26.

Benítez Vinueza, Leopoldo, ed. 1960. *Precursores*. Puebla, Mexico: J. M. Cajica, Jr.

Bennett, Herman. 2003. *Africans in Colonial Mexico: Absolutism, Christianity, and Afro-Creole Consciousness, 1570–1640*. Bloomington: Indiana University Press.

Bennett, Judith. 2006. *History Matters: Patriarchy and the Challenge of Feminism*. Philadelphia: University of Pennsylvania Press.

Benson, Nettie Lee. 2004. "The Elections of 1809: Transforming Political Culture in New Spain." *Mexican Studies/Estudios Mexicanos* 20 (1): 1–20.

Benton, Laura. 2002. *Law and Colonial Cultures: Legal Regimes in World History, 1400–1900*. Cambridge, UK: Cambridge University Press.

Berstein, Harry. 1946. "A Provincial Library in Colonial Mexico, 1802" *HAHR* 26 (2): 162–83.

Besse, Susan. 1996. *Restructuring Patriarchy: The Modernization of Gender Inequality in Brazil, 1914–1940*. Chapel Hill, NC: University of North Carolina Press.

Black, Chad Thomas. 2006. "Between Prescription and Practice: Governance, Legal culture, and Gender in Colonial Quito, 1765–1830." PhD diss. Albuquerque: University of New Mexico.

Black, Chad Thomas. 2007. "Between Prescription and Practice: Governance, Legal Culture, and Gender in Quito, 1765–1830." *CLAR* 16 (2): 273–98.

Bono y Huerta, José. 1981. "Los Formularios Notariales Españoles de los Siglos XVI, XVII y XVIII." *Anales de la Academia Matritense del Notariado* 23 (1): 287–317.

Borchart de Moreno, Christiana. 1998. *La Audiencia de Quito: Aspectos económicos y sociales (siglos XVI–VIII)*. Quito, Ecuador: Abaya Yala/ Banco Central.

Borchart de Moreno, Christiana. 2004. "Words and Wounds: Gender Relations, Violence, and the State in Latin Colonial and Early Republican Ecuador." *CLAR* 13 (1): 129–44.

Borrero, Manuel Maria. 1962. *La revolución de Quito, 1809–1812*. Quito, Ecuador: Editorial Espejo.

Boyer, Richard. 1995. *Lives of the Bigamists: Marriage, Family, and Community in Colonial Mexico*. Albuquerque: University of New Mexico Press.

Brading, D. A. 1994. *Church and State in Bourbon Mexico: The Diocese of Michoacán, 1749–1810*. Cambridge, UK: Cambridge University Press.

Bravo Lira, Bernardino. 1988. "El Derecho Indiano y sus Raíces Europeas: Derecho Común y Propio de Castilla." *Anuario de Historia del Derecho Español*, 58.

Burkholder, Mark A., and D. S. Chandler. 1982. *Biographical Dictionary of Audiencia Members in the Americas, 1687–1821*. Westport, CT: Greenwood Press.

Burns, Kathryn. 2005. "Notaries, Truth, and Consequences." *AHR* 110 (2): 350–79.

Butler, Judith. 1999. *Gender Trouble: Feminism and the Subversion of Identity*. New York: Routledge.

Caillet-Bois, Ricardo R. 1929. *Ensayo sobre el río de la plata y la revolución Francesa*. Buenos Aires, Argentina: Imprenta de la Universidad.

Cañeque, Alejandro. 2005. *The King's Living Image: The Culture and Politics of Viceregal Power in Colonial Mexico*. New York: Routledge Press.

Cañizares-Esguerra, Jorge. 2003. "Postcolonialism *avante la lettre?* Travelers and Clerics in Eighteenth-Century Colonial Spanish America." In *After Spanish Rule*, ed. Mark Thurner, 89–110. Durham, NC: Duke University Press.

Cardoso, Fernandno Henrique, and Enzo Faletto. 1971. *Dependency and Development in Latin America*. Berkeley: University of California Press.

Caufield, Sueann. 2000. *In Defense of Honor: Morality, Modernity, and the Nation in Early Twentieth-Century Brazil*. Durham, NC: Duke University Press.

Caulfield, Sueann, Sarah C. Chambers, and Lara Putnam, eds. 2005. *Honor, Status, and Law in Modern Latin America*. Durham, NC: Duke University Press.

Caulfield, Sueann, Sarah C. Chambers, and Lara Putnam. 2005. "Introduction: Transformation in Honor, Status, and Law over the Long Nineteenth Century." In *Honor, Status, and Law in Modern Latin America*, ed. Sueann Caulfied, Sarah C. Chambers, and Lara Putnam, 1–26. Durham, NC: Duke University Press.

Cevallos García, Gabriel. 1959. "El 10 de Agosto y Nosotros." *Anales de la universidad de Cuenca* 15 (3–4): 423–48.

Chambers, Sarah C. 1999. *From Subjects to Citizens: Honor, Gender, and Politics in Arequipa, Peru, 1780–1854*. University Park, PA: Penn State University Press.

Chambers, Sarah C. 2001. "Republican Friendship: Manuela Saenz Writes Women into the Nation, 1835–1856." *HAHR* 81 (2, May). http://www.jstor.org/stable/c1114510.

Chambers, Sarah C. 2005. "Private Crimes, Public Order: Honor, Gender, and the Law in Early Republican Peru." In *Honor, Status, and Law in Modern Latin America*, ed. Sueann Caulfield, Sarah C. Chambers, and Lara Putnam, 27–49. Durham, NC: Duke University Press.

Chatterjee, Partha. 1993. *The Nation and Its Fragments: Colonial and Post-Colonial Histories*. Princeton, NJ: Princeton University Press.

Cogliano Francis, and Susan Manning, eds. 2008. *The Atlantic Enlightment*. Burlington, VT: Ashgate Publishers.

Cohen, Jean L., and Andrew Arato 1994. *Civil Society and Political Theory*. Cambridge, MA: MIT Press.

Colloque International "La Condamine": Paris, 22–23 Novembre 1985, Museum National d'Histoire Naturelle. 1987. Mexico: IPGH.

Cutter, Charles R. 1995. *The Legal Culture of Northern New Spain, 1700–1810*. Albuquerque: University of New Mexico Press.

Deere, C. D., and M. León, 2005. "Liberalism and Married Women's Property Rights in Nineteenth-Century Latin America." *HAHR* 85 (4): 653–54.

Diaz, Arlene J. 2004. *Female Citizens, Patriarchs, and the Law in Venezuela, 1786–1904*. Lincoln: University of Nebraska Press.

Dore, Elizabeth. 1997. "The Holy Family: Imagined Households in Latin American History." In *Gender Politics in Latin America: Debates in Theory and Practice*, 101–17. New York: Monthly Review Press.

Dore, Elizabeth. 2000. "One Step Forward, Two Steps Back: Gender and the State in the Long Nineteenth Century." In *Hidden Histories of Gender and the State in Latin America*, ed. Elizabeth Dore and Maxine Molyneux, 3–32. Durham, NC: Duke University.

Dore, Elizabeth. 2006. *Myths of Modernity: Peonage and Patriarchy in Nicaragua*. Durham, NC: Duke University Press.

Dore, Elizabeth, and Maxine Molyneux, eds. 2000. *Hidden Histories of Gender and the State*. Durham, NC: Duke University Press.

Eagleton, Terry. 2005. *The Functions of Criticism*. New York: Verso.

Fiehrer, Thomas Marc. 1977. "The Baron de Carondelet as Agent of Bourbon Reforms: A Study of Spanish Colonial Administration in the Years of the

French Revolution." 2 vols. PhD diss., Tulane University, New Orleans, LA.

Foucault, Michel. 2003. *"Society Must Be Defended": Lectures at the Collège de France, 1976–1976*. New York: Picador.

Fraser, Nancy. 1992. "Rethinking the Public Sphere: A Contribution to the Critique of Actually Existing Democracy." In *Habermas and the Public Sphere*, ed. Craig Calhoun, 109–42. Cambridge, MA: MIT Press.

Freile Granizo, Carlos E., ed. 2009. *Cartas y lecturas de Eugenio Espejo*. Quito, Ecuador: Banco Central.

Gandhi, Leela. 1998. *Postcolonial Theory: A Critical Introduction*. New York: Columbia University Press.

Garafalo, Leo. 2001. "The Ethno-economy of Food, Drink, and Stimulants: The Making of Race in Colonial Lima and Cuzco." PhD diss., University of Wisconsin–Madison.

Gauderman, Kimberly. 2003. *Women's Lives in Colonial Quito: Gender, Law, and Economy in Spanish America*. Austin: University of Texas Press.

Gibson, Charles. 1964. *The Aztecs under Spanish Rule: A History of the Indians of the Valley of Mexico, 1519–1810*. Stanford, CA: Stanford University Press.

Gilmore, Robert. 1960. "The Imperial Crisis, Rebellion, and the Viceroy: Nueva Granada in 1809." *HAHR* 40 (1): 1–24

Gimeno Gómez, Ana. 1988. *Una tentativa monárquica en América: El caso ecuatoriano*. Quito, Ecuador: Centro de Investigación y Cultura, Banco Central del Ecuador.

Glic, Thomas F. 1991. "Science and Independence in Latin America (with Special Reference to New Granada)." *HAHR* 71 (2): 307–34.

Gomme, Alice Bertha. 1898. *The Traditional Games of England, Scotland, and Ireland*. Vol. 2. London: David Nutt.

González, Julio V. 1937–1938. *Filiación Histórico del Gobierno Representativo Argentino*, 2 vols. Buenos Aires, Argentina: Editorial "La Vanguardia."

González Suarez, Federico. 1970 [1892]. *Historia General de la República del Ecuador*. Vol. 2. Quito, Ecuador: Casa de la Cultura.

Goodman, Dena. 1992. "Public Sphere and Private Life: Toward a Synthesis of Current Historiographical Approaches to the Old Regime." *History and Theory* 31 (1): 1–20.

Gueda, Virginia. 1993. "The First Popular Elections in Mexico City, 1812–13." In *The Evolution of the Mexican Political System*, ed. Jaime E. Rodríguez O. Wilmington, DE: Scholarly Resources.

Guerrero, Andrés. 1989. "Curages y Tenientos Políticos: La Ley de la Costumbre y la ley del Estado (Otavalo 1830–1875)." *Revista Andina* 7 (2): 321–66.

Guerrero, Andrés. 1991. *La Semántica de la Dominación: El Concertaje de Indios*. Quito, Ecuador: Ediciones Libri Mundi.

Gunder Frank, André. 1967. *Capitalism and Underdevelopment in Latin America*. New York: Monthly Review Press.

Habermas, Jürgen. 1989. *The Structural Transformation of the Public Sphere: An Inquiry into a Category of Bourgeoise Society*. Trans. Thomas Burger. Cambridge, MA: MIT Press.

Hamerly, Michael. 1968. "Selva Alegre, President of the Quiteña Junta of 1809: Traitor or Patriot?" *HAHR* 48 (4): 642–53.

Hamerly, Michael T. *Bibliografía Histórica del Ecuador.* Vol. I Periodo Nacional. http://www.ecuatorianistas.org/bibliographies/hamerly/ec9.html.

Haring, Clarence H. 1975 [1947]. *The Spanish Empire in America.* New York: Harcourt Brace.

Haskins, Ralph. 1947. "Juan José Flores and the Proposed Expedition against Ecuador, 1845–1847." *HAHR* 27 (3): 467–95.

Herr, Richard. 1958. *The Eighteenth Century Revolution in Spain.* Princeton, NJ: Princeton University Press.

Herrán Baquero, Marío. 1988. *El virrey don Antonio Amar y Borbon: La Crisis del Régimen Colonial en la Nueva Granada.* Bogotá, Colombia: Banco de la República.

Herzog, Tamar. 1995. *La Administración como un Fenómeno Social: La Justicia Penal de la Ciudad de Quito (1650–1750).* Madrid: Centro de Estudios Constitucionales.

Hulme, Peter. 1995. "Including America." *Ariel* 21 (1): 117–23.

Hünefeldt, Christine. 2000. *Liberalism in the Bedroom: Quarrelling Spouses in Nineteenth Century Lima.* University Park, PA: Penn State University Press.

Christine Hünefeldt, 1996. "Las dotes en Manos Limeñas." In *Familia y Vida Privada en la Historia de Iberoamérica,* ed. Pilar Gonzalbo and Cecilia Rabell, 255–87. Mexico City, Mexico: Colegio de México.

Ibarra Dávila, Alexia. 2002. *Estrategias del Mestizaje: Quito a Finales de la Época Colonial.* Quito, Ecuador: Abya-Yala.

Jackson, Robert, ed. 1997. *Liberals, the Church, and Indian Peasants: Corporate Lands and the Challenge of Reform in Nineteenth-Century Spanish America.* Albuquerque: University of New Mexico Press.

Jara, Alvaro, and John J. TePaske. 1990. *The Royal Treasuries of the Spanish Empire in America.* Vol. 4. *Eighteenth-Century Ecuador.* Durham, NC: Duke University Press.

Jaramillo M., Juvenal. 1990. *José Pérez Calama: Un Clérigo Illustrado del Siglo XVIII en la antigua Valladolid de Michoacán.* Morelia, Michoacan, Mexico: Universidad Michoacana de San Nicólas de Hidalgo.

Johnson, Lyman L., and Sonya Lipsett-Rivera, eds. 1998. *The Faces of Honor: Sex, Shame, and Violence in Colonial Latin America.* Albuquerque: University of New Mexico Press.

Kagan, Richard. 1981. *Lawsuits and Litigants in Castile, 1500–1700.* Chapel Hill: University of North Carolina Press.

Kanter, Deborah E. 1995. "Native Female Land Tenure and Its Decline in Mexico, 1750–1900." *Ethnohistory* 42: 607–16.

Klor de Alva, Jorge. 1992. "Colonialism and Postcolonialism as (Latin) American Mirages." *CLAR* 1 (1–2): 3–23.

Klor de Alva, Jorge. 1995. "The Postcolonization of the (Latin) American Experience: A Reconsideration of 'Colonialism,' 'Postcolonialism,' and 'Mestizaje.'" In *After Colonialism: Imperial Histories and Postcolonial Displacements,* ed. Gyan Prakas, 241–75. Princeton, NJ: Princeton University Press.

Korth, Eugene H. and Della M. Flusche. 1987. "Dowry and Inheritance in Colonial Spanish America: Peninsular Law and Chilean Practice." *Americas* 43 (4): 395–410.

Kuethe, Allan J. 1990. "The Early Reforms of Charles III in the Viceroyalty of New Granada, 1759–1776." In *Reform and Insurrection in Bourbon New Granada and Peru*, ed. John R. Fisher, Allan J. Kuethe, and Anthony McFarlane, 19–40. Baton Rouge: Louisiana State University Press.

Kuethe, Allan J. 1978. *Military Reform and Society in New Granada, 1773–1808*. Gainesville: University of Florida Press.

Laclau, Ernesto. 1977. "Feudalism and Capitalism in Latin America." *Politics and Ideology in Marxist Theory*. London: NLB.

Lafuente, Antonio. 2000. "Enlightenment in an Imperial Context: Local Science in the Late-Eighteenth-Century Hispanic World." *Osiris*, 2nd Ser., Vol. 15. *Nature and Empire: Science and the Colonial Enterprise*: 155–73.

Landes, Joan. 1988. *Women and the Public Sphere in the Age of the French Revolution*. Ithaca, NY: Cornell University Press.

Lara, Jorge Salvador, ed. 1982. *La Revolución de Quito, 1809–1822: Según los Primeros Relatos e Historias por Autores Extranjeros*. Quito, Ecuador: Corporación Editora Nacional.

Larrea, Carlos Manuel. 1968. *Baron Luis Héctor de Carondelet; el Vigesimonono Presidente de la Real Audiencia de Quito*. Quito, Ecuador: Corporación de Estudios y Publicaciones.

Lavrín, Asucnión. 1989. "Introduction: The Scenario, The Actors, and the Issues." In *Sexuality and Marriage in Colonial Latin America*, 1–43. Lincoln: University of Nebraska Press.

Lavrín, Asunción, ed. 1989. *Sexuality and Marriage in Colonial Latin America*. Lincoln: University of Nebraska Press.

Lavrín, Asunción. 1989. "Sexuality in Colonial Mexico: A Church Delimma." In *Sexuality and Marriage in Colonial Latin America*, 47–95. Lincoln: University of Nebraska Press.

Lavrín, Asunción, and Edith Courturier. 1979. "Dowries and Wills: A View of Women's Socioeconomic Role in Colonial Guadalajara and Puebla, 1640–1857." *HAHR* 59 (2): 280–304.

Las Reales Sociedades Economicas de Amigos del País y su Obra. 1972. San Sebastian: Patronato "José Maria Quadrado."

Leonard, I. A. 1943. "A Frontier Library, 1799." *HAHR* 23 (1): 21–51.

Lesser, Ricardo. 2003. *Los Orígenes de la Argentina: Historias del Reino del Rió de la Plata*. Buenos Aires, Argentina: Editorial Biblios.

Lewin, Linda. 1992. "Natural and Spurious Children in Brazilian Inheritance Law from Colony to Empire: A Methodological Essay." *Americas* 48 (3): 351–96.

Lockhart, James. 1992. *The Nahuas After the Conquest: A Social and Cultural History of the Indians of Central Mexico, Sixteenth through Eighteenth Centuries*. Stanford, CA: Stanford University Press.

Lockhart, James. 1994. *Spanish Peru, 1532–1560: A Social History*. 2nd ed. Madison: University of Wisconsin Press.

Londoño, Jenny. 1997. *Entre la Sumisión y la Resistencia: Las Mujeres en la Audiencia de Quito*. Quito, Ecuador: Ediciones Abya-Yala.

Lynch, John. 1985. "The Origins of Spanish American Independence." In *The Cambridge History of Latin America*, ed. Leslie Bethell, 3–50. Vol. III. Cambridge, UK: Cambridge University Press.

Lynch, John. 1986. *The Spanish American Revolutions, 1808–1826.* 2nd ed. New York: Norton Press.

Lynch, John. 1989. *Bourbon Spain, 1700–1808.* Oxford, UK: B. Blackwell.

MacKay, Ruth. 1999. *The Limits of Royal Authority: Resistance and Obedience in Seventeenth-Century Castile.* Cambridge, UK: Cambridge University Press.

MacLachlan, Colin M. 1974. *Criminal Justice in Eighteenth-Century Mexico: A Study of the Tribunal of the Acordada.* Berkeley: University of California Press.

Maine, Sir Henry Sumner. 1861. *Ancient Law: Its Connection with the Early History of Society, and its Relation to Modern Ideas.* London.

Mallon, Florencia. 1995. *Peasant and Nation: The Making of Postcolonial Mexico and Peru.* Berkeley: University of California Press.

Mariátegui, José Carlos. 1969 [1928]. *Siete Ensayos de Interpretación de la Realidad Peruana.* Vol. 2. *Colleción obras completas.* Lima, Peru: Empresa Editora Amauta.

Mariluz Urquijo, José M. 1998. *El agente de la Administración Pública en Indias.* Buenos Aires, Argentina: Insituto Internacional de Historia del Derecho Indians; Instituto de Investigaciones de Historia del Derecho.

Martín, Luis. 1983. *Daughters of the Conquistadors.* Albuquerque: University of New Mexico Press.

Mangan, Jane. 2005. *Trading Roles: Gender, Ethnicity, and the Urban Economy in Colonial Potosí.* Durham, NC: Duke University Press.

McFarlane, Anthony. 1990. "The Rebellion of the Barrios: Urban Insurrection in Bourbon Quito." In *Reform and Insurrection in Bourbon New Granada and Peru*, ed. John R. Fisher, Allan J. Kuethe, and Anthony McFarlane, 197–254. Baton Rouge: Louisiana State University Press.

McFarlane, Anthony. 1993. *Colombia before Independence: Economy, Society, and Politics under Bourbon Rule.* Cambridge, UK: Cambridge University Press.

McFarlane, Anthony. 1998. "Identity, Enlightenment and Political Dissent in Late Colonial Spanish America." *Transactions of the Royal Historical Society*, 6th Ser., Vol. 8: 309–35.

Meiksins Wood, Ellen. 1999. *The Origins of Capitalism.* New York: Monthly Review Press.

Mena Villamar, Claudio. 1997. *Quito Rebelde (1809–1812).* Quito, Ecuador: Abya-Yala.

Milton, Cynthia. 2007. *The Many Meanings of Poverty: Colonialism, Social Compacts, and Assistance in Eighteenth-Century Ecuador.* Stanford, CA: Stanford University Press.

Minchom, Martin. 1994. *The People of Quito, 1690–1810: Change and Unrest in the Underclass.* Boulder, CO: Westview Press.

Mirow, M. C. 2004. *Latin American Law: A History of Private Law and Institutions in Spanish America.* Austin: University of Texas Press.

Mond, Rebecca Earle. 1993. "Indian Rebellion and Bourbon Reform in New Granada: Riots in Pasto, 1780–1800." *HAHR* 73 (1): 99–124.

Monterroso y Alvarado, Gabriel de. 1566. *Práctica Criminal y Civil: Instrucción de Escrivanos*. Valladolid: F. Fernandez de Cordova.

Moreno Yánez, Segundo E. 1985. *Sublevaciones Indígenas en la Audiencia de Quito: Deside Comienzos del Siglo XVIII Hasta Finales de la Colonia*. 3rd ed. Quito, Ecuador: EDIPUCE.

Murray, Pamela S. 2008. *For Glory and Bolívar: The Remarkable Life of Manuela Sáenz, 1797–1856*. Austin: University of Texas Press.

Nader, Helen. 1993. *Liberty in Absolutist Spain: The Sale of Habsburg Towns, 1516–1700*. Baltimore: Johns Hopkins University Press.

Nader, Helen. 2004. *Power and Gender in Renaissance Spain: Eight Women of the Mendoza Family, 1450–1650*. Baltimore: Johns Hopkins University Press.

Naranjo, Plutaro and Rodrigo Fierro-Benítez, eds. 2008. *Eugenio Espejo: Su época y pensamiento*. Quito, Ecuador: Corporación Editora Nacional.

Navarro, Juan Romualdo. 1984. "Idea del Reino de Quito." In *La Economía Colonial: Relaciones Socio-Economicas de la Real Audiencia de Quito*, ed. Manuel Miño Grijalva, 111–71. Quito, Ecuador: Corporación Editora Nacional.

Navarro, Marysa. 2002. "Against *Marianismo*." In *Genders Place: Feminist Anthropologies of Latin America*, ed. Rosario Montoya, Leslie Jo Frazier, and Janis Hurtig. New York: Palgrave.

Nazzari, Muriel. 1990. "Parents and Daughters: Change in Dowry Practice in São Paulo (1600–1770)." *HAHR* 70 (4): 639–65.

Nazzari, Muriel. 1991. *Disappearance of the Dowry: Women, Families, and Social Change in São Paulo, Brazil (1600–1900)*. Stanford, CA: Stanford University Press.

Navarro, José Gabriel. 1962. *La Revolución de Quito de 1809*. Quito, Ecuador: Instituto Panamericano de Geografía e Historia.

O'Connor, Erin. 2002. "Widow's Rights Questioned: Indians, the State, and Fluctuating Gender Ideas in Central Highland Ecuador, 1870–1900." *The Americas* 59 (1): 87–106.

O'Phelan Godoy, Scarlett. 1988. "Por el Rey, Religión y Patría: Las Juntas de Gobierno de 1809 en La Paz y Quito." *Bulletin de l'Institut Français d'etudes Andines* 17 (2): 51–80.

Onis, José de. 1951. "Alcedo's Biblioteca Americana." *HAHR* 31 (1): 530–41.

Owens, J. B. 2005. *"By My Absolute Royal Authority": Justice and the Castilian Commonwealth at the Beginning of the First Global Age*. Rochester, NY: University of Rochester Press.

Pacheco, Juan Manuel. 1984. *Ciencia Filosoíia y Educación en Colomiba (siglo XVIII)*. Bogotá, Colombia: ECOE.

Paladines Escudero, Carlos. 1988. "Estudio Introductorio." In *Pensamiento Pedagógico Ecuatoriano*, 23–50. Biblioteca Basica de Pensamiento Ecuatoriano Vol. XXXIII. Quito, Ecuador: Banco Central del Ecuador and Corporación Editora Nacional.

Paladines Escudero, Carlos, ed. 1996. *Historia de la Educación y el Pensamiento Pedagógico Ecuatorianos.* Quito, Ecuador: Instituto de Capatación Municipal.

Palidanes Escudero, Carlos. 2007. *Eugenio Espejo: Estudio, Selecciones, y Notas.* Quito, Ecuador: Campaña Nacional Eugenio Espejo por el Libro y la Lectura, Corporación Editora Nacional, Universidad Andina Simón Bolívar.

Paquette, Gabriel. 2008. *Enlightenment, Governance, and Reform in Spain and its Empire, 1759–1808.* New York: Palgrave McMillan.

Pateman, Carole. 1988. *The Sexual Contract.* Stanford, CA: Stanford University Press.

Pateman, Carole. 1989. "Feminist Critiques of the Public/Private Dichotomy." In *The Disorder of Women: Democracy Feminism, and Political Theory,* 118–41. Stanford, CA: Stanford University Press.

Peloso, Vincent C., and Barbara A. Tenenbaum, eds. 1996. *Liberals, Politics, and Power: State Formation in Nineteenth-Century Latin America.* Athens: University of Georgia Press.

Pérez Fernández del Castillo, Bernardo. 1994. *Historia de la escribanía en la Nueva España y del notariado en México.* Mexico: Colegio de Notarios del Distrito Federal, Editorial Porrúa.

Peset, José Luis. 2006. "Enlightenment and Renovation in the Spanish University." In *Universities and Science in the Early Modern Period,* ed. M. Feingold and V. Navarro-Brotóns, 231–39. Amsterdam: Springer.

Phelan, John Leddy. 1960. "Authority and Flexibility in the Spanish Imperial Bureaucracy." *Administrative Science Quarterly* 5: 47–65.

Phelan, John Leddy. 1967. *The Kingdom of Quito in the Seventeenth Century: Bureaucratic Politics in the Spanish Empire.* Madison: University of Wisconsin Press.

Phelan, John Leddy. 1978. *The People and the King: The Comunero Revolution in Colombia, 1781.* Madison: University of Wisconsin Press.

Platt, Tristan. 1984. "Liberalism and Ethnocide in the Southern Andes." *History Workshop Journal* 17: 3–18.

Platt, Tristan. 1987. "The Andean Experience of Bolivian Liberalism, 1825–1900: Roots of Rebellion 19th-Century Chayanta (Postosí)." In *Resistance, Rebellion, and Consciousness in the Andean Peasant World, 18th to 20th Centuries,* Steve J. Stern, ed., 280–323. Madison: University of Wisconsin Press.

Platt, Tristan. 1993. "Simón Bolívar, the Sun of Justice, and the Amerindian Virgin: Andean Conceptions of the Patria in Nineteenth-Century Postosí." *Journal of Latin American Studies* 25 (1): 159–85.

Poska, Allyson. 1996. "When Love Goes Wrong: Getting out of Marriage in Seventeenth-Century Spain." *Journal of Social History* 29 (4): 873–82.

Poska, Allyson. 2004. "Elusive Virtue: Rethinking the Role of Female Chastity in Early Modern Spain." *Journal of Early Modern History* 8 (1–2, January): 135–46.

Poska, Allyson. 2005. *Women and Authority in Early Modern Spain: The Peasants of Galicia.* Oxford, UK: Oxford University Press.

Powers, Karen. 1995. *Andean Journeys: Migration, Ethnogenisis, and the State in Colonial Quito.* Albuquerque: University of New Mexico Press.

Premo, Bianca. 2005. *Children of the Father King: Youth, Authority, and Legal Minority in Colonial Lima.* Chapel Hill, NC: University of North Carolina Press.

Rípodas Ardanaz, Daisy. 1977. *El Matrimonio en Indias: Realidad social y regulación jurídica.* Buenos Aires, Argentina: Conicet.

Ramos Perez, Demetrio. 1978. *Entre el plata y Bogotá: Cuatro claves de la emancipación Ecuatoriana.* Madrid: Ediciones Cultura Hispanica.

Rodríguez O., Jaime. 1998. *The Independence of Spanish America.* Cambridge, UK: Cambridge University Press.

Rodríguez O., Jaime. 2006. *La revolución liberal en la epocha de independencia: El reino de Quito, 1808–1822.* Quito, Ecuador: Universidad Andina Simón Bolívar : Corporación Editora Nacional.

Rojas, Rafael. 2003. *La escritura de independencia: El surgimiento de la opinion pública en México.* Mexico: Taurus/CIDE.

Ronan, Chares E. 1978. "Antonio de Alcedo: His Collaboratos and His Letters to William Robertson." *The Americas* 34 (3): 490–501.

Ruíz Guiñazú, Enrique. 1916. *La magistratura Indiana.* Buenos Aires, Argentina: Facultad de Derecho y Ciencias Sociales.

Saether, Steinar A. 2003. "Bourbon Absolutism and Marriage Reform in Latin Colonial Spanish America." *Americas* 59 (4): 475–509.

Said, Edward. 1993 [1978]. *Orientalism.* New York: Vintage Books.

Salomon, Frank. 1988. "Indian Women of Early Colonial Quito as Seen through Their Testaments." *The Americas* 44 (3, January): 325–41.

Salvatorre, Ricardo, Carlos Aguirre, and Gil Joseph, eds. 2001. *Crime and Punishment in Latin America: Law and Society since Late Colonial Times.* Durham, NC: Duke University Press.

Sanders, James E. 2004. *Contentious Republicans: Popular Politics, Race, and Class in Nineteenth-Century Colombia.* Durham, NC: Duke University Press.

Scardaville, Michael. 1994. "(Hapsburg) Law and (Bourbon) Order: State Authority, Popular Unrest, and the Criminal Justice in Bourbon Mexico City." *The Americas* 50 (4): 501–25.

Seed, Patricia. 1988. *To Love, Honor, and Obey in Colonial Mexico: Conflicts over Marriage Choice, 1574–1821.* Stanford, CA: Stanford University Press.

Seed, Patricia. 1991. "Colonial and Postcolonial Discourse." *LARR* 26 (3): 181–200.

Serulnikov, Sergio. 2003. *Subverting Colonial Authority: Challenges to Spanish Rule in the Eighteenth-Century Southern Andes.* Durham, NC: Duke University Press.

Shafer, R. J. 1958. *The Economic Societies in the Spanish World (1763–1821).* Syracuse, NY: Syracuse University Press.

Shelton, Laura. 2007. "Like a Servant or Like a Son: Circulating Children in Northwestern Mexico (1790–1850)." In *Raising an Empire: Children in Early Modern Iberia and Colonial Latin America*, ed. Gonzalez and Premo, 219–37. Albuquerque: University of New Mexico Press.

Silva, Renan José. 1981. *La reforma de estudios en el nuevo reino de Granada, 1767–1790*. Bogotá, Colombia: Universidad Pedagógica Nacional.

Silvestre, Francisco. 1950 [1789]. *Descripción del reyno de Santa Fé de Bógota*. Bógota: Ministerio de Educación Nacional.

Silverblatt, Irene. 1989. *Moon, Sun, Witches: Gender Ideologies and Class in Inca and Colonial Peru*. Princeton, NJ: Princeton University Press.

Smith, Teresa Ann. 2006. *The Emerging Female Citizen: Gender and Enlightenment in Spain*. Berkeley: University of California Press.

Socolow, Susan. 1989. "Acceptable Partners: Marriage Choice in Colonial Argentina, 1778–1810." In *Sexuality and Marriage in Colonial Latin America*, ed. Asunción Lavrín, 209–52. Lincoln: University of Nebraska Press.

Sousa, Lisa Mary. 1997. "Women and Crime in Colonial Oaxaca: Evidence of Complementary Gender Roles in Mixtec and Zapotec Societies." In *Indian Women of Early Mexico*, ed. Susan Schroader, Stephanie Wood, and Robert Haskett, 199–216. Norman: University of Oklahoma Press.

Spalding, Karen. 1984. *Huarochirí: An Andean Society under Inca and Spanish Rule*. Stanford, CA: Stanford University Press.

Spivak, Gayatri Chakravorty. 1990. *The Postcolonial Critic: Interviews, Strategies, Dialogues*. Edited by Sara Harasym. New York: Routledge Press.

Stavig, Ward. 1999. *The World of Túpac Amaru: Conflict, Community, and Identity in Colonial Peru*. Lincoln: University of Nebraska Press.

Stein Stanley J., and Barbara H. Stein. 1970. *The Colonial Heritage of Latin America: Essays on Economic Dependence in Perspective*. New York: Oxford University Press.

Stern, Steve J. 1982. *Peru's Indian Peoples and the Challenge of Spanish Conquest: Huamanga to 1640*. Madison: University of Wisconsin Press.

Stern, Steve J., ed. 1987. *Resistance, Rebellion, and Conciousness in the Andean Peasant World, 18th to 20th Centuries*. Madison: University of Wisconsin Press.

Stern, Steve J. 1993. "Feudalism, Capitalism, and the World-System in the Perspective of Latin America and the Caribbean." In *Confronting Historical Paradigms: Peasants, Labor and the Capitalist World System in Africa and Latin America*, ed. Federick Cooper, Florencia E. Mallon, Steve J. Stern, and Alan F. Isaacman, 23–83. Madison: University of Wisconsin Press.

Stern, Steve J. 1995. *The Secret History of Gender: Women, Men, and Power in Late Colonial Mexico*. Chapel Hill, NC: University of North Carolina Press.

Sublette, Ned. 2008. *The World that Made New Orleans: From Spanish Silver to Congo Square*. Chicago: Chicago Review Press.

Tao Anzoátegui, Víctor. 1999. "Ordenes Normativos y Prácticas Socio-Jurídicas: La Justicia." In *Nueva historia de la nación Argentina*, Vol. 2, 283–315. Buenos Aires, Argentina: Planeta.

Terán Najas, Rosemarie. 1988. *Los proyectos del Imperio Borbónico en la Real Audiencia*. Quito, Ecuador: Abya-Yala/TEHIS.

Terraciano, Kevin. 2004. *The Mixtecs of Colonial Oaxaca: Nudazahul History, Sixteenth through Eighteenth Centuries*. Stanford, CA: Stanford University Press.

Thompson, I. A. A. 1976. *War and Government in Habsburg Spain, 1560–1620*. London: Athlone Press.

Thomson, Sinclair. 2002. *We Along Will Rule: Native Andean Politics in the Age of Insurgency*. Madison: University of Wisconsin Press.

Thurner, Mark. 1997. *From Two Republics to One Divided: Contradictions in Postcolonial Nationmaking in Andean Peru*. Durham, NC: Duke University Press.

Thurner, Mark. 2003. "After Spanish Rule: Writing Another After." In *After Spanish Rule*, ed. Thurner, 12–57. Durham, NC: Duke University Press.

de Toro, Alfredo and Fernando de Toro, eds. 1999. *El debate de la postcolonialidad en Latinoamerica*. Frankfurt am Main: Vervuert/Madrid: Iberoamericana.

Torre Reyes, Carlos de la. 1961. *La revolución de Quito del 10 de Agosto de 1809, sus vicisitudes y su significación en el proceso general de la empancipación Hispanoamericano*. Quito, Ecuador: Talleres Gráficos de Educación.

"Tramite legal para declatoria de mestizaje." 1995. *Quitumbre* 9: 122.

Twinam, Anne. 1999. *Public Lives, Private Secrets: Gender, Honor, Sexuality, and Illegitimacy in Colonial Spanish America*. Stanford, CA: Stanford University Press.

Tyrer, Robson Brines 1976. "The Demographic and Economic History of the Audiencia of Quito: Indian Population and Textile Production, 1600–1800." PhD diss., University of California at Berkeley.

Uribe, Victor M. 1995. "The Lawyers and New Granada's Late Colonial State." *Journal of Latin American Studies* 27 (3): 517–49.

Uribe, Victor M. 1995. "Kill All the Lawyers!: Lawyers and the Independence Movement in New Granada, 1809–1820." *The Americas* 52 (2): 175–210.

Uribe, Victor M. 2000. *Honorable Lives: Lawyers, Family, and Politics in Colombia, 1780–1850*. Pittsburgh, PA: University of Pittsburgh Press.

Uribe-Uran, Victor M. 2000. "The Birth of a Public Sphere in Latin America During the Age of Revolution." *Comparative Studies in Society and History* 42 (2): 425–57.

Valencia Llano, Alonso. 1993. "Elites, Burocracia, Clero y Sectores Populares en la Independencia Quiteña (1809–1812)." *Procesos: Revista Ecuatoriana de historia* 3: 55–101.

Van Aken, Mark. 1981. "The Lingering Death of Indian Tribute in Ecuador." *HAHR* 61 (3): 429–59.

Van Aken, Mark. 1989. *King of the Night: Juan José Flores and Ecuador, 1824–1864*. Berkeley: University of California Press.

Vickery, Amanda. 1993. "Golden Age to Separate Spheres? A Review of the Categories and Chronology of English women's History." *The Historical Journal* 36 (2): 383–414.

Viforcos Marinas, Maria Isabel. 1993. "Los Recogimientos, de Centros de Integración Social a Cárceles Privadas: Santa Marta de Quito" *Anuario de Estudios Americanos* 50 (2): 59–92.

Walker, Charles F. 1999. *Smoldering Ashes: Cuzco and the Creation of Republican Peru, 1780–1840.* Durham, NC: Duke University Press.

Walker, Charles F. 2001. "Crime in the Time of the Great Fear: Indians and the State in the Peruvian Southern Andes, 1780–1820." In *Crime and Punishment in Latin America*, ed. Ricardo Salvatore, Carlos Aguirre, and Gilbert Joseph, 35–55. Durham, NC: Duke University Press.

Wood, Stephanie. "Matters of Life at Death: Nahuatl Testaments of Rural Women, 1589–1801." In *Indian Women of Early Mexico*, ed. Susan Schroader, Stephanie Wood, and Robert Haskett, 165–82. Norman: University of Oklahoma Press.

Yrolo Calar, Nicolás de. 1996 [1605]. *La Política de escrituras*, ed. María del Pilar Martínez López-Cano. Mexico City, Mexico: Universidad Nacional Autónoma de México.

Zahler, Reuben. 2006. "Bums, Vice, Poverty, and Honor in the Early Venezuelan Republic, 1821–1835." Paper presented at the *AHA*, Philadelphia, PA, January 8.

INDEX

patriarchy, 2, 7, 14, 258; and Bourbon law, 122; as conjugal right, 137; criticisms of the model, 10–11; defined, 9–11, 261–62; legal, 2; as metacategory, 9; misuses of, 11; and marriage, 136; and sexuality, 119; and Spanish law, 137

patrols. See *ronda*

pawned goods, 154, 156

pecado nefando, 115

pendolista, 210

peninsulares, 65

Peru, Viceroyalty of, 15, 29

Phelan, J. L., 37, 43

Pichincha, 16

Pifo, 50, 238–39

plebeians, 37, 51, 54–55; and the Rebellion of the Barrios, 50; as rebellious, 56

pobre de solemnidad, 221

police, magistrates, 229; regulations of 1825, 229–30, 241

policing, 31; and the barrios of Quito, 70, 81, 230–31; commercial, 57

Pomasqui, 147

poorhouse. See *ospicio de pobres* (poorhouse)

Popayán, 175, 179, 186, 189

Pragmática Real (on Marriage), 129

pragmaticas reales, 133

premisa la venia. See license

Primicias de la cultura de Quito, 170–71

private sphere, 228, 231, 242

procedure, civil, 251; and criminal cases, 73, 75–79; legal, 139–40

procurador (attorney), 76; for the declared poor, 76; for minors, 76

procurador general, 40

property, disputes, 256; marital, 121, 136; rights, and gender, 121

prostitute, as insult, 216

prostitution, 80, 235

protector de naturales (legal office for representing indigenous people), 76, 159

protocolo (notarized document), 152

prueba (magistrate investigation), 77–78

public good, 31, 39, 50; morality and the, 104, 231; and shaming and punishment, 108; and sin, 102–3

pueblo, as "the people," 176

Puembo, 50, 238–39

pulpería, 219

Quiroga, Manuel Rodriguez de, 174, 177, 181, 183, 184, 187, 192, 194

Quito, Ecuador, 1, 4–5, 14, 58, 59, 66, 175, 179; eighteenth century population of, 21; map of barrios in, 16

rape, 75, 80, 231, 241; statutory (*estrupo*), 100, 148

Real Caja (Royal Treasury), 37, 57

Rebellion of the Alcabalas, 176

Rebellion of the Barrios, 22, 27, 31, 101, 169, 176; May 22, 1765, uprising, 45–48; June 24 uprising, 51–55

Recopilación de Indias, 130, 166, 227

Recopilacion de leyes de Castilla, 96, 107–8, 130, 133, 136, 141, 166, 227

Regency (Spain), 180, 196, 198

republicanism, 163, 174, 257; in Quito, 166

Recio, Bernardo, 46

Riobamba, 68, 179, 225

Río de la Plata, Viceroyalty of, 29

robbery, 156, 159

ronda (street patrol), 48–49, 51, 53, 84–85, 89, 92, 97–98, 106–7, 110–12, 114, 118, 120, 222, 228, 233, 241

Rubio de Arevalo, President Manuel, 40, 51

Ruiz de Castilla, Conde, 168, 169, 174, 176–77, 185, 188–89, 190–92, 195

Sáenz, Manuela, 173, 185

Sala, Juan, 131

Salinas, Juan, 176, 181, 183

Sambiza, 238–39

San Blas, barrio of, 16, 38, 47, 49, 54, 56, 73, 88, 94, 101, 157, 181, 195, 219, 234; and Quito junta, 184; and social life, 118–19

San Felipe, 66
San Francisco church and monastery, 16, 48, 54
San Juan, festival of, 51
San Marcos, barrio of, 16, 54, 88, 118, 181; and Quito junta, 184
San Roque, barrio of, 16, 46, 47, 51, 53, 56, 88, 100, 110, 150, 181, 194, 207; and Quito junta, 184; textile factory, 69
San Sebastian, barrio of, 16, 46, 47, 51–52, 56, 88, 110–11, 113, 158, 181, 194, 238–39, 242, 243, 245; and Quito junta, 184
Santa Bárbara, barrio of, 16, 38, 46–47, 54, 56, 72–73, 82, 88, 94, 101, 160–62, 165, 181, 229; description of, 17–20; occupations in, 263–64; and Quito junta, 184
Santa Clara, convent of, 16
Santa Prisca, barrio of, 16, 38
Santo Domingo, church, 52, 55
Saquisili, 66
sex, anal, 116; illicit, 85, 241. *See also* adultery; *concubinato*; sodomy; solicitation
sexual crime, 84, 104–5; defined, 80
Siete Partidas, 86, 107–8, 117, 129, 133, 137–38, 166, 227, 233, 247, 249
slavery, and crime, 86
smallpox, 171
Sociedad de Amigos de País, 171–72
sodomy, 80, 115–19; female, 118–19
solicitation, 80, 242
soltera, 160
sovereignty, 165–66, 227; and juntas, 169; popular, 167; and royal legitimacy, 178
status, 12, 14; and ethnicity, 114, 130; and gender, 130; and honor, 257; Indian as fiscal category and, 68; and the law, 130, 145; marital, 99, 145, 257; in the republican period, 257; and use of doña, 98–99
sugar, 36, 41, 158–59
Superior Court (Ecuador), 244
Supreme Court (Ecuador), 250

taxes and taxation, 20, 41, 68, 239–40; collection of, 37; evasion of, 45; increase of, after the Rebellion of the Barrios, 66
teniente alguacil mayor, 4. *See also* *alguacil mayor*
tertulia (salon), 173
testaments, 139
textile economy, 41, 44
tobacco, 38, 112; and convict labor, 62–63; royal factories, 63, 92, 100, 102, 110, 113, 117, 119; royal factory and punishment, 98, 108; royal factory in Guayaquil, 118; royal monopoly, 62
torture, and criminal procedure, 78
tribute, 46, 51, 62, 66–69, 130, 145, 149; arrests for, 91; royal revenues from, 63–65
troops, 59–60; from Lima, 58, 60, 193–95; from Panama, 58, 60
Tumbaco, 4, 50, 97

vago (vagabondage), 229, 241
vecino/vecina, 3, 36, 49, 52, 160, 181, 198; as a corporation, 40; as participants in the Rebellion of the Barrios, 48
verbal hearing, 124, 152, 203, 246, 250, 255, 256. *See also* conciliation
Villadiego, Alonso, 131, 139, 145
violence, gender, 243–47
virginity, 100

War of Spanish Succession, 29, 33
weapons: cannons, 52, 53; fusiles, 52, 53, 55; lances, 52, 53, 55; ordered turned in after Rebellion, 61; stones, 52
widows, 2, 142, 144–45, 153, 233; and the law, 143
witnesses, 109; and criminal procedure, 77–78; and testimony, 73
women: and abandonment, spousal, 146; and access to law, 12, 137; and adultery, 93–94, 98; arrested at request of spouse or parent, 83; arrested for sexual offenses, 83–84; and changing notions of citizenship, 228; and

www.ingramcontent.com/pod-product-compliance
Lightning Source LLC
Chambersburg PA
CBHW020654270326
41928CB00005B/116